ASSESSING
ORGANIZATIONAL
CHANGE

Wiley Series on ORGANIZATIONAL ASSESSMENT AND CHANGE

Series Editors
Edward E. Lawler III and
Stanley E. Seashore

Assessing Organizational Change: The Rushton Quality of Work Experiment
by Paul S. Goodman

SCHEDULED BOOKS

Measuring and Assessing Organizations
by Andrew H. Van de Ven and Diane L. Ferry

Work and Well-Being
by Robert L. Kahn

Organizational Assessment: Perspectives on the Measurement of Organizational Behavior and Quality of Working Life
edited by Edward E. Lawler III, David A. Nadler, and Cortlandt Cammann

The New Plant
by Dennis N. T. Perkins, Veronica F. Nieva, and Edward E. Lawler III

Employee Productivity and the Quality of Work Life
by Richard E. Walton and Leonard Schlesinger

PROSPECTIVE BOOKS

Observing and Measuring Organizational Change: A Guide to Field Practice
edited by Stanley E. Seashore, Edward E. Lawler III, Philip H. Mirvis, and Cortlandt Cammann

The Bolivar Quality of Work Experiment: 1972–1978
by Barry A. Macy, Edward E. Lawler III, and Gerald E. Ledford, Jr.

ASSESSING ORGANIZATIONAL CHANGE

THE RUSHTON QUALITY OF WORK EXPERIMENT

Robert Manning Strozier Library

OCT 16 1979

Tallahassee, Florida

PAUL S. GOODMAN
Graduate School of Industrial Administration
Carnegie–Mellon University

with major contributions by

Edward Conlon
Dennis Epple
Eduard Fidler

A WILEY-INTERSCIENCE PUBLICATION

JOHN WILEY & SONS, New York
Chichester • Brisbane • Toronto

Robert Manning Strozier Library

OCT 16 1979

Tallahassee, Florida

Copyright © 1979 by John Wiley & Sons, Inc.

All rights reserved. Published simultaneously in Canada.

Reproduction or translation of any part of this work
beyond that permitted by Sections 107 or 108 of the
1976 United States Copyright Act without the permission
of the copyright owner is unlawful. Requests for
permission or further information should be addressed to
the Permissions Department, John Wiley & Sons, Inc.

Library of Congress Cataloging in Publication Data

Goodman, Paul S
  Assessing organizational change.

  (Wiley series on organizational assessment and
change)
  Includes index.
  1. Coal-miners—United States—Case studies.
2. Organizational change—Case studies.   3. Industrial organizational—United States—Case studies.
4. Coal mines and mining—United States—Management—Case studies.   I. Title.   II. Series.
HD8039.M62U6258   658.31′52   78-31857
ISBN 0-471-04782-1

Printed in the United States of America

10 9 8 7 6 5 4 3 2 1

Series Preface

The WILEY SERIES ON ORGANIZATIONAL ASSESSMENT AND CHANGE is concerned with informing and furthering the contemporary debate about the effectiveness of work organizations and the quality of life they provide for their members. Of particular concern is the adaptation of work organizations to changing social aspirations and economic constraints. The phenomenal growth of interest in the quality of work life and productivity speaks clearly to the existing concern with organizational life. Issues that not long ago were the quiet concern of a few academics and a few leaders in unions and management have become issues of broader public concern. They have intruded upon broadcast media prime time, lead newspaper and magazine columns, the houses of Congress, and the board rooms of both firms and unions.

A thorough discussion of what organizations should be like and how they can be improved must involve many issues and aspects. Some are concerned with basic moral and ethical questions. What is the responsibility of an organization to its employees? What, after all, is a "good job"? How should it be decided that some might benefit from and others pay for gains in the quality of working life? Should there be a public policy on the matter? Yet others are concerned with the strategies and tactics of bringing about changes in organizational life; advocates of alternative approaches are numerous, vocal, and controversial. Others are concerned with the task of measurement and assessment on grounds that the choices to be made by leaders, the assessment of consequences, and the bargaining of equities must be informed by reliable, comprehensive, and relevant information of kinds not now readily available.

The WILEY SERIES ON ORGANIZATIONAL ASSESSMENT AND CHANGE is concerned with all aspects of the debate over how organizations should be managed, changed, and controlled. It contains books pertaining to the basic moral and ethical issues, the assessment of organizational effectiveness, and the study of organizational changes that represent new approaches to management. The volumes in the series have in common a concern with work organizations, a focus on change and the dynamics of change, an assumption that diverse social and personal interests need to be taken into account in discussions of organizational effectiveness, and a view that concrete cases and quantitative data are essential ingredients in a lucid debate. As such, these books consider a broad but integrated set of issues and ideas. They are intended to be read by managers, union officials, researchers, consultants, policy makers, students, and others who are seriously concerned with organizational assessment and change.

In the present volume, Paul Goodman of the Carnegie–Mellon University, an accomplished analyst of organizational dynamics, presents an incisive description and interpretation of a joint union/management quality of work-life program carried out in an underground coal mine. Along with his research team, he observed the events over a span of three years, made measurements as needed, and drew his conclusions independently of the special interests of miners, union representatives, and managers who were engaged in the project. The book provides concrete examples of the ways in which moral and ethical issues arise during organizational change activity. It also provides some interesting insights into the conditions under which a particular strategy of change is likely to be effective. Finally, it represents the best example in the organizational change literature of the joint use of sophisticated quantitative data and direct personal observations in the search for understanding.

EDWARD E. LAWLER III
STANLEY E. SEASHORE

Pittsburgh, Pennsylvania
(January 1979)

Preface

This book started a long time ago. In 1971 I was a visiting professor at the School of Industrial and Labor Relations at Cornell University. There were frequent discussions about productivity and quality of working life. One consequence of this interest was a proposal by the School's Dean, Bob McKersie, to put together a Cornell team to develop a methodology for evaluating a series of quality of work experiments proposed by Ted Mills of the National Commission on Productivity, now at the American Center for Quality of Working Life. Mills initiated a series of experiments, conceived at the national level, to serve as demonstration projects for ways to improve productivity and the quality of working life. The Cornell team secured a grant from the Ford Foundation toward the development of an evaluation methodology for assessing these experimental projects. Working with the Cornell team of Lee Dyer, Leo Gruenfeld, Tom Kochan, Dave Lipsky, and Bob McKersie was exciting, exhausting, and rewarding. The task was complex, because there has not been a lot of work on organizational evaluation research, and the problem required multiple discipline inputs.

In 1973 the series of quality of work experiments was launched. One experiment was initiated in Pennsylvania. I had just moved to Carnegie–Mellon University in Pittsburgh and was asked to become the principal investigator for the evaluation side of that experiment. Eric Trist was principal investigator (with Gerald Susman and Grant Brown) of the actual intervention.

I entered into this role, which was to last for six years, because I wanted to test some of the ideas we had developed at Cornell, and the measuring of organizational change over time was a new learning opportunity for me. Also, the experience provided a unique opportunity for me to observe the activities of the Trist team; most professionals involved in organizational change are not open to another party's monitoring and observing their activities.

I would like to acknowledge the major contributions of Edward Conlon to Chapter 14, Dennis Epple to Chapters 11 and 16, and Eduard Fidler to Chapter 11. The open interdisciplinary perspective at GSIA permitted faculty members such as Tim McGuire, Bob Avery, Bob Atkin, Jone Pearce, and others to provide valuable inputs. Johannes Pennings worked in various phases of developing and analyzing worker attitudes.

One of the biggest jobs in the project was the preparation of data for analysis. When we were done we had a more elaborate information system than the company. This particular job required a lot of long, tedious hours. The major contributors were Mary Ann Janey, Debby Kress, Jane Hart, and Stephanie Keyes, who was the principal programmer. The manuscript to the publisher was around 600 pages, which had been retyped many times. Over the four-year period there were multitudes of memos, reports, and major reports. Joanne Austin and Rosalyn Tallet performed these typing chores well.

Many of the people at the Rushton mine have become friends. We saw or talked with each other almost weekly over a four-year period. It was hard to leave in early 1977. I think it is better not to name names, because there are too many, and I do not want to miss any. What the reader should appreciate is this: I wandered around that mine for four years, observing, asking questions, asking for data and never reciprocating because of my role as an independent evaluator.

Perhaps this preface is too full of acknowledgements, but it is important to note that the scope of this operation grew from the cooperation and contributions of many.

Warren Hinks, Jr., the president of the Rushton mine, helped me through every phase of the project. Basil Whiting, the program director at the Ford Foundation, had the foresight to see the need for systematic evaluation studies of these experiments. He provided both intellectual and financial support throughout the course of our study. Bob Shrank continued supporting the project when Basil left the Ford Foundation for a position in Washington. The Institute for Social Research at the University of Michigan was the prime contractor for the Ford Foundation; I was a subcontractor. Ed Lawler and Stan Seashore created an environment where I was free to develop and to experiment with new evaluation approaches. This was a new relationship for both of us because most of the initial evaluation efforts were conducted by Michigan people.

Lastly, conducting the project and writing this book required an inordinate amount of time away from my family. Mary, Jonathan, Jennifer, and Daniel then also contributed.

PAUL S. GOODMAN

Fox Chapel, Pa.
January 1979

Contents

PART IV
ANALYSIS OF ORGANIZATIONAL CHANGE

APPENDIXES

ASSESSING
ORGANIZATIONAL
CHANGE

RUSHTON EMPLOYEES' VIEWS OF EXPERIMENTAL SECTION —UNION, 1974

From interviews at the Rushton Mining Company.

Well you're your own boss . . . you go to your own section . . . run things your own way . . . talk things out when you have to . . . seems jobs now are divided more equitably . . . everything is kept up better . . . before when a timber [safety timber] was down, you'd say the hell with it. Now you do something . . . it's your section.

It's [the program] trying to get everyone to do the next man's job [job switching] . . . doing a real good job . . . the place is kept better . . . men seem to care. If something's wrong we fix it . . . everyone's part of it . . . just jumping to do it.

We see that the work gets done . . . that the law is kept up . . . learn how to run all the equipment . . . you want to come to work now.

Nothing different . . . once in a while they will change off [job switch], but that's all . . . when we started the men were careful . . . now they don't give a fuck . . . we're back to the way we were before.

The boss's job is easier, now the men take responsibility . . . we all work together . . . like a team.

. . . AND MORE THAN TWO YEARS LATER—UNION, 1976

We do a lot better work on our crew . . . know the laws better. I understand the plans better . . . before I didn't . . . all I knew before was running my car.

I don't really think there is a program now . . . only in the minds of some people [such as] Warren [company president] and Grant Brown [research consultant] . . . not in the minds of the men.

Well it worked . . . it worked in 2 South, not in the other sections . . . if anything the program is going backwards. Only real improvement was in safety and that did come from the program.

Don't mean much now . . . program is back to where it was [in the beginning]. All the joint committee meetings are a lot of talk . . . don't get nothing solved. Program [would be] good if it were run as it was intended to.

CHAPTER ONE

Introduction

The purpose of this book is to tell the story of the quality of work (QOW) experiment at the Rushton Mining Company. The story is exciting because it describes one of the most comprehensive attempts to improve productivity and the quality of working life. Since the early 1970s there has been a revolution in new forms of work organization. By revolution, I mean a fundamental change in the designing of work and work organizations. People are looking for new ways to structure jobs and to organize work in order to improve the economic viability of the organization and to make work a more satisfying and rewarding experience for the worker. Most of this organizational redesign work is done on an experimental basis; these efforts are labeled quality of work experiments or projects. We are in a phase of discovery, that is there are no set packages or programs to bring about a fundamental change in work organization. The goal of the experimental work is not simply to restructure one organization, but rather to discover the principles that will make restructuring activities successful in many different kinds of organizations.

The Rushton story is unique in a number of ways. It is one of the most comprehensive both in terms of changing multiple aspects of the organization and in terms of the new work organization projects currently underway. The Rushton experiment has been in existence long enough (since late 1973) to permit a review of its effectiveness. Rushton is also unique since it is probably the most systematically evaluated of all the major work restructuring experiments. By systematic, I mean that extensive data sets were gathered on a large variety of variables over a three-year period to determine the impact of the experimental intervention. This book brings together for the first time extensive econometric analyses of the economic results and

3

psychometric measures of work attitudes and beliefs and offers qualitative observations and interpretations of the process of change. In this sense the book adopts an interdisciplinary, multimethod orientation to measuring and analyzing organizational change. Another distinguishing aspect of the evaluation is that it was carried out independently (in terms of personnel and funding) from the research team that was responsible for introducing the change program.

The setting of the Rushton experiment is also timely. Rushton is a coal mine located in Pennsylvania. In terms of national energy policy President Carter wants to increase coal production to more than one billion tons by 1985. Coal clearly represents one of our major natural energy resources. Relative to other countries, the United States has the largest percentage (48.2%) of the estimated remaining coal reserves. However, despite the availability of coal and the demand for coal, output per employee has been steadily decreasing. Output per employee in 1970 was 97.2 (1967 = 100) and this rate fell to 73.7 in 1975 (U.S. Department of Labor, 1976). A critical question is how to increase coal productivity—one objective of the Rushton project. Increased productivity is not the only desired outcome. Mining is one of the most dangerous occupations. The experiment was designed to find new ways to improve the miner's safety. Improvement in the psychological quality of work (in terms of security, attractiveness of work, opportunities to develop new skills, etc.) represented another objective. The goals of increased productivity, safety, and attractiveness of work are of course important to all organizations.

The book is written for a number of different groups. First, it is directed to managers who want to learn more about recent innovations in organizational design. This account will provide details of why management participated in the experiment, the form of the experiment, and management's views of the results as well as different ways to approach the redesigning of organizations to increase productivity and the quality of working life.

The book is also directed to union leaders. Many QOW experiments have been joint labor-management ventures, and it is likely we shall find greater union participation in the future. Until now, however, there has been virtually no systematic information on the benefits and costs to the union of participating in these experiments. The results of the experiment from the union perspective as well as the consequences to the union organization of participating in a QOW experiment will be examined.

In addition, the experiment at Rushton represents a new approach in organizational development and as such should be of interest to specialists involved in introducing organizational change.

The book is also invaluable for social scientists interested in organizational theory and change, since QOW experiments provide a unique opportunity to increase our knowledge of organizational structure and process. For one of the first times there is a planned organizational intervention where the agent of change is separate from the evaluator of change. This division of labor provides an excellent opportunity to trace organizational interventions and processes over time. The QOW experiments also have stimulated the development of new measurement and analysis procedures to capture changes in organization. Both the substantive knowledge on organizational change and new technologies for assessing change should be of interest to organizational scholars.

In a recent article John Dunlop (1977) argued that there was little connection between academic research on manpower topics and policy decision making. He stated that academic researchers spend a lot of time claiming their research is policy oriented when it really is not. In order not to incur Dunlop's wrath, or that of the Federal Trade Commission (FTC) for false advertising, I do not claim that the Rushton experiment will reshape national policy. However, policymakers should study this book for two reasons: (1) The Rushton experiment is one of the first of a series of quality of work experiments initiated at the national level to improve productivity and quality of working life. After examining the results of Rushton and other independently evaluated QOW experiments, a policymaker should be in a better position to judge whether experimentation in new forms of work organization is a viable national strategy; (2) The Rushton experiment takes place in a coal mine. There are many ways to meet President Carter's goal of increasing production. Most of the national attention has been on technological improvement with little attention to the human and organizational factors that bear heavily on whether a mine is shut down by a walkout or on how much coal gets produced each day.

THE CONTEXT

Before beginning the story of Rushton, it is useful to know the context in which the project developed. Experiments in new forms of work organization have proliferated in the United States since 1970. These have taken many different forms and their impact on work, the work environment, worker attitudes, organizational effectiveness, and labor-management relations is potentially very significant.

While there is no simple cause and effect relationship, economic and labor-management conditions in the early 1970s clearly provided a climate conducive to the emergence of these experiments. Economic conditions in the 1970s were characterized by serious problems including two recessions, abnormally high unemployment rates, and acute inflation. Per capita gross national product (GNP), which had been rising slowly in the 1960s, dropped slightly during the first recession in late 1969–1970; it dropped again at the beginning of the second recession in 1974. In 1969 the total unemployment rate was less than 4%; in 1975 it was around 9%. These economic conditions probably stimulated the search for new ways to increase productivity and to resolve other unfavorable economic factors, such as inflation.

Labor-management relations reflected events in the economic sphere. In response to growing inflation rates the Nixon administration introduced a three-phase program to limit wage and price increases. This program focused attention on productivity by requiring justifications, in the form of productivity increments, for wage increases. There was a growing use of labor-management committees, at both the industry and local levels, to solve some of the economic dilemmas. Labor-management committees in the construction, food, and steel industries dealt with a variety of issues, such as wages, technological change, and employment security. The joint concern of both labor and management over productivity was also highlighted during this period. In the past productivity had been strictly a management problem. As foreign competition threatened jobs, however, management and labor initiated new programs (e.g., the Experimental Negotiation Agreement) to deal with productivity and job security. Increasing interest in productivity and joint labor-management problem-solving activities outside of traditional collective bargaining parallel the form of many of the current quality of work experiments. Again there is no simple relationship between economic and labor-management conditions and development of organizational experimentation (see Goodman and Lawler, 1977).

The initiation of the current set of organizational experiments came from a diverse set of "quality of working life" centers. The centers operate primarily on the national level; now some centers are focusing on statewide activities. The general objective of all the centers is similar: to increase productivity and to improve the quality of working life through new forms of work organization. While their strategies differ, all the centers provide information—through conferences, newsletters, and articles—about current QOW experiments and procedures for participating in the experiments. The centers serve primarily as catalysts for labor and management participation.

In 1972 a series of labor-management demonstration projects were initiated by what is now called the American Center for Quality of Working Life (ACQWL). The purpose of these projects, of which Rushton was one of the first, was to find new ways to structure organizations in order to increase productivity and quality of working life. The projects were not ends in themselves, rather they were to demonstrate the feasibility of work restructuring activities. The leaders of the center hoped that eventually other organizations would be stimulated to experiment in new forms of work organization. The framework that guided these demonstration projects was the following: (1) They were all union-management projects. That is, initiation and administration was a joint labor-management responsibility. The projects were jointly owned and benefits were to be jointly shared. At Rushton the partnership was between the company and the United Mine Workers of America; (2) It was expected that external resource people would be available to guide the research efforts. At Rushton this research team included Eric Trist (University of Pennsylvania), Gerald Susman (Penn State University), and Grant Brown, a mining engineer associated at that time with Penn State University; (3) Projects were designed to run for 18 months. Complete funding was to be provided by the center for the initial 6 months, during which time union and management would develop the design of the experiment. For the next 12 months one-half of the funding would be provided by the center, and the union and management would carry the other half in some proportion; (4) There would be an independent evaluation team to assess the effects of each experiment. It was expected that an independent and objective analysis of the process and outcomes of the experiment would be more widely accepted. The Institute for Social Research (ISR) at the University of Michigan was the prime contractor for the evaluations of all the center's projects.

Except for these four factors, the center's framework did not specify what the substance of each experiment should be. The premise was that no particular form of work organization was the "best." Therefore, the design of each of these projects was different, with the form of the experiment fitting the characteristics of each particular organization—its people, structure, and environment.

This four-factor framework clearly distinguishes work experiments from other attempts to improve the utilization of human resources within the firm. Some other novel characteristics of these and other QOW experiments are:

1. Their *dual* focus on improving both productivity and quality of work life dimensions. The latter includes physical and psychological safety at work as well as opportunities to learn new skills, to accept

greater responsibility, and for more satisfaction from work, and so on. The focus is not on either productivity or on the psychological outcomes of work, but rather on jointly improving both of these dimensions.

2. Their attempt to restructure *multiple* aspects of the organization simultaneously, rather than just one aspect, such as a job or pay system. Other organizational interventions often focus on single dimensions, for example, on a new pay system or a new appraisal system, for example, management by objective (MBO). A quality of work experiment restructures multiple dimensions of the organization, such as the authority, decision making, reward, and communication systems, rather than any one dimension. Therefore, a new job enrichment or supervisory training program does not fit our characterization of a quality of work experiment. The focus of the multidimensional change is generally to provide greater democratization of the work place, greater control for the worker over his or her environment, and greater joint problem-solving between labor and management.

3. The use of an internal mechanism for diagnosing, introducing, monitoring, and recalibrating change. Many organizational change projects are initiated and conducted by outside consultants. The source and direction of change is external to the organization. When the external consultant leaves the organization, in many cases so does the stimulus and direction for change. In the ACQWL projects a quality of work committee is designed as an internal part of the organization for diagnosis, planning, monitoring, and recalibrating change. By designing the change mechanism (in the Rushton case it was a labor-management problem-solving group) as part of the organizational structure the long-run viability of the experimental intervention is facilitated.

MY POINT OF VIEW

In 1974 I signed a contract with ISR to do an independent evaluation of the Rushton project for a period of three years. The design of the first QOW experiments required an evaluation team that was independent of the external consultants to management and the union. Funding for the evaluation team came from separate sources.

The major activities for the evaluation team were to design, collect, and analyze the data, and to write up the results of the experimental intervention at Rushton. We had complete access to all company data. We attended and made transcripts of all major meetings, with the exception of a few consultations of the research team with management or with the union. Members of labor and management were available at all times for interviews. At the end of three years vast amounts of information on job attitudes, productivity, costs, absenteeism, safety, strikes, and so on, had been accumulated from five attitude surveys, four years of daily economic data, extensive on-site observations and interviews. While our work was intensive, we did not contribute directly to the decisions relevant to the experimental program at Rushton. Our role was to observe and record, but not to intervene. I cannot, of course, argue that we were completely independent of the change process. Asking questions of union leaders, miners, or managers in some sense can affect the course of the experiment. The key idea, however, was that we did *not* participate in decisions relevant to the design or operation of the experiment.

Despite our independent measurement of the project, our values could possibly have affected the outcome of this report. That is, if we ideologically supported a particular form of change, we might be more likely to present data supportive of that type of change. Therefore my own values relevant to this and similar projects need to be stated. They are the following: I think management and labor should experiment with new forms of work organization to improve both the economic well-being of the firm and the psychological well-being of the workers. There is clearly no one solution. A period of experimentation is necessary to identify approaches that will work in specific situations. Eventually the projects will have to meet the test of economic viability or organization "owners" will have to change organizational goals explicitly to permit trading off social or psychological benefits for economic benefits. I am not a proponent of the theoretical framework (sociotechnical approach) or the major substantive change (autonomous work groups) that characterized the Rushton project. Therefore, while I support the general principles of finding new forms of work organization, I am not an *advocate* of any of the specific approaches used at Rushton. Basically, I feel that my value position, and that of the others on the evaluation team, has not biased the results.

PLAN OF THE BOOK

The book opens with a description of the Rushton setting. The organizational, technological, and social aspects of Rushton are defined to provide the reader a context for understanding the experiment. The major actors from management, union, and the research team are then introduced.

Part II of the book provides a historical account of the change. It opens with the decision to participate, delineates the development and proposed experimental plan, then moves into the phases of implementing the plan and diffusing it to the rest of the organization. That story ends in the first quarter of 1976. Part III is a description of the evaluation design and methodology, followed by an examination of the results. Part IV is a crucial section because it analyzes why change was successful and why it was not. Particular attention is given to why certain aspects of the change program did not remain stable over time. The last chapter tries to identify the critical issues in designing and implementing change.

WHAT SHOULD WE LEARN

The Rushton experiment was one of the most elaborate and innovative interventions in recent years. It attempted to change the total organization by restructuring the nature of the communication, decision-making, authority, reward, and other organizational systems. The Rushton experiment was also one of the most elaborately evaluated of all the QOW experiments. It therefore provides a unique opportunity for learning. The question is, what do we want to learn? Over the three years I have worked on this project, the most frequent question asked was whether Rushton was a success. I typically avoided answering that question, in the best academic tradition, by saying that I had not completed analyzing the data. Now that I have completed analyzing the data, I think that it is the wrong question to ask.

Rushton was truly an experiment—it was an attempt to learn about some fundamental processes in organizational change. There was little precedent to guide the research team, union, or management. This was not a traditional three-hour laboratory experiment with college students, it was a more than three-year venture into an ongoing organization. Successes as well as failures were inevitable, and they were distributed over different time periods. What is important is the unique opportunity to focus not on *what* happened, but on *why* events happened the way they did—not *what* did not change, but *why* it did not change. We want to be able to identify a set of problems that are likely to be recurrent in other QOW experiments. Why did certain planned interventions take, while others failed to take? Why did certain structures persist over the three-year period, while others gradually vanished? Why did problems occur in diffusing the change project throughout the mine? Why did other mines not adopt practices introduced at Rushton, despite the highly publicized nature of the experiment? We want to begin to understand the theoretical processes that surround the answers to these questions and other issues of organizational theory and practice.

PART ONE

BACKGROUND FOR THE EXPERIMENT

THE FOLLOWING CHAPTERS DESCRIBE THE BASIC institutions—the company and the union—affected by the QOW project and provide information that the reader needs in order to interpret and evaluate the experiment and its consequences. Chapter 2 deals with the company, its structure, technology, communication systems, and so on. Chapter 3 describes the characteristics of the union that bear on understanding the Rushton QOW experiment. The last chapter in this section provides a sketch of the employees prior to the initiation of the experiment. The delineation of contextual factors is important for understanding the rationale for participation, the form of the experiments, and the interpretation of the results.

CHAPTER TWO

The Company

The Rushton Mining Company is located near Osceola Mills, Clearfield County, Pennsylvania—a small rural community (population approximately 1,670). A review of the map of Pennsylvania shows Osceola Mills in the north-central section of the state. State College, home of Penn State University, is the most visible community of significant size in the area and is approximately 25 miles east of Osceola Mills.

Rushton is a medium-sized mine. There were approximately 180 employees when the experiment began late in 1973. Of these, some 35 were classified as managerial, the remainder were nonexempt and members of the United Mine Workers Union. At the beginning of the evaluation, there were three working sections in the mine (South, North, and East). The other working departments included maintenance, a general labor group, and the cleaning plant.

Data on the descriptive characteristics of the company were collected from: (1) the *Organizational Description Interview* and (2) informal interviews with management, and company records. (The formal interview is described in Appendix One and is available on request from the author.)

HISTORY

This brief identification of the critical points in Rushton's history is limited to events that bear on the interpretation of this QOW project.

Prospecting for the mine began in 1962 and 1963. Warren Hinks, the president of Rushton, was the principal individual involved in this activity. Prospecting includes a variety of activities, such as contacting people who are willing to lease coal rights, reading and evaluating

17

maps, taking core samples, and so on. Mr. Hinks is a mining engineer and had been involved with mining activities for some time. Prior to the Rushton venture he had operated a small mine outside of Pittsburgh.

During 1963–1964 contact was made with Pennsylvania Power and Light Company (PPL), a major electric utility in Pennsylvania. Since the power company relies on coal as a main energy source, it is always interested in securing an additional supply. It owns some mines and buys from others. Some interest in Hinks' exploration was expressed, and Hinks and his associates were asked to submit a feasibility study to PPL officials, who were then to decide whether to back the construction of the mine. Financial backing was necessary since construction of a mine is an expensive proposition.

In 1964 PPL approved the Rushton plan and provided funds for construction. Warren Hinks was president; his associate, Mike Cimba, was treasurer. At that time Rushton was run independently of PPL, although the latter provided the major source of funds. It was independent in the sense that Mr. Hinks made most of the decisions; there were no PPL people in management positions. Rushton developed its own system for mining and its own information system. It performed its own operational activities (e.g., purchasing, recordkeeping). All its production, however, went to PPL, which paid for the coal on a cost, rather than market-price basis, that is all operating costs were allocated over a tonnage basis and the cost per ton is what PPL paid Rushton.

By 1964–1965 construction activities had started, this included building the major outside buildings and the shaft (the entry) into the mine. During construction, recruiting, hiring, the buying of machines, and the setting up of procedures for mining and record keeping were underway.

In 1965 the mine began operation. It is interesting to note that we are dealing with a relatively young organization at the time of the experiment. The work force, then, is young in terms of length of service. Many of the participants in this experiment were around when the mining started.

During 1967 a major strike occurred over unionization. The company had started as nonunion. However, an organizing drive began in 1967 and there was a bitter strike. Management strongly opposed unionization. The strike ended with the company becoming unionized.

A new mine superintendent took over in 1969. Many people at Rushton see this change in superintendents as marking a turning point in union-management relations. There was a flurry of strikes after unionization and the original superintendent was a central actor in these disputes. After the change in superintendents, however, the general feeling was that union-management affairs moved on a more conciliatory basis. We do not wish to imply any casual connection. Rather, the point is that the change in superintendents marks a turning point in labor-management affairs.

Initial discussions on the feasibility of a QOW project at Rushton began in 1973. The experiment was launched on December 3, 1973, after an extensive planning period.

In 1974 PPL took over formal control of the mine. Mr. Hinks remained the major decision maker at Rushton, although he was now formally an employee of PPL, rather than under a contractual arrangement. Resulting organizational changes include the merging of the Rushton information systems into the PPL systems and PPL's supervision of certain activities, such as insurance.

ORGANIZATIONAL STRUCTURE

Figure 2.1 shows Rushton's organizational structure during the first experimental year. The owner and final authority over the policy and operations at Rushton is PPL. However, the president of the mine in fact directs the policy and operation decisions at the mine. Both he and the secretary-treasurer work from Johnstown, Pennsylvania, where they also supervise the operation of other mines. The superintendent is responsible for the mine's day-to-day operations, including both inside and outside (e.g., cleaning plant, offices) activities. The general foreman is responsible only for the inside operations of the mine. Mining sections are geographically defined. Each section (physical area) has three crews composed of a foreman, a miner operator, a miner helper, two bolters, and two carmen. One maintenance man works with each crew in the section, but he reports to the maintenance foreman. The general labor pool is another source of inside workers; they report to the assistant general foreman and perform support services, such as laying track or maintaining conveyor belts. They may be temporarily assigned to a crew or work in the "back area." The inside work force represents about 60 to 65% of the total work force, which varied from between 180 and 200 people.

The two outside operations are the cleaning plant and maintenance. One general foreman and three shift foremen supervise approximately 33 men in the cleaning plant which prepares (e.g., separating out rock, wash, drying) the mined coal for shipment. The outside maintenance operation, supervised by a general foreman and an assistant, consists

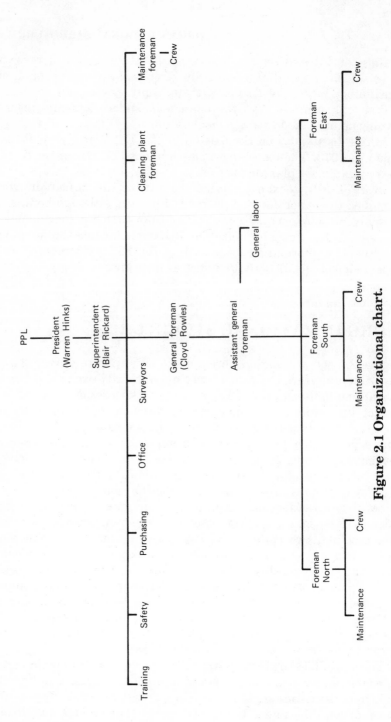

Figure 2.1 Organizational chart.

of men who repair and rebuild pieces of mining equipment. This group may also work on special maintenance projects inside the mine. The outside operation represents about 20% of the work force.

The staff functions that report to the superintendent include purchasing, safety, training, the office group that processes all the mine's records, and the surveyor's group that determines the amount of coal cut. This group, including the foreman, are in the management group, which constitutes around 20% of the work force.

The organizational chart in Figure 2.1 specifies not only reporting relationships, but also the major job functions at Rushton.

Due to the small size of the firm, many of the functions, such as record keeping, training, and purchasing, are performed by a single individual. For example, there is no personnel function as a specific nor is there a production-control or a quality-control job. Activities, such as time and method studies, are not formalized and may be handled, for example, by the training director. The nature of the relationship with PPL affects Rushton's outside or external functions. Since all the coal is sold to PPL, no sales functions are necessary. Other external functions, such as public relations, are nonexistent.

The authority structure of the mine is relatively centralized. Authority is defined here as action that can be taken on a decision without waiting for confirmation from above; the more the authority is concentrated at higher levels, the more centralized the organization. At Rushton the majority of operating decisions are made either by the president or by the superintendent. Most of these, with the exception of minor operation problems, require the confirmation of the president. The word "require" means that the superintendent would not make these decisions without getting the president's approval.

The character of the centralization can be clarified with a few examples. Purchasing new equipment or changing the mining plan (the map of areas to be mined) would be done only with the president's approval. The decision to hire a new foreman would be made by the superintendent. However, he would most likely review this decision with the president first. Following our definition of authority, this would mean that the decision is still in the hands of the president. The decision to hire a particular miner would be made solely by the superintendent. The number of new miners to be hired, however, would need the president's approval.

The relationship between the president and PPL is affected by the fact that Rushton began as an independent company. Since PPL did not become Rushton's formal owner until 1974, Warren Hinks was the chief officer and owner during the period when participation in the experiment was under consideration. Despite the formal change in ownership, most of the major mining decisions are still made by Mr. Hinks. The relative independence of Rushton from PPL was important in the decision to participate, to design, and to modify the experiment. There was simply a good deal of freedom and hence flexibility to shape decisions as local conditions warranted, without having to appeal to higher organizational levels.

DOCUMENTS

Except for the labor-management contract, which is an important document at Rushton, and federal and state mining laws, which are also available in written form, there are few formal documents (e.g., job descriptions or statements of policy) to guide Rushton's operation. The contract and the laws are generated outside of, rather than within, the firm. In general, Rushton is not run with many formalized documents.

TECHNOLOGY

Mining has often been described as a transportation system. That is, the technology of the mine is organized to transport coal from the coal face to the consumer. The coal is removed at the face and transported to a conveyor belt which carries it outside the mine. There it is transferred to the cleaning plant for processing and then transported to the finished coal pile. Subsequently it is loaded on coal cars for transportation to PPL.

Since the focus of the QOW experiment was the mining crew, this discussion will be limited to the technology used in each physically designated mining area or "section" in the mining plan of the company. Each of the three mining sections—North, South, and East—has unique physical conditions as well as specific machinery assigned to it. As opposed to a department in a company, the physical delineation of a section is dynamic since the section is continuously moving.

Physical Layout and Conditions

The sections are located about 200 feet underground, approximately one to two miles from the entrance to the mine. The average roof height is around 5½ feet. A typical entry or corridor width is approximately 20 feet.

The physical conditions of the section are critical to the mine's operations. For example, the roof is an important predictor of work behavior and production. Some sandstone roofs are so hard they need not be bolted, and thus production moves at a faster rate. A good roof also means less chance of accidents, obviously a preferred state. A bad roof, one that has a high probability of falling, necessitates special bolting procedures and is associated with a higher probability for accidents. It is an undesirable working state and one that impedes production.

The bottom is another physical dimension relevant to the mine's operation. Two aspects of the bottom are important: (1) steep grades impede the movement of the cars and (2) a wet bottom, a common occurrence, also leads to transportation problems.

At Rushton the coal seam, which defines the layer of coal versus other rock, was approximately five feet in height, and this figure was fairly constant across mining sections. Although samples are taken to approximate the direction of the coal seams, there is always some uncertainty about their direction and about the presence of faults. Faults are large rock concentrations cutting across the seam and are formidable obstacles. The problem is that it is hard to predict the character of an unmined coal seam despite the sampling procedure in which holes are bored from the surface into the unmined area.

Other significant physical conditions include complete darkness, wet areas, and a temperature level of approximately 50°. There is also a noticeable dust level, which is denser at the coal face and near the conveyor belt. This discussion of physical conditions and layout will be important later in understanding the context in which the Rushton QOW project unfolds.

Types of Mining

The mining system at Rushton is called "continuous mining." Continuous mining involves developmental mining and retreat mining. There are some important basic differences between these two types of mining which affect production costs and output.

Developmental mining, as the name suggests, concerns developing the coal field, that is, driving ahead in the coal field by developing a number of entries. As the entries are driven forward, cross cuts, openings from one entry to the next for ventilation and passage of equipment, are also made. Pillars (large blocks of coal left to support the roof) are the result of this entry and cross-cut work.

When a mine is opened, the initial entries driven to get at the coal are called main entries. Subsequently other entries are driven off the main entry to create smaller workable coal areas and these at Rushton are called "butts." Further subdivisions occur by driving rooms off these secondary entries.

Retreat mining or pillaring, as the name suggests, means moving back from the developed area. Hence the objective is to recover the pillars that have been left as supports during the developmental mining. In retreat mining productivity is generally higher because there is less set-up work than in developmental mining where the roof has to be buttressed by timbers and roof bolts after every pass of the continuous miner. In retreat mining the pillars are extracted and the roof is expected to fall. The fall obviously creates particular safety hazards; this is clearly the most dangerous time to be in the mine.

Actual production rates, costs, and safety hazards vary between these two methods. Therefore, it will be necessary to reflect these differences in the economic analysis of this experiment.

Equipment

Each section has major pieces of equipment. The largest piece is the continuous miner which has a large rotating drum with carbon bits. It is used to shear the coal from the wall. The miner operates by electricity fed to it by attached cables. The bolter is essentially a drilling machine used to place bolts in the roof and is also run by electricity. Large open mobile units, called cars, carry coal from the miner to the feeder. They run on electricity provided either through the cables or by batteries. The distance from the face to feeder varies; an average distance would be on the order of 200 feet. The feeder is a conveyor-like apparatus connected to the main conveyor belt. Coal is dumped onto the feeder which then feeds it onto the conveyor belt. The conveyor belt carries the coal outside the mine. Other pieces of support machinery, principally for transporting people or supplies, are a jeep, a supply bus, and a mantrip bus for taking the men from the bottom of the slope inside the mine to the face. (The trip from the surface to the face via cars takes approximately 30 minutes.) Each section has a large scoop to clean up coal. Since electricity is the source of power, there are several electrical installations (e.g., transformers) to supply and control the use of electricity in the section.

Most of the machinery can be classified as power equipment that is manually controlled. The machinery is not characterized as operating at an automatic self-feeding or feedback type, neither is the bulk of the technology at the level of hand tools and manual labor, as it had been in the past. The activities performed manually include setting timbers (roof supports), shoveling coal back onto the conveyor belt, and hanging brattice curtains (for ventilation).

Workflow

The nature of the workflow depends in part on the type of mining. Consider, for example, a developmental mining operation where five entries are being driven. Although the cycle is continuous and multiple operations are being conducted, let us start with the miner making its initial pass into area A. Coal is sheared from the wall, picked up by the miner's own conveyor, and temporarily stored. A car is driven up to the back of the miner and the miner's conveyor pushes the coal into the car. These processes of mining and filling up the car occur simultaneously until the car is full. (The estimated time for filling a car is less than two minutes.) The car then travels to the feeder and a second car moves into place behind the miner; the mining and filling operations are repeated. By this time car "1" has dropped its coal on the feeder. Car "2" is disengaging from the miner and heads to the feeder, while car "1" returns to the miner. The sequence continues until the miner completes its first pass. The first pass is necessarily completed when the miner can no longer advance without the miner operator working under an unbolted roof. At this point the operator backs the miner up and, with the assistance of his helper, prepares to make a second pass into area A. Before this can be done the operator, and sometimes a car operator, timber the unsupported area just mined. The same sequence of activities between the miner and cars continues until the miner completes its second pass in section A.

While these activities are underway, other activities are being completed. One important task, which imposes a constraint on the miner, is bolting. Unless an area is bolted, it cannot legally be mined. Other support activities, such as building brattices for ventilation, are in process during this time period.

Once the miner has completed area A and area B is bolted, the operator, with the assistance of his helper and car operator, moves his miner into B. The same sequence takes place, with the miner moving from area B to C and so forth. Eventually the distance from the feeder to the face becomes great enough to warrant a belt move. This means that the belt is extended to reduce the traveling time from the miner to the feeder. In this complicated activity mining stops and the whole crew plus support personnel undertake the move. A move generally lasts one and a half shifts.

If we review the workflow of the mining sequence within the section we can make a number of observations. First, the work is highly interdependent. If the miner or feeder belt break down, mining essentially stops. Most systems have at least two cars and sometimes two bolters. If one piece breaks down, the other continues and production is not completely stopped. Second, the sequence of operations is relatively inflexible. The miner is the common first point for all operations.

A second type of interdependence occurs between the crews (shifts) in a section. What one crew does in the mining cycle bears heavily on the activities the next crew must do. This interdependence is a critical source of conflict between crews. Since the work cycle includes both production and support activities, it is not surprising that a crew, which is evaluated on tons produced per shift, would orient its activities toward production, rather than support or set up. If one crew maximizes production, the other crew will have to do the support work and will be poorly evaluated due to low production. This causes intercrew conflicts.

Similar interdependencies occur between the section and the outside. Supplies come from the outside. Failure to have supplies on hand or to bring in the correct supplies can stop the section's production. Another type of interdependence concerns transporting coal out of the section. The belt provides the means of transporting coal out, yet long portions of the belt are outside the section's jurisdiction. If the belt stops, so does the section's production.

Job and Job Environment

There are five focal jobs in the section: miner operator, miner helper, bolter, car operator, and support man. These constitute the major jobs in each crew. The miner operator runs the continuous mining machine that scrapes the coal from the seam. The helper does set-up work to facilitate the work of the miner operator. The bolter bolts up the roof. The car men move the coal from the continuous miner to the feeder. The support men, who work in the back areas primarily, do set-up work, such as ventilation, wiring for communications, laying track, and rock dusting (to suppress gasses capable of exploding), in order to keep the section up to safety standards and ready for production.

Another way to describe the jobs is to rate them on a series of dimensions reflecting their inherent characteristics as well as their environment. To do this we used the *On-the-Job Observation Booklet* developed at ISR (Jenkins, et al., 1975). Two appraisers rated all of the jobs over a one-month period (December, 1973). There was 71% agreement across the categories for the two raters (see Appendix I).

Before examining some of the specific results, a number of general observations can be derived from the data. First, the job environment for the five jobs is quite similar, so there are common ratings across these dimensions. Second, there is similarity in the level of mechanization, so there is not a lot of variability among the descriptive job dimensions.

The job environment is dirty, noisy, and dangerous. The only illumination comes from the lamps on the miners' hard hats. The seam height varies, but is generally around five feet, so some of the workers cannot stand upright. When the machines are in operation, the dust level increases and the noise, particularly from the continuous miner, precludes conversation. Water is a common problem and leads to muddy bottoms and pools of water. In some sections the men mine with raincoats.

Sampling some of the ratings we see that the car job has the least amount of variety; the miner operator has the most autonomous job. Although the level of feedback from others is generally low, the miner, bolter, and car operators have clear outputs from their jobs by which to judge their progress. The most sophisticated skills are found in the miner and bolter jobs, but these jobs also have more uncertainty. In terms of control over the pace of work, the support men work alone and can set their own work pace. The miner and bolter have to determine the pace of their work within the constraints of their environment. The bolter is the most dangerous job in terms of possible fatalities, the support position is probably the least dangerous job. The miner operator is the highest status job in the crew and the operator often serves as the informal leader.

The semantic differential ratings provide another picture of the jobs. These ratings come from the worker, rather than from the observer (see Goodman, 1975). The most interesting factor is that the environment is not viewed by the worker in as hostile a way as it is by the observer. This follows from the simple notion of adaptation level theory. Most of the men at Rushton have worked only in mines, as have their fathers and relatives. There are few reference points in their lives for jobs with more desirable environments. Hence the moderately positive view of their work and its environment.

The technology of Rushton is the critical background factor in understanding the QOW experiment. The design of the experiment in many ways is a response to the technology of the coal mine. For this reason it is probably useful to repeat some of the crucial characteristics of the technology and its environment:

1. **The environment is hostile.** Two people died during the time the experiment was in operation. A casual observer at the mine can pick out men with missing fingers or who show other signs of working in the mine.

2. **There is a high degree of uncertainty.** It is difficult to predict what will happen as one works on a day-by-day basis. The physical conditions create this uncertainty and represent a major factor in the production process. A consequence of the physical conditions is that the miners react to their environment, rather than try to control it. Passive orientation toward work and fatalism are common.

3. **The layout and darkness** make it impossible for the supervisor to review the work of his subordinates.

4. **There is a high degree of interdependence within crews.** If one machine goes down, the whole production process goes down.

5. **There is a high degree of interdependence among crews.** Since the mining cycle extends over the shift cycle, there needs to be a high coordination between shifts. Shifts or crews are evaluated in terms of their productivity, so there is a tendency to focus on increasing a crew's productivity, often at the expense of the other crews in the section. This leads to intercrew conflict and lower production.

6. **There is a high interdependence between the inside section and the outside.** Failure to bring in the right supplies leads to long downtimes because travel in and out of a section takes at least an hour. Without adequate planning there can be a lot of downtime and production can be lost.

OUTPUTS AND MEASUREMENTS

The output from the mining operation is raw coal. The coal product is measured in terms of feet cut. This measurement is recorded and presented by the foreman and his miner operator. The foreman estimates the feet by tape measure or by the number of cuts made by the miner. The same information on feet cut is also generated independently by the surveyors on a section basis, rather than shift basis, and at varying time periods (generally every 10 days). The feet times width and height of the seam provides a cubic-feet figure. This is then multiplied by a density factor to estimate tons of coal produced.

There is no real measurement of the quality of coal produced by each section. After the coal is delivered, PPL assesses how much of the coal is acceptable, that is can be used in their power plants. Thus a general rejection factor is computed. But this is measured at the company level since all the mine's coal has been merged by the time it reaches the outside coal pile. There are procedures for taking core samples, but this is expensive on a section basis and not practiced by Rushton.

FINANCIAL POSITION

Rushton is a captive mine. All its production is sold to its owner. The price of the coal is determined by dividing the number of tons produced into the cost of producing the coal. In this sense Rushton is different from other firms selling or competing on the open market.

To get an idea of Rushton's general financial position, consider some of the following information. Raw coal production per section per week was around 4400 tons. There were three operating sections prior to the beginning of the experiment. There are roughly 48 production weeks per year. The clean coal shipped to the power company is approximately 72% of the raw coal. The assets of the mine were in the order of $5.5 million.

CONTROL SYSTEMS

In general, Rushton does not rely on elaborate or formalized control mechanisms. There is a budget, with standard costs derived from past experience and time-study or other analytic procedures. The budget, however, does not seem to be a major decision-making tool at Rushton.

As a matter of law the company has to develop a mining plan which indicates future areas to be mined. Planning, of course, could be done on other topics, such as manpower, capital requirements, and so on, but there is no planning of this sort at Rushton. Operations have a day-to-day quality.

One source of control is the information on production, delays, and accidents contained in the regular production and financial reports. These are reviewed daily and used by the superintendent to control the day-to-day operation. A good deal of attention is given to whether a crew's production is at an acceptable level.

Reward systems, such as pay or promotion, are not used as control devices. Nonexempt workers' salaries and job movement are determined by the United Mine Workers of America (UMWA) contract. Position, rather than performance, determines pay raises. Managerial salaries also seem to be a result of position, with across-the-board raises given rather than differential rewards based on performance. There is no formal performance evaluation system.

COMMUNICATION STRUCTURE

Overall, Rushton's communication system both at the managerial and employee level is fairly informal and unprogrammed. Data on communications came from semistructured observations and in semistructured interviews during the last few months of the baseline period (1973).

Memos placed in the foreman's room or in the nonexempt employees' waiting room are the closest thing to a formal communications mechanism. Most communication involving the operation of the mine is face-to-face. For example, discussions on day-to-day operational problems are carried on between the superintendent and the general foreman, between the general foreman and the other foremen. Problems in the cleaning plant are discussed between the superintendent and the cleaning plant foreman. The president and superintendent generally discuss operations each day.

At the employee level the physical area defines the unit of interaction. This is particularly true in the mine where a crew member sees only his own crew and actually only a limited number of them. The principal periods for informal communication occur as the shifts are changed (approximately 5 minutes), during a lunch break prior to work (10 minutes), at dinner break during the shift (30 minutes), and during work for those that do work with each other. The content of these discussions includes some task considerations, but most concern nonwork topics. The frequency of this communication is highly variable and is a function of the number of friendship pairs in each crew.

Informal communications outside of work are more difficult to determine. The fact that the work force is dispersed over many small communities has the consequence of limiting interaction and communication. What one then finds is small informal groups drawn together by location, age, and interests, such as hunting. These, however, are the exception rather than the rule.

Communication Flow

The flow of communication can be characterized by who initiates the communications, who receives them, the ratio of initiations, and the content. Consider the following dyads at Rushton.

1. President/Top Management of the Mine. Most of the initiations come from the superintendent to the president in the form of a daily status report or a question to be resolved by the president's decision.

2. Top Management/Section Foreman. The most frequent initiator is the superintendent. The ratio of initiations of interactions is greatly skewed from him to the supervisors. The content primarily concerns task-related matters. There is a heavy emphasis on evaluation of the adequacy of crew production.

3. Top Management/Staff. The principal initiator would be the superintendent; the receivers are primarily the safety and training directors. Staff groups, such as maintenance and the surveyors, receive less frequent communication from the superintendent.

4. Middle Management/Section Foremen. The character of communications is the same as for 2.

5. Staff/Section Foremen. The safety director is the most frequent communicator with the section foremen. He initiates many more communications than he receives, and the content is primarily evaluative. The general foreman of maintenance is primarily a receiver of initiations. Since he controls the resource of maintenance assistance however, he can control the interaction in terms of how and when he wants to respond.

6. Supervisor/Crew. The communications pattern between a supervisor and his crew is constrained by the physical layout of the section. It is impossible to see or communicate with the whole crew. Another characteristic of the mining work environment is that the men are relatively independent and begin their work with little direction. Therefore, the general level of interaction is low. Of the interactions that do occur the ratio of initiating interactions to receiving interactions is greater for the foreman—approximately 3:2.

7. Horizontal Communications. The horizontal communication among the production sections is at a minimum, occurring most often when the crews change shifts. The foreman is the only frequent communicator since he learns from the foreman just completing a shift what the major problems are in the section. Formal horizontal communication between managerial groups (e.g., staff positions) is almost nonexistent.

CONCLUSION

The above picture at Rushton—its authority, technology, control, and communication—was taken prior to the initiation of the QOW experiment. It is important for at least two reasons: (1) It provides the background on context for the experiment. The rationale for participation and the form of the experiment (discussed later) are intimately tied to these contextual factors; (2) Although the experiment had some stated goals, its impact might be broader than these intended consequences. One question we are to pursue is the extent to which the experiment changed the structure of the organization. For example, did the experiment change the control system or the communication system?

CHAPTER THREE

The Union

The union played a crucial role in the Rushton QOW project—a role that cut across many domains, including the initial decision to participate in the experiment, to negotiate conditions for a sheltered experiment, to be a productive partner in the experiment, and to evaluate the QOW project.

Data on the descriptive characteristics of the union were collected from: (1) the Union Description Interview which provides information on the characteristics of the union; (2) a baseline attitude interview (see Chapter 10); (3) informal interviews with management and the union, and (4) company records. (The formal interview is described in Appendix I and available on request from the author.)

HISTORY

Although the mine was started in 1965 as a nonunion mine and fairly strong attempts were made to keep it nonunion, in 1967 there was a major strike over unionization. Jock Yablonsky was the principal organizer from the UMWA. The strike from all accounts was extremely bitter. After a five-week period the company was unionized and the strike ended. Subsequently, particularly during the year following the unionization of the mine, there was a rash of strikes brought on by management's resistance to the union role and attempts by the union to establish its power base.

In 1969 a new superintendent took over, and the union-management relationship was gradually changed. The period from 1966 to 1969 can be characterized as a period when the union established itself as a new institution and when both union and

management tested the legitimacy of their roles. After 1969 relationships moved to a state of equilibrium, and respective territories were
better defined. This is not to imply that there was a resolution of
conflicts. It simply means there now existed a condition in which the
two parties accepted each other. In terms of conflict they were still in a
condition of bargaining (March and Simon, 1958). Both parties had
different goals, and negotiations had the quality of a zero-sum game in
which one party won and the other lost.

ORGANIZATION OF THE UNION

The union structure contained three major groups: the local, the
district, and the international (UMWA).

The local includes the work force of Rushton (membership is
mandatory) and pensioners in the area. The union has the traditional
set of officers (president, vice president, secretary, financial secretary),
and it has two committees, the safety committee and mine committee.
Both committees are a creation of the collective-bargaining agreement.
The safety committee's responsibility is to represent the workers'
interests in maintaining and evaluating the quality of the mine's
safety conditions. The mine committee is responsible for initiating and
processing grievances. Membership on these committees is by election.

The local's basic functions are to protect the safety and welfare of its
members, to insure they receive all the benefits due to them under the
contract, and to file and resolve grievances in their members' interests
if the contract is violated. The local performs these activities through
its leadership, the committee structure, and monthly meetings.

The district performs several functions for the local. First, it
determines if the local complies with the contract. Second, it serves as
a resource for the local union issues not covered by the contract (e.g.,
initiation of a QOW project), but relevant to a particular local.
Similarly, special grievances are brought to the district for suggestions
about strategy and processing. The district also provides legal services
to the local. An elected district representative provides the connection
between the local and the district.

The international's major role is to negotiate the contract and
establish the union's general policies. The international, for example,
had to approve the Rushton local's participation in the QOW project.
The international represents approximately 220,000 miners.

BARGAINING STRUCTURE

Collective bargaining in the mining industry is conducted at the industry level with a centralized negotiating group. For the coal producers, the Bituminous Coal Operators' Association (BCOA) is the principal bargainer. For the union, the major bargainer is the negotiation team of the UMWA. The Rushton Mining Company had no direct involvement in determining the collective-bargaining agreement reached by the BCOA and the UMWA, but once the agreement was reached, the company adopted the agreement as its own. At the time of the experiment Rushton was not a member of the BCOA, even though it abided by its agreement. This probably contributed to the ease of setting up the QOW project at Rushton. Members of BCOA are required to get the approval of other BCOA members before changes can be made in the agreement. It is conceivable that some BCOA members' objections might have delayed or halted the Rushton QOW project's introduction. Since Rushton was a nonsigner, the company was able to initiate the program with few constraints.

The local union has relatively little direct impact on the industry's negotiations. However, Arnold Miller, UMWA president, has attempted to democratize the union by creating greater opportunities for members to affect the affairs of the union. Now members can participate in the bargaining process through voting on the agreement. In addition, representatives are elected from locals to a district conference where they make recommendations to the international on items to be included in the union bargaining package.

CHARACTER OF LABOR-MANAGEMENT RELATIONSHIPS

One way to describe the character of labor-management relationships is to look at some of the traditional indicators, such as grievances and strikes, and then examine some of the views held by the leaders and membership about management-union relations and the union itself.

Grievances

The grievance procedure during the baseline period (January to November, 1973) was governed by the 1971 contract. This specified a five-step procedure, beginning with a discussion between the grievant and foreman and proceeding to the final step which required the use of an umpire. The *actual* grievance procedure was different. Rarely would a grievance be worked out by a union member and his foreman. A more typical route would be for the individual to talk with the mine committee which, in turn, would contact the superintendent (step 2). Most grievances were resolved at this step. In general, the actual grievance procedure was somewhat informal, and there were not good records concerning the initiation and disposition of grievances.

Although there are a few grievance records, some estimates of number and types of grievances are available from the union and management. During 1973 some three or four grievances were introduced per month. Most of these were direct discussions between the mine committee and the superintendent (step 2). No grievances were formally sent to the commissioners, high level management and district representatives who review unresolved grievances (step 3). The average time to resolve a grievance during the baseline was three months; a year and a half was the longest. The most typical grievances concern job bidding or pay issues.

We entered Rushton late in 1973, so we have only a limited picture of the character of grievance processes at Rushton. However it is our judgment that there was a high degree of conflict between the mine committee and the superintendent. The mine committee initiated grievance procedures very actively for its members. This committee had a strong orientation to win. The superintendent of the mine, in turn, took a hard line against union demands.

Strikes

In the early 1970s the number of strikes substantially decreased. In 1971 there was the traditional strike over a new contract. During the baseline period for this experiment (1973) there were four walkouts. The first, a single-day stoppage, concerned a worker allegedly caught sleeping at work and considered for firing. The union objected to any disciplinary action and walked out. Three production shifts were lost. The miner in question was not disciplined. The second concerned management's opposition to a particular union member becoming a member of the safety committee—a union committee which monitors safety practices. The strike lasted 4 days and 36 work shifts (4 days times 3 sections times 3 shifts). The miner retained his position in the safety committee. The two other walkouts were externally caused by pickets set up by miners from other mines. As a matter of tradition these pickets are always respected. Twelve work shifts were lost for these two strikes.

Labor-Management Perceptions

Another way to describe the character of labor-management relations is by the perceptions each held toward the other. These were gathered in the *Union Description Interview.*

Management tended to view its relationship with the union, prior to the QOW project, as primarily defensive. Meetings between the two parties were characterized by conflict, and management attempted to protect itself from encroachments on managerial prerogatives. Although the level of conflict has subsided since the union organization, management still questions whether the union is the best possible institution to represent the men's interests. This is still a source of underlying conflicts.

The parties see each other as slightly untrustworthy. From the union's point of view this distrust is expressed by trying to get everything in writing and by not taking management's word, saying management often changes its mind or will not take a hard position on an issue.

Another way to characterize labor-management perceptions is in terms of stereotypes. The respective interpersonal perceptions are not clouded by simple negative stereotypes, that is, management does not hold undifferentiated negative perceptions of the union and the same is true with the union leaders' views of management. Although the interpersonal perceptions are somewhat differentiated, they can best be described as skewed toward the negative side. The differentiations in perceptions that do exist on both sides tend to fall into the range of neutral to negative.

Analysis of the union's and management's goals is another way to describe the relationship between these two groups. Union members described their goals in terms of obtaining the best working conditions, carrying out the contract, and insuring the men all their rights. In addition, there was an implicit goal to get anything above the contract they could get. Management's views of the union's goals were quite similar, that is, management thought the union wanted to get all the money and benefits it could for the workers. Production was viewed by management and the union as management's goal. Although each of the parties viewed each other's goals realistically, clearly some basic conflict existed between the goals. The concept of a fair share or equal distribution of profits was not considered. Rather, the union's underlying theme was to maximize what it could get from the company, while the company's view, of course, was to minimize what the union got.

CHARACTERISTICS OF THE LOCAL

Some characteristics of the local are relevant for understanding the QOW experiment at Rushton. These are drawn from our observations of the Rushton scene from November 1973 to December 1977.

First, prior to the beginning of the experiment there was no major figure or opinion leader in the local union officer hierarchy. There was no one person who was generally respected by all and could rally the opinions and behavior of the union membership.

Second, the views and experiences of the miners toward their union were not homogeneous. One group (approximately 25 men) within the union was the original core of organizers at Rushton. These workers tended to be older and to work more in outside jobs than in the mining sections. Because of their role in the bitter unionization of Rushton, they were, in general, less trusting of management and held more negative stereotypes about management. This group was also much more likely to participate in the monthly union meetings and to believe strongly in the union as an institution. Other members in the union were younger and had only worked at Rushton since the 1970s. They did not experience the organizing activities and were less committed ideologically to the union. As we shall discuss later, these groups reacted differently to the QOW program.

Third, although tension between these groups was reported in the interviews, it in no way affected the solidarity of the union in its actions against management. This UMWA local acts together. If one person walks out, they all leave.

BASELINE ATTITUDE MEASURE

The baseline interview administered in December 1973 was another means of obtaining information about the union. A set of structured items covered topics such as union decision making, union influence structure, and member participation. (More information on the interview is found in Chapter 10.)

External Union Influence

The respondents were asked to indicate how much say the union had in determining a variety of work outcomes. Table 3.1 illustrates the percent of respondents who thought the union had some say or a great deal of say in determining a set of extrinsic and intrinsic outcomes.

Table 3.1. Percent of Respondents Indicating the Union
Has Some Say in Determining Work Outcome
(N = 119 Union Respondents—December 1973)

Work Outcome	% Respondents
Physical conditions	87
Better job	63
Pay	94
Security	94
Interesting jobs	24
Successful	29
New things	30
Amount of work	18
Amount of freedom	24

The results illustrate what would be expected—the union has an important voice in determining extrinsic work outcomes, but not in determining intrinsic outcomes, such as the interest of the job, the success of the worker, and so on. This question was introduced to establish a baseline measure, reflecting feelings prior to the experiment. The hypothesis was that the QOW project might lead to changing the type of work outcomes a union considers in its bargaining domain. Since many quality of work projects focus on intrinsic outcomes and since these outcomes may be subject to labor-management discussion outside the QOW project, they might become new areas for union-management negotiation.

Internal Union Influence

The control graph (Tannenbaum, 1968) was used to describe the influence structure in the union. Again this item was introduced as a baseline measure to determine if the QOW project would change the union's internal influence structure. One hypothesis was that a QOW project would lower the influence of the local officers and committee

40 THE UNION

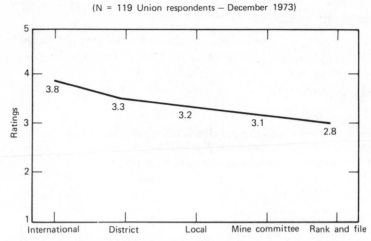

Figure 3.1 Control graph for union: Influence structure.

men. The initial picture (Figure 3.1) is of a relatively flat control graph. The international is the most influential of the five groups, but there are no major differences among the groups.

The shape of the control graph may be accounted for by the following: First, there had been an attempt to democratize the union and our respondents were aware of this. Perhaps if we had used a control graph during the Boyle (UMWA president before Miller) era, the slope of the graph would have been steeper. Second, the question focused on influence of the respective parties at the level of the local union. Actually the international's influence on local union policy is felt primarily at the three-year intervals when new contracts are established. Therefore, the saliency of the international's influence on the union is not great except during those periods. Since the baseline measurement occurred some 9 to 10 months prior to the 1974 negotiations, it may be that the saliency of the international's influence was low. Hence its influence rating was no higher than within the three to four range. A similar argument can be made concerning the district. During the prior year the district representatives had not been visible at Rushton. Their role has been to serve as a resource for the local, and this kind of consulting does not lead to high ratings of influence.

Another factor affecting the slope of the control graph is the personalities of the individuals in these respective groups. For example, some members of the mine (grievance) committee were very vocal as compared to the local union officers. This might contribute to the similar rating between these two groups.

Union Participation

Two items in the baseline interview concerned union participation. The first dealt with attendance at the regular meetings. The second dealt with meetings that are called for issues, such as a strike or a special grievance. The question was whether a QOW project would affect the level of participation in union meetings. Table 3.2 shows that approximately 18% of the members attended no regular meetings; more than 50% attended at least half of the regular meetings; and the remaining members fall into the 7 to 12 meetings category.

For the special meetings some 24% did not attend any of them, while 61% attended at least half of them.

Since there may be inconsistencies between reported and actual attendence in union meetings, we attempted to check participation rates through reports of attendance at actual meetings: 20 to 25% is a good estimate of attendance at regular meetings; 50 to 100% describes participation in special meetings.

Table 3.2.   Percent of Members Attending Regular Union Meetings (N = 119 Union Respondents—December 1973)

Meetings Attended	Percent of Members Attending
0	17.8
1–6	50.9
7–12	31.3

Internal Union Conflict

Earlier in this section the character of union-management conflict was examined. Two questions in the baseline measure were included to examine conflict within the union. Respondents were asked to rate how well members agreed about the way grievances were handled and the amount of agreement about the quality of their current contract (1973). There seemed to be considerable disagreement on the handling of grievances. Some 58% perceived little or no agreement among the men and 31% said there was only some agreement on how grievances were handled. Concerning their contract, some 42% of the members thought there was some agreement. In general there was more consensus among the men concerning the quality of the contract. The research question was whether a QOW project would change the level of internal union conflict.

CONCLUSION

The structure and character of the union on the international, district, and local levels had a major impact on the outcome of the Rushton project. As the reader moves through the historical development, the design, the initial results, and current status of the project, the character of the international as well as the nature of local union leadership and divisions within the membership (organizers versus nonorganizers) will play an important role in the understanding of the Rushton experiment.

CHAPTER FOUR

The Employee

The third central actor in this experiment is, of course, the employee—both in labor and management. In this section we shall present a brief picture of the employee, drawing from company records and our baseline attitude survey as well as from our own observations.

DEMOGRAPHIC CHARACTERISTICS

Table 4.1 presents some of the basic demographic characteristics of the union and managerial personnel. The data are drawn from company records and include only those individuals who were involved in our baseline survey, some 80% of the total work force. Other analyses indicate that this sample is representative of Rushton's total work force. The average age of the union workers is high and it does not

Table 4.1. Demographic Characteristics of Baseline Respondents

Demographic Characteristics	Union N = 119	Supervisor N = 22
Age	$\overline{X}$ = 39.71	$\overline{X}$ = 42.91
Education (years)	$\overline{X}$ = 10.3	$\overline{X}$ = 10.8
Marital status (married)	89%	82%
Number of dependents	$\overline{X}$ = 2.8	$\overline{X}$ = 3.6
Length service (years)	$\overline{X}$ = 3.7	$\overline{X}$ = 6.04
Prior coal experience	68%	82%

reflect the bimodal character of that group. The mine started with an older, experienced work force, which in most cases is still at Rushton. As Rushton expanded relatively younger and less experienced workers were hired.

In terms of education level the workers and management are quite similar. The union group is split, however, since many of the older men did not finish beyond eighth grade, while several of the younger workers had completed high school. The majority of employees at Rushton are married with dependents. The years of service are low because Rushton was only eight years old at the time of our baseline measures. During those eight years employment gradually built up, with much of the increase in hiring occurring in the last few years. Although it is not stated in the table, the work force at Rushton is predominantly male. One female works in the office, but office personnel are not included in our sample.

EMPLOYEE ATTITUDES

Another perspective on the employees at Rushton can be derived from their responses to the baseline attitude survey conducted in December 1973. Here we shall present a general picture of the Rushton miners' feelings about their jobs and the company prior to the beginning of the experiment. We shall concentrate on the miners, rather than the managers, since the miners are the target population in this experiment. Also, the technical discussion of the instrumentation used for the baseline survey will be deferred to Chapter 10 where attitudes are discussed in detail.

We asked the miners how they felt about their work, and some 70% were satisfied with their current job. Some 53% reported their job permitted them to make decisions on their own; 54% viewed their job as challenging; and 69% felt their work was interesting. In general, the miners seemed to feel positive about their work.

In terms of their work environment, 44% reported they were satisfied or very satisfied. Another 19% reported being slightly satisfied. Given the environmental conditions, which include darkness, high dust levels, danger, low ceilings, and dampness, these ratings are relatively high. They reflect, of course, the reference point used by the miners in making that judgment. Most used other mines rather than other work settings (e.g., a bank) as a reference.

The work group is a critical part of the miner's life: 75% of the miners felt positively toward their work group; 90% felt they were really part of their group; and 89% reported they were satisfied with the people they worked with. These data suggest a strong degree of cohesiveness among the work groups and indicate a higher level of positive attitudes than one probably would find in most work situations.

The foreman or boss is another critical factor in the employees' work life. In general, the Rushton employees viewed their boss favorably— about 70% were satisfied or very satisfied with their supervisor. In terms of specific supervisory behaviors, most respondents (84%) saw the boss as deciding what work would be done (prior to the experiment the major work areas were controlled in the traditional hierarchical manner). The men, in general, felt their boss was fair (73%) and looked out for their interests (73%). Most respondents did not see their supervisors actively engaged in providing rewards or punishments, keeping workers informed, or providing opportunities for participation (all current themes in the leadership literature). At least at the time of the baseline survey, attitudes toward a supervisor were more conditioned by whether he was fair or whether he was "breathing down your neck," rather than how he created opportunities for participation, for example. Supervisory control or sharing of responsibility and authority did not become an issue until after the experiment.

Since the concepts of control and authority were important in the experiment, we explored them during this baseline period. Figure 4.1 presents employee perceptions of the amount of influence on the operation of the organization held by various positions. The picture is

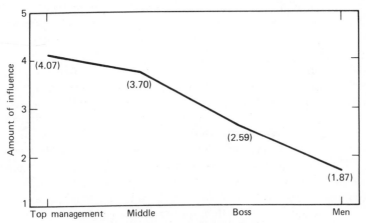

Figure 4.1 Control graph time.

one of a hierarchical structure, with the top management (president) and middle management (e.g., mine superintendent) exhibiting most of the power and influence. We also asked: How much control workers exercised in decisions, such as how the work was to be divided up, how much should be done, and how it should be carried out. The majority of the respondents (80%) perceived that they had little say in these decisions.

Pay, promotional opportunities, as well as other forms of organizational rewards are an important part of the worker's life. At the baseline period most (80%) of the workers were satisfied with their pay, and 65% reported that they were satisfied with their opportunities for getting a better job. Opportunities for freedom, for learning new things at work, and to participate were viewed as satisfactory by 60 to 70% of the respondents. When we asked about how satisfied they were with Rushton as a place to work, some 67% responded they were satisfied or very satisfied. The general picture, then, was that most of the respondents were content with the rewards they received at work.

Another area we probed concerned the workers' general perception of the climate of the organization. Here we find a somewhat different picture. Less than one-half of the respondents (41%) reported being proud of working at Rushton; 60% felt that not enough reward and recognition was given; and approximately 50% said there were many communication problems at Rushton and that productivity suffered from lack of organization and planning.

In general the miners viewed their job, work group, supervisor, and the rewards available at Rushton as satisfactory. These satisfactory arrangements occur in an organization that is fairly traditional in terms of hierarchical structure. We did not find identifiable sources of discontent in the miners' everyday work experience (e.g., supervision, work group) prior to the experiment. Only the area of organizational climate varies with this picture. Here the respondents seem more negative about the organization in terms of communication problems, lack of recognition, and poor planning. The stronger negative feelings in this area may be explained by the following: the referent for these items is probably more at the managerial level (e.g., top and middle-line managers); historically there has been a great deal of conflict between labor and management. Responses to the climate items may reflect this history. During the course of the experiment we observed continual "battles" between the workers and some members of management and the responses may have reflected this state of affairs. Another example of how differences in the referent may explain differences in response patterns can be found in the items concerning satisfaction with Rushton as a place to work and how proud the men felt about working at Rushton. The data which indicated miners were satisfied with Rushton (67%), but not always proud of being there (only 41% reported being proud), are not necessarily inconsistent. Rushton is the largest and best employer in the area in terms of pay, job security, and so on. It is not surprising that workers would find Rushton a satisfactory place to work. This does not mean that they would also be proud of working there.

Our general picture then is of a relatively satisfied work force, at least in terms of the factors immediately affecting the miners' work. There are, nevertheless, some strains between labor and management of the mine.

CONTEXTUAL AND CULTURAL FACTORS

To close this background discussion of the workforce, some qualitative observations will be presented. Rushton is located in a rural area in north-central Pennsylvania. The mine is surrounded by many small communities. Osceola Mills, Philipsburg, Houtzdale, Snowshoe are some of the small towns in which the miners live. Some men have a few minutes to commute, others take more than a half-hour to get to work. This geographical location bears on understanding the men at Rushton. First, there is no dominant community-company relationship—the men are spread in a 50-mile radius around the mine. Second, this dispersion prevents the development of cohesiveness in nonjob activities. After work the men go in different directions. Third, their life experiences have a narrow focus. Most were born in this area and will probably stay there. Few of the men have traveled, so their experience is limited. Clearly, television exposes them to mainstream events, and some will go to ballgames in Pittsburgh, but the focus of their everyday activities is in this geographical area where opportunities to broaden their experience are few.

The work experience for most of the men has been in mining (68%), and almost all of them have relatives who have been in mining. Many of those with no experience in and/or connections with mining have worked in jobs similar to mining, such as construction or timbering.

While our data collection did not focus on developing a description of the mining culture surrounding Rushton, some general themes did appear that are relevant for understanding the QOW experiment.

First, mining is a legitimate, desirable job. It is a job that has been performed through the generations, and it is a socially acceptable occupation. We informally asked the men if their children should be miners. In most cases they preferred that their brightest child go to Penn State, but it was quite acceptable for one of the children to go into the mines. Although some outsiders wonder why people accept this kind of job, for the men mining activities are legitimate.

A second cultural theme is one of autonomy or independence. The men exhibit strong preferences for behaving autonomously. Mining throughout the years has been a very autonomous activity and very likely the nature of the work has reinforced the miners' personal preference for independence. As we shall develop later, this orientation was consistent with some of the values of the experiment.

Third, a noticeable theme of fatalism appeared in many of the observations and conversations at Rushton. All the miners do not exhibit the same degree of fatalism, but it is a pervasive theme. It is best represented by the frequently used phrase at Rushton, "my name is on a rock," meaning somewhere and at sometime "I will be hit and die from a rock fall." This fatalism is not surprising, given the danger and uncertainty attached to the mining environment. The behavioral consequence of it is that the men are more likely to be passive or reactive to their environment. The QOW experiment, in contrast, requires active manipulation of the mining environment.

Fourth, performing concrete, physical, "masculine" activities was a major dimension of the worker's life, both on and off the job. We often asked the men how they spent their holidays or free time. Building a house, rewiring a room, or doing plumbing work were not uncommon responses. Hunting and fishing were also popular. Although the beginning of doe season was a regular working day, few men appeared at the mine. To some extent this emphasis on physical, rather than intellectual, activity was to contrast with aspects of the experiment, which focused on abstract ideas and day-long learning and discussion meetings, often dealing with questions or problems that were not easily resolved.

In this description of the worker, it is important to comment on the place of work in the miner's total life activities. Most of the men (60%) felt that their job was not the central part of their life; home and other nonwork activities were more central. Similarly, few were personally involved in what went on at the company.

Most of the men (67%) expected to be at Rushton five years from the date of our baseline interview (December 1973). But this was because Rushton was the best employer (in terms of wages and job security) in the area, rather than because of any personal involvement in the job or in the company.

CONCLUSION

The nature of the employees had a major effect on the introduction and maintenance of the QOW program at Rushton. As we unfold the decision to become involved in a QOW project, the nature of the intervention, the initial successes and attempts to diffuse the experimental intervention, the reader should keep in mind the employees' general attitudes about work, about management, and the cultural themes that characterize the work force.

PART TWO

THE RUSHTON
EXPERIENCE:
CRITICAL
HISTORICAL EVENTS

IN THIS PART WE REVIEW THE MAJOR PHASES OF the Rushton experiment to give the reader its historical development. Phase 1 (Chapter 5) concerns the decision to participate in the program. Phase 2 (Chapter 6) includes the period from April to December 1973 when the structure of the change at Rushton was being planned. During phase 3 (Chapter 7) the first experimental section was started. Phase 4, (discussed in Chapter 7), covers the period from March 1974 to April 1975 and is defined by the research team as the first experimental year. This phase has two parts. The first runs to the creation of the second experimental group in October 1974 and the beginning of the national coal strike in November 1974. The second begins after the coal strike and runs to April 1975. Phase 5 (Chapter 8) also has two parts. The first runs from April 1975 to August 1975 when plans for extending the experimental concept to the whole mine were being developed. This period ends with the men's vote in August not to extend the autonomous program. The last part runs from September 1975 through 1976. This period included the extension by management of the program throughout the mine (Chapter 8). Table 5.1 identifies the major historical events.

CHAPTER FIVE

The Decision to Participate

Two parties, the Rushton Mining Company and the United Mine Workers of America, decided in 1973 to enter into a QOW project agreement. Analysis of this decision is important for several reasons. First, it helps us understand why labor and management would participate in such a project. Neither the UMWA nor other mining companies have become involved in similar work experiments. A QOW project requires substantial change and the parties involved must give up traditional ways of doing things for some potential benefits. An analysis of the Rushton case will provide some insight into why management and the union did accept new risks.

A second reason to examine the decision to participate is simply that such an analysis provides a context for interpreting and examining the results of a QOW effort. In examining the reasons for participation the goals of the participants can be uncovered and used in the evaluation of the project. We expect divergence in the goals and hence differences in the meaning of the project's effectiveness.

Another reason for examining the decision to participate is to deal with the issue of selection bias. A potential problem in the QOW program is that certain firms might select themselves into it. Since participation is voluntary, organizations that are not necessarily representative of their general class of organizations might volunteer. This would lead to a selection bias that might detract from the generalization of results from the project. By investigating the decision to participate, one can better evaluate the significance of the selection bias.

There is a limited amount of data relevant to Rushton's decision to participate. Since the evaluation group was brought into the Rushton project some nine months after decisions concerning the project were under way, all the information is retrospective in nature. Being able to observe the development of the agreement would have been preferable. While it was possible to learn about the decision to participate from the point of view of the management and to some extent from the external research team (i.e., Trist, et al.), there has been less opportunity to review this decision from the international's point of view. The first real access to the international's position was obtained in 1977. Despite these limitations, it will be possible to identify some of the major factors contributing to the decision to participate.

BACKGROUND TO THE DECISION

Rushton's president, Warren Hinks, attended a safety seminar in February 1973 at Penn State. Mr. Hinks was attracted to the orientation of the training. He said:

> I liked . . . the talk about positive reinforcement. . . . We needed more than the carrot and stick approach. Needed more from a man's inner motivation. . . . I was encouraged by this line of thinking.

This meeting provided one of the initial contacts between Hinks and Grant Brown, a trainer who was to become part of the research team for the Rushton QOW experiment.

During this period Brown, a mining engineer by training, had established a relationship at Penn State with Gerald Susman, a social scientist in the business school. Susman's doctoral work had been undertaken at UCLA where he had come in contact with Eric Trist, an internationally known social scientist, who had been deeply involved in work design and organizational restructuring in coal fields in Great Britain. As the Hinks, Brown, Susman relationships were being formed, activities were happening at the United Mine Workers' headquarters. Davitt McAteer, head of safety at UMWA under the new Miller administration, was looking for new ways to improve safety. He read Trist's book, *Organizational Choice* (1963), which described work experiments in British coal mines and documented improvements in safety. McAteer contacted Trist, chairman of the Management and Behavioral Science Center at the University of Pennsylvania, to explore the feasibility of setting up an experiment to improve safety in a UMWA mine.

Since Trist and Susman had maintained contact this connection brought together the two groups interested in a QOW experiment in the coal mines. Discussions among Trist, Susman, and Brown eventually led to a meeting in New York City where the research team was formed. Then the three members of the research team met with Ted Mills who was then with the National Commission on Productivity. The plan was to draw up a quality of work proposal for Ted Mills, with the expectation that Mills could obtain funds to conduct a QOW experiment. At this point neither the company nor the union had made any commitments.

At a second training session at Penn State, still early in 1973, Brown talked with Hinks about trying an autonomous work group experiment in one of the Rushton sections. Hinks' recollections of this meeting include:

> I knew something about the autonomous idea from things I had read. . . . I brought over our superintendent [Blair Rickard] to talk with Grant Brown. Grant said we might lose some productivity, but there was a good possibility to make it up. Blair said it might be worth a try. . . . I think we were positive enough with Grant that he said he would talk to another company about participating.

The other company, Eastern Associated Coal Company, also agreed to explore participation in a QOW experiment. The existence of two interested organizations had a mutually reinforcing quality. Rushton's exploration continued because they knew that Eastern Coal was interested.

The next major event was a meeting in Washington on April 17, 1973, with all the major actors—Hinks and his co-owner, Mike Cimba; Brown; Susman; Trist; McAteer from UMWA; and Tom Faulkie, head of mine engineering at Penn State, who helped in the initiation of the project. The Eastern Coal representative could not come. At this meeting the concepts of a QOW experiment were explored, and everyone's views were expressed. The general position was that both Rushton and the union would participate. At the end of this meeting the participants met with Arnold Miller, president of the UMWA, and reviewed the basic concepts of the QOW program. Miller and Hinks then signed a letter which approved the purpose of a QOW project at Rushton and provided the opportunity for each of the parties to withdraw from the agreement whenever they saw fit. (The local union was not a party to this agreement.) Some of the text of the letter addressed to Ted Mills at the National Commission on Productivity follows:

> We have agreed to collaborate on a program, the purpose of which is to seek new approaches and, where indicated, new job designs so that all people in the company can experience increased satisfaction and increased quality of work and working life.

> We are conversant with the principles and objective of your quality of work program. We agree with the principles and agree to explore together the possibility of establishing a quality of work demonstration project at Rushton at a certain coal mine of Eastern Association Coal Corporation. We agree that Dr. Eric Trist will serve as consultant.

THE DECISION

Why did the company and union join into this agreement? The fact that both the union president and company president were willing to participate in a QOW program is a significant event. The past relationship between the company and union had been characterized by open hostility. In addition, quality of work concepts were fairly abstract and ill-defined, at least at this point in time. The president of the company said:

> There were a lot of questions going through my mind [such as] Is this a communist plot? . . . I was concerned we were getting into a communist concept . . . I did a lot of soul-searching.

The representative from the international, Davitt McAteer, also had misgivings:

> I was a bit scared. . . . I didn't know how far this thing was going to go.

The decision was also significant because the new venture was likely to be a risky one. There was no precedent in the United States for this kind of experiment. As McAteer said:

> I was very nervous . . . if this backfired . . . my head would be on the line.

The following analyzes this decision from the point of view of the company and then the union.

The Company

Why did the company join into this agreement? The president's values bear heavily on Rushton's decision to participate in the program. Autonomy, responsibility, and freedom of choice are all cornerstones of the project. These are values that are held and frequently articulated by Warren Hinks. The congruence between the values inherent in the Rushton experiment as articulated by the research team (Trist, Susman, and Brown) and the philosophy of the president is the key to the company's participation. Here are some excerpts from an early interview with Hinks:

> I had a clear philosophy . . . that everyone had the position of an associate rather than some hierarchical relationship.

> I liked doing things on my own . . . the freedom attached to doing things completely on my own . . . freedom is very important to me . . . it's very valuable for any individual. I read a lot . . . well, recently I finished *Pagan to Christian*. I got concepts from that book . . . man being his own self-governor . . . that propelled me . . . each person can self-govern themselves *[sic]*.

Hink's rationale for participation was not solely on ideological grounds:

> I enjoy a challenge. . . . I feel everyone should have the opportunity . . . but one thing that gave me concern was our younger people . . . just out of high school. They were better educated than their fathers. . . . I don't think they would stick with the boring repetitive work in a coal mine. If we were going to attract workers we needed the type of organization for them to grow. . . . Over time I can visualize the development of a professional coal miner . . . who can do many different jobs in a coal mine; a person who will have self-respect.

While the Rushton president was debating whether to participate, another mine was being considered by the research team as part of their two-mine design for a quality of work project. The second mine was larger and had different seam and technologies for mining. It was hoped that a common intervention in different mines would legitimatize QOW projects in the industry. Warren Hinks' perception that the other mining company would participate provided another force for signing the QOW project agreement.

The regard that Hinks held for the other participants also contributed to his decision to participate. The president of Rushton seemed to have positive perceptions about the competence of both the research

team and Ted Mills, who were serving as catalysts to bring the
company and union together. Hinks' view of Trist was generally
positive after some initial meetings:

> By the end of the day . . . we talked out a few more things. . . . I was
> more favorably impressed about his experience and commitment to help
> the worker. . . . I liked him . . . but still had questions about the
> political ideology.

About Grant Brown:

> I had met him before in the training sessions. . . . It's easy to like him
> . . . he seemed dedicated, to me. . . . I'm sure he also wanted the project
> because it brings bucks into Penn State.

The president exercises considerable influence over the management
of the mine. Although there was little explicit rejection of the experiment, it is clear members of management differed considerably in their
attitudes toward the plan. However no one really challenged the
feasibility of the QOW project. The influence or power structure at
Rushton is such that once the president supports a project it is likely to
be followed.

The history and structure of the mine bears on the decision to
participate. First, the fact that the president started the mine and
knows many of the men personally provided a base of power or
influence other than legal or formal power. The mine has the atmosphere of a family-run operation, rather than a large corporation.
Second, although PPL owns the mine, most of the decisions about
joining the QOW project were at the president's level. There was no
need to go through multiple organizational levels to get approval.
Dealing with a simple bureaucratic structure simplifies the process of
getting a project accepted.

As mentioned before, the company did not participate in the
labor-management contract created by the UMWA and the Bituminous Coal Operators Association. A signer of the BCOA agreement
cannot change it unless the other members concede. Since Rushton was
not bound to the agreement as a signer, when the QOW proposal was
generated, there was no need to get approval from the BCOA.

The Union

The international's participation in the QOW project at Rushton was
largely determined by Davitt McAteer. Although Arnold Miller signed
the letter, it was largely on the advice of McAteer, who was the prime

Table 5.1.   Rushton Timetable

	1973	1974	1975	1976
January				
February				
March		South section officially autonomous	End first experimental year	Strikes
April	Union/management sign QOW agreement in Washington			Mine training and development (steering committee) meets monthly
May			Preparation for mine-wide program	New role of union safety coordinator instituted
June				
July				
August	Development of program		Mine-wide vote rejects plan	
September			Management's extension of program mine-wide	
October	Local union approves program	New section introduced	Training initiated for new experimental work areas	
November		National coal strike		
December	Program launched in South section			

mover in this decision. McAteer was head of the safety department for the UMWA, and he was dissatisfied with the slow pace of improvement in mine safety. A QOW project at Rushton looked like a new way to improve safety, given some of the results of Trist's earlier work. McAteer said:

We were willing to try anything that looked promising . . . this was one of several projects. . . . We were anxious to improve safety . . . our interest was safety. . . . It was different from Trist's interest in quality of working life . . . but that was fine.

The people involved also influenced McAteer's decision to go ahead:

> I liked Eric [Trist] . . . he was a very decent guy. . . . Grant—I had known him before and we could get along. . . . Penn State [Brown, Susman, and Faulkie] was a relatively good place . . . at least better than the other mining schools. Tom Faulkie [Penn State mining engineer head who was involved in the initial planning] was a main player for me . . . we had different views but I could work with him.

The basic point is that *safety*—not the values of autonomy, responsibility, or greater control over work—dominated the decision of union participation.

CONCLUSION

The decision to participate was a momentous decision for both parties. It was clearly an adventure in uncharted waters with high levels of risk. It is interesting to note that the Eastern Coal QOW project never became operational (see Trist, Susman, and Brown, 1977) and that no other mine has joined into a quality of work experiment. Participation by management was due to Hinks' values and to his practical concern to make mining more attractive to young miners. The unique characteristics of Rushton, such as its size and lack of bureaucratic entanglements, enabled Hinks to dominate the decision. On the union side it was McAteer's need for new programs to improve safety that led to union participation. It is important to note that up to this period in our account the local union officials had not been involved.

What is important is that *single individuals* from the company and union determined the decision to participate. There was no attempt to gain consensus within either the union (international or local) or company. Indeed there was no consensus within either organization. This top-level commitment rather than system-wide commitment was later to have significant impacts on the project.

CHAPTER SIX

The Development and Structure of the QOW Program

This chapter is divided into three sections. First, our story moves from Washington to the involvement of the Rushton employees in the QOW project. Second, the nature of the initial experimental plan at Rushton is revealed. Third, the steps to implement the experimental plan are reviewed.

INTRODUCTION OF QOW CONCEPTS AT RUSHTON

After the signing, a series of correspondences passed among the major participants. Issues raised in these correspondences became in part the agenda of the next formal meeting attended by all participants (company officials, international union officials, the research team, and Ted Mills). This meeting, held in Harrisburg, Pennsylvania, in June 1973, concerned topics such as how gains would be allocated among labor and management, costs to be shared by labor and management, the role of the evaluation team, training, handling of grievances, and so on. (The evaluation team did not join this project until late October of 1973.)

The QOW ideas were still new for the participants. This and other meetings served to clarify some of the concepts but strains of ambivalence were still evident. The president of Rushton commented on the Harrisburg meeting by saying:

> [It] gave me a new appreciation of the issues . . . made me re-evaluate a number of concepts about participation. . . . I could see areas where we might not be willing to change . . . I was not at ease about these changes . . . [such as] giving up the right to direct the work force. . . . I was skeptical about the union members. . . . Davitt brought out a few things . . . that led me to believe that the UMWA still wanted to get more control of the industry.

During this same time period meetings were held with federal and state officials to review the consequences of the QOW project at Rushton in the light of federal and state mining laws.

In August 1973 the focus of activities turned to the mine. On August 13, McAteer met with officers of the Rushton local to acquaint them with the purposes of the project. The next day management, union, and the research team (Trist, Susman, and Brown) met at the mine and formed a labor-management steering committee that was to design the QOW project at Rushton. Management had seven members and was represented by the president, superintendent, other staff personnel (e.g., safety director), and two foremen. The union, with nine members, drew its representatives from its officers and members from the mine (that is, grievances) and safety committees. It is interesting to note that during the course of the experiment there was some variability in who attended the steering committee meeting. Sometimes the district representatives from the UMWA would show up. At other times work at the mine kept some management personnel away. Occasionally federal or state safety officials were there. The research team was always represented. Generally about 20 people attended the meetings, but there was fluidity in the membership. The nature of the meetings did not call for formal voting, so there was not undue concern over having an equal number of representatives from labor and management.

A second meeting in August by the steering committee focused on the role of the supervisor, grievances, selection of an experimental section, how to deal with overtime, and other issues related to designing the experimental intervention at Rushton.

Hinks, commenting on the first two meetings, said:

> Generally they were harmonious and productive. . . . I was pleased with the discussions . . . it was a real revelation to see them [union] able to make significant and intelligent contributions . . . with objectivity, that was being expressed as we worked out the contractual questions.

The president's comment is interesting given that there had been a strike at Rushton early in August where conflict rather than coopera-tion had characterized labor-management relations. The strike oc-curred when a union member was elected to the safety committee, but management objected to his presence on the committee because they believed he would "keep stirring up problems." After a week the men returned to work and the individual in question took up his position on the committee.

The steering committee continued to meet throughout September to draw up the plan for change. In October the document, *A Proposal for an Experimental Project in Work Quality at the Rushton Mine,* was submitted to the local union and ratified by a narrow margin (25 to 21). Management also agreed to the provisions of the document.

From the first steering committee in August, costs of the research team were sponsored by a grant from the U. S. Department of Commerce. The company bore all the other costs (e.g., loss production, meeting rooms, travel to conferences, etc.).

NATURE OF THE EXPERIMENTAL CHANGE

This section outlines the basic ingredients of *A Proposal for an Experimental Project in Work Quality at the Rushton Mine.* First an overview of the proposal.

The goals of the experimental change program at Rushton were: (1) a higher level of safety; (2) a higher and all-around level of skill and responsibility; (3) a higher level of productivity; (4) greater earnings, and (5) greater job satisfaction. These goals were to be accomplished by reorganizing one work section (three shifts) along the lines of an autonomous work group (hereafter AW). Basically this means that the responsibility for production and for directing the work force would be delegated to the working crew. The foreman no longer would have production responsibilities; safety was to become his greatest responsi-bility.

The specific design and outcome of the project were jointly developed and owned by labor and management. The program was to be guided by a joint committee including representatives from both labor and management. We shall now discuss the major aspects of the document for change.

Nature of the Experimental Section

Prior to the experiment at Rushton, the crew consisted of six employees (miner operator, miner helper, two shuttle car operators, and two roofbolters). In the experimental section, two support men who lay tracks, work on wiring, and so on, became regular members of the crew. These two support men were traditionally drawn from the general labor force and assigned to a section only when support work was needed. Therefore 24 (8 × 3 shifts) men were in the experimental section, plus three mechanics (one per crew) who reported to the head of maintenance, and three foremen (one per crew). All the work in the section was to be done by the crews. Only when special expertise was needed were other men brought in.

Autonomous Work Group

Management gave up the right to direct the work force in the experimental section. This meant that day-to-day decision-making about the mining work would be done by the crew. Mining is a fairly regulated industry and proceeds under a federally approved mining plan that indicates where mining can take place. Roof and ventilation plans are other governmentally approved documents that determine mining practices. The point is that the miners were not free to do what they wanted. The above plans provided clear constraints on their activities. Still there was room for decision-making on a day-to-day basis on where to mine, how much to mine, when to move, and so on. The general understanding was that the miners use of this new authority would occur gradually and probably be exercised by the informal leader of the crew.

Foreman

The foreman was no longer responsible for production or assigning the work force. These responsibilities were delegated to the men in the experimental section. The foreman was responsible for insuring that all safety regulations were followed. In addition he was to develop the men by focusing on new activities, such as training, planning, and integrating work in the section with activities in the rest of the mine.

Job Switching

All men were expected to exchange and to learn other jobs within their crews so that the crew would be multiskilled. The multiskilled arrangement would provide greater flexibility for the crew in terms of its ability to react to environmental changes and to staff any position. From the miner's point of view it would enhance opportunities for variety at work as well as the opportunity to become a professional coal miner, that is to be able to perform multiple job skills.

Payment

All members of the experimental section received the same top rate of $50 a day (plus shift differentials). The rationale for the same high pay rate was that all men assumed equal responsibility for production and maintenance of equipment. The learning and sharing of tasks included clean-up and support work as well as the regular mining work. Movement between jobs did not require bidding, as is the case under the labor-management contract. In the control sections, wages were paid by job category with only the miner operator receiving the top rate. The wage differential between the highest and lowest paying job within the control sections was approximately $7 per day during the first experimental year.

The Joint Committee: The Coordinating Mechanism

A joint labor-management committee, with equal representation from labor and management, supervised and monitored the experiment after it had been in operation for 75 days. The original and larger steering committee of management and union officers, who drew up the proposal, still remained intact and dealt with broader policy issues, while the joint labor-management committee dealt with day-to-day operations. The joint committee was composed of five members each from labor and management. The labor component involved a committee representative from each of the three crews on the experimental section plus two other union officials.

Grievances

Grievances were not initially processed through the traditional grievance machinery. The expectation was that grievances would be resolved within the experimental section. If not, they were to be brought by the section representatives to the joint labor-management committee, which would attempt to resolve them. Employees who were not members of the experimental section came under the grievance machinery specified in the regular union contract.

Training

A major part of the experiment was to move the men toward being professional miners. One way to accomplish this was to provide training on mining law, safety practices, ventilation, roof control, and rock dusting. A six-day formal training program was initiated early in the program.

Allocation of Gains

No gain-sharing plan was worked out by the initial labor-management committee. Rather some general principles were established. If no gains resulted from the project, the company would assume its costs for the experiment. If gains occurred, then management was to be reimbursed for costs (e.g., meeting time) related to the experiment. Thereafter a plan would be drawn up to work out an equitable sharing plan.

Volunteering

Selection of men for the experimental section was done through a volunteer procedure specified in the proposal. Essentially the men volunteered as they did in regular bidding, that is, within a job classification and with seniority as the main criterion for selection. A volunteer retained the rights to his original classification throughout the experiment and could leave the experiment at any time. His previous job remained open for 60 days. After that time he could bid for any opening according to his seniority and use any experience gained in the experimental section to his advantage.

The two topics described thus far, the labor-management steering committee meetings and the document for change, are significant points in the Rushton story. The meetings represented the first time labor and management were placed in a problem-solving situation, rather than an adversary relationship. All of the participants were pleasantly surprised by the ability of labor and management to work together. My own reaction to the first steering committee meeting I attended in late October 1973 was also one of surprise and admiration.

There were difficult problems to be solved, many could have been of the "I-win-you-lose" variety. There were heated arguments. There was some institutional harassment—"You management guys never want to give in." But all in all, difficult problems were resolved in a problem-solving, rather than bargaining or adversary climate. A number of factors probably contributed to this. The project was a new event and there was some motivation to make it work. The steering committee meetings took place in a different physical social arena with new actors. Previously labor and management met in the superintendent's office to fight over grievances. Now meetings were held outside the mine at a local motel and others, such as the president, the research team, members of management besides the superintendent, and union officials not on the grievance committee, were present. This created a new environment where new behaviors could be tried out.

The other significant event was the document itself. It represented a contract. This is unusual, since most unions are unwilling to modify an existing contract. A second and related point is that both the union and management gave up rights they previously enjoyed. Management gave up its right to direct the work—a prerogative most managers are unwilling to relinquish. The union, on the other hand, relinquished pay differentials for different jobs. Grievances appeared in the joint labor-management committee before they went through the contractual grievance machinery. The union also gave up claims on job bidding, since the men could switch jobs within the section.

A third feature of the document was that it substantially changed how work was to be conducted. Miners now had the opportunity to perform multiple jobs, rather than one job. In addition the hierarchical character of work was modified; foremen and other members of management were to shift control downward.

These changes are clearly dramatic and substantial. They occurred in a particular context. In the initial agreement between Miller and Hinks, it was stated that the project was experimental in nature and that either party could terminate it. This "out" clearly facilitated the opportunity for both parties to take risks.

SOURCE OF THE DOCUMENT FOR CHANGE

I have often been asked about the source of the ideas that surround the plan outlined above. Who really provided the ideas behind the design? Was it an individual or did it evolve from the steering committee's deliberations?

The basic design of the intervention at Rushton was the research team's creation, particularly Eric Trist's. Trist had done a landmark piece of research in the British coal fields examining the impact of autonomous work groups on economic, safety, and psychological outcomes of work (Trist, et al., 1963). This key book has become one of the principal examples of how to utilize successfully autonomous work groups in a work setting. It is not surprising then to find the use of autonomous work groups at Rushton. Perhaps more important than the autonomous work group concept is the basic theme of sociotechnical analysis that underlies Trist's and Susman's prior work and the Rushton project. Sociotechnical analysis has been one of Trist's major contributions to the field of organizational theory.

Basically, sociotechnical analysis assumes that work organizations have two interdependent systems: the technical system and the social system. The technical system includes the machinery, layout, workflow procedures, information, and so on, that are necessary to transform some material into a new state. The social system includes the human component of work. This refers to the attitudes, beliefs, abilities, and energies of individuals as well as the norms, traditions, and culture that ties individuals into a social network or system. The technical system has always been the province of the engineer, while the social system has traditionally been designed by the social scientist. Sociotechnical designers argue that the engineer and social scientist have erred by considering only their own system and that trying to optimize one system (e.g., improving work methods) will not necessarily improve organizational effectiveness. Single-system optimization fails to recognize the interdependency between the two systems. Therefore, sociotechnical designers propose that optimizing both the technical and social systems, that is, trying to find the best match between them, will enhance organizational effectiveness.

If we follow the premise of finding the best match between the social and technical system, the rationale for the design of the Rushton QOW project will quickly unfold. In order not to repeat in detail our analysis of the technology at Rushton, let us remember three central characteristics: (1) there is a high degree of uncertainty, (2) there is a high degree of interdependence within and between crews, and (3) the nature of the work layout isolates the men from themselves and their supervisor. Given these conditions, the innovations at Rushton represent an attempt to find a match between the social and technical system. Job switching increases the number of skills held by each crew member. As the number of skills increases so does the flexibility of the work group. The greater the flexibility of the social system to adapt to technical uncertainty, the greater the match between the two systems. Another innovation at Rushton was to have section conferences, in part to create a section (versus crew) consciousness. The nature of the work required that there be close coordination between crews. If the crew members were oriented toward the section, rather than their own crews, suboptimization would less likely occur and section effectiveness would be enhanced.

This identification of particular members of the research team as the principal architects of the Rushton QOW project is not made evaluatively and does not minimize the work of the steering committee. The steering committee, after many long hours of discussion, was able to translate these general ideas into a written document and subsequently into an operational plan. Thus the Rushton program had its roots in prior work done by the research team; the steering committee did not meet and suddenly create such a comprehensive program.

PUTTING THE PROPOSAL IN OPERATIONAL FORM

After the local union approved the proposal in October 1973, the next task for the steering committee was to translate the proposal into an operational plan. One important task was to select an experimental section. The position taken in the proposal was that the project would start with a single section. Although their theoretical framework called for an eventual total system transformation, the research team felt that neither management nor the union was ready for a change of the total system at Rushton. After a year the steering committee would evaluate the results of this pilot project and then decide whether the project would be extended. This action would reflect the joint ownership of the project.

The South section was selected by the steering committee as the first experimental section. The committee felt that this section was operating under normal physical conditions and that its mining machinery was representative of the equipment at Rushton (one section used special cars to haul the coal from the miner to the feeder).

Another task was to set up the procedure for selecting men into the section. Twenty-four voluntary bids (3 eight-men crews) were posted for these jobs. Given the values of the program in terms of increased responsibility and autonomy, the steering committee felt that the miners should make their own choice about participation. The bids were reviewed by the steering committee and men were chosen on the basis of qualifications and seniority. To protect the worker, previous jobs were held open for 60 days. If a worker wanted to leave the experimental section after 60 days, he would return to the general work force until an opening was available in his former work classification. Only one worker left within 60 days. His reason was that his new job was more difficult physically than his previous job.

There were sufficient volunteers for all the jobs except mechanics. No mechanics bid into the experimental section. At this time there was conflict between the mechanics and the company over whether the company should pay for certain maintenance training. This was a hot issue and probably explains why the mechanics were unwilling to cooperate with management in the experimental program. Finally, three mechanics were assigned by management to the South section.

CONCLUSION

This chapter unfolds the basic structure of the Rushton QOW project. Although modifications occurred over the course of the experiment, the core of the program in this chapter remained intact. The process of developing the program is important because it represents in part the product of labor and management problem solving. In the past labor and management had only met on an adversary basis. The program itself is significant because it represents substantial changes on the part of the union and management as to the nature of work at Rushton. The program is also significant because it represents a substantial commitment to change the total organization, rather than just some part of the system, that is, the proposal includes changes in the authority, communication, decision making, reward systems, and so on. Relative to other experimental work in the mining or related industries, the Rushton design represented a major attempt to restructure work and the organization.

The chapter also provides some detail on how the general plan was put into operational form. The next chapter explains how the project was introduced.

CHAPTER SEVEN

Introducing Change

On December 23, 1973 the experimental section began its operation. For the next three months a series of training and other meetings were used to introduce the new experimental plan. At the end of February the experimental section was declared officially autonomous by the labor-management committee.

The period March 1974 to April 1975 was defined as the first experimental year. A 13-month period was used because of the month-long national coal strike in the latter part of 1974. In effect, the experimental year contains 12 working months. The end of the first experimental year marks the end of this chapter.

Our discussion of this period follows two paths: (1) a description of the mechanisms or institutions used to introduce the experimental program detailed in the previous chapter and (2) a discussion of some of the critical events during the first year of the program.

NEW INSTITUTIONS

Classroom Training Program

A training program launched the experiment. The experimental section (South) attended six classroom training sessions, generally on Monday and Friday, during December and January. These all-day sessions were designed to bring the men up to date on the technical aspects of mining as well as to understand the nature of the new program. Topics included the laws relevant to mining, roof and ventilation plans, and the mining cycle. Jobs were analyzed so that members of the experimental section would be familiar with all the jobs in the section. This information was to facilitate job switching, one of the primary parts of the new program. A job-safety analysis was presented for each job in the section. In addition federal and state laws were reviewed. This focus was consistent with the safety objective in the Rushton QOW project. The principles of autonomous working were also discussed, and the men were exposed to some experiental learning exercises in group relations and problem solving. Members of the research team and selected outside experts served as the trainers.

Section Conference

Late in December the first section conference was introduced. The section conference—a meeting of all the members of the experimental section plus management, some union officers, and the research team—has four functions: (1) to review past performance, (2) to provide communication opportunities across crews, (3) to solve problems, and (4) to plan future activities. A wide range of problems were generated during the section conferences, which were held monthly for the first three months and then at six-week intervals during the early part of the experiment. Some of the topics included: defining the boundaries of the experimental section (i.e., areas they were responsible for); determining overtime procedure for members of the section; defining the proper role of the foreman; coordinating clean-up activities across crews; coordinating supply needs; determining pay for non-AW members working in the experimental section, and so on. Thus the section conference was a critical new arena for labor-management problem solving; for facilitating communication among all parties; and for providing the opportunity to develop section, rather than crew, identity and thus minimize intercrew conflict. As part of the evaluation process we kept transcripts of these section meetings.

Joint Labor-Management Committee

A joint labor-management committee began meeting at the end of the first quarter in 1974. This committee, composed of five members of labor and five members of management, had the responsibility of resolving day-to-day problems that arose within the experimental section. Three of the labor representatives were committeemen elected by each of the three crews in South. The South section elected the other two from the union officers. Some of the problems concerned technical issues. In one meeting, for example, there was a discussion of flat tires and how to prevent them. During that same meeting proper safety practices for dealing with a machine's electricity cables were discussed. Proper timbering was also discussed in several labor-management meetings. Other meetings dealt with coordination problems across shifts, one recurrent problem is clean-up. Sometimes issues relevant to labor-management practices were considered, for example, whether a job should be put up for temporary or permanent bid. Other meetings were concerned with issues specific to the experimental intervention.

One of the problems in establishing groups, such as a joint labor-management committee, is the role of its members. There was some ambiguity about how the committeemen should play their respective roles, particularly among the labor members, who at times felt a conflict between their roles as crew representatives and their roles as union members. For example there were problems as to whether they could direct or discipline their union brothers.

Foremen Meetings

The foreman's role was affected most immediately by the experiment. Originally the foreman was responsible for production and safety; now his only responsibility was safety. Partially in response to this change, a series of foremen meetings were instituted. Their function was to clarify the foreman's role, provide better communication exchanges among the foremen and between the foremen and management, and to solve problems. Members of this group included the three foremen in the experimental section, management, and the research team. These foremen meetings began in January 1974.

Management Meetings

During the planning and introduction of change at Rushton the focus was on the experimental section and the work force. Little time was allocated to discussing the impact of the program on management. As the project began to evolve, problems were raised by the research team, the experimental section, and some members of management as to whether the management at the mine was committed to supporting the program. A series of meetings in December of 1974 was initiated to deal with the interrelationships of the mine management and their role relevant to the program.

Steering Committee

The steering committee, which drew up the original document for change, continued to function during the experimental year, although it met only twice. The first meeting concerned opening up a new section at Rushton and focused on whether that section should be a second experimental section. The second meeting was an evaluation of the first experimental year and consisted primarily of reviewing a report submitted by the research team.

QOW Conferences

Another type of meeting came into the picture in late 1974. Although not specifically part of the Rushton project, it did affect the project's activities. Regional QOW meetings, which generally contained presentations from QOW projects, were starting up around the country. A Rushton contingent began attending these meetings to present the facts of the Rushton experience. The contingent included members of management, the union, the first experimental section, and the research team. The meetings were important because they substantially increased the visibility of the Rushton project and in this context served as a diffusion vehicle. In addition, they tended to support Rushton's commitment to the project since these presentations required a public commitment to the project's value by members of management, union, and the experimental section. Explaining the benefits of the program in public required a certain amount of personal belief. A related point is that since Rushton was in the limelight in these conferences, the participants felt reinforced and thus probably were more supportive of the program.

Our account of this phase of introducing change has been in terms of different groups or meetings. We have organized our description this way because these groups represent the critical institutions in the development of the change effort of Rushton. They represent new structures for problem solving, that is, they represent the mechanisms through which the change program is carried out in a dynamic context.

CRITICAL EVENTS

Another way to review the introduction of change at Rushton is through the series of critical events that took place during the first experimental year. These incidents are pulled from the data collected by the evaluation team through interviews and on-site observations in the mining sections. The semistructured interviews were conducted weekly by the principal investigator with members of management or the union. The semistructured on-site observation was conducted approximately every three weeks by the same individuals during the first part of the experimental year.

Initial Changes

The QOW proposal (detailed in Chapter 6) contained fairly specific goals and principles about the nature of the change. But there was a major gap between the principles and the day-to-day operations of the mine. This, of course, was to be expected. Most of December and January 1974 focused on trying to implement the document. There were ambiguities about work, the foreman's role, how autonomous the section could be, the overtime procedure, and so on. One typical problem that came up early in January concerned when management could ask the members of the South section to work in other sections. An excerpt from our on-site observer's notes illustrates this point:

> I talked with a bolter and support man from 2 South. The [continuous] miner was down and most of the work in the section was done. . . . The question is whether they could be asked to work in some other area outside the experimental section. The men were initially resistant . . . this point—about what was their territory and whether management could ask them to work outside—had never been worked out before. They didn't want to work outside the experimental section. They wanted to get paid, but there was no work to do. [January 1974]

As one would expect, change did not occur right away. Much of the time from December 1973 to February 1974 was spent getting acquainted with the jobs, the section, and the concepts in the program. The safety director, during an inspection in January 1974 of the South section, said:

> The place is not cleaned up as it should be. They are supposed to do gas checks. . . . They heard this in the classroom but they don't do it yet. . . . As far as timbers go, it's better than it was.

A crew member in the experimental section observed:

> . . . things pretty much the same . . . safety not much different. I turn around in my seat [on the shuttle car], but only when the inspector is around. Nothing changes. [January 1974]

A mechanic had a stronger point of view:

> Those fucking autonomous guys. . . . They can't fix anything . . . nothin's changed around here. [January 1974]

The experimental section did not operate in a vacuum. The South section was receiving a good deal of attention, many of its members were earning higher wages, and the program permitted the South section workers to spend time on nonmining activities, such as meetings. This situation naturally generated resentment. One boss from a nonautonomous section said:

> Why should my men break their ass . . . they do it and get less than those other guys in South. [January 1974]

In February, three months into the project, evidence of change began to appear. Consider two excerpts from South miners:

> Definitely it is better now than it used to be. You know what you are supposed to be doing. . . . If you need help, now others will help . . . before they wouldn't . . . they had one job and that was it. [Bolter, February 1974]

> Just different now, there is no pushy foreman . . . here I am on my own . . . there is a different atmosphere. The other sections . . . I've talked to guys in East, they call us the communist crew . . . they complain about us getting better treatment. [Carman, January 1974]

These interviews are interesting because they identify behavioral areas where change has occurred and indicate that members of the experimental group held positive feelings about the changes in the section.

While behavioral and attitudinal changes began to appear toward the end of February, the process of change did not occur smoothly. Certain problems continually needed to be resolved, for example conflicts continued between the experimental crews over which crew was responsible for what. A member of management commented on this issue:

> The men didn't realize that they had to be working together, one crew felt they were doing all the [clean-up] work . . . but they didn't realize what the other crews were doing. There was bad feeling, but we talked it out in the joint committee and I think we got a way to work it out. [March 1974]

Another source of conflict and one of the most persistent themes in this experiment was the mine management's attitude toward the experiment. The general view from the workers, research team, and some members of management was that the superintendent, general foreman, and other management personnel did not support the experiment. As a South crew foreman and a worker commented:

> Well . . . the only reason why the program is really on line is because of Warren [president]. I don't think Cloyd [general foreman] or Blair [superintendent] feel very comfortable with the program. . . . Blair and Cloyd are production men; the program takes away their whip and I'm not sure they like that. [Foreman, March 1974]

> Blair is really quick to blame us . . . all the problems are because of autonomy. . . . Cloyd is about the same. Sometimes for it, sometimes against it. [Miner, April 1974]

The mechanics also posed another problem for the experiment. From the initial bidding for the experimental section, the mechanics had decided not to participate in the program. They had a long-standing conflict with management over whether they should be paid for additional training. As the program progressed, the mechanics worked in the experimental section, but did not participate in the autonomous project. One mechanic in South said:

> I tried to help out . . . and do some shoveling . . . but the other mechanics heard about it and let me have it. [April 1974]

While there were conflicts, there was also progress:

> The section seems to run pretty much by itself. . . . The men arrived at South around 8:30 A.M. and had a brief lunch and went off. . . . This happened without any direction. Production was underway by 8:37. [On-site observer, April 1974]

Greater autonomy became more evident by May 1974. Below is an excerpt from the on-site observer's report:

> For the three hours I was in that section there was only two interactions between the boss and the men. One of the bolters had a question which [the boss] answered. And there was a discussion on how to mine, but the miner operator made the decision. I observed that the boss was primarily watching the mining operation. . . . Everyone knew what their job was and they were doing it. Before [the experiment] the boss would have been more active in making decisions. [On-site observer, May 1974]

A research team member described the same phenomena, but with a different vocabulary:

> I saw the men demonstrating systems thinking . . . I saw them deploy
> themselves to the belt on their own . . . I saw planning by the miner
> operator and bolter. [May 1974]

Structures such as intershift communication began at this time and
persisted in a fairly stable manner:

> I arrived in the waiting room about 7:50. Most of the guys from South
> were together when the mantrip came up. . . . There was the regular
> rush to get out. The carman stopped to talk with the waiting carman. I
> also saw the supply men talking. It all happens fast. From what else I can
> see no one stopped to communicate in the other [control] sections except
> the bosses. [On-site observer, May 1974]

Other proposed changes did not proceed as smoothly. When the experiment began in December 1973, the general rule was to become
familiar with one's job and not to job switch. After the section was
considered fully autonomous (March 1974) by the research team, job
switching became more prevalent, but not all felt that they were
capable of switching or that they wanted to switch:

> Well . . . the miner operator on that shift doesn't want to exchange jobs
> . . . maybe he is afraid of losing it. I know that [two other miners] are
> unhappy—they told me that in confidence. One guy said how can you get
> that guy's fingers off the miner. [Miner, June 1974]

> It [job switching] seems to work better in other crews. . . . I know in
> [one] crew they exchange on the miner during lunch. [Management, May
> 1974]

An issue in any experimental intervention is whether the experimental changes will be adopted by other areas in the organization, that is,
to what extent would the other mining sections adopt the practices of
the experimental section? To check on this we periodically observed
mining practices in the other sections. We found no evidence of
borrowing. The other crews rarely engaged in intershift communication, the boss took a fairly directive role, and there was little evidence
of problem-solving activities by the men in the crews.

New Mining Section

In August 1974 management decided to open up a new mining section.
The energy crisis was at hand and PPL wanted to increase its supply of
coal. Rushton was selected because its costs per ton were better (prior
to the experiment) than PPL's other mines.

The decision to add the new section was made by the president of Rushton. There was no consultation with the research team and indeed there was no plan to make the section an experimental section. When the research team learned about the new section, they wanted it to be an autonomous section. One major reason for their position was that they did not think the program could survive if all the other sections were nonautonomous. They felt a growing hostility toward the project from certain levels of management and the other sections. As one member of the research team said:

> I had just learned about the idea of a new section. . . . It seemed natural that it would be an extension of our project. We called Warren . . . he hadn't thought about making the new section autonomous, but he was excited about the idea. I have long felt that it would be important to get another section going . . . given the size of the mine and the number of sections. I don't see how the original experimental section could run over time, alone. [September 1974]

The proposal to make the new section experimental was then presented to the steering committee in September 1974. The union's reaction to this new issue was interesting. In general, it saw the decision to extend the autonomous concept to the new section as management's and not a joint decision as previous problem solving had been. One union official commented:

> There was no general discussion of expanding the experiment to a second section. It was a foregone conclusion on the part of management . . . the discussion [in the steering committee] was devoted to how the new section should be made autonomous, rather than whether it should be operated autonomously. [September, 1974]

The meeting concluded with the steering committee endorsing a new autonomous section along the concepts laid out in the original document.

The new proposal was brought before the union membership and passed by a vote of 25 to 6. Of those attending this meeting, 17 came from the original experimental section. This level of participation from any section was quite unusual. Most of these men generally did not come to meetings. It demonstrates that the experiment created a new interest group that could substantially influence the outcome of union votes.

The introduction of the new experimental section (Section 5 Butt) was one of the key events during the first experimental year. On the one hand it represented a substantial change in the firm's productive capacity. This required the acquisition of equipment, and a major effort was undertaken to prepare the new area. There were also major changes in personnel. To staff the new section men in other work areas bid into the new section. In one case a whole crew bid into the new section. To replace the men and crews who had bid out, other switching occurred within the work force and additional men were hired. Only the first experimental section remained the same. At the managerial level one change took place. An assistant safety director was appointed, partly because the regular safety director was allocating more of his time to the QOW program, and also because he was needed to monitor the regular sections because of more frequent federal and state inspections. The increase in inspections was independent of the experiment.

The procedure for setting up a second experimental section followed the same general plan as had been followed for the first section. The overall document was the same. The content and teachers of the initial training were the same. The only major difference was in the timing of the training sessions. For the first experimental group the six training sessions were concentrated in a two-month period, with most coming in the first month. For 5 Butt the sessions began in October and continued into February 1975. This spread in training was partly caused by the national coal strike, but it also reflects the design of the research team and members of the labor-management steering committee.

While the focus turned to the set up of the 5 Butt section, the first experimental section continued its development. As one manager said:

> They have a pride in having no accidents . . . one guy said to me we aren't going to have accidents . . . it's a pride I've never seen. . . . South is definitely different from the other sections. Men stop in the other sections when they go out of work . . . not in South, they stay busy. [October, 1974]

National Coal Strike

The national coal strike stopped production for essentially the whole month of November. Since both the company and the local union were not involved in developing the collective-bargaining agreement, the strike did not represent a period of increased conflict or tension between management and its employees. Any tension generated was between the local and the international leadership. Under Arnold Miller's tenure, the local unions, for the first time, were given the opportunity to vote on the contract. The Rushton local voted against the contract approved by the international. As one miner said:

> The contract was bad. [There were] no real benefits to the men . . . the five-day sick leave was ok . . . but the wages were not enough.

Post-Strike Activities

After the strike the activities during the last month of 1974 represented a continuation of the institutions (e.g., section foreman meetings) and activities of the past. Most of the changes introduced in South were in place. There were noticeable levels of intercrew and intracrew coordination. The bosses had backed off and the men were involved in making decisions. There were increases in work satisfaction, pride in work, and overall safety. Not all the changes were successfully introduced. The process of job switching had not become a regular work procedure. Planning sessions prior to each shift really never got underway. Probably most important was a perceived strain between the mine management and the quality of work experiment. Most of the work force, including members of management, believed the top management at the mine did not support the project.

The development of the second experimental section did not proceed as smoothly as expected. Not enough men volunteered into that section, so a relatively high proportion of inexperienced miners worked there. This created a problem, because 5 Butt was a new section with new equipment. Since there were enough problems just learning to make the section go, the concept of autonomous work groups was pushed to the side:

> There was a lot of discussion among the men about intershift relations. [One boss] said that the men don't communicate with each other, and there are lots of ways that the shifts do not help each other. He felt he was not getting much production out because he [was] spending a lot more time on support work. . . . He did expect that, . . . but safety was poor. There were a lot of potential violations. In my own observation there was a high initiation of activities from the boss to the men. The boss is also actively involved in doing things (e.g., setting up curtains). This is quite a contrast to South where the men initiate their work activities. [On-site observer, January 1975]

Final Quarter

The period from January to March 1975 represented the last quarter of the experimental year. Much of the activities during that time period were a continuation of previously initiated activities. The South section conferences were held in January and March. Topics in these meetings included problems of obtaining equipment, procedures for cleaning the miner, rules for job switching, and the need to support the committeemen. The training sessions continued in the new experimental section, 5 Butt. Also, the foremen's meetings were held. Members of management, the union, and the first experimental section participated in QOW conferences.

During this period the South section continued its progress along the experimental lines; the 5 Butt section was still getting organized. The on-site observer reported:

> South's clean-up is good . . . production's up . . . they are doing a good job . . . [the men] do everything on their own . . . keep the boss informed . . . ask his opinion, but don't wait for orders. 5 Butt is still a hassle . . . still having problems keeping things in order. Clean-up not good . . . too much loose coal . . . other violations are noticeable. . . . Men [i.e., crews] still are separated until the foremen get together. They have three separate subsystems. [February 1975]

We will conclude this section by describing two interesting events that closed out the first experimental year. Davitt McAteer, from the international, visited the mine during this quarter. After discussions with some of the union officials, it appeared to him that the company was trying to divide the union. The issue was gain sharing, and it was McAteer's understanding that only the South section was to receive benefits from the QOW project. In his view this would divide the union. McAteer viewed the company's approach to gain sharing as another form of union busting. Bitter words were exchanged between Hinks and McAteer with no resolution at hand. This created ambiguity as to the international's support of the program. Gain sharing was in preliminary discussions at this time.

The second event concerned a new form of power created by the experimental intervention. On March 3 one of the crews from the South section met with the superintendent and asked for the removal of their boss and their mine operator. One member of the research team met with that crew to review these demands. The meeting was run by the committeeman of that crew. The basic complaint against the boss was that he was behaving like an old-line manager, that is, he was still very directive. The meeting unfolded by having each crew member provide his perception of the boss. The boss then gave his perception, which essentially viewed the men as very dependent on him. The men made some suggestions to create a change in their boss's behavior, but the research team member considered the solutions quite diffuse. No resolution was defined.

The discussion then switched to the miner operator. Tension had been growing in this crew between the miner operator and the men because they perceived that he would not exchange his job with the members of the crew. The crew members presented their opinion of the operator and said they did not want to work with him. The miner operator expressed surprise over the men's feelings, but he said he would let others run the miner.

These two incidents are significant because they highlight the growing identity and power of the crew. The prevailing working norms do not sanction workers disciplining their boss; union norms are that brothers do not criticize brothers. The fact that the crew would publicly attack its boss and a crew member indicates that new structural forms were emerging.

CONCLUSION

This chapter has portrayed the initial development of the experimental intervention. The experimental plan was translated into a real set of activities. In addition, a whole new set of institutions (e.g., section conference, foremen meetings) were introduced to support the experimental intervention. By the end of the experimental year the total experimental program was in operation in the first experimental section. These changes led to modifications in the miners' behavior toward improving safety, production, intershift coordination, and so on. The growing cohesiveness of the experimental section was illustrated by their public censuring of their boss and a fellow union member. A new social system was in the process of being created.

By the end of 1974 the second experimental section was still not underway in terms of adopting the new experimental practices. Differences in training and composition of members considerably slowed the introduction of new quality of work practices in this section.

As we looked ahead, the basic problems were whether the experimental program could be extended to the whole mine, whether the first experimental section would retain its development, whether the second experimental section would adopt practices congruent with the intervention, and what would be the effects of the deteriorating relationship with the international.

CHAPTER EIGHT

Diffusion of the Experiment within the Mine

The diffusion or spread of the experiment to the whole mine, which this chapter describes, can be broken into three periods. The period from April to August 1975 focuses on the development of a mine-wide QOW document for Rushton; it ends with a close (79 to 75) vote by the union membership not to extend the experiment to the rest of the mine. The second period concerns the extension of the project to the rest of the mine on management's initiative. Management had the formal right to introduce some features of the project under the existing labor-management contract; the project was no longer a joint labor-management endeavor. The introduction of a mine-wide program continued through the first quarter of 1976. The last period in the chapter runs through the first quarter of 1977. It portrays the decline of many of the program characteristics (e.g., behaviors and outcomes) that had characterized the first experimental section in 1974.

In our previous chapter, an historical account was provided by detailing new institutions and critical events. Since most of the institutions of the project have been identified, our focus in this chapter will be on critical events.

PERIOD I: THE CHALLENGE

Perhaps the most dramatic event during the second quarter of 1975 was a challenge from the union that either the whole mine participate in the QOW or none of the mine participate. This challenge was raised during the South section conference in April by the local union president, who said that the local union (in their last meeting) had passed a resolution demanding immediately either total participation or no participation. The basic issue was the inequity in wages among the sections. Members in the South and 5 Butt sections were getting higher rates than other men in the mine doing the same job. The company president's reaction was the following:

> I do not think there should be an ultimatum. I realize there are jealousies. We're in an experiment. We shouldn't be stampeded. . . . If the whole mine had to go autonomous, I would say no. I couldn't pay the high rate. . . . It will take time. One section at a time. Our goal is to make the coal miner a professional. I don't want to be stampeded.

The union president's response was:

> If these men [union members] want something, that's what they are going to get. The men in the South section are not running this mine.

Members in the experimental section reacted differently to the union resolution. Some said that management should just pay the men in the other sections more. Other members of the South section pointed out that pay was not the issue—the concept of working in an autonomous work group was more complex and demanded more work and responsibilities.

The union's action forced a decision on whether to continue and to extend the project. The research team began some informal discussions with union officials, although the issue had to wait until the May union meeting for further clarification. The meeting took place on the first Sunday in May. Forty of the 54 men in the two experimental sections came. This represented a majority of the 60 participants at that meeting. Their voting power was not needed, as a review of April's minutes showed that although there was a call for a mine-wide program or no program, there was no formal vote and no deadline. This permitted planning time for the development of a mine-wide program, a position which had been lobbied for by the research team. A member of the research team's reaction to these events was:

> It worked out because of a technicality [there had been no formal union vote or deadline] . . . it looks good for us. We have the flexibility to work now. [The union's] original statement was non-negotiable. [May 1975]

The union position now was that a new document specifying the operation of a QOW project at Rushton was to be drawn up by the steering committee and then voted on by union members. The vote was to be after the miner's holiday in July.

After this meeting, local union-management relations moved back to the problem-solving mode that had characterized their relationship prior to the union's challenge. Relationships with the international, however, had become strained after McAteer's inspection visit of the project in March. He viewed the project now as a way to break the union. The research team contacted McAteer and asked others, for example, a senior union official in the United Auto Workers of America (UAW), to help them with the international. The following comments identify the problem and show the research team's difficulties in working out a strategy to deal with the international.

> I had a meeting with Davitt . . . he's very negative . . . opposes the program . . . wanted to call off today's meeting. If the international says no, it will kill the program. There is still the old animosity . . . I think Davitt doesn't want to make Hinks look good . . . and Hinks' statement that he wants a separate contract [for Rushton] really hit Davitt [interview with research team, April 1975]. We're not sure about how to deal with the international. Eric wants to keep them at arm's length for awhile. . . . Grant wants active collaboration, and I'm in between. Davitt wants to slow this thing down. [Interview with research team, May 1975]

It was not until July that the international representatives reappeared at Rushton to review the emerging document.

Writing a New Document

The task of developing a document that would fit the whole mine was begun by the steering committee in May. Meeting biweekly, they worked through August with the assistance of the research team to draw up an acceptable program dealing with such issues as grievances, movement within areas of the mine, and job bidding. The most persistent problems concerned the pay rate and how to qualify for the top rate. Under the original document, members of the first experimental section received the top rate when the program started. The rationale was that they would be learning multiple tasks and assuming more responsibilities. In the new negotiations the company did not want to pay the top rate unless it was tied to training and qualifications. The union, on the other hand, argued for equity with the two experimental sections. If they received top rate without training or demonstrating qualifications on multiple jobs, so should the rest of the areas in the mine. Eventually a compromise was reached. It included paying the top rate for the job area for 120 days. During this time the miner would have to demonstrate that he could perform multiple jobs. The document included different combinations of job paths the worker could follow to demonstrate competence and qualify for the top rate. This issue of pay and qualifications was an emotional one, as indicated by management's comments:

> It is abhorrent for me to pay high rates just to deal with someone's feelings. . . . I see it as a temporary thing [paying high rates]. Originally we used it as bait. . . . We are still buying bait . . . but it is probably a necessary cost. . . . Maybe I rationalized it because of the overall goal. . . . It's worth it . . . I want something for it . . . I want to see some increased responsibility for training. [July 1975]

While the pay and qualifications issues were central themes in the steering committee, many other problems arose as the committee tried to work out a useful document. One problem was that the project was no longer dealing only with the mining sections. The mine-wide program had to include the cleaning plant, outside workers, and special inside workers, such as pumpers. Since the work and technology surrounding these jobs was different, this complicated drawing up the document.

As the document began to take form, representatives from the research department of the international began to attend the steering committee meetings. They played an active role in working out some of the more complicated issues (e.g., pay).

The final document incorporated most of the basic goals, institutions, and practices that formed the initial experimental plan. Some of the basic changes included qualification procedures for obtaining top pay rate and grievances were to pass through the formal contract procedure, rather than beginning in the joint labor-management committee. A set of communication meetings were instituted parallel to the steering committee meetings. Their purpose was to explain the nature of the program and the document and to obtain ideas from miners (not in the experimental project) that could be used in the document. Two types of meetings were held. The first was run by members of the research team. These half-day meetings involved all men in the mine who were not in the QOW experiment. Two series of these meetings took place at the mine and were attended by groups of approximately 20 to 30 men. The format was primarily a presentation by the research team and management. Our observations indicate that interactions in the meetings were primarily from the speakers to the men. The participation that did occur from the miners was limited to a few individuals. As one member of management said:

They're [the meetings] still a little shaky . . . not much talk . . . no one [in the union] says the program's great, but neither are they talking it down. [May 1975]

The union officers ran the second type of meeting with no participation from management or the research team. It was felt that better understanding of the program might be achieved in this type of meeting. As one member of the research team put it:

It's the right strategy if the officers can carry it out. Some people might think we [the research team] are in with management. We're only trusted to a certain extent. [June 1975]

While the research team members had proposed this second type of communication meeting, they did feel ambivalent about the outcome:

I have doubts whether [the union officers] can do it. . . . They do believe they can sell it . . . [but] they're not proponents of new values. I was surprised that they asked questions about things I thought they knew about . . . [for example] they weren't sure who was funding.

Our evaluation of the communications meetings were that they were not effective in providing the nonautonomous miners a good understanding of the program. In Chapter 18 we shall examine this issue in more detail, but consider the following protocol from an on-site observer about his conversation with one of the foremen:

I was talking with a boss who had gone to several communications meetings. He wanted to know who was paying for the classrooms and lower production brought about by the experiment. He heard it was the Ford Foundation. Later . . . he said he was in favor of autonomy and hoped the whole mine would adopt that system . . . yet he also felt that a man needs a boss and without a boss the men would tend to goof off. [July 1975]

This boss did not have a clear picture of the program. Who was paying was discussed several times in the communications meetings; it was not the Ford Foundation. The concept of not having a boss in an autonomous section was one of the most persistent misconceptions.

Another strategy to extend the program was to bring foremen from the nonexperimental sections into the experimental sections to see how autonomy worked. This idea came late in the planning and did not involve all the bosses. One boss reported to our on-site observer:

I think the only difference is that South has 2 extra men and for that reason South is kept a little bit nicer . . . I feel my men do almost as much work as 2 South. [July 1975]

That observation is important because the boss's view of the new program can influence how his crew votes—he is an opinion leader.

While all this dissemination was going on, intershift communication occurred in the two experimental sections, but not in the other sections. South continued to run an autonomous section with much of the decision making done by the men and their crew leaders. The behavior of the 5 Butt crew was a function of the bosses. One boss had a fairly laissez-faire attitude, so the crew ran similar to the South crews. Other bosses ran their crews in a more directive fashion that bore no relation to the program. Conflict between some of the crews, evident early in 1975, continued. It is our view that 5 Butt never closely approximated the goals of the QOW program. We continued our on-site observations of the nonexperimental sections during this period to determine whether the discussions about the experiment were leading to any early adoptions. There was no evidence to support any contamination effect. The nonexperimental sections had not changed their behavior; they were not being run along autonomous lines.

The regular union meeting held in August was to review the final document. Davitt McAteer made a presentation on behalf of the international. He supported the program, while still leaving room for the local members to decide for themselves. A strong minority group responded after McAteer's presentation by attacking the idea of a QOW project and dominated the rest of the meeting. There was no time, as was originally planned, to review the document.

As the election neared there were lots of predictions about the outcome. A member from the research team said:

> I just feel unable to see where it's going to go. . . . The union officers are optimistic . . . it's rather a close thing. We've tried to make a tally . . . it came out in favor. . . . There seems to be a core emphatically opposed . . . they are not listening to what was said. . . . They are an all-or-nothing mentality. . . . We lost heavily in the union meeting . . . the major issues [were] not really discussed. . . . The idea of doing this on a trial basis never came up. It's really hard for them to vote, they don't know what they are experiencing. [August 1975]

Management tended to see a close vote, with the edge given to expanding the program. We tried informally to sample members from the nonautonomous section. Opinions ranged from "I think it is a good thing . . . you get more pay" to a note written across the proposed document near the pumpers' work area which said "How to fuck up your mine in 16 pages." Overall opinions from the nonautonomous section were skewed more to a neutral, slightly negative position.

There were few outspoken proponents. Members in the autonomous sections wanted a positive vote.

The election was held by secret ballot at the mine on August 20, 1975, and the program was defeated in a close vote, 79 to 75. This vote was to be one of the major turning points in this experimental intervention.

PERIOD II: EXTENDING THE PROGRAM

This phase begins after the vote and extends until March 1976. It includes the immediate reaction to the vote, the development of a new plan to extend the QOW concepts throughout the mine, and an intense training program both at the worker and managerial levels.

The reaction to the "no" vote was obviously one of disappointment. The company president said:

> I had a slight pang of disappointment but . . . I have been preparing in my mind for either eventuality. . . . It shows a lack of understanding of what is good for the working man. I don't see the vote shutting off the experiment. I don't see why management can't come up with new policies, but keeping within the contract and still forwarding the autonomous idea. The vote is a matter of misunderstanding . . . there is a way to fall back and regroup . . . we could go back to the old system, but I think we've passed that. [August 1975]

This position did indeed become the description of what was to happen during this phase. The experiment was not over, management took over the program and implemented it throughout the mine.

Other members of management and the research team expressed similar disappointment. Management did some proselytizing immediately after the vote to change some of the "no" votes. Also skirmishes were reported between some of the "yes" and "no" voters. During the first few days after the vote, there was continued talk of calling a second vote. The research team opposed this idea because the outcome of such a vote was unclear. It never became a viable course of action in the union meeting that followed shortly after the election.

Developing New Relationships

In the week after the vote the superintendent convened a meeting composed of the steering committee members. The president made clear his intention of continuing the program. At the end of the meeting the common position of the members was reflected in the following announcement issued by the union:

> Due to the recent vote, the autonomous joint steering committee has been abolished; but under Article 16, Sec. G, p. 67 of the contract a new committee has been formed called the MTDC (Mine Training and Development Committee) which is strictly a management committee but may have union representation.

> The management now retains the right to direct the work force. All wages will be paid according to the contract rates and Article 19, Sec. E, J, two extra support people will be assigned to each crew under the direction of the foreman to provide the same opportunity as 5 Butt and 2 South.

> Classes on mine law, mine safety, and section performance will continue under the direction of the company. All foremen and general men will remain the same until a training program is arranged.

This announcement was significant because it signaled a new direction in the experiment. The official joint labor-management program was cancelled. Management, however, elected to continue the program for the whole mine. It had this right under the regular union contract. Training was to be given to all workers, specifically those in the nonautonomous section. In the announcement the right to direct the work force was retained again by management. However, during the August 25 meeting, top management stated that the experimental sections were to work as they had in the past. The issue of who had the right to direct the work force remained fairly ambiguous through the fall of 1975. It, of course, limited the degree of autonomy exercised in the two original experimental sections.

Now that the official program was over, all members of the experimental sections went back to the contract pay rates. This meant that the two car operators and two support men in each autonomous crew could no longer draw the top rate (pay loss per day was approximately $6.50). One consequence of this was that some of these men bid for higher paying jobs outside the experimental section. Another consequence was a new arrangement (discussed at the August meeting) of ways members in the autonomous sections could still get top rate within the context of the union contract. This could be realized by having men on low-paying jobs switch to high-paying jobs for a minimum of one-half hour. Although this procedure was privately acknowledged, it was never made legitimate or practiced publicly. The major mechanism for labor-management discussion, the steering committee, remained in reality much the same, although it had a new name, "Mine Training and Development Committee," and union members were to be advisors only.

On September 8 a meeting of the new MTDC was held to draw up a revised document that would provide the guidelines for extending the program to the whole mine. The research team continued its role as outside consultants. As in the past they played an active role in setting agenda and providing direction for joint problem-solving activities during the course of the meetings. The focal issue in this meeting was determining the appropriate pay rate and qualifications, the same issue that had plagued prior steering committee meetings. The initial position of the union was that people had voted against the program because the routes to the top rates and the qualification system were inequitable. They argued that the two experimental sections had been given top rate immediately with no conditions or qualifications. This same procedure should be extended to the other sections. Management's position was that people should be paid for services rendered; the original decision on pay was made in the context of an experiment, and now that the experiment was over, new approaches for payment should be considered.

The final resolution was to pay the men the top rate for their work area. Some redefinitions of work areas were drawn to provide the men more opportunities for job switching and for higher rates. The qualifying factor was that after 60 days if any of the men decided not to participate in the training program, they would revert to their contract rate.

Concerning his decision to pay the top rate, the president said:

I firmly believed we should pay for services rendered. The thing that bothered me was to pay people not deserving. The 60-day idea . . . seemed ok. . . . If [workers] didn't cut it, I wanted the right to cut them out. . . . I also felt we wouldn't make progress [with the men] if we didn't pay the top rate.

It is interesting to note, and this point will be discussed later in more detail, that no procedure was established for determining in 60 days if the men wanted to participate in the new training program.

During the period right after the vote, the research team asked the evaluation team to suspend any data collection because of the critical stage of the program. Since we could not go into the sections, we relied on information reported by company employees who were in the mine. Consider this report from a member of management:

The men in South were initially disappointed. They were really down after the vote . . . the program was down the drain. . . . There was a feeling of hostility against the other sections. Now things seem to be back to normal. I was in there the last two and a half days and I could see little differences . . . intershift communication was still going on, . . . I didn't see much difference in the boss . . . maybe he checked a few more things, like when the belt went off. . . . The section is in good shape. I was also in North and East . . . they're not so quick to voice an opinion . . . they know the company put people on high rate and they are waiting to see what happens. Some of the guys . . . who were against it in the beginning say [management is] changing the contract. Others I talked to said, 'I guess we're going AW whether we like it or not.' [September 1977]

New Training Effort

Another major decision from the meeting was to begin a training program for the workers who had not been in the two experimental sections. Training was to represent one of the major activities of the extended program for the next six months.

Training began in late September and continued to April 1976. The substantive part of the training was much the same as that presented in the earlier training programs for the two autonomous work groups. Each area was to receive six sessions. The training sessions for each area were spread over six months. Training for the original autonomous section was completed within a two-month period (six meetings). Another change was that training was conducted primarily by management people. Prior to this the research team had performed the major training function.

The joint committees staffed by crew representatives were set up during this time to deal with day-to-day problems in the implementation of the QOW program.

A new phase of training for managers began in January 1976. One of the issues after the vote was the need to improve supervisory skills. Six sessions were conducted by the research team for all the personnel.

During this phase the research team remained active participants in the project, attending the major meetings and playing a major role in the design and implementation of the training program. Members of the research team described their changing role:

We're trying to do more planning with the training director . . . work out agenda . . . [We're] not running those meetings anymore . . . we're stepping back. [December 1975]

One of the most significant events during this time was a series of walkouts that began in mid-September. Before this, no internal walkouts (those initiated by the Rushton local) had occurred since the program's start in December 1973. Three days were lost in September 1975 and a day in October. September walkouts were due to a new safety regulation that required canopies on the continuous miner and cars. The requirement was a matter of law, and while the company asked for a variance, the federal inspector wanted the canopies installed. In this situation the company is really a third party. Two men objected to the canopy and initiated the September walkout. The walkout in October was due to a dispute over pay received for the time of the September walkout, that is, the men had gone to work and then walked out and the question was whether the time they worked was accurately remunerated.

Elaborating the New Program

While the training activities were underway and while resources were directed to coping with the labor-management conflicts, some effort was allocated to further revising the document. The MTDC with the assistance of the research team continued to meet at least on a monthly basis to review current issues and expand the document. For example, a number of proposals were acted on in the latter part of 1975. The time when crews switch was expanded to 10 minutes to permit greater intershift communication; previously only a few minutes were available to talk. There was also an attempt to regularize the meetings of the important committees in the program. In the past there had always been some confusion about when the different committees were to meet. Another issue that was discussed during the MTDC meetings concerned follow up. Some attempt was made to develop procedures that would follow up on decisions made in the different committee meetings. An important realization—made explicit in the December MTDC meeting—was that many of the decisions initiated in the meetings were never followed up to see if they were implemented. Mr. Hinks commented:

> The emphasis on follow up was a feature of management I hadn't thought out. . . . It wasn't until Repasky kept laying on it that I said yeah, boy have I been stupid. I had an idealistic approach that the men would work through on their own decisions. [December 1975]

While these attempts to revise and expand the document were under way, the issue of joint labor-management collaboration was again brought before the local union at their December meeting. The membership agreed (there was no formal vote) to allow its officers to develop a document that could then be submitted to the membership for another vote.

Through the end of 1975 attention was focused on the new training program, expanding the AW concepts to the whole mine, modifying the document, and the flurry of walkouts. Meanwhile, in November, the evaluation team was allowed to continue its data collection; on-site observations of the two experimental sections were resumed. These sections were clearly out of the limelight during this period. Selections from the following reports provide a picture of South and then 5 Butt:

> I watched during the shift interchange; there was less talking than I had observed before. . . . They worked like clockwork . . . until the belt went off . . . then the boss took over with the mechanic . . . before [the vote] the support people would have gone down [to work on the belt] . . . the men said they didn't because they weren't autonomous. The men said they have the concern they had before the vote. . . . Since the vote they do not seem verbally to support the program as they used to. . . . As far as the section goes, there seems to be a number of small violations. . . . The clean up is not as good as it was. [December 1975]

In this description we see that much of the day-to-day production work is done as the crew did it prior to the vote. There are signs, however, of a decay in their earlier behavior. Intershift communications were letting up as were some of the safety practices. When the belt went down, the men did not take the initiative as they would have prior to the vote. The description of 5 Butt by the on-site observer indicated that not much had changed:

> In this crew . . . there never were any substantial changes . . . the boss was directive then, but he is even more so now. The boss felt that a great deal of surveillance and direction were necessary in order to keep the crew moving. . . . The committeeman for this crew felt he had no say in decision-making at all. . . . The men wondered why there hadn't been any section conference since the vote. [December 1975]

We also conducted site visits in the other sections that were undergoing training. There was some indication of more intercrew communication, but within the sections there were no noticeable changes. This is not surprising since most of the sections had attended only a few training sessions by the end of the year.

The following comments by the president of Rushton as he reviews the project at the end of the year reflect the tension and ambivalence caused by the vote, ambiguities in the role of the first experimental section, and the labor-management conflicts:

> As a general impression . . . there still seems to be a substantially greater desire on the part of the coal miner to receive than to give. . . . I'm not saying the program is a failure, there are people who are giving. But there still is that feeling that cooperation has not dominated money. . . . I felt when we got into the document . . . we moved to an

earlier rapport . . . we had something to work on . . . something that brought us together . . . even though it was rejected. . . . Now things aren't as harmonious. . . . There is a conflict in my own thinking. . . . I have been feeling it's management's job to keep the goals shined up . . . more coal and a low cost. It seems to be in conflict with the idea of the program, that is the idea to increase the quality of working life . . . that goal is an end in itself. I'm ready to put complete emphasis on that. . . . I don't know if AW leads to [the miners'] assumption of providing better service.

1976 was characterized by a series of dramatic labor-management events, the continuation of old institutions, the introduction of new practices, and a set of recurrent themes or problems.

A Decline in Labor-Management Relations

A series of walkouts plagued the first quarter of 1976. In one case a man who had been absent returned to work without a doctor's excuse and was not permitted to work. This precipitated a walkout. In another case a worker with frequent absenteeism was given a warning letter which indicated that further absenteeism might lead to dismissal. Since the union objected to a formal absentee policy and the letter was interpreted by some as the superintendent's attempt "to arbitrarily rewrite the contract" by instituting an absentee policy, the men walked out. Increasing absenteeism rates were a persistent problem during this year. The third incident involved a job-bidding problem. When a dozer operator job opened, the senior man applying for the job was not selected. The union claimed in a formal grievance:

> The 1974 wage agreement (Section C) clearly states that the senior employee shall be given preference in filling a temporary assignment. Goss was the senior employee on the bid . . . and he feels discriminated against, in relation to Article 16, Section C.

Management's formal response was:

> Section A states seniority . . . shall be recognized . . . on the following basis: length of service and ability to step into and perform the work on the job at the time the job is offered. Robert Goss was given an opportunity to operate the dozer, he didn't know how to start the machine let alone operate it. He then was offered another job in connection with this job classification wherein he could be trained . . . he refused the offer.

This walkout was to be one of the most critical events in the history of the Rushton project.

The mine committee (the union-elected committee for processing grievances) and superintendent met, but to no avail. The mine committee then suggested putting the grievance through arbitration; instead, on Monday at 6 P.M. (during the second shift) the men walked out. A special meeting was called on Tuesday in which the men voted to stay out, on the grounds that arbitration takes too long. That night some of the men met and decided to picket other mines owned by Hinks. Their rationale was that one-day strikes were not effective, and picketing was the best way to get at Hinks. The pickets went up the next day at several of Hinks' mines. The district then became involved and applied pressure on the union leaders to get the men back. Meanwhile the company sent letters of "intent to discharge" to all the men involved in the picketing. At the union meeting held on Thursday, the men agreed to go back to work on Friday. Because of the discharge letter, a formal hearing was called with union and management officials. After some discussion management withdrew the dismissals, but suspended the picketers for two weeks and removed two of the picketers from the union mine committee (which is part of the contract) and from the Rushton labor-management committee. The level of tension was quite high.

> Hinks was really mad. . . . I've never seen him like he was. . . . He was so mad he was shaking all over. . . . When [the men] heard what happened, they were really burned up. . . . I think a lot of damage has been done to the program. [Miner, April 1976]

A manager involved in the strike said:

> We feel some of the union guys say one thing to us when we are in the quality of work meetings, but say another thing when they get back to the men . . . we've really had it.

The international became involved and threatened to pull out of the program because of management's actions. Hinks described his conversation with McAteer as the "most vitriolic message . . . it was unbelievable . . . full of threats." The district continued to mediate to find an acceptable solution. Further discussion continued during the weekend. On Saturday management agreed to reinstate the two miners to the mine committee and quality of work committees. The phone call from the international probably affected that decision, which had been the least defensible position management had taken, since membership on the mine committee results from union election and not from management's decision.

On Monday the discussions resumed. Management felt they had the union "cold" and planned to enforce the suspensions. The discussions revolved around the grievance procedure and the use of grievance machinery to prevent strikes. During this discussion the company president changed his position and withdrew the suspensions.

> I felt if we could talk about [the union officials'] responsibilities during a strike . . . the idea of getting the men back to work . . . to build trust through discussion versus persuasion. . . . All I was trying to do was to prove that strikes are unnecessary. . . . After we talked about this until 1:30, we felt we had smoked out a lot of ideas. . . . I said to Blair, "Let's do without the suspensions, and everyone go back to work tomorrow."

On Tuesday everyone was back at work, but the problems or tensions were not resolved. We detected increased hostility from the men toward management because of the suspensions and the arbitrary way management pulled men off union committees. Relations with the international were strained. Conflict within the union was increased. Many of the managers at the mine felt that the president had again capitulated to the union. They perceived the union's walkout and pickets as arbitrary and harmful to the mine. From either perspective, union or management, the events surrounding this walkout were antagonistic toward the QOW principles and objectives. Unilateral hostile acts had replaced bilateral problem-solving. Although a project such as this one is made up of a series of interrelated events and no one event is the critical event, this walkout did highlight the differences between labor and management and opened up a tendency toward more adversary, rather than problem-solving, activities.

PERIOD III: A HOLDING PERIOD

During 1976 many of the old institutions continued. The training program to extend the QOW project concluded at the end of the first quarter of 1976. A management training program for foremen was also under way during that period. The major decision-making mechanisms, the MTDC, continued to meet almost monthly to modify parts of the earlier document and deal with major problems. Some meetings of the joint committees also continued. The research team continued its role in forming the agenda of these meetings and providing direction for joint problem-solving activities.

New Innovations

At the same time new institutions were introduced. Early in 1976 another role was incorporated into the program. The MTDC did not feel well informed about the daily events at the mine. The new role was to develop an effective communications channel between the committee and the mine: a union man (who would have a greater access to the work force than a member of management) was to go daily into different sections and collect data about safety and the functioning of QOW behaviors. Lem Hollen, an experienced miner at Rushton, was elected by the union members of the MTDC and was to report monthly. The job was considered temporary and would be renewed at the discretion of the committee. This role was a significant addition to the structures created at Rushton, as it provided data that was previously not available. It was not a position, however, without conflict. In Hollen's first days on the job he was called a "scab" and a "company suck." This point of conflict was later resolved at a union meeting. Other strains occurred, including some tension over whether Hollen should go where he wanted or where management needed him.

While the new role of the data collector and communicator was a creation of labor and management discussions in the MTDC meetings, other new QOW activities were initiated primarily by the research team.

A goal-setting procedure was instituted by which the bosses would estimate production one month in advance. This figure would then be broken down by the crews on a weekly basis to evaluate progress in production. The goal also represented an "agreement" between the superintendent and the section as to how much they should produce.

The research team presented a deployment model that concerned allocating resources among the face, bolting, and support jobs. This framework was described in training and section conferences. The plan was to have the training director and his assistant work with the bosses in practicing the use of the model.

A related proposal concerned planning, which represents one of the critical behaviors the research team wanted Rushton to adopt. Planning behaviors were to be learned with the help of the training director and his assistant, who were to help each boss plan out the next three hours of work whenever they were in the section. The training director and his assistant were members of management who were trained in this planning activity by the research team.

A similar proposal was directed at the general mine foreman (who supervises all inside work). The research team wanted this individual to formulate a one-day planning horizon in advance. Currently, they felt, "He worked out of his hip pocket."

Another goal was to revitalize the section conferences, which the research team felt were not effective and needed a new design to facilitate problem-solving.

It is our view that a new design of section conferences was never successfully implemented. The activities of goal-setting and goal-planning never became a permanent part of the Rushton fabric. Only the new role of the data collector and the communicator were successfully institutionalized. The reasons for this will be discussed in Chapter 18.

The other major innovation that occurred during this period was a new preventive maintenance program. Although not directly part of the QOW project, its adoption was influenced by the strong training emphasis in the QOW activities. It also generated a series of problems that were dealt with by the MTDC.

Recurrent Issues

To provide the reader with another view of 1976, we shall enumerate a set of general themes or problems that appeared fairly regularly during this year. They were repeated in the MTDC and in the interviews we conducted with the participants.

Absenteeism was a major concern. It precipitated two of the strikes in the first quarter and it was greater in 1976 as compared to prior years. Management wanted a formal policy, for example, that a certain number of unexcused absences leads to dismissal. The union, of course, fought such a policy. The early discussions on this topic in the MTDC generated dialogues in an adversary mode; there was little joint problem solving to reach an acceptable position:

Union 1: Why don't you hire an extra guy to help with absenteeism?

Management 1: That would cost $130 a day. If we need an extra guy, your job is in jeopardy.

Management 2: The program was supposed to make people want to come to work . . . what does the union want to do?

Union 1: Does the company have a policy?

Management 1: We did, but you struck over it.

Management 3: From the absenteeism point of view, QOW stinks.

Union 2: We need an incentive for the men.

Management 2: Only way is to fire a man.

Management 1: If you do that you have a strike.

The union agreed in some cases to talk with a particular individual, but there was no general strategy to deal with absenteeism. Later in the year a union member proposed that people be paid weekly rather than biweekly, as a way to reduce absenteeism. Management felt that there was no evidence to support the validity of that proposal and that it would increase clerical costs:

Union 1: You got to try any proposal to see if it works.

Management 1: That's not the point, is it good?

Union 2: We should try it.

Management 2: I can jump off Brooklyn Bridge . . . I am not going to do it . . . I want to see if it will work.

Union 1: I'm trying to help the program.

Although the proposal surfaced in several meetings, it was never acted on. Without judging the quality of that proposal, we should note the following: the proposal was made by a union officer and member of the South section, he was an informal leader in that section and played an important role in implementing the experimental program. By 1976 a casual review of his comments in the MTDC shows that he was becoming disinterested. The rejection of the absentee proposal further alienated him from the program.

There was one activity jointly agreed on to deal with absenteeism. Gerald Susman, a member of the research team, interviewed absentee individuals to determine causes of absenteeism. This diagnostic phase extended into 1977.

Another major issue that persisted throughout the year concerned qualifying new miners, or "yellow hats." When the program went mine-wide, everyone received high pay rates except the new hires. A procedure was set up to qualify these men for high rates. Dissatisfaction with the qualification procedure was raised by the union in April 1976. The union argued that many of the men were qualified, but were not given the high rate. One of the underlying problems was who should do the qualifying? Although the union was dissatisfied with the procedure, it did not want to become part of a mechanism to judge the qualifications of fellow miners. Disagreements within management about whether an individual should be qualified created problems in resolving the labor-management definition of qualification. In June a new procedure was jointly laid out to qualify new miners. The problem reappeared, however, toward the end of the year. The union finally became more involved when it assigned one of its members to review informally the qualifications of a given miner. Nevertheless the areas of conflict were not fully resolved.

Gain sharing was another major issue in 1976 and had a critical bearing on the viability of the program. It was originally discussed in 1976, but no program had been worked out. During 1976 the research team increased their efforts to draw up a plan. They tried to involve the union in deciding on some of the basic principles (e.g., percent to be shared by company and union). The union's response was, "First let's find out what we're getting." Ultimately, the union decided that developing a gain-sharing program was too complicated and delegated the activity to the research team subject to international approval. By September a program had been worked out. The company president said:

> We do have a technical plan that's easy to understand . . . the men from PPL gave it tacit approval. But right now I have mixed emotions about gain sharing. . . . I felt there was too much emphasis toward incentive plans. . . . The men aren't working because the program's a good thing . . . we're hanging bait. . . . Also I had a problem in my mind how easy it would be to come up with a number to represent relative improvement [productivity gains] . . . maybe there is pressure just to give out more . . . I don't like that . . . I've been hammered by _____
> [union mine official] enough. [September 1976]

In response to the question, "Why do it?", Hinks said, "It's unfair to do nothing. I believe in gain sharing." In response to the question, "Are there benefits?", Hinks said, "I don't have any good measure to say there has not been benefits . . . maybe I'm going on the bait idea. . . . The amount we're talking about is small, relatively, to our total labor bill." By the end of the year however no plan had been implemented. The credibility of the research team, management, and the program was hurt by this delay.

Other pay issues appeared throughout the year. For example, the union argued that many of the miners were at the top rate when the program went mine-wide. These men did not benefit from the program, and the union felt a special top rate should be introduced. Other discussions focused on the rates given to the pumpers and the apprentice mechanics. The union argued that these jobs should have higher rates; management held the rates at their current levels.

CONCLUSION

We can conclude this account of 1976 by briefly reviewing the status of the sections at the end of the year in regards to the QOW program as well as some strains that persisted throughout the year.

In South the AW beliefs and practices seemed to be slowly eroding. At the crew interchange only the bosses and miner operator talked. There was little evidence of job switching. Two of the major informal leaders of the program withdrew from their leadership roles. One skilled miner operator had "bid off" that machine to the bolter because he felt "the men were not doing their job, and [he] did not want to take the rap for not getting the coal out." The other miner psychologically withdrew because he found the other management committee meetings were ineffective, and he felt his idea of moving to a weekly pay period to reduce absenteeism was not seriously treated.

The picture we are painting is *not* one of an inefficient section. In fact, the South section was consistently described as the best or one of the best sections in the mine. All the training the men had was not lost. In routine situations the men did work well together. They were knowledgeable and responsible miners. But many of the behaviors exhibited within the crew in 1974, such as planning, making decisions about production matters, coordinating within- and between-shift activities, were on the decline. Also, any identification with the program had all but disappeared.

The 5 Butt crew was the second experimental section. It never approximated the autonomous work group form found in South. Behavior in 5 Butt was largely a function of the boss or foreman. In one crew the boss held a laissez-faire attitude; in another the boss was authoritarian. A persistent rumor during this period was that one of the 5 Butt crews wanted to get out of the program. Although this crew was identified, the rumor was never confirmed.

The East section showed the greatest movement toward autonomy of the work areas involved in the mine-wide extension. Intershift communication increased in this section, and two of the foremen modified their behavior from a more authoritarian to a more cooperative mode. Nevertheless, the change in East did not approximate the level of autonomy achieved in the South section in 1974. There was not the same emergence of informal leaders, active decision making within the crew, or level of identity toward the program.

The North section never achieved any substantial level of change. This was partly due to the bad physical conditions (the worst in the mine), which hampered experimenting with autonomy. Also, and related to the physical-condition problem, some of the bosses in that section did not develop enough competency in running a crew to experiment with autonomy.

Other work areas of the mine (e.g., the cleaning plant), except for the training sessions, were not involved in the program and did not seem substantially to change their style of work. Our observations of these areas, however, were quite limited.

Our view of 1976 is that the concept of autonomy, which was the basic value underlying the QOW project, was weakening at Rushton. A variety of other strains appeared in the meetings and interviews that seem congruent with this point of view. Discussions continued about whether the bosses were giving the men enough room for decision making. What makes this strain interesting is the position taken by the research team. They stated:

> What exists now in the program is a delegation model. . . . Management has not given up the right to direct the work force . . ., [but] it is really a personal matter now. . . . How much autonomy there will be depends on the bosses.

This statement in effect created a dilemma. Although there were general beliefs that the program focused on the development of autonomous work groups, this statement permitted the level of autonomy to be determined by the boss and created a natural tension. In the original South experiment in 1974, although individual variations were expected, all three supervisors were urged to achieve an autonomous working relationship with their crews.

The purpose of the last four chapters was to give a detailed view of the structure of the Rushton experiment up to this period. Chapter 20 will update the Rushton story through 1978.

PART THREE

EVALUATION DESIGN AND RESULTS

THIS SECTION COVERS TWO MAIN TOPICS: THE DE-
sign for evaluating change and the results of the experiment. By delineating the major objectives, concepts, and methods that guided the evaluation, Chapter 9 describes how we went about measuring the experiment at Rushton. The subsequent chapters (10–16) examine the results of the experiment in terms of specific models, operational procedures, and data.

CHAPTER NINE

Design and Measurement of Change

EVALUATION OBJECTIVES

The evaluation activities at Rushton had four objectives. The first was to provide an independent assessment of the effectiveness of the Rushton QOW project. Basically we wanted to know if the program had any effects. Questions relevant to assessing effectiveness included: What were the effects, if any, of the program on productivity, safety, attitudes, job skills, and so on? At what time during the experiment were these changes most pronounced? Did the changes persist over time? Why did these effects occur, persist, or dissipate?

The second objective was to provide managers, union leaders, and policymakers with guidelines for using QOW programs in other settings. We were interested in what could be generalized from the Rushton experience to other settings. Questions related to this objective included: What factors affect the successful introduction of a program? What are the problems of implementing a QOW project? What factors affect whether a newly introduced structure will persist over time? What factors facilitate or inhibit the diffusion of a project to other settings?

The third objective was to design and conduct the evaluation in a way that facilitated comparing the results at Rushton across other QOW projects. An objective was to compare programs. The strategy in the Rushton project was to use measures that could be used at other

113

sites and to develop analysis procedures and models that could be generalized to other QOW projects.

The fourth objective of the QOW program evaluation at Rushton was to provide data for the participants about the results of the project. This project had required and received high levels of cooperation from management, the union, and the workers. There was a need for meaningful feedback.

To achieve these evaluation objectives, five criteria were adopted to guide the design of the evaluation:

1. **Comprehensiveness.** To assess the effectiveness of any QOW project it is important to cast as broad a net as possible to capture the many consequences of such an intervention. Because these experiments are complex, however, they are likely to have many unanticipated consequences. When a QOW project is introduced, it is difficult to know what will happen over time. The task for the designer is to anticipate as many consequences as possible, but also to collect more data than might appear to be necessary.

2. **Flexibility.** A change project by definition is dynamic; the evaluation design cannot be fixed. Mechanisms must be used to inform the principal investigator when and what recalibrations in the design are necessary. The unexpected introduction of a new experimental section in the fall of 1974 substantially affected the evaluation design by changing the work force composition in the control groups. It was necessary to resurvey the Rushton work force at that time and to modify some of the instruments. Failure to react would have limited the effectiveness of evaluating attitude changes over time.

3. **Standardization.** If results in one site are to be compared to another, it is necessary to use a common core of measures and common analytic models. Standardization can occur at many levels. At one level it would be to have the same items across sites. At another level, only the domain of items (e.g., perceptions about supervision, absenteeism) would be the same.

4. **Translatability.** If these projects are to have any impact on the immediate participants or on the industry at large, then the information from the evaluation must be understood and perceived as useful. A potential danger of studies created by professionals is that they can only be read by professionals. Therefore, each decision about the evaluation design should generate the type of information that is perceived as understandable and useful by managers, union officials, and government personnel.

5. Cost-Benefits. The purpose of the evaluation component is to compare the benefits in relation to the costs of the experiment. The evaluation activities themselves, however, should be subject to this same analysis; that is, the principal investigator must be able to weigh the benefits and costs of the various evaluation procedures. If QOW projects in the future are to be run on company resources, firms will need to know the most efficient and economical approach to evaluation.

EFFECTIVENESS OF QOW PROJECTS

A basic objective is to determine whether the Rushton project was effective. A basic problem, however, is to determine what effective or successful means. The purpose of this section is to outline a framework that can be used to define effectiveness or success in QOW projects. The purpose of the framework is to provide some intellectual organization for data collection, analysis, and interpretation of the Rushton evaluation design. Although the following discussion is tied to the Rushton project, it can be generalized to other QOW projects. (See Goodman and Pennings, 1977 and 1979, for more detail.)

Social System and Constituencies

QOW projects take place in complex social systems. The common design is a joint labor-management effort that brings together two major constituencies: the organization (represented by management) and the union (represented by its leaders). The workers as members of both the union and organization represent the third major constituency. These three subsystems—the organization, the union, and the workers—are highly interdependent and relatively stable entities over time and form the basic social system for a QOW project.

They can also be considered as independent entities, representing quite different goals. For example, union and management have different goals, which are often in conflict with each other. We considered the workers as a separate constituency because: (1) some QOW program outcomes are at the individual level, reflecting interest in the workers' attitudes, motivations, and other variables independent of the union or management and (2) the workers' interests are not always identical to management or union interests.

Our framework, then, begins by defining the social system of a QOW program as comprising the organization, the union, and the worker. Each of these constituencies is a distinct, independent entity with different goals. It was possible to identify a much broader social system that would include, for example, economic (suppliers, competitors), political (funding agencies), or community systems in the firm's environment. We have elected not to use this broad definition of social system because of the resources available for the evaluation effort. (A broader definition would have required data collection from these external systems.) It probably is more useful to demonstrate first that the project had a significant impact on the major constituencies (organization, union, and workers), before tracing out its effects on the extended environment.

Although we chose to define the social system in terms of the company, local union, and workers, we recognize the need to take into account the effect the program might have on organization-environment relations—for example, the experiment at Rushton could change the character of the relationship between the company and government regulators or between the local union and its international. This change bears on the effectiveness of the project and needs to be included in the analysis. Therefore, although the company, union, and workers are the principal constituencies, the boundaries of this investigation extend beyond these three groups to their relationships with external constituencies.

To conclude, it is important to note that we have considered the company, union, and workers as single entities. However, where the program has had different effects on different groups within each constituency, these will be made explicit. For example, the effectiveness of the program was viewed differently by top management, middle management, and first-line management.

Dimensions of Effectiveness

Given the definition of the social system in terms of three relevant constituencies, the next issue concerns delineating dimensions on which effectiveness is to be assessed. Two classes of dimensions were considered: explicit and implicit goals.

Explicit goals are those stated by members of the different constituencies. In a QOW project such as Rushton these goal statements appear in the document (see Chapter 6) for the change effort. Since this is a mutually designed and agreed-on document by labor and management, the goals are valid indicators for assessing effectiveness. The major goals included in that document are increased safety, increased production, increased earning, job satisfaction, and greater job skills. If we were to assign goals by constituencies, management's goals would include safety, production, job satisfaction, and job skills; the union's goals would include safety, earnings, job satisfaction, and job skills; and the workers' goals would be, in this case, the same as the union's goals. Although the latter two constituencies' explicit goals appear to be the same, the relative weights for these goals probably differ between the union official and the union member. The explicit goals are the most obvious standards by which the effectiveness of the Rushton project can be judged. They were formally agreed to by the three major constituencies.

Implicit goals are also important in assessing effectiveness. They are derived from the systems-model perspective in the organizational effectiveness literature. Basically, this perspective holds that organizations must deal not only with immediate or explicit goals (e.g., producing coal), but also with maintaining the organization as a system both internally (e.g., training members, improving communications, dealing with conflict) and externally (e.g., dealing with government regulators). Adaptability of the organization is a sign of effectiveness.

Translating this perspective into our constituency framework means we can view Rushton as an organization not only in terms of how well it meets its explicit goals (e.g., production and safety), but also in terms of how well it is able to maintain itself as a system both internally and externally. For example, it would be possible to maximize production in the short run at the expense of creating conflict or strain for the foremen. The organization is effective in terms of explicit goals, but ineffective in terms of implicit goals. That is, increased levels of role strain for the foremen may reduce the organization's adaptability to future changes in technology or regulations. Or it could be that production does not increase, while relationships with external regulators (e.g., state mine inspectors) improve. Here effectiveness would appear in the implicit goals. Similar examples can be generated for the union. While safety levels may increase, rivalry within the union may also increase. In this case effectiveness appears in the explicit goals, ineffectiveness in the implicit goals.

Two types of implicit goals can be used in QOW projects. The first concerns the character of the organization's internal relationships, focusing on levels of conflict, coordination, and skill-development among organizational members. The second concerns the character (e.g., the degree of conflict-cooperation) of the external relationships between the organization and its environment. In the case of Rushton this could refer to relationships between the local, district, or international union. Implicit goals are stated for systems (Rushton organization or the union), not for individual workers.

Other Issues

Social systems, constituencies, explicit and implicit goals are the main concepts of our framework for assessing effectiveness. There are a number of related issues that need to be explored briefly to provide closure to this discussion.

First, there are no operational referents or standards imbedded in the goal statements that would permit assessing the degree to which a goal is achieved: Management wants to increase productivity, but there is no standard established to determine how much is an effective increase in productivity. What does it mean to improve safety? What amount of accident reduction is necessary to constitute an effective QOW project? There is no easy resolution to this problem, since it is unlikely that members in the constituencies could articulate clear referents or standards. Therefore, our strategy will be to chart changes in goal achievement (e.g., in productivity) and to provide some information on the statistical significance of these changes in relation to the control groups. The final interpretation of the magnitude of any changes must be left to the judgment of the constituency members and other readers.

Another issue concerns the relative weights assigned to the different goals. Although there are a variety of procedures for generating these weights, our strategy was to treat the goals as equal. The additional data collection and the analysis costs to determine weights did not seem warranted, given the many problems confronting the evaluation team. The data as they are presented permit the reader to assign weights to the relevant goals or outcome variables.

A related issue, which follows logically from assigning relative weights, concerns developing a single indicator of effectiveness for each constituency. This option was rejected and would have been rejected regardless of our position in determining weights. A QOW project is a complex activity. Many outcome variables change, and the nature of the changes varies over time. In addition, the pioneering nature and scope of the change effort makes it difficult to identify all the outcomes and their relationships with each other. Therefore, a single index of effectiveness would be an oversimplification. We felt that it was necessary to chart all the relevant costs and benefits of the project, but not to reduce these to some simple indicator.

The last issue concerns the time period used to assess effectiveness.

Major change projects in the field take a long time to set up, and their impact often extends over a long period. Therefore, it is difficult to know when to begin the assessment or when to take periodic assessments. It is clear that the period selected for assessment will determine to some extent our view of the effectiveness of the project. For example, let us assume significant effects from an intervention occur three years into a project. If the assessment occurs only at the end of the first year, then our evaluation of the project will be greatly constrained. Our position has been to select time periods bounded by the critical events in the project (the specific time periods are discussed at the end of this chapter).

DESIGN STRATEGY

Intervention in an ongoing organization is a complicated process. Measurement of the effects of that intervention is also complicated. It is impossible to introduce many of the traditional features of an experimental design into such a setting. Random assignment of workers between experimental and control groups is unlikely. Control over external events (e.g., changes in physical conditions in the mine or in mining regulations) that bear on the effects of the intervention is also unlikely. The dilemma is to identify experimental effects in a situation where tight experimental controls are impossible.

We dealt with this dilemma by using the following strategies. First, we tried to approximate as closely as possible many of the traditional features of an experiment. One work section—2 South—was the experimental group, and two other sections served as control groups. The tasks, work group composition, policies, and regulations were the same across all three sections, but there were some differences in equipment and physical conditions. The evaluation team could do nothing to change these similarities or differences. Another traditional feature used at Rushton was the comparison of data from before and after the intervention. This allowed us to examine the amount of change and to use each section as its own control, that is, we were able to compare South's performance in the baseline with its performance after the intervention. In this comparison, equipment and physical conditions were the same. *

A second strategy in our design was to use multiple regression procedures to improve the precision in estimating experimental effects. Since the experimental and control groups were operating under different physical conditions that affected productivity, noting differences between sections without controlling for physical conditions would have been improper. Measures of external circumstances, such as physical conditions or new timbering plans, were introduced as external variables into some of our models, and their impact determined. The use of multivariate procedures permitted dealing statistically with variables that might generally be labeled uncontrollable.

The third strategy in our design was to collect data with multiple measurement methods. Reliance on any one method or instrumentation (e.g., self-report, observation) was clearly not advisable. Each method has its own properties and limitations. The complexities of assessing organizational change require multiple methods. While multiple methods provide greater opportunity for convergent validity, some events in an intervention can be best captured with only certain methods and others with different methods. We can illustrate the use of multiple methods by the following example of experimental- versus control-group productivity. An important part of the analysis was to verify that the experimental changes were in place only in the experimental section. It was possible that foremen in the control sections had borrowed and implemented changes in their own crews that would have confounded interpretation of the productivity results. At Rushton we collected survey data and conducted informal interviews and on-site investigations to determine if the control sections were borrowing experimental changes. We found convergence among these measures: there was no borrowing of experimental changes.

The fourth strategy was to anticipate and collect data that would bear on different explanations for experimental results. For example, one problem in the design was that the first experimental crew volunteered. This surely created a selection bias. How significant this bias was depends on why the men volunteered. Anticipating this problem, we collected data on the reasons for volunteering, which helped us to place the volunteering issue in perspective. In other words, anticipating and collecting data on varying explanations improves one's ability to identify the experimental effects.

ISSUES IN EVALUATING CHANGE

We shall now examine how four design parameters relate to some issues in evaluating change.

Identification and Control of Contamination Factors

The basic objective of the evaluation was to determine the effect of the multiple interventions on a set of outcome variables. Unfortunately, there were a variety of contaminating factors that could have confounded interpreting the consequences of the experiment. The problem was to identify these factors and try to isolate or control their effects. Some potential contaminating factors (see Campbell and Stanley, 1966) included:

1. External factors. These refer to events outside of the experiment that affect the results of the experiment. The energy crisis and the greater demand for coal led to the introduction of a new production section. The new section led to changes in the experimental intervention strategy and thus had noticeable consequences on the project. The national coal strike in 1974 represented another external event that bore on the working life at the mine.

The most traditional way to deal with these contaminating factors is to use a control group. If the experimental and control groups have been exposed to the same stimuli, then differences between these groups should represent effects of the experiment. Another way we dealt with this phenomenon was to collect systematic data before and after the external event occurred. A third procedure was to incorporate the external variables into a multivariate model.

2. Maturation. A more subtle contaminating factor occurs when there are maturation changes underway within the experimental system prior to and during the experiment that are parallel to, but independent of, the planned changes. For example, at Rushton a gradual improvement in labor-management relationships had been underway. This was in sharp contrast to an earlier period of bitter labor-management relationships. Since one goal of the intervention was to improve the quality of labor-management relations, it was necessary to separate the experimental effects from the maturation effect. This was no simple task. In this case control groups were not useful since the effects of union-management relationships impacted on the whole mine, not on a single section. Similarly, one could not rely on analytic procedures since the number of observations (e.g., number of walkouts) was small. Collecting data on different explanations and using that data to interpret changes over time is the procedure we adopted in analyzing this phenomenon.

3. **Selection and mortality bias.** Another contaminating factor occurs when there is differential selection between the control and experimental groups. At Rushton the miners volunteered into the experimental group. If the men in the experimental and control sections differed on variables relevant to the intervention, then the equivalence of the two sections would have been questionable and the value of the control group lost. The problem of equivalence in the experimental and control groups was a reality in this experiment. We approached this issue by using differing control groups that were less contaminated by the selection bias. For example, using a production section as its own control (i.e., comparing the baseline year with the experimental year) provided some of the advantages of a control group without the selection bias. Another approach was to examine whether the experimental and control sections at the beginning of the experiment were similar on a set of relevant variables (e.g., age). If no differences were found, then the selection bias was less significant. A third approach was to determine the reasons for volunteering.

A related issue in this study concerned subject loss or mortality. One problem in any longitudinal study is that respondents leave their job section or the organization. A consequence of this is that the sample size becomes smaller and thus precludes certain types of data analysis. Subject loss also confounds interpreting the results. Would those subjects who left have changed in the same direction as those that remained? An analysis of the characteristics of people who leave versus those that stay is one major strategy for determining whether mortality is a significant contaminator.

4. **Measurement.** Another source of error resides in the measurement instruments. Standard problems of unreliability and lack of validity affect interpretation of results. Changes in record keeping procedures over time create problems, as do instruments that elicit socially desirable responses. Another problem concerns reactivity effects, where the measuring process itself affects the nature of the responses. Our general strategy in dealing with these measurement problems was to use standard instruments that have demonstrated reliability and validity as well as to use multiple measures (both reactive and nonreactive) of the same phenomenon. If different independent measures portray the same results, then one can be more confident in interpreting the data.

Multiple Intervention

One characteristic of this experiment was that it incorporated a multiple intervention strategy. The structure of the experiment required changes in Rushton's pay system, communication system, authority system, training practices, and so on. A problem posed by this multiple intervention was to separate the effects of the different structural changes. To what extent were changes in worker attitudes or production a function of the change in the pay system, communications, or authority structure? If one could isolate these effects, strategies for future change activities could be more effectively implemented.

The design of this study did not permit identifying systematically the separate effects of the different changes introduced in the Rushton experiment. This would have required several experimental groups (each with different combinations of experimental factors) and several control groups and would have been difficult (if not impossible) to implement.

Our view is that most significant organizational changes require multiple intervention. The organization is a complex entity. It seems unlikely that changes in only one dimension (e.g., pay) will have substantial effects on the total organization. Another reason for using a multiple intervention strategy is that it represents the most likely condition for creating change. If no change occurs with a multiple intervention strategy, chances for change in any of the separate interventions is less likely. The initial problem for an evaluation of these interventions is to determine whether the intervention has produced an overall effect. If it has, then future analyses can try to separate the impacts of the different components in the multiple intervention.

MAJOR VARIABLES AND METHODS

The evaluation design incorporated multiple variables and multiple methods to measure these variables. Table 9.1 lists the major variables.

The attitudinal variables represented one of the major outcome variables in this study. We were interested in whether attitudes and beliefs about work changed as a function of the experiment. Also, changes in attitudes might have affected other variables, such as absenteeism, turnover, accidents, and production.

The change process variables refer to specific activities that took place during the change effort. For example, a major part of the change process concerned problem-solving activities in labor-management committees. The behavior of union leaders, management, and the

Table 9.1.   Major Variables for Evaluation

Major Area	Representative Variables
Attitudinal	Attitudes toward the company, job, supervision, working conditions, organizational reward systems, influence structure, feedback systems, life in general.
Change processes	Process of problem-solving, modification and learning new roles, learning new social relationships, levels and modifications of commitment to change.
Decision to participate	Perception of goals for change effort, congruency among goals for different participants, perceptions of change effort as a means of reaching goals.
Economic	Quantity and rate of output, direct labor costs, direct material costs, productivity indices, downtime, costs of investments for change, predictors of production function.
Job attachment	Absenteeism rates, reasons for absenteeism, costs of absenteeism, turnover rates, reasons for turnover, costs of turnover.
Labor-management	Climate of labor-management relations, characteristics of grievances, attitudes toward grievance procedure, internal structure of the union, influence of union on organizational decisions, level of union participation.
Organizational structure	Size, market, conditions, organizational structure, financial structure, information and control systems, personal systems.
Safety	Frequency of safety violations, cost of violations, number of accidents, costs of accidents, quality of compliance with safety laws.
Task-technology structure	Characteristics of machinery, workflow, physical layout, physical work conditions, structure of tasks, characteristics of job.

change team in these committees was an important aspect of introducing and administering the change effort and needed to be examined.

The decision to participate refers primarily to background material concerning why the different parties became involved in the QOW program. It is an important area since there had been resistance to participating in such a program from both management and labor. By investigating why the Rushton experiment got under way, one would be better able to assess which firms might become involved in QOW projects, and the generalizability of the Rushton findings.

Economic information comprises the largest body of data in this study. Some of the major outcome variables in this area include tons produced, productivity, and cost per ton.

The job attachment information concerns the traditional indices of absenteeism and turnover.

Another major outcome variable concerns the character of labor-management relationships (e.g., frequency of grievances, lost time due to strikes, etc.). Within the labor-management area the internal structure of the union also will be examined since a potential QOW program consequence is to modify this structure.

The organization area primarily concerns information on topics such as organizational size, structure, division of labor, and market conditions. One function of these data is to provide a bench mark for comparing the results of this project with other QOW projects. That is, to compare results across studies it is necessary to have some descriptive information on the different organizations. The organizational data, however, are not simply background data. They could be used to assess change. For example, if a program leads to new organizational arrangements, these will be documented; since we are dealing with a single observation, there will be no data analysis.

The safety information is critical, given the hazardous nature of the mining industry. Statistics on accidents, costs of accidents, and frequency of safety violations are the variables in this area.

The last area includes the technological description of the firm, including such topics as workflow, level of mechanization, and characteristics of the focal jobs.

Table 9.2 identifies the methods used in this project. Existing record systems provided most of the economic, job attachment, and safety data. The office force at Rushton was small, and there was little slack to undertake administering new data systems. This did not lead to any significant limitation in the data, since the existing systems seemed adequate.

There were three separate structured interviews. The *Baseline Interview* dealt with attitudes and beliefs. The *Organizational Description Interview*, as the name suggests, described the structure of the company, while the *Union Description Interview* did the same for the union.

An unstructured interview was used primarily to keep in touch with the daily events at the mine. It was usually conducted by phone with members of management, and therefore, was descriptive in nature, picking up critical events during a particular period. A similar type of interview was conducted with members of the training and develop-

Table 9.2.   Major Methods for Evaluation

Existing record systems	Much of the data for economic, job attachment, and safety is derived from existing record systems that are available.
New record systems	Some new systems, primarily in the economic area, have been set up to supplement existing record systems.
Structured interviews	These include most of the standard instruments that have been validated in other organizations and that are used to measure work attitudes, organizational characteristics, and so on.
Unstructured interviews	These include instruments specifically designed to measure the change process.
Structured observational rating forms	These are standard forms used to record behavior and dimensions of work. This represents data collected by observation versus some self-report format. Rating of job components using the ISR schedule would be an example.
Semistructured observational rating forms.	These forms were developed for the project and primarily concern the change effort.

ment team. This provided information about their plans for future activities which helped to plan the evaluation activities. This interview also provided some data on the training teams' evaluations of events that occurred.

One significant innovation of the change effort at Rushton was a set of problem-solving groups composed of people in management, the union, and the experimental section. A structured rating form was developed to catalogue the activities of these meetings. This method entailed three steps: (1) a transcript of the meetings was made. This served as a useful log of major events during the history of the project; (2) the transcript was coded from categories in the rating scheme; (3) the codes were collapsed into indices for analysis. One example of an indicator would be the amount of conflict between labor and management for a given meeting.

The semistructured rating form was designed for examining the evolving structure in the change process. Information for the form was collected by observation in the work place. The form was semistructured in that a series of categories were to be described in each observation. What got described was, of course, specific to the situation. One example of a category would be coordination between shifts. This was measured by describing who communicated with whom during the shift interchange. Greater communication between shifts was a goal of the intervention. Table 9.3 shows several methods for the

Table 9.3. Evaluation Variables × Methods

Evaluation Areas	Records Existing System	Records New System	Interview Structured	Interview Unstructured	Observation Structured	Observation Semistructured
				Evaluation Methods		
Attitudinal	—	—	X	X	X	X
Change processes	—	—	X	X	X	X
Decision to participate	—	—	X	X	—	—
Economic	X	X	X	—	X	X
Job attachment	X	—	X	—	—	—
Labor-management	X	—	X	X	X	X
Organizational structure	X	—	X	X	X	X
Safety	X	—	X	X	X	X
Task-technology structure	X	—	X	X	X	X

127

measurement of each variable. Attitudes, for example, could be measured in four different ways. The major method was the structured interview. However, the unstructured interview provided global assessments of attitudes. Attitudes could be inferred from the pattern of interactions in the structured observation form. On-site observation provided additional information on attitudes.

TIME PERIOD

The baseline period for this study ran from January through November 1973. During this period the experimental mining system was not in operation. Intensive planning for the change began around August 1973 and continued until the experiment started on December 3, 1973. There was a training and start up period until March 1, 1974, when the experiment began.

The second time period ran from the beginning of the experiment to the introduction of the new experimental section in October 1974. We used this event to bound the second period because it had a substantial effect on crew composition in all sections but South. The third period began after the national coal strike (December 1974) and continued until the vote on August 20, 1975. The second and third periods represent a relatively uncontaminated period to examine the first experimental intervention and can be combined to compare the first experimental section to the control sections. The last period began after the vote and represented the extension of the program to the whole mine and runs through December 1976. Although much of the data is presented using these periods, other time periods were examined. For example, the research team defined the first experimental year from March 1974 through March 1975. We looked at this period.

ROLE RELATIONSHIP BETWEEN EVALUATION AND RESEARCH TEAMS

A unique aspect of the Rushton experiment was the existence of an evaluation team and a research team. A brief exploration of this relationship, which is rare in organizational interventions, is important for understanding the analyses that are to follow.

First, the evaluation team was not involved in any of the design or strategy issues in the Rushton intervention. We attended all the major activities (e.g., training, steering committees) but did not actively participate.

Second, the evaluation team had access to different information sources (i.e., informants) and collected different types of information (e.g., attitude surveys). Most members of management and the union understood the difference between the two teams and often provided differential information.

Third, there was very little transfer of information from the evaluation team to the research team. Although our rule was to make available any data we had from commonly available sources (e.g., record data on absenteeism), there was very little exchange. In many cases the research team collected its own data from sources we had used. On the other hand, the research team was very open in providing us with their view of the change process.

Fourth, the two teams differed in their intellectual frameworks. The research team was a strong advocate of sociotechnical analysis. The two groups also differed in their research methods' orientation; for example, the survey method (one approach used by the evaluation team) was not embraced by the senior member of the research team. There were significant differences in the way both teams analyzed data. The evaluation team combined econometric and qualitative analysis, while the research team focused more on the latter. (See Trist, Susman, and Brown 1977 versus Chapters 10 and 11.)

Lastly, the groups were independently funded.

While this model is only one of many that might be adopted in organizational interventions, it has a number of advantages. First, the existence of differential roles permitted the access to different types of data. Second, changing an organization is a role requiring great time investments and personal commitments. It is difficult to see how a person in such a role can stand back and objectively view the process of change. The separation of the two roles permits this activity. Third, evaluation and change activities require different skills. There are few "great people" that possess both sets of skills. Therefore, the existence of both roles permits a division of labor that facilitates the maximum use of both skills. Lastly, the role relationships we described worked. There was a high degree of cooperation between both teams over the three years of this experiment.

CONCLUSION

The purpose of this chapter was to provide an overview of the assessment goals, strategies, and procedures. Basically I wanted to lead the reader through a series of decisions I made relevant to the Rushton project. The underlying assumption, however, is that these decisions are generalizable to other QOW or related projects. The first decision is to delineate the concept of effectiveness. Then, the dilemma of assessing an experiment in a context where traditional experimental controls are absent requires an articulation of design strategies pertinent to this dilemma. Four strategies were developed. Lastly, the methods, variables, and time periods for assessment were identified.

The following chapters present the findings. The results are arranged in terms of the explicit goals and implicit or indirect effects.

CHAPTER TEN

Beliefs—Attitudes

One goal of the experimental program was to change beliefs and attitudes about work. This chapter examines whether any changes occurred as a function of the experimental intervention.

The basic results, captured by a set of different measures, were that attitudes changed in a manner consistent with the experimental interventions. Changes occurred in attitudes toward the work group, supervision, the reward system, decision-making practices, authority, and responsibility systems. However, after the vote that rejected the mine-wide program, there was a regression in scores toward the baseline for the first experimental section, while those trained under the management's mine-wide program exhibited some moderate changes consistent with the experimental plan. Readers who prefer a summary and interpretation of the results rather than the technical issues in assessing attitude change should turn to the discussion section.

BASIC HYPOTHESES

The basic hypothesis for this chapter is that the experimental intervention changed workers' beliefs and attitudes. This hypothesis is based on the assumption that the experiment introduced structural changes, which, in turn, affected belief and attitude systems. Following this line of reasoning, the beliefs and attitudes most likely to change were those directly related to the new structures. In this experiment structural changes were most closely tied to the work group, supervision, the job, and work motivation. (Those not exposed to the intervention, of course, should exhibit no changes.)

The experiment provided workers in the experimental group with more authority and responsibility to make decisions. Therefore, it should have produced feelings of greater autonomy. Also, changes in the number of new activities performed in the experimental section should have enhanced perceptions of job variety. Beliefs about the supervisor (foreman) should also have changed; he should have been seen as less directive and more facilitative. The use of meetings to develop section identity and of intershift communication to enhance cooperation should have led to changes in how the miners perceived their work group. The above are illustrations of the relationship between the intervention and changes in work attitudes. Attitude areas other than those discussed above were also considered.

The motivational model used for this analysis is the expectancy model (Mitchell, 1974). Our study incorporates two features of that model: (1) the belief that if one tries hard, performance can be increased (self-expectancy) and (2) the belief that certain rewards are contingent on increasing performance (system expectancy). Given the structural changes that occurred in the experiment, we hypothesized that self-expectancies ("If I try, how likely is it that I can increase my performance?") and beliefs about behavior-reward contingencies would increase. For example, the concept of gain sharing is included in the intervention document. Implicit is the idea that gain sharing will be possible if people produce more. To verify this hypothesis we shall see if the perceived relationship between pay and performance changed in the experimental group.

The basic hypotheses have been phrased primarily in terms of a direct relationship between the experimental intervention and other classes of variables. While there may be a more complicated analytic model, the design of the experiment and of the evaluation did not permit testing it. For example, it could be that supervisor behavior changed, that this then modified job perceptions, and that both of these factors affected work group perceptions. The multiple intervention design of the experiment, which introduced many factors simultaneously, and the lack of a continuous series of measures precludes testing this causal chain.

GENERAL DESIGN

We shall now examine how the measurement of beliefs and attitudes was carried out. First we shall look at the measurement periods; then the sample, the instruments, and the analysis model will be reviewed. The specification of the attitude measures will be discussed on pp. 136, 154, 160, 168.

Measurement Periods

Five different measurements were taken by interview after this evaluation began. The baseline interviewing began in the first week of December 1973. This was the first access we had to the experimental population, and it was early enough in the program to avoid any contamination. A second measurement was conducted in June 1974. The purpose of this measure was to see whether any of the changes had "taken," that is, was there any evidence that the new structures had an effect? We planned this additional measurement because we felt that by using only annual measurements we would sacrifice learning about some of the critical change processes. A third measurement occurred in October 1974 because of the introduction of the new experimental section. This changed the composition of the work force in the sections we were using as control groups. Since our design was based on matching people by sections and jobs over time, this change was going to prevent this matching process, therefore we reinterviewed everyone in October. For some people we conducted a prior and current interview. If a person had been in control group E during the first two measurement periods, but was moved to a new section in October, he was interviewed twice. The prior interview focused on his beliefs and attitudes in control group E. The current interview, which included the same items, focused on the respondent's attitudes and beliefs about his new section. The two interviews were conducted at the same time, some three weeks after the person had moved into the new section. This time period was selected so that the person would remember events in his prior section, yet have been in the new section long enough to form impressions of the work and supervision. If a person in October 1974 was in the same section he had been in during the first or second interviews or had never been surveyed, he received only one interview.

The fourth measure occurred in April 1975. This period was selected because it represented the research team's definition of the end of the first experimental year. The last measurement was completed in August 1976 just before we withdrew our active association at Rushton; it also represents a year into the post-vote mode of operation.

Sample

The sampling strategy was determined to a large extent by the nature of the workers, the experiment, and the work. Given our decision to interview, we had to do our data collection in the work area. Since the intervention focused on the mining sections, most of our interviews were conducted near the coal face. We could not have asked the miners to come outside since it takes an hour to go in and out. This would have tied up all the inside transportation facilities. Also, we wanted to work with the men in their own territory. Once we arrived at the face we had to stay for the full shift. The costs of going to the coal face to interview just three people were rather high. Therefore, our general strategy was to interview everyone in the experimental sections and then as many as possible in the other control sections. Given these constraints to interviewing, we did not keep returning to the control sections to interview all the workers. Instead, we spent one shift per crew interviewing in the control sections. We selectively sampled (to get diversity in jobs and length of service) in other areas, such as maintenance, cleaning plant, and outside laborers. Most members of management were interviewed.

The average interview lasted 50 minutes. None of the processed interview data were fed back to the miners. We did complete interim reports in 1974 and 1975 that contained analyses of the attitude data and these were available to the research team. To the best of my knowledge the research team never used these data with the miners.

The total number of people interviewed was 147 in period 1 (December 1973), 137 in period 2 (June 1974), 155 in period 3 (October 1974), 156 in period 4 (April 1975), and 123 in period 5 (August 1976). This represents approximately 80% of the work force for those time periods. Table 10.1 represents the sample for the experimental and control groups. The major focus on the attitude analysis was on these groups since the experiment took place primarily in the mining sections. We have not included the second experimental section in the main analysis since it did not come into being until period 3. Results for this section are discussed in the body of this chapter, where appropriate. Similarly we are not including in the main analysis work areas that are not comparable to the mining sections. Miners in the cleaning plant, for example, have different jobs and working conditions and they were not appropriate control groups. It could be, however, that these nonmining section areas borrowed concepts from the experimental intervention and these areas became, in that sense, new

Table 10.1.   Sample for Experimental and Control Groups

	Experimental	Control N	Control E
Period 1 (12/73)	29	20	18
Period 2 (6/74)	30	24	24
Period 3 (10/74)	26	19	14
Period 4 (4/75)	29	20	20
Period 5 (8/76)	25	17	14

N = North section
E = East section

experimental groups. The data from our on-site observations indicated this was not the case. Therefore, since these areas were not appropriate control groups and since they did not borrow experimental innovations, they are not included in the main analysis. We, of course, did look at the data and any changes that did occur in the nonmining sections will be reported.

To do this analysis properly we also had to match respondents over the time periods. That is, if we asked a respondent questions about his work group at different time periods, it is important that the referent to his answer was the same work group. If an individual changed work groups, any changes in attitudes about work groups could have been a function either of differences in work groups or the intervention. To facilitate this analysis, we matched the respondents on dimensions, such as section, work group, and job. One consequence of the matching procedure is that, given the subject loss, the analysis sample is small (see Table 10.2).

Instruments

Different types of attitude measures were used to enhance the validity of the measurement process. The first was a set of standard structured

Table 10.2.   Sample of Matched Respondents

	Experimental	Control N	Control E
Period 1—2 (6/74)	21	13	14
Period 1—3 (10/74)	18	13	10
Period 1—4 (4/75)	21	6	4
Period 4—5 (8/76)	21	9	8

items in a Likert form. These items are common to all QOW projects and were selected because of their validity and reliability. Respondents were presented a statement and asked the degree to which they agreed with that statement. The second measurement was a set of global rating items designed specifically for the Rushton project and focused on outcome variables, such as, "What effect, if any, has the QOW project had on safety at Rushton?" Basically, we wanted to tap respondents' overall judgments of the success of the program. Third, we used a set of semistructured items that asked the respondent to describe what the autonomous project was all about in his own words, with an open-ended response category. A coding system was developed for these questions. The three sets of measures were collected by interview, rather than by questionnaire because: (1) The interviewer's personal nature would maximize response rates over time; (2) It provided for a broader range of questions; (3) It was a better check on social desirability responses; and (4) It was more suited to a population where literacy is generally low.

In addition to the interview, belief and attitude data were collected by an on-site observer and by an analysis of interactions during the meetings. Also, unstructured interviews conducted periodically with members of labor and management provided some information on attitudes. Data from the on-site observer and unstructured interviews are presented here; the analysis of meeting interactions is found in Chapter 14.

STANDARD STRUCTURED ITEMS

Method

A core of 21 items and scales was introduced to assess the effect of the intervention on attitudes and beliefs. These items were drawn from previous studies where they had indicated reasonable levels of reliability and validity (see Goodman, 1975 for more detail). They were representative of a standard set of items being used across different QOW sites and thus provided an opportunity to compare results. These items were also selected because of their relevance to the experimental intervention at Rushton.

The core items are presented in Table 10.3 and are grouped in five classes. The classification is somewhat arbitrary and is used to facilitate the presentation and discussion of the results.

The wording of the characteristic items of all the scales as well

Table 10.3. Description of Dependent Variables with Their Mean, Standard Deviation, and Number of Observations at t_1

	Item	Mean	SD	N
Group Variables				
Productivity (factor) (.56)[a]	I look forward to being with people I work with.			
	People I work with have high performance standards.	4.57	0.91	48
Cohesiveness (factor) (−.36)	Mine is a one-person job. (R) I depend on others for suggestions.			
	I work a great deal with others.	4.13	1.03	48
Innovativeness (.68)	People I work with come up with new ideas to work more efficiently.	3.36	1.23	47
Supervisory Variables				
Consideration (.88)	My boss criticizes and punishes if I perform poorly. (R)	4.06	1.53	48
Initiating structure (factor) (.62)	My boss decides what shall be done.			
	My boss decides how it shall be done.			
	My boss makes all the decisions.	4.82	0.80	48
Feedback (.70)	My boss maintains definite standards of performance.			
	My boss gives recognition and praise.			
	He encourages his people to participate in important decisions.	4.03	0.96	48
Task Variables				
Autonomy	I make decisions on my own.	4.35	1.16	48
Challenge	My job is very challenging.	4.35	1.25	48
Accomplishment	I always feel I am accomplishing something.	4.81	0.99	48
Interest	I find my work interesting.	4.63	1.13	48
Job involvement (.75)	The most important things which happen to me involve my job.	4.51	0.75	48
Role overload (.62)	I don't have enough time to do everything.	3.39	1.09	48

137

Table 10.3.—*Cont.*

	Item	Mean	SD	N
Repetitiveness	*I do the same work every day.*	4.29	1.47	48
Motivation Variables				
Expectancy	*If I tried I could increase my performance.*	2.54	1.19	48
Pay	*There is a relationship between performance and more pay.*	1.10	0.60	47
New skills	*There is a relationship between performance and better skills.*	3.15	1.33	46
Recognition	*There is a relationship between performance and more recognition.*	2.79	1.26	48
Criticism	*There is a relationship between poor performance and criticism.*	3.58	1.13	48
Decision-Control Variables				
Divide work	*How much say do you have in determining how the work will be divided?*	1.45	0.67	20
How much work	*How much say do you have in determining how much work shall be done?*	1.55	0.74	20
What methods	*How much say do you have in deciding on the methods to be used?*	2.10	0.83	20

[a] = internal consistency estimate for multiple-item scales.
(R) = items that have been reserved for scale construction purposes.

as their means and standard deviations are presented. All of the variables have been scaled in such a way that high value is consistent with the objectives of the research team. For example, cohesiveness is scaled so that a high value indicates a high degree of collaboration and dependence on peers.

Results

This section presents the results for the structured items. Before we examine the effects of the intervention on the 21 structured items,

Table 10.4.   One-way Analysis of Variance of Demographic
Variables (means and F)

Variable	South	North	East	N	F	df	$p<$
Age	35.29	39.00	39.29	48	0.53	2,45	NS
Length of service	3.86	3.62	3.00	48	1.22	2,45	NS
Education	10.81	10.54	10.07	48	0.61	2,45	NS
Number of union meetings attended	5.10	3.77	3.79	48	0.81	2,45	NS
Authoritarianism	3.65	4.33	3.68	48	2.15	2,45	NS
Marital status	1.00	0.54	0.86	48	—	—	S^a
Prior work in mining	0.33	0.85	0.71	48	5.98	2,45	NS
Future work in mining	0.81	0.46	0.71	48	2.38	2,45	NS
Same job in future	0.40	0.54	0.46	48	0.30	2,45	NS
Reading ability (interviewer rating)	0.76	0.77	0.79	48	0.01	2,45	NS

[a] South versus North comparison $p < .01$ by χ^2 test
South versus East comparison   NS
NS = not significant

the equivalence of the experimental and control sections is analyzed. Then, some alternative models for assessing the intervention effects are presented, and the rationale for the selected analytic model is discussed. Third, the results for the 21 core items are examined. A comparison of the findings with the alternative analytic models is also reviewed.

Equivalence of experimental and control groups. Table 10.4 presents the comparison of the three sections on the demographic and individual-level variables gathered at the baseline period (December 1973). Many of the variables should be self-explanatory. Authoritarianism is a short form of the F-scale (internal consistency reliability = .66). This scale was included as a possible moderator of changes in the core variables. Three items were written to determine prior coal experience and expectations about future work. The last item is a rating by the interviewer of the respondent's ability to read the response categories (see Goodman, 1975, for more detail on these items).

Except for prior work in mining and marital status (measured by percent married) the three sections are highly equivalent, indicating that the problems of self-selection may not be significant. The men are roughly equivalent in length of service, education, union affiliation, and authoritarianism (although the North scores are slightly higher).

The concern for nonequivalence centers around the mine attachment variable. (It is not clear that being married should moderate the effect of the intervention.) As can be seen from Table 10.4, the employees in the control sections are more likely to state that they have worked in mining before joining Rushton. Also, although not statistically significant, the mean age is higher in these two sections. This dimension of greater age and experience might point to some potential for resistance to mining innovations.

In summary, given that we could not match people to sections prior to the experiment, the three sections in the mine appear sufficiently equivalent with respect to these demographic variables. However, there is a need for caution in treating these three sections as identical. In testing some of the alternative analytic models we can insert some of these demographic variables (e.g., age) to determine whether they moderate changes in attitudes or beliefs.

To further examine the equivalence of the three sections, the analysis was complemented by a similar investigation of the 21 core dependent variables. These variables are descriptive of those aspects of the employees' work and work environment that are the targets of the research team.

Table 10.5 shows the means of these variables for the three sections separately. It is this contrast between the sections that is crucial in determining their equivalence.

1. **Group Variables:** Table 10.5 shows that there are differences among the three sections in group cohesiveness and innovativeness. North is highly cohesive and innovative; South is intermediate; and East is at the bottom of these attributes. The differences between the sections are highly significant: F (cohesiveness) = 4.15; $p \leq .01$; and F (innovativeness) = 3.59; $p \leq .05$. In addition the variables in question are important as far as the intervention strategy is concerned. Later we shall return to this problem.

2. **Supervisory Variables:** There is a strong similarity in leadership styles among the three sections. The foremen in North appear higher on consideration, but overall the differences among the sections are not significant.

3. **Task Variables:** The same statement can be made with respect

Table 10.5.   One-way Analysis of Variance of the Dependent
Variables (means and F)

	South	North	East	F
Group Variables				
Productivity	4.57	4.73	4.43	0.35
Cohesiveness	4.18	4.65	3.57	4.15[a]
Innovativeness	3.35	4.00	2.79	3.59
Supervisory Variables				
Consideration	3.33	4.18	3.14	0.97
Initiating structure	4.83	5.23	4.71	1.24
Feedback	4.17	4.46	4.19	0.32
Task Variables				
Autonomy	4.20	4.18	5.00	2.31
Challenge	4.48	4.54	4.00	0.78
Accomplishment	4.71	5.00	4.79	0.32
Interest	4.57	4.39	4.43	0.80
Job involvement	4.45	4.61	4.50	0.17
Role overload	3.30	3.14	3.76	1.21
Repetitiveness	3.95	4.64	4.58	1.01
Motivation Variables				
Expectancy	2.81	2.54	2.14	1.31
Pay	1.10	1.31	1.00	0.87
New skills	3.05	3.23	3.23	0.08
Recognition	2.57	2.92	3.00	0.56
Negative criticism	3.48	3.08	4.21	3.92[a]

[a]$p \leq 0.5$

to the task variables. There are no noticeable differences among the
three sections on the autonomy and repetitiveness variables.

4. Motivation Variables: Among the expectancy, reward contingency, and performance variables, there is only one item on
which the three sections differ. This is the expectancy about the
relationship between performance and criticism from peers. The
people in East are prone to criticize each other if performance is not
considered adequate, while the people in North refrain from such
punitive action ($F = 3.92; p \leq .05$).

5. Satisfaction: As part of our investigation an 11-item satisfaction scale (internal consistency reliability = .81) was also administered. Comparison among the sections indicated no differences. In

fact, the level of satisfaction was quite high (the scale varies from 1 to 6; 6 = very satisfied) across all sections (range 4.9 to 5.1). The high positive skewness in that scale, although interesting in its own right, restricts the room for movement to greater satisfaction, and therefore, limits the utility of this measure in the over time analysis.

The above dissimilarity of group variables among sections presents comparability problems. Whether such dissimilarities are related to the issue of self-selection bias is difficult to determine. However, since there is a self-selection danger, the analysis was supplemented with an investigation of people who volunteered (one-half of the new section was composed of volunteers) into the experimental section versus those who chose to remain in that section. One hypothesis is that those who volunteered into South may have been different from those who remained. The latter respondents during the interview told us they chose to remain in the experimental section because they liked working in South quite independent of any of the planned features of the experiment. An analysis of all the items listed in Table 10.3 indicates only one significant difference between those that stayed in South and those that volunteered into South; those remaining reported higher group innovativeness. In general, there do not appear to be differences between the volunteers and nonvolunteers.

To examine this issue further we interviewed all the respondents at the baseline period to determine why they signed up for the South section or why they did not. The principal reason given for joining South was money (50% of the 36 volunteers selected this category). The next two major reasons given were: (1) the opportunity to learn and (2) preferring to remain in their own section. The principal reasons given for not volunteering were that miners preferred to remain in their present job or section (38%) or that the nature of their job or seniority precluded them from successfully bidding into the new section (28%). For example, a miner working on the surface would generally prefer that job to an inside job, or a person with low seniority would have a low probability of successfully bidding into South. Those not volunteering gave other reasons, such as "It will never work." But these responses were infrequent (2%).

To conclude this analysis we can make the following observations. Given that the experiment permitted volunteering versus random assignment, there has to be some selection bias. A review of the demographic and attitudinal measures shows no consistent pattern of differences. The greater group cohesiveness in the North section may be due to the poor physical conditions in which those miners worked in the baseline period. A hostile physical environment might have led to greater cohesiveness. In the analysis of the "movers into" and the "stayers in" the South section we found no pattern of differences among the attitudinal items, although we hypothesized that the movers might have different attitudes.

In the analysis of those who volunteered versus those who did not we found that the volunteers cited money as a major reason for joining South. These individuals also reported that learning opportunities were attractive. This would probably indicate a willingness or an openness to change, a possible biasing factor. The nonsigners opted out primarily because of the attractiveness of their own job or section or inability to bid. We do not find in this analysis an ideological or value basis for participation in South, that is, the volunteers did not sign into the experimental section because of chances for greater autonomy or responsibility. Their choices were instrumental in nature—more money and the opportunity to learn new job skills. Our position is that, although some self-selection bias exists, the various analyses indicate it is not a major factor in explaining the results. It will be important, however, to examine statistically for its possible effect. In the next section a set of analytic models is posed; some deal with this problem.

Analytic models for examining change. In this section we examine the standard structured items' measurement of changes in attitudes and beliefs over time that are attributable to the experimental intervention. In our analysis we used the following models. Model 1 assumes that the change in attitudes is a function of the experiment and of events external to the experiment. Given such an assumption, the simplest mathematical model can be written as:

$$A_{t+1} - A_t = B_1 + B_2 D_E + E_{t+1} \qquad (1)$$

This model states that the attitude change is a simple additive process consisting of effects external to the experiment (B_1), effects due to the experiment for the experimental section (D_E), and some random error term (E_{t+1}). D_E represents a dummy variable, having the value 1 for individuals belonging to the experimental sections and 0 for other individuals. This represents the traditional change model, which compares experimental and control groups.

The second model we propose ignores the effects of factors external to the experiment and assumes that a systematic attitude change should occur only for individuals in the experimental group. This model tests whether changes in the experimental group are statisti-

144   BELIEFS—ATTITUDES

cally different from zero. Mathematically we can write this model as:

$$A_{t+1} - A_t = B_2 D_E + E_{t+1} \qquad (2)$$

The third model we postulate is an extension of the first model by assuming that the effect of the experiment interacts with various individual characteristics such as F-scale (FS), education (Ed), age (A), and length of service (LS). The basic assumption in this model is that changes occur in the experimental group, but only for those with certain demographic characteristics (e.g., level of age, education). Mathematically this model can be written as:

$$A_{t+1} - A_t = B_1 + B_2 (D_E FS)_{t+1} + B_3 (D_E Ed)_{t+1} + \\ B_4 (D_E A_{t+1}) + B_5 (D_E LS_{t+1}) + E_t \qquad (3)$$

Another change model that could be postulated considers, instead of interaction effects between individual characteristics and experimental effects, the simple individual characteristics and experimental effects. This model assumes changes occur as a function of: (1) membership in the experimental group and (2) certain demographic characteristics. We consider it the least plausible of the four models, since it assumes that positions on certain demographic characteristics are associated with changes in attitudes without regard to the experiment. We included the model primarily because we could not randomly assign respondents to experimental conditions and controlling on these demographic characteristics appeared to be a conservative way to deal with selection bias. This model, written as:

$$A_{t+1} - A_t = B_1 + B_2 D_E + B_3 FS_{t+1} + B_4 Ed_{t+1} + \\ B_5 A_{t+1} + B_6 LS_{t+1} + E_{t+1} \qquad (4)$$

tests whether, after controlling for individual differences, experimental and nonexperimental effects influence attitude change.[1]

---

[1]In our previous models we assumed that attitude change $(A_{t+1} - A_t)$ is a function of various factors. There are, of course, other formulations available for modeling the effects of the experiment on attitudes. One possible and freqently used model of attitude formation is static and does not reflect the previous attitudes explicitly in the model, for example,

$$A_t = B_1 + B_2 D_E + E_t$$

Such a static view of behavior, however, is, in our opinion, not the most appropriate way for modeling attitudes because the attitudes in one period are very likely affecting our attitudes in the next period.

Another possible model would be to allow the coefficient of A_t to be different from 1, that is

$$A_{t+1} = \alpha A_t + B_1 + B_2 D_E + E_{t+1}$$

Changes in Attitudes/Beliefs over time. The following analysis will be organized around model 1, which examines changes in the experimental group relative to the control group. This is probably the most appropriate model in that it captures changes due to the experiment compared to external events. Then data for the other models will be reviewed.

1. Time $T_2 - T_1$: The T_2 measure was introduced to determine to what extent the experimental intervention had "taken" at Rushton. Here we were borrowing an idea from the experimental laboratory where manipulation (or intervention) checks are always introduced. We wanted to ascertain whether the miners themselves perceived a difference in the decision-making and work structure. It is one thing to say that the research team, union leaders, and management introduced changes in the decision-making structure; it is another thing if the workers perceive that change. Seven months separate the T_1 and T_2 measures. By the time of T_2 there had been no significant external events and the experimental group was declared officially autonoumous (March 1, 1974) and was running smoothly.

When I decided to conduct a survey to determine the status of the experiment, only items that were likely to capture the initial impact of the intervention were introduced. So an item about job autonomy, for example, was used, but not one about job challenge, since it was unlikely that changes in job challenge would occur seven months into the project. A reduction of items was also necessary to reduce costs and to minimize demands on our respondents. The disadvantages of the mini-instrument are that it sacrifices content area; and to some extent, reliability. It did, however, permit getting a better picture of the attitude change process by conducting more than annual measures. My assumption is that feelings of job challenge may follow the establishment of feelings about autonomy.

During this time period, the experimental group reported (see Table 10.6) significantly greater changes in the level of group innovativeness, compared to the control groups; positive changes in cohesiveness

---

If in this model α is less than 1, this implies that attitudes automatically lower over time. An α greater than 1, on the other hand, means that attitudes would increase steadily, given there are no other external effects offsetting such as automatic increase or decrease of attitudes. We tested this model with our data and found that α is less than 1. Given that information we reanalyzed all the data from the different time periods using the model:

$$A_{t+1} = \alpha A_t + B_1 + B_2 D_E + E_{t+1}$$

The results using this model are consistent with those reported from model 1.

Table 10.6. Attitude/Belief Changes for $T_2 - T_1$ (Model 1)

	Beta	t Values
Group Variables		
Productivity	0.35	0.99
Cohesiveness	0.30	1.16
Innovativeness	1.10	2.38
Supervisory Variables		
Consideration	0.04	0.23
Initiating structure	-1.78	-1.67
Feedback	0.42	0.91
Task Variables		
Autonomy	0.71	2.28
Repetitiveness	0.00	0.00
Motivation Variables		
Expectancy	-0.47	-1.51
Pay	0.47	2.06
New skills	0.42	1.71
Recognition	0.33	1.21
Criticism	-0.50	-1.73
Decision-Control Variables		
Divide work	1.70	7.40
How much work	1.37	5.18
What methods	1.00	3.79

t value: $p < .1 = 1.687$ $p < .05 = 2.10$ $p < .01 = 2.68$
$t = 1.68$

and productivity were also evident, but were not statistically significant. Since we reported some lack of equivalence among the groups in the baseline scores, these results may be artifactual. However, we analyzed the data with the control sections combined or treated separately and found the same relationships. Also, the scaled scores on innovativeness for all three groups are in the intermediate range. There was plenty of room for either the experimental or control groups to shift in a positive or negative direction. These data simply indicate that the change score in South is significantly different from scores in the control sections.

The major attitude change in the supervisory items indicated that the miners in the experimental section found their bosses significantly less directive. This is congruent with the autonomous task item where

STANDARD STRUCTURED ITEMS **147**

miners reported that they made more decisions on their own ($p < .05$).

In the motivational items the belief that performance and pay are more closely linked ($p < .10$) is congruent with the idea that a gain-sharing plan would be instituted for the experimental section. There should be little or no perceived relationship for the control group since their pay was determined by position, not performance.

Some trends in the other motivational items are worthy of comment. In the South section there is a strengthening of the tie between performance and acquiring new skills and recognition. Although not statistically significant, these trends are congruent with the experimental changes. For example, as the experiment progresses we would expect a greater connection between work performance and acquiring new skills. The negative change in the expectancy scores, although not hypothesized or statistically significant, is congruent with the other changes. The referent for this item is expected future performance. Respondents were asked whether they could increase performance over existing levels. If we assume that the South section miners perceived themselves as having increased the amount of effort they expended at work, then it is not surprising that they saw limits to future increases in energy expenditure (our on-site observations indicate that by six or seven months into the experiment, the experimental miners were more actively involved in work activities).

The change scores indicate a clear trend in the decision-control items. There were significant changes in the South miners' beliefs about their ability to make decisions at work.

The data in Table 10.6 fit the basic hypothesis that structural changes introduced by the intervention would affect the beliefs and attitudes of the men. Changes in the authority, decision-making, supervisory, and task structures are fairly well represented by the changes in the belief items. Changes in the group-innovation dimensions probably reflect the greater opportunities for group decision-making brought about by the many meetings that were part of the experiment. Changes in supervision, jobs, and the decision-control structure reflect the emergence of the autonomous work group.

Before we leave this time period, it is instructive to ask whether the results would have differed if we had selected any of the other three analytic models (see pp. 143–144). The only model that indicates any real differences over those reported is model 2. It asks whether changes in the experimental group are significantly different from zero? The t values indicate greater levels of statistical significance for the experimental group. The expectancy scores and the supervisory feedback scores in this model are now significant for the experimental

148 BELIEFS—ATTITUDES

Table 10.7. Attitude/Belief Changes for $T_3 - T_1$ (Model 1)

	Beta	t Values
Group Variables		
Productivity	0.19	0.06
Cohesiveness	0.17	0.27
Innovativeness	0.70	1.93
Supervisory Variables		
Consideration	−0.47	−1.56
Initiating structure	−1.50	−3.97
Feedback	0.64	−0.19
Task Variables		
Autonomy	0.44	1.70
Challenge	0.05	0.13
Accomplishment	0.52	1.39
Interest	0.44	1.17
Job involvement	0.74	−0.68
Repetitiveness	−0.55	−0.85
Motivation variables		
Expectancy	−0.46	−0.36
Pay	0.83	2.62
New skills	0.05	1.06
Recognition	0.88	0.82
Criticism	0.29	1.75
Decision-Control Variables		
Divide work	2.00	7.74
How much work	1.71	5.76
What methods	1.06	3.84

t values: $p < .1 = 1.68$ $p < .05 = 2.02$ $p < .01 = 2.70$

group. For reasons discussed above, however, model 1 is preferable. It compares changes in South against the control group changes. Basically we do not learn any more about the T_2 versus T_1 period by using the other three models.

2. Time $T_3 - T_1$: A third attitude survey was conducted in October 1974. A new mining section was introduced at this time. This caused members of the control sections to change sections and in some cases jobs. Since our strategy was to match people over time in similar sections and jobs, this external change forced us to reinterview respondents to capture their attitudes and beliefs about the section and job covered in the first two interviews, and to establish a new section and job baseline for those respondents who were changing. The main point is that nothing about the experiment per se led to this survey. From other methods (e.g., on-site observation) we learned that the experiment was running under full steam. The experimental subjects understood their roles and were strongly committed to the experiment.

A review of Table 10.7 indicates relationships similar to the T_2 versus T_1 period. However, the level of the beta and significance values are lower. The changes—more group innovativeness, less supervisory initiating structure, and greater decision control for the workers—still exist, but at a lower level. It may be that the T_2 measure captured some of the newness and the excitement of the experiment, which had subsided by the time of the third measurement. The changes in the belief about the pay-performance contingency remain essentially the same in T_3, probably because there were frequent discussions up to this period about gain sharing.

An analysis of the data by the three other models does not shed any new light on these relationships.

3. Time $T_4 - T_1$: We instituted a fourth data collection in April 1975 to capture beliefs and attitudes at the end of the first official year of the Rushton project. The research team at Rushton defined the first official year as March 1974 (when the South section became autonomous) through March 1975 (because of a month's loss in the national coal strike). At the time of data collection no major external events had affected the results. The union had challenged management on either extending the program to the whole mine or discontinuing it. This issue had not been resolved at the time of the interviews, but it did not seem to be of major importance during the survey.

The results for T_4 compared to T_1 parallel the results for the earlier comparison (see Table 10.8). The South section miners still perceived their work group as more innovative than the control groups. The bosses were still perceived as less directive. A significant complementary change is that the South miners perceived their jobs as more autonomous. In terms of future performance, the South miners felt less able to increase their performance level (expectancy factor). The picture I get as I review all three time periods for the group, supervisory, and task variables, and the expectancy item, is that the most change in attitude and beliefs appears in the second time period. These changes are less pronounced when we compare T_3 and T_1. Then, at T_4, the same changes are more pronounced.

Another similarity across time periods is the changes in the decision-control items. The South miners compared to those in the control group report that they have much more say on how they conduct their work.

Table 10.8.   Attitude/Belief Changes for $T_4 - T_1$ (Model 1)

	Beta	t Values
Group Variables		
Productivity	0.53	0.65
Cohesiveness	0.61	1.53
Innovativeness	1.50	2.87
Supervisory Variables		
Consideration	0.29	0.002
Initiating structure	−2.09	−3.98
Feedback	0.35	0.91
Task Variables		
Autonomy	0.76	2.19
Challenge	0.42	−0.22
Accomplishment	0.60	1.25
Interest	−0.57	−0.06
Job involvement	−1.11	−1.63
Role overload	0.64	0.02
Repetitiveness	−1.00	−0.69
Motivation Variables		
Expectancy	−0.76	−2.48
Pay	0.23	0.78
New skills	0.44	2.76
Recognition	0.47	0.81
Criticism	0.88	1.67
Decision-Control Variables		
Divide work	1.85	7.74
How much work	1.68	6.16
What methods	1.35	5.95

t value: $p < .1 = 1.69$ $p < 0.5 = 2.04$ $p < .01 = 2.75$

There are, of course, differences among the time periods. The belief that pay and performance are related (in T_2 and T_3) is no longer held by the experimental section in T_4. This is congruent with the fact that a gain-sharing system had been discussed almost a year prior to the survey, but that no system had been implemented. There is also in the $T_4 - T_1$ comparison a stronger expectation that increasing levels of performance will lead to new skills. After 16 months of extensive training it is not surprising that the men in the experimental section see a closer connection between what they do and learning new skills.

The data on the criticism variable, although not statistically significant, are worthy of speculation. At the $T_2 - T_1$ comparison, experimental respondents were less likely to criticize their peers for poor performance. As we move to $T_3 - T_1$ or $T_4 - T_1$ we find experimental subjects more likely to criticize their peers for poor performance. My hunch is that at initial states of the project (T_2) experimental miners would withhold criticism of each other, hence the negative beta in the $T_2 - T_1$ comparison. However, after the identification with the project and experimental section was enhanced, within-group criticism was more likely to be tolerated. Early in 1975 the South section called for the removal of a boss and one of the miners for not following autonomous work group practices. It is most unusual for miners to criticize publicly one of their fellow union members. The incident supports the hypothesis that the miners became more willing to criticize peers as their work group became more cohesive.

We examined these data with models 2, 3, and 4. In model 2, as expected, the results that we reported for $T_4 - T_1$ were more pronounced. That model, however, is not the appropriate one for it does not contrast the experimental and control groups. Models 3 and 4 have no systematic results that would contribute to our analysis of changes in attitudes and beliefs.

4. Time $T_5 - T_4$: Data for the fifth survey were collected in August 1976. Its purpose was to reflect the attitudes and beliefs in the post-vote period. At the time of the survey there were no major external events (e.g., strikes). This comparison $(T_5 - T_4)$ presents the best picture of changes in pre- and post-vote attitudes.

Table 10.9 indicates some interesting changes. Members in the experimental section reported that their work groups or crews were significantly less cohesive and innovative. In the supervisory scales there is a big reversal on the initiating structure dimension. South miners report their bosses are significantly more directive. In the task items there are declines in autonomy and challenge from work. The decision-control items complement these changes indicating that the workers in South have less to say about decisions in their work place. There are no significant contrasts in the motivation items.

Further analysis of the $T_5 - T_4$ comparison provides insights into the extension of the program to the whole mine. The control groups for the first time are now part of the experiment. Although East and North did not receive as intensive an indoctrination as South, there should be some evidence of their training. An analysis of changes in the control groups as contrasted with South indicates significantly greater feelings of cohesiveness and innovativeness and greater control over decisions about how the work is to be divided up. The picture, then, is

152 BELIEFS—ATTITUDES

Table 10.9. Attitude/Belief Changes for $T_5 - T_4$ (Model 1)

	Beta	t Values
Group Variables		
Productivity	−0.00	0.11
Cohesiveness	−0.13	−2.04
Innovativeness	−0.17	−1.95
Supervisory Variables		
Consideration	−0.05	−0.54
Initiating structure	1.29	4.123
Feedback	0.16	−0.13
Task Variables		
Autonomy	−0.05	−1.92
Challenge	−0.11	−2.00
Accomplishment	−0.33	−0.57
Interest	−0.26	−0.41
Job involvement	−0.16	0.97
Role overload	−0.14	1.28
Repetitiveness	−0.05	−0.10
Motivation Variables		
Expectancy	0.10	0.07
Pay	0.12	−0.97
New skills	0.11	0.52
Criticism	−0.93	−0.87
Decision-Control Variables		
Divide work	−0.78	−3.96
How much work	−0.61	−2.99
What methods	−0.44	−1.70

t value: $p < .1 = 1.68$ $p < 0.5 = 2.02$ $p < .01 = 2.70$

of changes in the same direction, but not as pervasive as those experienced by the South section. Use of the alternative models (2 to 4) does not change any of our observations of the changes in the experimental and control sections.[2]

[2]One problem with this analysis is that the residuals for the different models may be correlated over time. This would affect (i.e., reduce) the efficiency of our estimates. If the data were rearranged into the $T_2 - T_1$, $T_3 - T_2$, $T_4 - T_3$, and $T_5 - T_4$ periods, we might consider reanalyzing the data with a procedure suggested by Zellner (see Johnston, 1972, p. 238). However, since the variables are the same in our models across all time periods, this procedure cannot be adopted. Therefore, there remains a problem of the efficiency of our estimates. It is important to note that this problem leads to an understatement, rather than an overstatement of our findings.

5. **Nonmining work areas:** Before we conclude this discussion of attitude change as measured by the structured items, a word should be said about the other work areas. Data were collected from the inside general workers, who do special work (e.g., laying track), but, who are not attached to any section, and from surface workers (e.g., cleaning plant), maintenance men who work inside and out, etc. We have not focused on this group, because they were not part of the experiment until after the vote, and even then, they received less attention than the mining sections. These work areas were not considered controls because the nature of their work is different from the mining section. Still, we collected data from their work areas to determine if there was any spillover effect. An analysis of these groups showed no effects from the experiment through T_4. The T_5 to T_4 comparison showed some slight effects from the experimental intervention. That is, after the vote these work groups received training similar to but less extensive than that received by the original South section. Some positive shifts were found in measures concerning greater job autonomy, group cohesion, and greater control over decisions pertaining to work.

A word should also be said about the second experimental group that started in October 1974. We have not focused on this group because comparison data were available only from T_4. By T_4 there were positive shifts in attitudes about autonomy, work group innovativeness, and productivity. However, the magnitude and scope of change is less than for the first experimental section during a comparable time period $(T_4 - T_3)$. This is consistent with the fact that the training and total intervention practices (e.g., number of section meetings) were less intensive in the second experimental section than in the first. In comparing scores before and after the vote we find decreases in perceived group productivity and in the chances that the group would recognize increased productivity. The pattern of decline in attitudes scores is not as pronounced as we reported for the first experimental section.

Summary

As the experimental intervention introduced changes in the nature of supervision, the work group, the job, and the decision and reward systems, there were corresponding changes in miner beliefs and attitudes as captured by the structured standard items. Over time many of these initial changes remained stable until the post-vote period. After the vote there was a gradual deterioration in the QOW program. This initiated a reversal in some of the previous attitude changes in the first experimental group. On the other hand, the original control groups became the experimental groups in the post-vote period and demonstrated shifts in attitudes parallel to, but not as pervasive as, the first experimental group in time periods $T_2 - T_1$.

GLOBAL EVALUATION MEASURES

Method

A global evaluation measure was also introduced to assess the miners' perceived consequences of the Rushton QOW project. The main item was, "What effect, if any, has this program had on _____?"—a choice of outcomes (e.g., job satisfaction) was listed. The respondent could then indicate on a five-point scale from "no effect" to "a very great effect." If the respondent indicated "at least a slight effect" (2), then he would also indicate if the effect was primarily positive or negative.

The data analysis for this measure uses a cross-tabulation format, rather than the regression models used for the structured items. The rationale for the different procedure is due to the nature of the item. Our interest was in the absolute values in the scale: Did the intervention have an effect? There was no need to compare the change scores in the experimental section with those in the control sections. If both groups had reported a great effect, then that information would help us to understand the consequences of the experiment. Also, many of the respondents did not have the information to answer all the global rating questions. They simply did not know enough about the experiment in the South section. The standard structured items could be answered by all respondents.

Only four items are relevant to this analysis. The other items on job skills, safety, and labor-management relations appear in those chapters. Not all individuals responded to all of these questions. Everyone was asked if the program had any effect on their job, crew, or boss. If the respondent said no to these questions and was not associated with any of the labor-management committees, he was not asked about job satisfaction or intershift relations. These questions were asked selectively because miners outside the experimental crew knew little about the program. If the program had any effect, it would have been on something the miner was well acquainted with, that is, either his job, crew, or boss. If no effect was perceived, the miner probably had no knowledge of more subtle areas, like intercrew communication in the experimental section.

Results

Tables 10.10 to 10.12 examine the perceived effects of the program on the worker's job, crew, and boss for all respondents from the periods T_2, T_3, T_4 and T_5. (Because of the time pressure to complete the interview, there are fewer respondents in period T_5.) What can we learn from these three tables? First, the initial effect of the program was fairly isolated to the South section. If we look at T_2 scores we find that most of the respondents did not think the program had an effect on their job, crew, or boss. Those who did perceive an effect were respondents in the South section. For example,

Table 10.10. Perceived Effect of AW Program on Worker's Job

	T_2		T_3	
	Union (N = 111)	Management (N = 21)	Union (N =118)	Management (N = 22)
Effect				
None	82%	57%	78%	55%
Some	13	28	12	22
Great	5	15	10	23
Direction				
Negative	10	11	5	13
Negative-positive	0	11	0	0
Positive	90	78	95	87

	T_4		T_5	
	Union (N = 124)	Management (N = 23)	Union (N = 84)	Management (N = 18)
Effect				
None	56%	39%	43%	22%
Some	31	30	38	50
Great	13	31	19	28
Direction				
Negative	0	0	0	22
Negative-positive	0	0	0	0
Positive	100	100	100	78

Table 10.11.   Perceived Effect of AW Program on Worker's Crew

	T_2		T_3	
	Union ($N = 109$)	Management ($N = 21$)	Union ($N = 119$)	Management ($N = 21$)
Effect				
None	72%	38%	62%	47%
Some	17	33	27	34
Great	11	29	11	19
Direction				
Negative	23	54	25	45
Negative- positive	0	0	0	0
Positive	77	46	75	55

	T_4		T_5	
	Union ($N = 121$)	Management ($N = 23$)	Union ($N = 81$)	Management ($N = 15$)
Effect				
None	47%	30%	28%	13%
Some	29	26	49	47
Geat	24	44	23	40
Direction				
Negative	36	31	5	29
Negative- positive	4	0	2	14
Positive	60	69	93	57

only 38% of the South miners said the program had no effect on their job as compared with 82% of the union respondents in Table 10.10.

Second, an analysis of responses to these questions over time, by sections, gives us some understanding of the evaluation of the program. If we compare responses by section between periods T_4 and T_5, we learn that respondents in the control sections after the mine-wide program was introduced were much less likely to say that the program had no effect on their crews (68% in T_4 versus 24% in T_5) or their jobs (94% in T_4 versus 18% in T_5). Respondents in the control sections reported that the program had no major impact on their bosses. This is consistent with our on-site observations at the North and East sections. Other data suggest a decline in the attitudes and AW behaviors for the South section. For these three items South

Table 10.12.   Perceived Effect of AW Program on Worker's Boss

	T_2		T_3	
	Union $(N = 108)$	Management $(N = 19)$	Union $(N = 118)$	Management $(N = 18)$
Effect				
None	83%	79%	81%	83%
Some	12	21	11	17
Great	5	0	8	0
Direction				
Negative	20	0	10	0
Negative-positive	0	0	0	0
Positive	80	100	90	100

	T_4		T_5	
	Union $(N = 121)$	Management $(N = 23)$	Union $(N = 80)$	Management $(N = 12)$
Effect				
None	61%	65%	51%	56%
Some	20	17	37	31
Great	19	18	12	13
Direction				
Negative	17	0	5	29
Negative-positive	3	0	3	0
Positive	80	100	92	71

respondents were more likely to report in T_5 (versus T_4) that the project had little or no effect. This is also consistent with our on-site observations that many of the traditional behaviors of the foreman returned after the vote.

Third, the program had slightly more of an effect on the crew than on the job or boss. This is consistent with the project since it focused less on job redesign than on restructuring the relationships within the work group. However, it is surprising that the supervisory item does not pick up the changes captured in the structured items, which did portray significant shifts. This inconsistency might be due to the nature of the items. The global item may be less sensitive to capturing change than the structured items which focus on specific supervisory behaviors.

Fourth, the reported effects of the program are primarily posi-

Table 10.13.   Perceived Effect of AW Program on Intershift Behavior

	T_2		T_3	
	Union (N = 38)	Management (N = 17)	Union (N = 12)	Management (N = 17)
Effect				
None	18%	18%	27%	24%
Some	60	35	54	29
Great	22	47	19	47
Direction				
Negative	7	7	10	0
Negative-positive	0	0	0	0
Positive	93	93	90	100

	T_4		T_5	
	Union (N = 62)	Management (N = 17)	Union (N = 81)	Management (N = 25)
Effect				
None	3%	12%	24%	12%
Some	60	35	46	56
Great	37	53	30	32
Direction				
Negative	9	0	9	9
Negative-positive	0	0	2	4
Positive	91	100	89	87

tive, and the assessments by union and managers are fairly parallel.

Two other global ratings were used—one on intershift coordination and the other on job satisfaction. These were used only for those respondents reporting an effect on their job, crew, or boss. The results for intercrew coordination are similar to those discussed above. The program had some effect and it was positive. Individuals in the South section were more likely to state that the program had a greater effect, and the percentage in that category decreased slightly from period T_4 to T_5 (see Table 10.13).

Table 10.14 shows the percentage of respondents who believed that the program affected job satisfaction. The results show that the program had a positive effect on job satisfaction. As we move from T_2 to

Table 10.14. Perceived Effect of AW Program on Job Satisfaction

| | T_2 | | T_3 | |
	Union (N = 38)	Management (N = 18)	Union (N = 55)	Management (N = 19)
Effect				
None	13%	17%	18%	5%
Some	39	44	40	37
Great	48	39	42	58
Direction				
Negative	6	0	11	0
Negative-positive	0	7	0	9
Positive	94	93	89	91

| | T_4 | | T_5 | |
	Union (N = 63)	Management (N = 18)	Union (N = 84)	Management (N = 27)
Effect				
None	0%	6%	19%	15%
Some	43	22	59	63
Great	57	72	22	22
Direction				
Negative	2	0	3	8
Negative-positive	0	12	2	4
Positive	98	88	95	88

T_4, the degree of that effect increases. At T_5 there is a decrease in the percentage of respondents reporting a great effect and an increase in those reporting no effect. This reversal seems congruent with the decline of the program, which occurred in the post-vote period (after T_4). The perception that the program had less of an effect at T_5 was common across all the mining sections.

Summary

The global ratings provide another way to measure attitudes and beliefs. Using a different format, these items show a set of relationships that parallel the results for the standard structured items. Respondents reported that the experiment had a positive effect on beliefs and attitudes related to work. The changes were modest and restricted to the South section. In contrasting the time periods before and after the vote, we see slight declines in the experimental section and slight increases in the control sections.

SEMISTRUCTURED ITEMS

Method

Another approach to evaluating the effect of the experimental intervention was to use semistructured interview items with open-ended responses. This was another way to tap beliefs and attitudes. In particular, it helped us to learn more about beliefs and attitudes from the respondents' point of view. By not requiring an agree-disagree response, we were able to get a more individual, personal definition of the QOW program.

This measure focused on the miners' views of what the program was all about; respondents were asked to describe in their own words what the program meant. Since the words "program" or "autonomous work group" were not familiar to all, the interviewer had to select words that clarified the question. Most respondents understood the standard clarifying phrase, "the project in 2 South." After the initial response, the interviewer used a predetermined set of probes to elicit more information. A coding scheme was constructed, and a coder classified the respondent's open-ended responses in a form for data analysis.

Hopefully, this question tapped people's conceptions of what the project was all about. By asking the same question over time, we were better able to get an idea of whether conceptions changed. The simplest hypothesis is that the respondents' conceptions should have become more differentiated over time. Also, understanding of the program's concepts, such as greater autonomy, responsibility, and so on, should have increased.

Results

1. **Qualitative Results:** To give the reader a feeling for what the AW program meant to the miners, we provide the following representative protocols:

> To me it is a challenge . . . [it provides] more money . . . it gives the men more responsibility . . . it's doing different things.

. . . I think it will give the boss more time for safety. [Experimental section, T_1]

It's to get more coal out and be safer. . . . I will be doing different jobs so it will not be so tiresome to do the same thing every day . . . the autonomous idea . . . I'm not sure. [Experimental section, T_1]

I don't know. [Control section, T_1]

Well, it's something altogether different . . . should benefit us and the company . . . if everyone works together . . . know laws better . . . make more money. [Experimental section, T_2]

No idea. [Control section, T_2]

Men operate the section . . . the boss is there for safety. . . . It is a safer and easier way to work. . . . Production is up when the shift is running good . . . less man hours [are] lost. . . . We don't have too much idle time. . . . Money's a good incentive. . . . I think we get the supplies better. [Experimental section, T_3]

No different from here [control section] . . . they have a school . . . that's about it. [Control section, T_3]

They're not doing much . . . we [control section] outload them [experimental section]. . . . They're no different from us except they get paid better for doing the same job. [Control section, T_3]

It's a lot better way; men know they have their say . . . the boss doesn't know everything . . . it's smoother, more challenging. Everyone gets along better. [Experimental section, T_4]

Autonomy is a hell of a nice thing if you can keep unity among the men . . . but I don't care where you get men from, some will slack off and others won't. . . . They say it [experimental section] keeps violations down, but I see more slips from these guys [experimental]. [Control section, T_4]

The above are complete protocols per respondent. We found that the first question elicited the longest response, while the two standard probes did not add much to the data. These miners are not very verbal, hence the protocols are short. A quick reading, however, indicates important differences between the experimental and control sections and gives the reader an idea of the quality of the responses.

   2. Quantitative Results: Here we cross tabulate the results by sections, time periods, and codes. Coding was done by one rater across all time periods. The codes were reviewed by the principal investigator and discrepancies were resolved through discussion. Table 10.15 shows the percentage of respondents using a particular

Table 10.15.   Percent of Codes Selected Describing AW Program
(Experimental Section)

$$\left(\text{Percent} = \frac{\text{Number of mentions per code}}{\text{Total number of mentions}}\right)$$

	Time Periods				
	T_1	T_2	T_3	T_4	T_5
Positive Codes					
Greater responsibility	7.4%	3.8%	4.0%	3.5%	0.0%
Coordination—men	25.9	38.5	32.0	35.0	12.5
Coordination—shifts	3.7	7.7	4.0	7.0	4.1
Safety	18.5	11.5	36.0	35.0	25.0
Job satisfaction	11.1	15.4	12.0	10.5	12.5
Variety	18.5	3.8	0.0	7.0	0.0
Learning opportunities	44.4	42.3	28.0	45.0	37.0
Freedom	0.0	0.0	4.0	14.0	0.0
Less supervision	77.8	73.1	60.0	87.0	66.7
Pay	33.3	26.9	36.0	3.5	21.0
Efficiency	25.9	23.1	24.0	10.5	4.1
Labor/management relations	0.0	3.8	4.0	3.5	0.0
Understanding of work	0.0	7.7	0.0	0.0	0.0
Recognition of individual achievement	0.0	7.7	0.0	0.0	0.0
Negative Codes					
Men will not cooperate	0.0	3.8	0.0	0.0	29.0
Job exchange will not work	3.7	3.8	4.0	0.0	0.0
Program will break union	0.0	0.0	4.0	0.0	0.0
Safety	3.7	0.0	0.0	0.0	0.0
Pay inequity	0.0	0.0	0.0	0.0	0.0
Program eliminates supervision	3.7	0.0	0.0	0.0	0.0
Company interferes with AW	0.0	7.7	0.0	0.0	0.0

code in the experimental section over the five time periods. The percentage represents the frequency of codes selected over the number of respondents at that time period. The frequencies for any column should *not* add up to 100% since a respondent can generate multiple codes. In T_1 (before formal training launched the program), experimental respondents thought about the program in terms of greater opportunities for coordination among the men, greater safety, greater variety on the job, greater opportunities to learn, less direct supervision, more pay, and more efficiency. The most salient dimension here is that the men would be under less direct supervision. In their words, "there would be no one breathing down [my] neck." New opportunities for learning, which primarily means being able to learn new jobs through job switching, ranked next. Greater pay and greater efficiency follow in importance.

In examining the percentages over the five time periods for the experimental group, the absence of direct supervision remains the dominant concept in the workers' view about the program. By T_5 the number of salient dimensions has decreased. Pay, for example, which was frequently mentioned in the first three periods, receives less attention. This decline is not surprising. Initially, getting top rate was a unique and visible aspect of the program, but this wore off over time. Also, by T_5, the men were less likely to believe a gain-sharing plan would be instituted. The decline in the positive code, "coordination among the men," is (in T_5) complemented by an increase in the negative code, "men not cooperative." These two codes plus the modest decline in the dominant codes of less supervision, learning opportunities, and safety probably signal a decline in the experimental operation in South after the vote. It is important to qualify the discussion of the percentages over time by two points. First, the percentages are based on approximately 25 individuals; changes generated by one or two individuals can alter the percentages significantly. Therefore, it is important to focus on the main trends discussed above. A second qualification concerns whether the responses are stable over time; that is, does the person who mentions less supervision in T_1 also mention less supervision in T_3? While the percentages might be the same over different periods, the composition of respondents might be different. If this is so, one would have to interpret the percentages over time differently. To examine this point, we traced respondents' answers over different time periods; that is, we determined whether a person who said greater pay in T_1 had repeated that response over time. The results over the salient codes we identified above were that the codes were repeated over time by slightly more than one-half of the respondents. Therefore, there is some stability in the responses.

Tables 10.16 and 10.17 present the percentage of codes selected by respondents in the control sections describing their view of the program. Safety, learning new things, less supervision, and pay are the dominant themes in the control sections. These results parallel those reported for the experimental section. The only difference is that the percentage of respondents selecting each of these items is slightly higher in the experimental section. Indeed, a review of the number of codes selected over the five time periods shows that respondents in the experimental section selected more codes than those in the other sections. It is interesting, however, that the conception of the program over time did not become more differentiated for those in the experimental section, at least through period T_4. That is, experimental respondents did not increase the

Table 10.16.   Percent of Codes Selected Describing AW Program (Control Section East)
$$\left(\text{Percent} = \frac{\text{Number of mentions per code}}{\text{Total number of mentions}}\right)$$

	Time Periods				
	T_1	T_2	T_3	T_4	T_5
Positive Codes					
Greater responsibility	0.0%	0.0%	5.3%	0.0%	0.0%
Coordination—men	0.0	16.7	21.1	5.0	7.1
Coordination—shifts	0.0	0.0	0.0	0.0	0.0
Safety	10.0	12.5	15.8	10.0	7.1
Job satisfaction	0.0	0.0	0.0	5.0	7.1
Variety	10.0	0.0	0.0	0.0	14.2
Learning opportunities	30.0	33.3	31.6	15.0	64.0
Freedom	0.0	0.0	0.0	5.0	0.0
Less supervision	65.0	62.5	42.1	45.0	0.0
Pay	35.0	16.7	36.8	20.0	7.1
Efficiency	10.0	12.5	5.3	20.0	7.1
Labor/management relations	0.0	0.0	0.0	0.0	0.0
Understanding of work	0.0	0.0	0.0	5.0	7.1
Recognition of individual achievement	0.0	0.0	0.0	0.0	0.0
Negative Codes					
Men will not cooperate	5.0	4.2	0.0	5.0	14.2
Job exchange will not work	0.0	4.2	0.0	25.0	14.2
Program will break union	5.0	0.0	5.3	0.0	0.0
Production down	10.0	8.3	5.3	0.0	0.0
Pay inequity	15.0	0.0	0.0	5.0	7.1
Program eliminates supervision	0.0	4.2	0.0	5.0	14.2
Company interferes with AW	0.0	4.2	0.0	0.0	0.0

number of codes they used to describe the program. Instead, the number of ideas they generated dropped from 3.0 during the baseline period to 2.08 in T_4.

There are two other differences between Table 10.15 and Tables 10.16 and 10.17. First, coordination among the men and efficiency are not mentioned as frequently by the control sections as they are by the experimental section. Second, more negative codes are selected by respondents in the control sections, although the frequency per category remains low.

Table 10.18 recasts the data in still another form. To determine whether the program was viewed primarily as positive or negative by the respondents, we created five different coding categories: positive, negative, descriptive, mixed (positive and negative), and don't

Table 10.17. Percent of Codes Selected Describing AW Program (Control Section North)

$$Percent = \frac{Number\ of\ mentions\ per\ code}{Total\ number\ of\ mentions}$$

	Time Periods				
	T_1	T_2	T_3	T_4	T_5
Positive Codes					
Greater responsibility	5.6%	4.2%	7.1%	0.0%	0.0%
Coordination—men	5.6	12.5	28.6	0.0	0.0
Coordination—shifts	0.0	4.2	7.1	0.0	0.0
Safety	33.3	12.5	28.6	5.0	7.1
Job satisfaction	5.6	0.0	0.0	5.0	0.0
Variety	0.0	0.0	7.1	0.0	0.0
Learning opportunities	44.4	20.8	50.0	45.0	64.0
Freedom	0.0	0.0	0.0	0.0	0.0
Less supervision	61.0	33.3	50.0	10.0	21.4
Pay	27.8	12.5	28.6	30.0	35.7
Efficiency	38.9	16.7	7.1	5.0	7.1
Labor/management relations	0.0	0.0	0.0	0.0	0.0
Understanding of work	0.0	0.0	7.1	0.0	0.0
Recognition of individual achievement	0.0	4.2	0.0	0.0	0.0
Negative Codes					
Men will not cooperate	0.0	0.0	0.0	25.0	43.0
Job exchange will not work	0.0	8.3	0.0	5.0	0.0
Program will break union	11.0	0.0	0.0	0.0	0.0
Production down	11.0	0.0	0.0	0.0	0.0
Pay inequity	5.6	4.2	0.0	5.0	0.0
Program eliminates supervision	11.0	0.0	0.0	5.0	0.0
Company interferes with AW	0.0	0.0	0.0	5.0	0.0

know. "Descriptive" is the only category we have not yet used; it consists of phrases used by the miners that primarily described the program, for example, "the AW is a six-man group" or "the AW is a management-labor plan." The percentages in Table 10.18 represent the number of workers responding in that category. In this table the categories are mutually exclusive, and the percentages add to 100.

The picture we get from Table 10.18 is that at the baseline the experimental respondents are slightly more positive toward the program. Over time the positive features of the program continue to grow for these individuals; 93% view the program in positive ways in period T_4. In period T_5 there is a substantial drop in the positive coding category and more ambivalence is recorded by those

Table 10.18.   Evaluation of the AW Program from Coded
Responses

| | Experimental Section | | | | |
	T_1	T_2	T_3	T_4	T_5
Evaluation Categories					
Positive	69.0%	74.1%	88.0%	93.1%	62.5%
Negative	3.4	3.7	4.0	0.0	8.3
Descriptive	17.2	7.4	8.0	6.9	4.2
Mixed	6.9	7.4	0.0	0.0	20.8
Don't know	3.4	7.4	0.0	0.0	4.2
N	29	27	25	28	24

| | Control Section—East | | | | |
	T_1	T_2	T_3	T_4	T_5
Evaluation Categories					
Positive	50.0%	44.4%	64.3%	20.0%	50.0%
Negative	22.0	22.0	14.3	5.0	7.1
Descriptive	11.1	16.7	0.0	15.0	14.3
Mixed	11.1	5.6	0.0	30.0	28.6
Don't know	5.6	11.1	21.4	30.0	0.0
N	18	18	14	20	14

| | Control Section—North | | | | |
	T_1	T_2	T_3	T_4	T_5
Evaluation Categories					
Positive	52.6%	62.5%	70.6%	50.0%	57.1%
Negative	15.8	12.5	0.0	25.0	14.3
Descriptive	15.8	12.5	17.6	0.0	0.0
Mixed	5.3	0.0	0.0	20.0	28.6
Don't know	10.5	12.5	11.8	5.0	0.0
N	19	16	17	20	14

using the mixed (positive and negative) category. In the two control
sections we find that positive codes are most frequently adopted,
but the rate is lower than in the experimental section. Negative responses are slightly higher. By period T_5 the pattern of responses
in the control groups more or less resembles that of the experimental group.

We also reclassified the codes into intrinsic rewards, extrinsic
rewards, or system rewards. Intrinsic rewards are mediated by the

Table 10.19.   Percent of Extrinsic, Intrinsic, and System Codes Selected

Evaluation Categories	T_1	T_2	T_3	T_4	T_5
			Experimental Section		
Extrinsic	30.6%	27.5%	19.7%	23.4%	48.8%
Intrinsic	48.6	44.9	54.1	55.8	39.5
System	20.8	27.5	26.2	20.8	11.6
			Control Section—East		
Extrinsic	68.7%	59.5%	60.0%	39.1%	10.0%
Intrinsic	25.0	21.6	23.3	47.8	80.0
System	6.3	18.9	16.7	14.1	10.0
			Control Section—North		
Extrinsic	55.0%	51.7%	48.3%	12.5%	36.8%
Intrinsic	25.0	20.7	32.3	50.0	57.9
System	20.0	27.6	19.4	37.5	5.3

work experience and include greater responsibility, job satisfaction, freedom, greater understanding, and learning new skills. Extrinsic rewards are mediated by some external source and include safety, greater pay, less direct supervision. System rewards represent changes related to the organization as an entity. This includes better coordination, greater efficiency, and better labor-management relations. The rationale for this breakdown is to see whether experimental section miners used more intrinsic reward codes over time.

Table 10.19 presents the percentage of codes in the three categories. Intrinsic codes are more often used by the experimental section, while the control sections select more extrinsic rewards, at least through period T_3. In the last two periods intrinsic rewards are more frequently selected for the control groups. There is no increase in the selection of intrinsic codes as might have been expected from the experimental group. The drop in the percentage of intrinsic codes might reflect the general decline in AW attitudes found after the vote.

Summary

This approach to attitude and belief measurement provides a new and different way to view the effect of the intervention on attitude and belief change. The measure's unique characteristic is that it taps the respondent's cognitive map of the program, that is, his personal view of the Rushton intervention.

The absence of direct supervision on production was the dimension most mentioned by the miners across all time periods. Opportunities to learn new skills and the pay system where everyone received top rate were also frequently mentioned by both the experimental and control groups. At the baseline the experimental group endorsed these and other categories more frequently than the controls. The greater differentiation of views about the program by South miners during T_1 may bear on the problem of the selection bias. We shall review this in the discussion section (pp. 176-177).

In terms of general feelings about the program over time, the experimental section generates more positive codes especially up to period T_4, but thereafter the post-vote decline is evident.

ON-SITE OBSERVATIONS AND UNSTRUCTURED INTERVIEWS

Method

Two other methods were employed in this study, which can be used to capture changes in beliefs and attitudes. On-site observations were collected periodically in the mining sections (see pp. 224-225). for further description). Also, weekly telephone interviews were conducted with members of management and the union. These interviews focused on what was going on in the mining sections during each week. Their purpose was to generate a weekly account of activities. The data are rich in qualitative observations.

To analyze these data I arranged all the on-site observations and interviews chronologically and tried to pull out their major themes. These were then arranged in terms of the major historical events of the project (e.g., the vote).

Results

At the initiation of the project past practices, behavior, and attitudes were dominant. None of the new behaviors had become institutionalized. The foremen did not understand their new role, intercrew conflict was still evident, production and safety factors had not changed. As one member of management said:

> There is not too much change yet . . . I think it [the experiment] happened too fast. . . . I am not sure if the boss knows his role. . . . Safety . . . well the place is not cleaned up like it should be . . . when the miner went down they didn't get repairs moving as soon as they should. . . . It's too early for any change. [Management, 1974]

While this description is about behavior, it indicates that past beliefs and attitudes were in place.

By March 1974 the first experimental group was declared officially autonomous. Our on-site observer reported that by this time the crew members were experimenting with new job activities (e.g., laying track) and achieving success in problem-solving activities (e.g., resolving intercrew conflicts). In the production tasks more intracrew cooperation was evident. These new activities created by the experiment began to shape the identification with the experimental section and generate positive attitudes toward the program. The underlying process seemed to be that performing new activities led to more positive attitudes about work, the experiment, and the experimental section. In other words the greater the opportunities for responsibility and for new skills, the more positive the attitudes. At this time the changes in behavior and attitudes were noticeable but modest. The total experiment was not yet in place.

As we move toward the second interview wave (June 1974), much of the AW behavior was being exhibited. Most important was the behavior of the foreman:

> When the section started there was no initiation of activites from the foreman . . . once the section was going, he primarily observed. During the first two hours he initiated one activity with an older bolter operator and consulted with his miner operator. The section was running by itself. [On-site observation, May 1974]

The AW activities became more predominant in the fall of 1974. The on-site observer reported the emergence of informal crew leaders. The foremen continued to operate with their crews in an autonomous fashion. There seemed to be greater enthusiasm among the men:

> The crew was really running by itself. . . . [The informal leader was guiding activities during a production downtime problem. The men were engaged in their tasks . . . coordination was at a high level. [On-site observation, August 1974]

This evolution of new forms of work behavior pushed attitudes to a new level. It was difficult to go into the South section and not sense a new level of enthusiasm. The section was operating in an autonomous manner and the men in general were pleased with the new set of activities and responsibilities. While there was a movement toward new forms of work behavior, some of the old conflicts (e.g., between crews) persisted, but at a reduced level. Conflicts between the experimental section and top management at the mine continued. A basic question throughout this project was whether the top management at the mine supported the project.

Our observations in the last quarter of 1974 (the third attitude survey was in October) indicated the same AW behaviors we had reported earlier. Intershift communication, job switching, self-directing crews, and so on, were all in place. The men demonstrated more interest in their jobs and expressed identification with their section and positive feelings toward the experiment:

> I feel South is in A-1 shape—their advance work is up. . . . The section is clean . . . stoppings are all up. They do everything on their own . . . still keeping their boss informed. Their attitude is very good. [Management, February 1975]

The momentum of South continued into 1975 as indicated by the above remarks from a manager. The group's cohesion was demonstrated during this first quarter when the section called for the removal of a boss for acting in a too authoritarian manner and of a crew member for not switching. This was an unprecedented activity. Union members do not (in the case of the miner) censure their brothers in front of management. This action was a fairly clear indication of the high level of section identification created by the program.

From about April to August 1975 the focus of the experiment turned toward planning for a mine-wide program. Data from our interviews and observations indicated that the South section continued to perform the behaviors initiated by the experiment, and attitudes toward job, crew, and the experiment remained positive.

The initial reaction to the negative vote was, of course, one of disappointment for the South section. The vote formally cancelled a project that had been a major part of their working lives. There were reports of scuffling between South and the control sections after the vote. Also, four of the crew members tried to bid out of the section in the early fall. Some of these probably bid out because, with the top rates for all jobs rescinded, they could earn more elsewhere. When the top rates were reinstituted, two of the crew members withdrew their bids. Two other individuals bid out because they wanted better jobs. They probably would have left regardless of the vote.

While there were negative reactions to the vote by the South section, their work did not seem to change substantially:

> I spent several days in South and I could see little difference. They still communicate well and coordinate their activities. The foreman gave very few directions. [Management, September 1975]

In the last quarter of 1975 changes in behavior began to appear gradually. There was less intershift communication, less coordination, and safety practices were poorer. An on-site report for South on November 4, 1975 indicated they "worked like clockwork" when everything was normal, but when a belt broke down the men did not take responsibility as they had in the past. Although we cannot document cause and effect relationships, we consider the changes in behavior illustrated by this example to signal a decline in beliefs about and identifications with the AW practices.

As we move into the first quarter of 1976 the on-site reports indicate that many of the old behaviors, such as intershift communication and coordination of intracrew activities, still continued. There were, how-ever, other signs of deterioration. Two of the major informal leaders of the South crews withdrew from their active leadership roles because they were disappointed with the AW program initiated by manage-ment after the vote. Safety practices were somewhat lax. Some crews could get no one to serve as a committeeman—another sign of lack of commitment toward the program. All during this period (fall 1975 through spring 1976) there was a proliferation of walkouts. While none of the walkouts concerned AW issues, alienation generated by the walkouts spilled over to other attitudes people held, particularly during the major walkout in April 1976. From an on-site observation on April 21, 1976, the men indicated strong negative attitudes toward management because of management's tactics (i.e., suspending some of the strikers) and low interest in the AW program.

Any change in attitudes and behavior through 1976 was gradual. Most changes from earlier AW practices occurred slowly and were hard to detect:

> There was very little foreman initiation to the men . . . the crews worked well together. There was no complaining; they seemed to have a high regard for each other. Yet the idea of whether there is a program is ambiguous to the men. Job switching seems to be nonexistent; intershift communication is lower than it had been. . . . South . . . doesn't have that vitality or excitement that we had seen before. [On-site observer, June 30, 1976]

The above protocol captures the character of the South section for the rest of 1976. The program behaviors and the related identification with program ideas had changed from the peak period in late 1974 through the vote in August 1975. By that time strong section identification, attitudes and behaviors had been created. After the vote there was a gradual decline in these behaviors. It is important for the reader to understand that the South section was still a strong section. They did communicate between shifts, but not as much as they had. They did coordinate their activities better than most of the crews, but not as well as they had. They still had good safety practices (and related attitudes), but not as strong as they had had during the peak period. One day in November 1976 the slope car that takes the men into the mine broke. The men had the option of walking in (which is possible but difficult) or going home. Only a South crew walked in. This is one of several possible examples that illustrates that the South section was willing to put out a little more than most crews. So, despite the change in attitudes and behaviors by the end of 1976, the men had not reverted to their baseline beliefs, attitudes, and behaviors. The experiment had had an effect.

DISCUSSION

The purpose of this chapter is to determine whether the intervention had an effect on attitudes and beliefs. To accomplish this goal we used multiple methods and analytic procedures to identify whether there was an experimental effect. A careful review of the methods indicate that they are different yet overlapping. The structured items focused primarily on beliefs about work and the work environment (i.e., job, supervisor, group, reward system, decision system). These items captured whether the miners perceived the structural change initiated by the research team. The global evaluation tapped general perceptions of the effectiveness of the program, particularly whether the program led to changes in dimensions (e.g., job, crew, intershift relations), about which the workers often express attitudes. The semistructured measure captured attitudes and beliefs about the program. The last set of measures—unstructured interviews and on-site observations—generates information about attitudes through descriptions of behavior.

What can we learn from these different measures? The most general statement is that the intervention caused changes in worker attitudes and beliefs. The nature of the changes, although not always large in magnitude or exhibited in all the attitude measures, is consistent with the nature of the initial change effort and its eventual evolution. In the global items the experimental-section workers indicated changes in their working groups. These changes appeared to be in terms of innovativeness (a structured item), which would have been facilitated by the section meetings. Improvements in intershift relations are also reported (global item). In the on-site observations and interviews during late 1974 and the first half of 1975 we find reports of high levels of crew cooperation (also in the semistructured measure) and enthusiasm about the program. All these changes in the group area are regarded as positive.

Changes in supervisory behavior complemented changes in the work group area. In the structured and semistructured measures, miners in the experimental section reported that their bosses were much less directive. The same effect was reported in the on-site observations, unstructured interviews, and to some extent, in the global items. These changes are viewed as positive. The fact that there were no changes in other supervisory dimensions is not surprising. The intervention strategy focused more on what the bosses should not do (i.e., initiating structure) than on what they should do (i.e., providing feedback).

Changes also appeared in the job items. Miners in the experimental section felt that they could make more decisions on their own (structured measures) and that they had new opportunities to learn about mining (semistructured measure). In the global items the majority of respondents, both experimental and nonexperimental, felt that the program had some effect on job satisfaction in a positive direction. It is interesting that no significant changes occurred in feelings about challenge, accomplishment, and interest in the job, variables that the research team might have expected to shift in a positive direction. Also we might have expected less repetitiveness in the miner's job. One explanation is that although job switching did occur (a strategy to reduce repetitiveness), it was not pervasive throughout the experimental section and it declined over time (see p. 231). Another explanation for the lack of support for these hypothesized relationships is that the experiment at Rushton did not change core job activities. The job of the miner operator or roof bolter never really changed. What did change was the decision context in which the job was performed. The men had more control of the conduct of their crew's activities and this contributed to positive attitudes. We can think of work as two concentric circles—the inner circle or core activities of the miner did not change, and these activities were defined by the miner as his job; the outer circle encompassed the new set of decisions the miners were involved in as a function of the experiment, including decisions about how the group functions (i.e., how should they divide up the work). It is not surprising, then, that questions focusing on feelings of accomplishment did not change substantially, while questions concerning outer circle activities did change.

In the motivational area the data were consistent. Expectancy scores decreased over time (through T_4) because the experimental subjects believed their levels of effort were increasing (see Goodman, 1976). The more the workers perceived that they had increased their effort level at a particular point in time, the less they perceived that their level of effort would increase in the future.

The focal role of pay was captured in the structured and semistructured measures. Initially, through T_3, there was a perceived connection between pay and performance. The failure to introduce a gain-sharing plan, however, led the miners to change their beliefs about the connection. The perceived connection between improving performance and learning new skills (structured measure) is consistent with the data collected in the semistructured measure, where opportunities for learning was a dominant theme.

The decision-control questions parallel the results in the job areas. The miners in the experimental section felt that they had more say over decisions relevant to their crew's work.

The above discussion has focused on changes before the vote. Post-vote changes provide additional evidence for the validity of the measures, in the sense that the measures reflect changes in the program. All the measures record a decline (in T_5) in the AW beliefs and attitudes of the experimental miners, at least as compared with their scores before the vote. In T_5 they perceived their group as less innovative and cohesive, their supervisor as more directive, and themselves as having less say in a variety of decisions about their work. Enthusiasm in their work crew or about the program was absent according to the on-site observer. Our conclusion is not that the men were dissatisfied, but that changes in their boss and crew led them to be less satisfied than they were prior to the vote.

Those in the control groups who now had the opportunity to participate in the program had positive shifts in beliefs and attitudes similar to those in the South section in T_2 and T_3. However, the changes were smaller in magnitude.

Our measurement strategy was to select items that might be sensitive to the experimental intervention. We did, however, include some measures on organizational climate and overall satisfaction. There were no systematic differences in these items as a function of the experiment. This is not surprising, since the experiment was not directed at changing organizational climate and the miners expressed a high level of overall satisfaction at the baseline measurement.

Although attitudes and beliefs appear to have changed, it is important to review some other explanations for these movements. External factors could have had an effect on the results, but there were no major external events that would have systematically modified the beliefs and attitudes under investigation. Similarly any maturation effect was limited to attitudes about labor-management relations, which are not included in this chapter.

Some of the changes (or lack of changes) in attitudes may be explained by measurement factors, rather than by the experimental intervention. Low levels of reliability in some of the group scales may explain why more consistent results did not appear. Another measurement problem concerns social desirability, that is, subjects may be responding in a way they think they should respond. In this case there would be a measurement-section interaction effect, that is, the experimental subjects would respond to the measurement process differently from those in other sections.

While there are no single techniques in this study that we can use to separate the confounding effects of social desirability, a number of procedures were used to minimize its effect. *First,* we used different measurement formats. Some, such as the global items on the effect of the program, are much more susceptible to social desirability responses than are the structured items that are more specific, and in most cases, have clear behavioral referents. If we had found changes in only the global items and not in the structured items, the results would be much more suspect.

Second, we collected the data through an interview. The level of rapport developed with the interviewer through meetings over time and the nature of the interview process minimized to some degree the socially desirable responses, that is the interview, through probing for examples, probably minimized the level of social desirability.

Third, we also collected some data through less reactive procedures: through observing behavior without asking questions. Data from the on-site observer do indicate that there was a greater level of enthusiasm, cohesiveness, and cooperation in the experimental section after the first quarter in 1974. The miners were more active and initiated more work activities than they had done in the past.

Another problem is a possible selection bias that could affect the equivalence of the experimental and control groups. In order to attribute the belief-attitude changes to the experimental intervention, our strategy has been first to investigate the possibility of a general selection bias. In general the sections are reasonably similar, although we have noted whether differences occurred (e.g., group factors). Because of these differences we examined the control sections separately and together and found no differences in the reported result. Other analyses examined whether people who volunteered into the experimental section were similar to those who elected to remain in that section; no differences were found. Also we looked at people who dropped out of the section versus those who remained. Again there were no consistent significant differences among the core attitude variables.

We have treated each group as its own control to minimize the problem of selection bias. Model 2 examines the changes in South, using this section as its own control. Again the results are consistent with what we have reported.

To push the analysis further we examined two other analytic models. The first assumes that there is an interaction effect between being in an experimental section and having certain demographic characteristics on the degree of attitude change. For example, let us assume that only younger people in the experimental section change attitudes in the hypothesized direction. This model is relevant if individuals with certain demographic characteristics are found in more abundance in the experimental sections. We did find that the miners in South were younger than in the other sections. Therefore, testing for these interaction effects seemed reasonable. We tested model 3—using age, education, length of service, and authoritarianism—and found no support for experimental and demographic effects. Model 4 assumes attitude changes are a function of the experiment and demographic characteristics, no interaction is postulated. For example, younger individuals, whether in the experimental or control groups, will be more prone to change. No data were found to support this model.

The comparison of $T_5 - T_4$ is also instructive. There was a shift in the control groups that paralleled the shift observed earlier in South. Those men in East and North who were taking part in the program were not volunteers. So changes in their scores after training and participation in section conferences cannot be attributed to some selection bias. Therefore, while it is clear some level of selectivity bias exists, it is doubtful that it is a major predictor of the results.

In summary, conducting an experiment in an ongoing organization without having control over the many possible dynamic factors inevitably leads to contaminating factors. We have adopted procedures to minimize the effect of these factors. Taking all the measures together, we can conclude that changes do occur, and they seem congruent and related to the experimental induction.

CHAPTER ELEVEN

Economic Analysis

The purpose of this and a subsequent chapter is to assess the economic impact of the QOW program at Rushton. The economic evaluation problem can be usefully divided into two subproblems. The first—to be taken up in this chapter—is to determine whether the experimental changes resulted in a gain in productivity. The second subproblem, addressed in Chapter 16, is to examine the relationship between benefits and costs.

The general results from this chapter are that the experiment had a slight positive effect on productivity. The chapter also includes a comprehensive strategy for measuring productivity changes in organizational experiments. Since most studies of organizational change have not systematically examined productivity changes, the analytic strategies discussed here represent an important methodological contribution to the field. For the reader who prefers to skip this technical analysis, the essence of the results can be found in the discussion section.

BASIC HYPOTHESES

To analyze and interpret the productivity data, it is useful to review the conceptual framework for the economic variables. Tons of coal produced (or the rate of tons produced) are a function of a number of input variables. Some of those variables are uncontrollable; others are controllable. Uncontrollable variables are primarily physical conditions, such as the quality of the roof and runways, that can have an important bearing on production. They are called uncontrollable because they cannot be affected by management or the workers.

178

Controllable variables (those which management or labor can influence) include the traditional economic variables, such as the number of laborers and the actual production time. The capital-technology factor is fairly constant across all sections, so it is not treated as a separate variable in this study. In mining there are other controllable variables, such as the type of mining. This variable indicates whether developmental mining or pillaring is being used by a work crew. These two types of mining have different productivity yields and therefore must be reflected in the production equation. The equation then, prior to the experimental intervention, is that production is a function of uncontrollable and controllable variables (i.e., the production function).

The basic hypothesis underlying the QOW project at Rushton is that the experimental intervention will increase productivity through more efficient utilization of the controllable variables and more productive behavior under different physical conditions (uncontrollable variables). The rationale for this hypothesis is based on the following intervening factors: First, that the men will work smarter, not harder. This is a statement often enunciated by the research team. It means that the experimental intervention will provide more knowledge, which, when applied, will lead to better decisions at work and thus to improved productivity. A second factor is that the men will be more likely to make productivity-related suggestions. Third, there will be better coordination across the crews. This, in turn, will improve the efficiency of completing the mining cycle and hence productivity. A fourth factor is that there will be less absenteeism and the crew will work at a more optimal size. The rationale for changes in these four factors is that the experimental induction will increase the level of motivation and knowledge. The training meetings and section conferences, which provided frequent feedback on performance indicators, and the greater responsibility and autonomy given to the miners are some structural features of the intervention that will enhance knowledge and motivation. The basic paradigm therefore is that the intervention will lead to changes in motivation and knowledge. These variables, in turn, predict changes in the quality of decisions at work, suggestion-making behavior, coordination, and absenteeism, which, in turn, lead to higher levels of productivity.

In this analysis production is the dependent variable and the uncontrollable and controllable variables represent the independent variables. The two sets of intervening variables (motivation and knowledge and the four factors discussed above) are used for explanatory purposes, that is, they will aid in tracing why the intervention does or does not have an effect. The analytic problem is to determine if the experimental intervention had an effect on production over and above the effects created by the controllable and uncontrollable variables.

METHOD

Sample

The data set is divided into four periods. The baseline runs from January 1973 to November 1973. It includes 46 actual production weeks; weeks are the unit for the economic analysis. The second period begins as the experiment is initiated on December 3, 1973 and runs until the national strike begins on November 9, 1974 (46 weeks). The third period begins after the strike's end in December 1974 and runs through August 1975 (35 weeks) when the program was voted on in the mine-wide election. The last period runs from September 1975 through March 1977 when the program was run under management auspices (79 weeks). These four periods parallel the major aspects of the evaluation design. The baseline (period one) is the pre-experimental period. Periods two and three capture the development and performance of the first experimental section; the fourth period represents a new phase of the experiment initiated by management. The South section (beginning December 3, 1973) is the experimental section. The other two sections are the control groups. We focus on the South section because it represents the best prototype of the experimental intervention and because it has the most production data under the experimental mode of operation.

Variables

Table 11.1 describes the major variables used in the analysis. The label or acronym, variable name, and meaning (description) are given; then the operational form and source of the data are identified. The means and standard deviations are for all three sections for the 1973 and 1974 time periods.

Analysis

The basic analytic problem is to determine whether changes in productivity resulted from experimental versus nonexperimental variables.

It should be clear that a simple comparison of average production in the experimental section to average production in the control sections will not be a satisfactory means of evaluating effects of the experiment on productivity. Observed differences in production could potentially be due to differences in physical conditions having nothing to do with the experiment. Unfortunately, the research team presented their analysis of productivity in this manner (Trist, Susman, and Brown, 1977).

Since it is not possible physically to control nonexperimental variables that differentially affect the experimental and control groups, it is necessary statistically to control for these differences. This is precisely what the technique of regression analysis is designed to do. We have adopted two alternative methods for testing for productivity changes after correcting for changes in uncontrollable variables across the experimental and control sections. (Unless otherwise indicated we shall refer to the experimental section prior to the experiment and to the nonexperimental sections as the control sections.)

Both of these testing procedures rely on the use of estimated production functions for the experimental and control sections. A production function is the physical relationship that specifies the amount produced as a function of the resources used and working conditions. The method of estimating the coefficients of the production function is multiple regression. The idea underlying this estimation procedure can be easily understood in the context of a simple production function in which only one variable, say "crew working time," affects production. Then production for each week of the year can be plotted against working time for each week as shown in Figure 11.1. Regression analysis is simply a method for finding the line that "best" fits the data. If the estimated production function is the solid line shown, and working time is W, then predicted production based on this line is at point P. If actual production is P', then the prediction error for that week is e. The regression procedure chooses the line so that the sum of the squared prediction errors is as small as possible.

Clearly the production function will provide more accurate predictions if there is relatively little scatter of the points about the

Table 11.1. Variable Descriptions

Acronym	Variable Name	Meaning of Variable
ROOF	Roof conditions	Quality of roof
RUNWAY	Runway conditions	Quality of runway
PILLARING	Pillaring	Average number of shifts pillaring
AVMAN	Average man days	Average man days worked per day of the week
AVMSHIFT	Average men per shift	Average number of men per shift
DWWO	Days per week worked	Days per week worked
PCWOT	Potential crew working time	Potential crew working time
ACWOT	Actual crew working time	Actual crew working time
AMWOT	Actual men working time	Total number of man minutes worked per week
SMWOT	Standardized men working time with standard crew of six men	Total number of standard man minutes worked per week for six-man crew
DIMWOT	Difference men working time with standard crew of six men	Difference between actual and standard man minutes worked per week for six-man standard crew
DU 1 N73	Dummy variable for the first week in North 73	Measuring the effect of two cars not working at the same time
DU 1–18 N73	Dummy variable for the weeks with runway condition 5 in North 73 (i.e., weeks 1 through 18)	Measuring the effect of very good runway conditions
DU 1–5 S73	Dummy variable for the first five weeks in South 73	Measurement of joint occurrence of low roof height, bad runway, and bad roof

182

Operational Form	Source	Mean	Standard Deviation
1 to 5 scale 1 very bad; 5 very good	Rating from superintendent	3.9	1.3
1 to 5 scale 1 very bad; 5 very good	Rating from superintendent	3.5	1.7
Number of shifts pillaring per week	Company records	1.13	3.4
Total man days worked per week/days per week worked	Created by analysts based on company records	18.4	2.6
Average man days/3	Created by analysts based on company records	6.1	1.5
Potential crew working time/ maximum crew working time per day. (1190) (Measured in days)	Created by analysts based on company records	4.76	0.57
Maximum crew working time (5850 per week) less holiday delays, strike delays, short-shift delays. (All in minutes)	Created by analysts based on company records	5573.	665.
Maximum possible crew working time (5850 per week) less total delays/ minutes	Created by analysts based on company records	4231.	894.
Actual crew working time multiplied by average men worked per shift	Created by analysts based on company records	25847.	10699.
Actual crew working time multiplied by standard crew of six men (except in East 73 where eight men worked weeks 1 to 7 due to conventional mining)	Created by analysts based on company records	25579.	5400.
AMWOT – SMWOT	Created by analysts based on company records	268.	3415.
1 in week one in North 73 and 0 in all other weeks and sections	Created by analysts based on company records	+	+
1 in the weeks with runway condition 5 in North 73 and 0 in all other weeks and sections	Created by analysts based on company records	+	+
1 in the first five weeks in South 73 and 0 in all other weeks and sections	Created by analysts based on company records	+	+

183

Table 11.1—*Cont.*

Acronym	Variable Name	Meaning of Variable
DU 69, 85–89 N74	Dummy variable for week 69 and weeks 85 to 89 in North	Representation of mining in bad area where machinery could not be moved around
DU 92–101 E 75	Dummy variable for weeks 92 to 101 in East	Unique physical conditions —steep slopes and water
DU 118–126 N 75	Dummy variable for weeks 118 to 126 in North	Unique physical conditions —water
DU TIMB	Dummy variable in all sections for weeks 91 to 206	———
DU CWOT TIMB	Product of CWOT and DU TIMB	———

estimated line. The sum of squared errors about the regression line provides a means for measuring how accurately the line fits the data, and can be used to determine whether a particular variable has a significant effect on production. The significance of the individual coefficients can be assessed by use of the t statistic. The value of the t statistic for a particular variable depends on the tightness of fit of the estimated production function (as illustrated in Figure 11.1) and on the amount of variation of the variables appearing in the production function. A common, if arbitrary, rule of thumb is that a coefficient is significant if it has a t statistic greater than 2. A t value of 2 means that a value as large as the estimated coefficient would be obtained by chance only 1 time in 20 if the true coefficient is in fact 0. When more than one variable affects production, it is more difficult to illustrate the production function diagrammatically, but the principle of minimizing the sum of squared errors and testing coefficients by use of the t statistic is still applicable.

Each estimated production function must pass the test of reasonableness as reflected in the algebraic signs before each coefficient in the equation. The appropriate positive or negative signs can be specified *a priori* for almost all variables in the production function equation. For example, output should be positively related to working time and to the roof and runway condition variables.

Table 11.1—*Cont.*

Operational Form	Source	Mean	Standard Deviation
1 for week 69 and weeks 85 to 89 in North 74 and 0 in all other weeks and sections	Created by analysts based on company records	+	+
1 in weeks 92 to 101 of East and 0 in all other weeks and sections	Created by analysts based on company records	+	+
1 in weeks 118 to 126 in North and 0 in all other weeks and sections	Created by analysts based on company records	+	+
1 in weeks 91 to 206 in all sections, and 0 in weeks 1 to 90 in all sections	Created by analysts based on company records	+	+
CWOT multiplied by DU TIMB	Created by analysts based on company records	+	+

Before accepting the estimated equation for an individual section, we have required that all coefficients that are significantly differ-

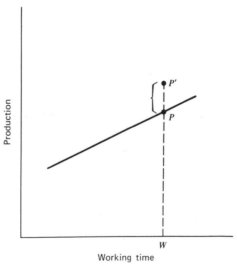

Working time

Figure 11.1   Illustrative relationship between working time and production

ent from zero have the predicted sign. In the few instances in which initial estimates did not satisfy the requirement, we have attempted to determine whether exceptional circumstances in a particular section might have given rise to an unreasonable coefficient estimate. Variables introduced to account for such special circumstances will be discussed in more detail when the results are presented.

The first method of testing for productivity changes is to test for differences in the structure of the production function between the experimental and control sections. This requires testing for differences in the estimated coefficients of the production function across the sections. The maintained (null) hypothesis is that all the coefficients in the production function are the same in all sections. The alternative hypothesis is that one or more of the coefficients differ across sections. Thus, if the experiment resulted in a significant change in the production function in the experimental section, the maintained hypothesis should be rejected when the experimental section is compared to the control sections.

For the standard linear model, the test described above is referred to as an analysis of covariance.[1] (The derivation of the test and an explanation of its use is provided in Johnston, 1972, Chapters 5 and 6.) If the true production function is in fact the same across all sections, then the equation requiring the coefficients to be the same in all sections should fit the data almost as well as the equations that allow the coefficient to be different in each section. The analysis of covariance determines whether the variance in production not explained by changes in resources, outputs, or physical conditions is significantly higher when the coefficients are the same as when the coefficients are different.

The maintained hypothesis in the first step of the test is that the coefficients in all sections are the same. The alternative is that the coefficients in all sections are different. Since the tests are sequential, the form of each subsequent test will depend on the outcome of the one preceding. One simple sequence is as follows: If the null hypothesis of the first test is rejected, the production functions of the sections are not all alike. The second step would then be to test whether the production function is the same for all control sections. If so, the control groups would be combined to yield a single

---

[1] The terms "analysis-of-covariance" and "analysis-of-variance" will be used interchangeably.

production function; this function would then be compared to the production function for the experimental section. Selective testing of subsets of the coefficients would determine more precisely which of the coefficients differ between the experimental and control section production functions.[2]

A great many other outcomes are possible. The control sections might be found to differ among themselves. The sections might be the same in each year and different across years. The control and experimental sections might be found to be all alike. Rather than enumerate all possible sequences, we shall defer further discussion until the results section (p. 191), where the actual test sequence is presented.

The testing procedure described has several limitations. As with any statistical test, one may make two types of errors. One may accept the null hypothesis when it is false or reject the null hypothesis when it is true. The test is generally constructed so that the significance level—the probability of rejecting the null hypothesis when it is true—is small, say 5%. One would then like the power of the test—the probability of rejecting the null hypothesis when it is false—to be high. However, for a given significance level, the *power* of the test increases with the number of observations of data on which the test is based and decreases with the number of coefficients being estimated. Thus the power of the analysis-of-variance test described above will be much greater, for example, when one uses a single production function for the control sections in a test against the experimental section than when one tests the control sections, each with a different production function, against the experimental section. For a given level of significance, one may get ambiguous results from the analysis-of-variance test because the power of the test changes when different combinations of coefficients or sections are tested.

Another problem is that individual coefficients may be different in the experimental section relative to the control sections, but some may be higher and others lower, so that the net effect on productivity would not be clearly defined.

The second method used to test the experimental section against the control sections is designed to provide an alternative that would

[2]To make the test procedure tractable, we treat each test in the sequence as an independent trial even though, strictly speaking, the probability of a particular test being conducted is dependent on the particular test sequence chosen.

potentially be conclusive if the analysis-of-variance test was ambiguous for either of the reasons identified above. The first step is to estimate a production function for each of the control sections, again applying the test of reasonableness to the algebraic signs of the coefficients. The second step is to substitute the values of the variables observed in the experimental section into the estimated production functions for the control sections. This provides a prediction of the amount that would have been produced had the resources from the experimental section been used in the control sections under similar physical conditions. The actual average weekly production from the experimental section can then be compared to the predicted average from the equations for the control sections. If the predicted amount from the control sections was significantly lower (higher) than actual production from the experimental section, one would conclude that under identical physical conditions the experimental section was more (less) productive than the control sections. The relevant test statistic has the t distribution. The derivation of the test statistic is provided in Appendix II.

The second method of comparison has the advantage of simplicity. The information on productivity is summarized in a single statistic comparing mean actual output of the experimental section with mean predicted output, using the same resources in the control section. The second advantage is that one need not estimate a production function for the experimental section. For purposes of this test, any shifting of the production function of the experimental section will be reflected in the production of that section. Finally, the power of this test is greater than the analysis-of-variance test because the latter test compares the sections along several dimensions (as many dimensions as there are estimated coefficients), while the former test is based on a single dimension (production).

The evaluation results reported below will not be based exclusively on either of the above tests. The multidimensional nature of the analysis-of-variance test enables one to identify differences among the sections that may not be reflected in the production figures. These differences are of interest in themselves as a supplement to the simpler test of differences in productivity.[3]

---

[3]A third choice is to use dummy variables to test for differences in the intercept or slopes of particular variables. There is no *a priori* reason for the experiment to affect only one coefficient in the production function. Therefore we feel that there is little to be gained by use of the dummy variable procedure. See Epple, Fidler, and Goodman (1977) for a more extensive discussion of different tests.

It should be emphasized that no test of significance can offer a simple yes or no to the question of whether the experiment affected productivity. Instead, the tests provide evidence concerning the probability that the sections were or were not the same. This evidence should be used with other evidence in evaluating the experiment without requiring that a particular arbitrarily chosen level of significance be achieved for a particular test.

The testing methods described measure the effects of uncontrollable variables that may cause differences in production among the sections; they simultaneously allow for random variations among the sections of the sort that would arise in more conventional experiments.

Though the basic strategy for the evaluation has now been established, some questions of judgment arise in the application of the methods. One such question is the choice of the level of aggregation of the data used in the analysis. Should the production function be estimated with data by shift, by day, by week, or by some other time unit? There are no well-developed formal methods for choosing the appropriate degree of aggregation. In general, increasing the number of observations by choosing shorter time intervals will yield more precise estimates of the parameters of interest. However, as the number of observations increase, data collection and processing costs increase. In addition, if the time interval is made too short, the activities carried on within a given time period may not be representative of the usual range of activities involved in the normal production cycle. By informally weighing the issues identified above, we chose to conduct the analysis with weekly observations.

A separate but related issue arises concerning the choice of the time interval over which the experiment is to be evaluated. The effects of the experiment may vary over time after the experiment is begun. It may be quite some time before the response stabilizes sufficiently to enable one to identify the permanent effects of the experiment. Fortunately, we have data over a four-year period, which permits us to test for transitory and permanent effects.

The methods of evaluation described earlier enable us to adopt several different treatments of these experimental effects. The first evaluation method described requires a test to determine whether the production function differs between the experimental and control sections. If differences are found, the following tests of effects over time may be conducted. In the estimation of the production function for the experimental section, we can explicitly introduce time variables to capture the transitory effects of the experiment. Alternatively, we can estimate the production function in the experimental section for two or more subperiods after the experiment is introduced and then test to determine if the production functions differ among those subperiods. The production function for these subperiods can also be compared to the production function of the control sections. We have chosen to use the latter procedure for the results reported below.

For the second method of evaluation described, changes in the experimental section affect the results only if those changes affect production. Since no assumptions are made about the form of the production function in the experimental section, changes in the form of that function over time need not be considered except as they affect output. The test can, however, be applied to various subperiods after the experiment is introduced in order to determine if productivity relative to the control sections is different among those subperiods. The results for different subperiods will be reported below.

When all is said and done, the precision of any statistical test will depend on the accuracy with which the variables are measured and the applicability of the assumptions by which the tests are derived. Before turning to the results, it is appropriate to discuss briefly issues of measurement and key assumptions underlying the statistical analysis.

The most important measurement problem is the measurement of physical conditions in the mine. Both roof and runway conditions are measured on an integer scale from one to five, with one indicating poor conditions (e.g., wet runway) and five indicating excellent conditions. To be valid, a one-unit change in the scale should have the same effect on productivity, regardless of the point along the interval at which the change occurs. Since one cannot be sure *a priori* that the subjectively determined variable satisfies this requirement, tests for possible nonlinear effects of changes in conditions were conducted as part of the evaluation. We found no systematic evidence of departures from linearity, so the initial scaling was not changed.

There are undoubtedly errors in measurement of all variables used in estimating the production function. The largest errors are probably in reported production tonnage since those figures are estimated. Since this is the dependent variable in our production function, random errors of measurement will not cause a bias in our results. Independent measures of production were available, and these were used to test for systematic errors in reported production. No evidence of systematic differences was found, but random variations between the two measures were quite large. Though there is no reason to think that there are substantial errors in measurement of other variables, no independent evidence is available on those variables.

RESULTS

The purpose of the analyses reported below is to determine what changes in productivity occurred in the experimental section relative to the control sections. As discussed, two alternative procedures for testing changes were developed. The first procedure involves testing whether any variable or group of variables had a different effect on production in the experimental section than it did in the control sections. For the second procedure, the values of all independent variables from the experimental section are substituted into the production function for the control section. This provides a prediction of the amount that would have been produced if the resources from the experimental section had been used under similar conditions in the control sections. The test then involves determining whether the average weekly output predicted, using the production function for the control sections, is significantly higher or lower than the actual output of the experimental section.

Stage-One Analysis

The first stage of our analysis was devoted to four activities. First, the production functions for the mining sections were estimated because the derived production models were critical for our subsequent examination of the experimental effects. Second, and a related point, was to select which model of the production function was most theoretically and empirically pertinent to our examination. The third issue was to test for the homogeneity of groups we labeled control groups. Lastly, we wanted to employ our two analytic analysis models to determine if there had been any experimental effects between the baseline and the first experimental period.

The four different models tested in the stage-one analysis are listed in Table 11.2. The first three models differ in the treatment of delays. Our prior expectation was that the effect of a delay on the amount produced would be fully reflected by way of its effect on lost working time. This motivated the specification of the ACWOT (actual crew working time) variable in which all delays have been deducted from PCWOT (potential crew working time). If our hypothesis is correct, coefficients of the delay variables should not be significantly different from zero since the delays have already been deducted in computing the ACWOT variable. The validity of our hypothesis about the effects

Table 11.2. Predicted Signs of Variables Included in Production Function Models

Independent Variables	Model 1	Model 2	Model 3	Model 1'
Roof condition	+	+	+	+
Runway condition	+	+	+	+
Type of mine pillaring	+	+	+	+
Average man days	+	+	+	
Car delay	0			
Moves delay	0			
Miner delay	0			
Machinery delay	0			
Physical delay	0			
Outside delay	0			
Miscellaneous delay	0			
Moves and miner delay		0		
$C + B + MA + PH + MI$ delay		0		
Actual crew time	+	+	+	
Man minutes standard crew				+
Man minutes above or below standard crew				+

Note: $C + B + MA + PH + MI$ = car, bolter, machinery, physical, and miner delays.

of delays is tested in models 1, 2, and 3. In model 1, delays are included in disaggregated form, in 2 they are partially aggregated, and in 3 they are removed entirely. If our hypothesis is correct, model 1 should not fit the data significantly better than model 3.

Since the time worked by miners is the major variable resource used in production, we have tested two ways of reflecting time worked. In models 1, 2, and 3, ACWOT (the time the section was producing regardless of the number of crew present) is used as the measure of working time. Average man days, AVMAN, is included separately in these models to measure the effect of varying crew time. In model 4 man minutes, rather than crew minutes, is the measure of working time. The two variables included in 4 are man minutes that would have been worked if a standard crew had been present, SMWOT, and the difference in man minutes actually worked and the standard, DIMWOT. The latter variable is designed to measure the productivity change associated with variations above or below the standard-size crew. This model was introduced because the experimental intervention added six extra men to the crew, so variation in man minutes was an important consideration.

An example will serve to clarify the different working time variables. Potential crew working time, PCWOT, in a normal week is 5850 minutes (390 minutes per shift for 15 shifts less strikes, holidays, and short shifts). Suppose that 1350 minutes are lost during the week due to delays. Then actual crew working time, ACWOT, is 4500 minutes. If there are six men in the standard crew, then standard man working time, SMWOT, would be 27,000 minutes (six men per crew times 4500 minutes per week). If five unreplaced absences occurred during the week, the time lost would average one-third of a man per shift. The deviation in man working time from the standard, DIMWOT, would then be 1500 (one-third of 4500 minutes). Finally, the average number of men working per day, AVMAN, would be 17 (six men for three shifts less one absence).

Our prior expectations about the coefficients are indicated in Table 11.2. Since we are using a linear approximation to the production function, and the conditions variables may shift the function up or down, we do not have a prior expectation concerning the sign of the constant term. Improvements in conditions should increase production as indicated by the positive signs on the physical conditions variables in the table. Since pillaring is more productive than developmental mining, we expected a positive effect on the pillaring variable. Increases in crew size should enhance production and give a positive sign to the man-days variable. As explained earlier, delays were expected to have no effect beyond the reduction in working time. Since delays have been deducted from potential crew time in constructing ACWOT, we expect zero coefficients on the delay variables when delays are entered separately. Crew time should also have a positive effect on production in models 1, 2, and 3. In model 4, we expect that the time of men in the standard crew should have a larger effect on production than variations above or below the standard. However, both of these variables should have positive coefficients.

With the exception of the pillaring variable (some sections did not pillar), the variables shown in Table 11.2 appear in the production

194 ECONOMIC ANALYSIS

Table 11.3. Production Functions for Baseline and First
Experimental Period

Variable	South 73 Estimate	t Statistic	South 74 Estimate	t Statistic
Constant	−406.	−0.36	−3353.	−2.25
Average man day	14.23	0.22	89.44	1.4
Roof condition	122.5	1.5	441.3	4.28
Runway condition	−37.25	−0.38	−47.04	−0.57
CWOT	1.028	10.	1.082	9.39
DU 1–5 S73	−1996.	−5.	—	—
Gamma	0.32		0.60	

Variable	North 73 Estimate	t Statistic	North 74 Estimate	t Statistic
Constant	−3219.	−3.24	−2375.	−1.9
Average man day	155.2	2.92	75.38	1.15
Roof condition	59.59	0.64	56.79	0.64
Runway condition	22.13	0.27	100.9	1.47
CWOT	0.9553	10.7	1.152	9.4
DU 1–18 N73	2053.	5.98	—	—
DU 69, 85–89 N74	—	—	−1469.	−4.75
DU 118–126 N75	—	—	—	—
Gamma	0.32		0.28	

Variable	East 73 Estimate	t Statistic	East 74 Estimate	t Statistic
Constant	−1420.	−2.21	2312.	−1.86
Average man day	47.36	1.74	69.97	1.25
Roof condition	−103.8	−1.8	340.5	2.6
Runway condition	187.0	4.06	−42.40	−0.61
CWOT	1.200	22.7	1.059	13.4
Pillaring	—	—	21.43	1.96
DU 92–101 E75	—	—	−1059.	−2.08
Gamma	0.62		0.18	

function for all of the sections. Additional variables particular to the
individual sections have also been introduced to deal with specific
problems that arose in conducting the analysis. Those variables are
defined in Table 11.1.

Table 11.3 presents the estimated production functions for the
experimental section and the North and East sections. The interpretation of coefficients may be illustrated by the roof coefficient for
South 74. The condition of the runway is measured on a scale from 1 to
5 with 1 representing very bad conditions and 5 very gοod conditions.

The estimated coefficient indicates that a one-unit improvement in roof conditions would result in an increase in production of 441.3 tons per week.

The second column presents the t statistic that provides a measure of the accuracy of the estimated coefficients. As explained earlier, a coefficient is normally considered significant if it has a t statistic greater than 2. A t value of 2 means that a value as large as the estimated coefficient would be obtained by chance only 1 time in 20 if the true coefficient is in fact 0. The estimated roof coefficient for South 74 has a t statistic of 4.28. If runway conditions actually had no effect on production, the probability of obtaining a coefficient as large by chance is less than 1 in a 1000. Statistically insignificant coefficients can occur for three reasons. It is possible that the variable in fact has no effect on production, or if it has an effect, that there was so little change in that variable during the year that its effect cannot be accurately measured. For the reasons given above, the sections in which a variable is significant will generally be those in which a substantial amount of variation in the value of the variable occurred over the course of the year. Also, multicolinearity can account for statistically insignificant coefficients.

The estimated coefficients of the production functions were largely consistent with the *a priori* signs identified in Table 11.2. There were a few instances in which the coefficients were significant and differed in sign from our expectations. This can occur because of sampling error; the frequency of occurrence of anomalous coefficients was consistent with the frequency one would expect with sampling error. On the whole, then, the estimated models were consistent with our prior predictions.

After estimating the production functions for the four models, we conducted tests for each model to determine whether there were differences across the sections in the estimated coefficients. We also tested to determine whether models 1 and 2 fit the data significantly better than model 3, and we tested whether the variables introduced to measure experimental startup effects significantly enhanced the fit of the model. These tests are based on the variance of the errors in the respective production functions. The testing procedure is termed analysis of variance (ANOVA), and the f statistic is used to measure significance.

Our findings with regard to the separate treatment of delays in models 1 and 2 confirmed our expectations. Delays cause a loss of working time and thereby a loss of production. However, there was no consistent evidence that delays had any effect on production other than the effect attributable to the loss of working time. We concluded that nothing was to be gained by separately including the delay variables in the production function. Therefore, in work conducted after the completion of the baseline analysis, we have used only models 3 and 4. Because of the conceptual differences in the treatment of crew size and working time, both of these models were retained (see Goodman, 1976, Chapter 7, for more detail).

To determine whether there were startup effects in South 74, we introduced a series of variables to measure possible variations in productivity during the initial 13-week training period. We found that production was low during the early weeks of the experiment, then increased rapidly, and finally declined again during the latter part of the startup period. As a result of this finding, all comparisons among sections in this analysis were done both with and without the startup variables in the production function for the experimental section. The results of these comparisons were not affected by the presence or absence of the startup variables (see Goodman, 1976, Chapter 7, for more detail).

Our conclusion from this stage-one analysis was that there were startup effects, but that they did not affect the outcome of tests of the desirability of the experimental intervention. As we continued our analysis and obtained additional data after completion of the baseline report, we again included variables to measure startup effects at the beginning of South 74. However, with this more extensive data series for the experimental section, the startup variables were no longer statistically significant. This suggested that the previous evidence of startup effects may simply have been due to sampling error in a relatively short data series. In any case, this new result, coupled with our earlier finding that the startup variables did not affect the outcomes of tests of the experimental intervention, led us to drop the startup variables in subsequent analysis.

In order to examine fully our production models, we also investigated the linearity assumption, that is, we assumed that a linear equation will serve as an adequate approximation of the production function. One analysis examined the linearity of our measures of physical conditions. Another analysis considered possible interaction effects of the physical condition variables on production. The use of working time and the square of working time provided another way to empirically assess the linearity assumption. Our judgment through all these, as well as other tests, was that the linearity assumption was acceptable because none of these extra terms were significant nor did they significantly improve the fit of the model.

Having selected two production function models (3 and 4), we then investigated possible control groups. Two classes of control groups were possible. First we could use the baseline (South 73) as the control group for that same section (now the experimental group) in 1974. The use of the experimental section as its own control (South 73 versus South 74), is based on the assumption that the production function for that section would not have changed in the absence of the experiment. This hypothesis, that individual sections would not have changed over time in the absence of the experiment, can be tested by comparing East 73 to East 74 and North 73 to North 74. The second control group is composed of all the nonexperimental sections. This would include East, North, and South 73, and East and North 74 (ENSEN). The basic question is whether the sections composing ENSEN are homogenous.

We conducted an extensive set of tests comparing production functions among the various control sections to test for homogeneity. The results of tests among the control sections supported the hypothesis that the control sections were homogenous. Separate production functions for each control section did not fit the data significantly better than a single production function for the sections combined. Some significant differences were found when comparisons were made among subsets of the control sections, but on balance, it was our conclusion that the evidence was not strong enough to reject the hypothesis of homogeneity (Goodman, 1976).

The fourth objective was to determine whether there was a significant difference between the experimental and control sections. When a single production function for the control sections was compared to the production function for the experimental section, they were found to differ significantly. Thus the conclusion of this portion of the analysis was that there was evidence of differences between the experimental (South 74) and control sections (South 73 or ENSEN).

The finding that the production functions are different indicates only that the experiment had an effect; it does not indicate whether the effect was desirable or undesirable. To assess the effect of the experiment on productivity, the production function for the control section was used to predict output for the experimental section by using the conditions and working-time variables that actually occurred in the experimental section. This prediction was then compared to actual production in the experimental section, with the finding that production was slightly greater than predicted in the experimental section, but that the difference was not statistically significant.

The results of this baseline analysis (1973 and 1974) established that our estimation and testing procedures were operational and also

Table 11.4.   Estimated Production Functions for South
December 1973—March 1977

Variable	Model 3		Model 4	
	Estimate	t Statistic	Estimate	t Statistic
Constant	−689.3	−1.32	−976.	−3.86
Roof	195.9	4.35	197.4	4.38
Runway	93.6	2.1	92.75	2.1
Pillaring	89.55	9.8	89.56	9.8
CWOT	1.126	18.7	—	—
AVMAN	−15.14	−0.62	—	—
SMWOT	—	—	0.06135	15.6
DIMWOT	—	—	0.0017	0.26
DU CWOT TIMB	−0.166	4.6	—	—
DU SMWOT TIMB	—	—	−0.00895	−4.45
Gamma	0.40	—	0.38	—

enabled us to reduce the set of models to be considered in subsequent analysis. This analysis also pointed to a number of technical problems (e.g., autocorrelation of the residuals) that would require attention in the following analysis.

Stage-Two Analysis

This analysis includes the data for the baseline and all the experimental periods. The basic procedure in this analysis was to: (1) Estimate the production functions using the full data set; (2) Investigate any statistical problems that might cast doubt on the validity of the models; (3) Examine the homogeneity of the control groups; and (4) Determine whether there had been any experimental effects.

Table 11.4 presents the estimated production functions for the experimental section for the whole experimental period (December 1973 to March 1977) for models 3 and 4. An examination of this model indicates that the coefficients and t statistics are congruent with the predicted signs (Table 11.2) and with the estimated models for the baseline and the first experimental period (Table 11.3). We also examined the production functions of the other sections with the extended data set and found the estimated production functions in the same general order of magnitude as the predicted data (Table 11.2) or the actual data (Table 11.3).

After estimating the production function we looked for potential problems in the data that might confound our subsequent testing procedures. The first problem concerned autocorrelation among residuals. Coefficient gamma measures the extent to which residuals in the estimated production function carry over from one week to the next. A positive value for gamma, which characterized our data, indicates that if production (after controlling the variation in inputs) is above or below average for a given week, then there is a better than even chance that production will be above or below the average for the following week. The existence of autocorrelation is an important issue since it leads to biases in the standard error and thus in the t test and f test estimates. To avoid this bias, we re-estimated the data using the method of maximum likelihood; the likelihood ratio then becomes the appropriate test statistic. The use of the maximum likelihood method did not change the specification of the production functions we have discussed above. It did have an effect on our tests for homogeneity of control groups, which will be discussed shortly.

Another problem occurred as we pursued our analysis of the existing data set. We found evidence that productivity had dropped substantially beginning in late 1974; for example, when data for 1973 through 1975 were combined for a given section, predominantly positive residuals tended to occur for weeks in late 1974 and in 1975. This indicates that the production function was predicting greater output than was being achieved for those weeks. Inquiries led to the finding that a new timbering plan had been introduced in October 1974 because of an accidental death earlier that year. This installation of additional timber was estimated to require about 30 minutes per shift, or roughly 10% of the working time per shift. We therefore introduced a dummy variable, where the timbering plan was introduced to permit the working time coefficient to change. The coefficient on crew working time indicates that roughly 1.126 tons per minute were produced by the crew working prior to October 1974. The coefficient on the timbering variable indicates that 0.166 fewer tons per minute were produced after the introduction of the new timbering plan. A drop of this magnitude is consistent with the estimate of the percentage of working time lost per shift and lends support to the hypothesis that the new timbering plan was responsible for the fall in productivity.

Next we move to testing the homogeneity of the control groups. The two methods used in this analysis were also used in testing for experimental effects. The first method of testing will serve to indicate whether there were differences in any of the coefficients of a particular model across the sections. As explained earlier, the test measures whether the production functions for individual sections fit the data significantly better than a single production function fitted to the

Table 11.5.   Analysis of Variance

Sections Being Compared	Chi-Square Test		f Test	
	df	X^2	df	f
E73, N73, S73, E74, N74 E75, N75 versus ENSENEN	32	100.6 +	32,255	2.07 +
E73, N73, S73, E74, N74 versus ENSEN	21	61.4 +	20,198	2.2 +
E73, N73, S73 versus total ENSEN	10	36.5 +	10,119	2.84 +
E73, E74, E75 versus EEE	11	39.32 +	11,108	2.10 −
N73, N74, N75 versus NNN	9	18.66 −	9,108	1.27

+ = significant beyond $\alpha = .01$.   − = significant at $\alpha = .05$.

combined data for those sections. In the standard linear model, the test, based on the variance of the errors in the respective production functions, is referred to as an analysis of variance (ANOVA). The f statistic is used for this test. The value that the f statistic must assume for a given level of significance depends on the number of coefficients in the production functions being compared and on the number of observations of data on which the test is based.

Since we have adopted an estimation procedure that takes account of serial correlation in the residuals, a likelihood ratio test is appropriate and the appropriate test statistic has the chi-square distribution. The conceptual underpinnings of this test are the same as those of the f test, namely, the relative variance of the error terms in the production functions being compared. While the f test is technically not appropriate in the present context, the adjustment for the number of observations used in estimating the functions is heuristically appealing. Therefore the f statistics as well as the chi-square statistics are presented below.

These results of the likelihood ratio tests reported in Table 11.5 indicate that the control sections are not homogenous.[4] One reason for the lack of homogeneity may be traced to how we specified our model.

[4]This result differs from the finding in the baseline report. This is mainly due to the correction for serial correlation. Also, there were some changes in the models in the two analyses. A few statistically insignificant variables (e.g., coal and boney height), which were not easily justified theoretically or captured by other variables, were deleted in stage-two analysis.

Table 11.6. Control Section Predicted and Actual

	Control: East 73		
	Predicted	Actual	Error (Actual-Predicted)
East 1974	5508	5448	−60
East 1975	3951	3841	−110
	Control: North 73		
North 1974	3373	3530	+157
North 1975	3407	3821	+414

Since the estimated function is a linear approximation of a potentially more complex function, one could introduce additional terms, for example, the square and cross-products of the variables already in the equation. We tested the effects of introducing the square of working time and the cross-products of both the working time and the conditions variables, but the outcomes of the tests were unchanged. Since we found no systematic evidence of nonlinearities in the individual sections, we have chosen not to employ this strategy because it would result in the introduction of many variables whose individual coefficients are statistically insignificant.

Method two is based on a different testing model but it is also appropriate for examining for homogeneity. It is restricted, however, for examining similarity within sections (East 73 versus East 74) as opposed to the control groups made up of different sections (i.e., ENSEN). The procedure is to define one group as the control (e.g., East 73). Then substitute the actual values in East 74 (e.g., roof condition) into the 1973 East production model. The predicted tonnage figure derived from this procedure is then compared to actual tonnage for 1974. The difference between actual and predicted is a measure of homogeneity.

In East the prediction error was -60 tons for 1974 and -110 in 1975 (see Table 11.6). In North the error was 157 in 1974 and 414 in 1975. Since the standard error of the residuals for East 73 and North 73 estimated production functions are 394 and 404 tons respectively, the prediction errors from method two would not be considered significant. Therefore there is some indication in method two for the homogeneity of the within comparisons over time for the East and North sections.

There is clearly ambiguity between methods one and two concerning whether there are appropriate control groups. The problem of identifying appropriate control groups still exists and cannot be ignored. One approach is to accept the proposition that there are inherent differences among the sections and there are no control groups; that is, the control sections are different, to ENSENEN is inappropriate. Also, since there were differences over time within the sections (East 73 versus East 74) we cannot use South 73 as a control for the experimental section.

A second approach we have adopted is to use multiple control groups and determine whether there are common findings when testing for the experimental effects; that is, if we observe the same findings using different controls (South 73, ENSENEN, and so on), we may be more confident about the observed differences between experimental and control groups. We have adopted the second approach in part because theory leads us to expect a common production function across all sections. All sections use the same technology with comparable equipment under the same mine-wide arrangement. Furthermore, when we look at the data combined across the different periods, we find a theoretically reasonably estimated model. It is not surprising to find differences across sections for particular periods, even if the true production functions are the same. We know that the linear form is an approximation of a more general production function, and we know there are measurement errors in the data. The larger the sample size, the greater the power of the test. Thus a finding of statistically significant differences in coefficients is inevitable as sample size increases. The important issue is whether these significant differences in coefficients across sections give rise to unacceptably large prediction errors. The evidence from the means test (method two) is that use of the production function for one period to predict output for the subsequent period resulted in a prediction error of less than 5% in both East and North. This occurs despite the fact that the production functions for the two periods in East had been found to be significantly different by the analysis-of-variance test. We therefore believe that the productivity comparisons based on predictions from the control sections will give an accurate reflection of the effects of the experiment, but we shall continue to emphasize the fact that all comparisons are subject to prediction error.

Given these qualifications about the comparison groups, we move to an analysis of experimental effects. ENSENEN and South 73 were the control sections. Method two was selected to examine the differences because it provided a clear single summary measure of differences in productivity. In method one we detected differences primarily in multiple coefficients. Since there may be differences among coefficients in different directions between the control and experimental sections and since the net effect of these differences is unclear, it is preferable to use method two for the final analysis.

Under method two the values for an experimental period are substituted into the production model for the control group. For example, predicted output is obtained by substituting the values of the explanatory variables from South 74 into the estimated production function for the control group—consider the South 73 equation in Table 11.3. If actual working time in South 74 was 4000 minutes, this would be multiplied by 1.028. By multiplying the value of each variable in a given week in South 74 by the coefficient for that variable from the South 73 run and adding the results one would obtain an estimate of how much the control group would have produced had the same resources been used under the same conditions.

Predicted average production from the South 73 and ENSENEN equations are compared to actual production from the experimental section for three subperiods. To assess the amount of production lost because meetings associated with the experiment, predicted output is calculated first with time deducted for meetings, then without deducting meeting time. The t statistic can be used to test for differences. As with previous applications of the t test, a value of 2 or more indicates that a difference as large as the one reported in the averages would occur by chance only 1 time in 20.

The results of these tests are presented in Table 11.7 using the model 3 production function. For the results in the upper half of the table, the production function for South 73 was used to obtain predicted average weekly production. This prediction is obtained by substituting the independent variables observed in each week in the experimental period into the estimated production function of South 73. The average of these predictions, denoted $\bar{y}$, was then subtracted from actual production in the experimental period to obtain the estimated difference, d. The difference is an estimate of the amount by which average weekly production in the experimental period exceeded the amount that would have been produced had the same resources been used under similar physical conditions in South 73. The results in the bottom half of the table were obtained by applying the same procedure using the production function estimated when the data from all the control groups were combined.

The means test (Table 11.7) indicates no significant difference between the experimental section and the control sections. This is true for each subperiod of the experiment with either South 73 or ENSEN-

Table 11.7.   Tests for Differences between Predicted and Actual
Mean Output in the Experimental Section

	Control: South 73				
	Actual	Predicted ($\bar{y}$)	Difference (d)	Standard Error	t
South 74 (a)	4716	4501	215	428	0.5
(b)	4716	4790	−74	442	0.18
South 75 (a)	4656	4424	233	445	0.52
(b)	4656	4549	107	442	0.24
South 76 (a)	4299	4223	76	390	0.19
77 (b)	4299	4273	26	389	0.07
	Control: ENSENEN				
South 74 (a)	4716	4634	82	134	0.61
(b)	4716	4945	−229	134	1.70
South 75 (a)	4656	4409	247	153	1.61
(b)	4656	4545	111	154	0.72
South 76 (a)	4299	4206	93	131	0.71
77 (b)	4299	4260	39	132	0.30

(a) meeting time excluded   (b) meeting time included

EN serving as the control. In South 74, if the production time lost because of QOW meetings is excluded from the analysis, the actual production of the experimental section exceeds the control groups (i.e., predicted production). If production time lost is included (i.e., considered part of actual working time), predicted production increases and the difference between actual and predicted production is negative; that is, during South 74 the loss of time because of meetings resulted in a loss of production large enough to counterbalance the increased productivity. This is perhaps not surprising since the introduction of the experiment during the initial part of the 1974 period required that a substantial amount of time be devoted to meetings. In the remaining periods of 1975 through 1977, less time was devoted to meetings. The results indicate that productivity in the experimental section during these two subperiods was higher than that in the control sections by an amount more than sufficient to compensate for time lost due to meetings.[5]

[5] We did similar analyses with model 4. The results indicate that the coefficients in the production functions and the differences between the actual and predicted means are similar to the results for model 3.

Overall the results of the means test suggest that the experiment may have had a positive effect on productivity in the South section. The effect, if any, is not statistically significant by the usual standards. In this connection it should be emphasized that the usual standards applied in testing statistical significance are arbitrary. We view the differences calculated in Table 11.7 as the best estimates of the effects of the experiment. However, these estimates lack the precision one would like. For example, a difference as large as 93 tons, the amount calculated for the 1976-1977 period using ENSENEN as the control, would have occurred by chance about 1 time in 4. The lack of precision is a consequence of the fact that a mine section is subject to large variations in physical conditions that are not perfectly captured by our measures of roof and runway conditions. Thus some imprecision in predictions is inevitable.

A second point should be emphasized. Even if we were certain that the experiment were responsible for increases in productivity of exactly the amount predicted by a given control section, that increase in productivity might not be worth the cost. This aspect of the problem will be addressed in the cost-benefit analysis chapter.

DISCUSSION

The general results do not indicate any major increase or decrease in productivity. Our best estimate is that there was a slight positive effect on production: weekly tonnage in the experimental section was greater than in other comparison groups. These positive differences, however, are not statistically significant, and thus we must be cautious about this estimate. The fact that there was not a decline in productivity is significant. Often when there are improvements in other behaviors, such as safety practices, production declines. This was not the case at Rushton.

In order to interpret these summary judgments on the effect of the QOW project on productivity, it is important to examine some other explanations that are primarily of a methodological nature. One problem that might confound our interpretation of our results is that the production-function models were incorrectly specified. For example, an important variable might be missing or some of the selected variables incorrectly operationalized. A review of the multiple models used in this analysis reveals the signs of some coefficients that are different from what we would have predicted; in some cases we have introduced dummy variables to deal with special problems (e.g., special physical conditions) not captured by our regular measures. To deal with these issues we thought carefully about the appropriate conceptual model and let neither techniques nor the data primarily guide our analysis. When anomalies appeared in the data, we went back to the original data sources to identify actual daily events. To avoid an *ex post facto* solution from this more detailed analysis, we always recast these findings into our conceptual framework. The major elements in the model make sense, and the findings across the many models used appear reasonably consistent. Also, as a function of sampling error, we expected some anomalies to occur.

Another methodological issue concerns the control groups. The lack of improvement in productivity might be explained by the fact that the other sections are not equivalent to the experimental section and the comparison with these groups is inappropriate. We responded to this by developing a theoretical model that was generalizable across sections. Indeed, the analysis of the production functions across the different sections showed a great deal of similarity among sections. The problems with homogeneity, however, have also been noted. Our overall strategy was to acknowledge that there were problems of equivalence, but to examine theoretically reasonable control groups at different times. Consistent differences across the different control groups provided evidence that the comparison was valid.

A third issue concerns problems of measurement. Unreliability or lack of validity in either the independent or dependent variables clearly would confound the analysis. To some extent this problem was out of our hands since we lacked the resources to set up our own measurement system for the economic variables. We did, however, analyze some of the ordinal scales used for measuring physical conditions to assess the validity of those measures. For the dependent variables, we examined other measures and found reasonable levels of convergent validity. In all of these analyses we found no evidence that measurement error was a major contributor to the differences or lack of differences in our results.

Another measurement issue concerns potential biases in the measures. This would result in a high degree of consistency (reliability) among measures, but validity would be low. That certain bosses overstated production as a reaction to the experiment is an important consideration. Bosses in the experimental section might have wanted to make the section look better, while bosses in the control groups wanted their sections to look comparable to the experimental section. Our own observations of this problem are the following: first, if overstating production figures by the foremen occurred, it was generally a reaction to management's demands for greater production. Our information suggests that this pressure existed during the baseline and experimental years and was constant across sections. Second, our observations and interviews with the foremen in the experimental section indicated that overstating production did not occur primarily as a function of the experiment, but might have occurred from production pressure. Third, some evidence exists that the control crews' production was overstated as a reaction to the experiment. This behavior, however, was temporary and not widespread; it should not have affected comparisons over the three years of the experiment.

The fourth issue concerns the level of aggregation used in this analysis. Our data were examined on a weekly basis. It could be argued that estimates would have been better if we had calculated production functions on the basis of daily data. Some preliminary comparisons between daily and weekly data, however, indicated that the general form of the production functions was the same.

In conclusion, therefore, although many possible confounding factors, such as model specification, control group equivalence, measurement error, and level of aggregation were present, the strategies that we used to deal with them were reasonable and effective. Therefore we do not feel that our estimates of the experiments are methodological artifacts.

Another approach to understanding the productivity results is to examine why we found only marginal positive increases in productivity and not major increases.

First, the experiment led to increases in energy or motivation expended at work. These changes in motivation level were directly related to experimental changes in the nature of work, supervision, work group structure, and the nature of the decision-making system. The attitudinal measures, on-site observational measures, and on-site interviews indicated that the experimental workers were investing more of themselves in their work. In the past, if a section was down because of equipment failure, the men waited until the machine was back in operation. During the experimental period and through the mine-wide vote, when a machine broke down, one was more likely to see men turning to other tasks that eventually needed to be done, such as rock dusting. The increased level of energy accounts in part for the positive versus negative effect of the experiment on productivity. Why was not the effect more substantial? Principally because the increased energy was expended on improving safety practices (e.g., rock dusting, timbering, shoveling loose coal), which indirectly affect the production process but not the direct production activities of producing coal. From our on-site observations it was clear that the men, after the experiment, expended more effort on keeping the section up to safety standards than on producing more coal.

The second assumption was that there would be more productivity-related suggestions. The experiment's many different meetings (section, foremen, joint committee) represented a forum for generating new ideas. In reviewing the transcripts of these meetings, we concluded that technical discussions were not the dominant theme and that no suggestions constituting a major technological breakthrough or substantially changing the core mining activities were made. To put this observation in a clearer perspective consider some of the following technical problems. A major source of discussion concerned when to service (maintenance) the miner. After much debate, it was decided to do this during lunchtime (midshift). Servicing also could have been completed in the beginning of the shift or during other downtime. This suggestion represents an attempt to minimize downtime and clearly could have affected tons produced because of increased production time. The downtime in this case, however, is short, relative to other delays, and would not have substantially increased tons produced. Also, the delay did not immediately affect the *rate* of production (tons/time). Other problems discussed during the foremen's meetings concerned ventilation, the mining cycle, maintenance problems, how to deal with flat tires, and so on. Suggestions related to these problems were clearly important to the mining process, but did not result in major changes in the basic mining activities. A related observation about the discussions on technical issues is that problems were raised, but specific solutions were not often proposed or implemented. In contrast, discussions about labor-management issues (e.g., rate of pay for experts coming into the experimental section) received many more formally proposed and implemented solutions.

The basic argument, however, is that there were no major productivity suggestions that would cause major productivity increases. The goal of increased productivity was not a major goal of the work force, so it was not surprising that the miners did not devote themselves to finding new ways to increase productivity. Improving safety was a much more legitimate goal. In addition, the section conferences, the major meeting place for the experimental section, was not a suitable setting for solving complicated productivity problems. The conference was much too big (more than 30 men) for effective problem solving. Suggestions related to productivity did occur, and we did report a positive productivity effect. What we did not find was productivity suggestions that significantly affected the mining process.

An important stimulus for increased productivity (in terms of actual output or productivity-related suggestions) is the contingent relationship between some valued rewards and increased effort for productivity, that is, the miners needed to see some relationship between increasing productivity and rewards. This relationship did not emerge for two reasons. First, the nature of the mining environment makes it difficult to build a close relationship between increasing productivity and rewards. As we have discussed, mine productivity is affected by many uncontrollable factors. Even if there were a contingent reward system available, it would be difficult for a worker to affect productivity. Second, a gain-sharing program, which might have provided a reward visibly related to productivity, was not instituted during the experimental periods under investigation. The Rushton miners were not going to increase productivity unless there was some kind of financial return. Increases in responsibility, autonomy, and job variety were considered attractive rewards. But our observations and interviews indicated some monetary reward should follow increases in productivity.

Another assumption was that there would be better coordinating within and among the experimental crews and this would improve productivity. The on-site observer consistently reported communication during the shift interchange. The section, foremens', and joint committee meetings all served to facilitate communication. These changes in coordination probably contributed to the positive, though marginal, increases in productivity we reported. Why then did greater coordination not lead to greater productivity? Many variables in the production model affected productivity, and these (e.g., physical conditions) probably dominated the increase in coordination. Of the other factors discussed so far, we would expect greater energy investment by the miners in direct mining activities and suggestions about these activities to have a more direct effect than coordination would have on productivity levels.

It was also theorized that the program would result in lower absenteeism, that this would lead to a more optimal crew size, and thus to greater productivity. The data in this analysis do not support that assumption for at least two reasons: (1) absenteeism was not reduced in the experimental periods and (2) the intervention encouraged job switching which increased group flexibility. Under the new situation, if someone was absent, the crew was sufficiently flexible to absorb this loss. So in one sense the nature of the intervention itself minimized the effects of absenteeism on productivity.

In conclusion, the experiment did lead to behavioral changes in the work place. Some of these changes contributed to productivity increases. Given that there were increases in other work behaviors, such as safety, it is important to note that production did not decrease. Some mining experts we interviewed expected that improvements in safety would lead to reductions in productivity. That did not occur. On the other hand, the research team hypothesized that there would be significant productivity increases. This also did not occur. Many of the behavioral changes that did occur were not directly related to increasing productivity or to productivity-related suggestions. In addition, there were no reward systems linked to behavior necessary for productivity increases. These results on productivity reflect the design of the program; other designs might produce different effects.

CHAPTER TWELVE

Safety

One of the goals of the QOW project at Rushton was to improve the level of safety. This goal was embraced by both labor and management. Preventing injury to human life is a value that transcends the particular interests of labor and management. The overall finding in this chapter is that the experimental intervention did lead to an improvement in safety practices.

BASIC HYPOTHESIS

The basic hypothesis is that the experimental intervention will improve safety practices and the safety record by reducing accidents and violations. The changes which should facilitate this are: (1) the experimental group received more formal training about safety practices and the law; (2) the experiment introduced a new reward system to motivate the workers toward good safety practices. Intrinsic rewards were increased: the work group had been restructured to provide the men greater opportunities for feelings of responsibility and accomplishment if safety levels improved. Extrinsic rewards were also increased through formal feedback sessions for the workers concerning their performance on such activities as safety. The nonexperimental groups received none of these increases in intrinsic or extrinsic rewards; they operated under the simple message "if you do not work carefully you will get hurt"; and (3) the foremen in the experimental section were no longer caught in the conflict between production and safety. They could expend all their energies on safety. Foremen in the nonexperimental sections had continually to balance production and safety demands.

The basic methodological problem is to evaluate the effects of the QOW project on safety practices and results at Rushton. Ideally this would be done by controlling the other variables that might affect accidents, that is, we would hold other variables constant (e.g., age and experience of the worker, physical conditions of the mine) and then see if the QOW project influenced the number or type of accidents. However, since frequency of accidents is very low and the distribution very skewed, the accident data do not lend themselves to this type of multivariate analysis.

Another analysis strategy is to examine the relationships among several independent indicators of QOW project effects on safety and to examine whether these indicators differentiate between the experimental and control groups. This is the procedure used in this analysis. Safety was measured by the number and type of accidents, the number and type of violations, ratings on the quality of safety made by independent observers as well as by the union and management, and by qualitative reports from the on-site observers. A high degree of convergence among these different indicators would yield more confidence in the validity of the data. If all the indicators point to differences between the experimental and nonexperimental sections, then this is evidence that the QOW project has affected safety. If there is a divergence in the measure, then one is less confident in attributing any effects to the program on safety.

ACCIDENT DATA

Accidents refer to illness or injuries that occur on the job as a direct result of exposure to the work environment. Accident data are divided into two general classes: (1) frequency and type of accident and (2) accident costs. The data are presented in terms of four periods: the baseline (January through November 1973); the first experimental period (December 1973 through November 1974); the second experimental period (December 1974 through August 1975); and the mine-wide extension of the program (September 1975 through December 1976). The focus will be on the sections since they were the main target of the intervention and are relatively comparable work areas.

Frequency and Type of Accident

Method. When an accident occurred it was recorded in the foreman's production report. At the end of a shift an accident report was filled out. If there was no lost time or medical expense, the accident report was the final document identifying the injury. If there was lost time, this was recorded in the biweekly payroll data and reflected as one class of absenteeism. If a claim for medical expenditures or compensation for lost time was made by the injured worker, this was recorded on the form that lists injuries and payment for injuries.

The potential error in accident reporting is to under-report lost-time accidents. Lost-time accidents can lead to bad feelings on the part of the workers, poor internal relations, inquiries from the state and federal inspectors, as well as substantial expenses. Some companies keep the injured worker on the payroll to avoid reporting these accidents. My own observation of the Rushton situation is that under-reporting did not occur systematically. Also there is no reason to suspect that it occurred in one section and not in another. The mine management indicated that there was an increased emphasis on reporting all accidents in 1974. This emphasis is more likely to be reflected in minor injuries (e.g., bruises), which, prior to 1974, were left unreported because they did not require lost time or medical assistance. The consequence of this shift in reporting is that the frequency of low-severity accidents might appear higher in 1974. However, accidents in this category show no major increase.

Results. Table 12.1 presents the accident data for the three mining sections for the four time periods. The South section was the first experimental section. In the fourth time period all sections were considered part of the experiment.

1. Frequency of Accidents: The frequency of accidents during this four-year period is low for the mining sections relative to other mines. In the baseline the South section had the lowest accident frequency. In the first experimental period the experimental section remained the same, while the number of accidents increased in one section and remained the same in another. There is a general increase in accidents in periods 3 and 4, with the total frequency being less in South than in the other sections. The same advantage to South appears if we compare only the experimental periods (2 and 3).

2. Accident Rate: This represents the total number of accidents per section divided by the total work days per year. This is an important indicator because the number of men was increased in the South section during periods 2 and 3, but not in the other sections until 1974. This, in turn, increased the chances for accidents. The accident rate is lower in the baseline for South. Analysis of the rate data indicates a gradual increase through time period 3

214 SAFETY

Table 12.1. Accident Data

	Period 1 1/73– 11/73	Period 2 12/73– 11/74	Period 3 12/74– 8/75	Period 4 9/75– 12/76
South				
Frequency	2	2	9	12
Accident Rate	0.00156	0.00109	0.00686	0.00455
Severity	1–2	1–2	1	1–2
No. of lost-time accidents	1	1	1	0
No. of lost-time days	39	21	1	0
Lost t rate (frequency)	0.00078	0.00055	0.00076	0.0
No. of man days	1284	1832	1312	2640
Lost t rate (days)	0.0304	0.0115	0.00076	0.0
East				
Frequency	6	10	7	15
Accident Rate	0.00467	0.00728	0.00711	0.00591
Severity	1–2	1–4	1–2	1–2
No. of lost-time accidents	4	2	2	1
No. of lost-time days	352	49	43	240
Lost t rate (frequency)	0.00312	0.00146	0.00203	0.00039
No. of man days	1284	1374	984	2540
Lost t rate (days)	0.27414	0.03566	0.04370	0.09449
North				
Frequency	4	4	10	17
Accident Rate	0.00312	0.00291	0.01016	0.00669
Severity	1–3	1–2	1	1–2
No. of lost-time accidents	1	2	0	5
No. of lost-time days	250	113	0	326
Lost t rate (frequency)	0.00078	0.00146	0.0	0.00197
No. of man days	1284	1374	984	2540
Lost t rate (days)	0.19470	0.08224	0.0	0.12835

and a slight drop in period 4. In all comparisons the rate is lower in the first experimental section.

3. Severity: Severity of accidents was rated on a four-point scale where 1 equaled a minor accident (e.g., muscle pull), 2 equaled a moderate accident (e.g., broken bone), 3 equaled some type of permanent disability, and 4 equaled a fatality. The mode across all sections for the different periods is 1; ranges of the severity scale are presented in Table 12.1. In general severity of accidents is low across all sections. There are no major section differences, with the exception of the fatality that occurred in East in period 2.

4. Frequency of lost-time accidents. The number of lost-time accidents is low across all the sections. The first experimental section has the fewest lost-time accidents; the differences between sections, however, are very small.

5. Number of lost-time days. Since this measure contains a high degree of variability—one accident can account for all the lost time—it must be viewed fairly conservatively. At best it can be considered a rough measure of severity. The first experimental section throughout the four time periods has the fewest number of lost days. In other sections the number drops in period 2 and increases again in period 4.

6. Lost-time rate. The lost-time rate either in frequency or in days provides the same information as above.

Accident Costs

Method. Costs related to accidents can be fixed or variable. The fixed costs include such things as preventive measures and installation of safety equipment. At Rushton this would be done across the board so that one section would not be in a preferred position. Another fixed cost is insurance. Here Rushton is in a peculiar position. During the baseline period the company paid premiums to an insurance company to cover medical and compensation costs. During the experimental year the company was self-insured by the parent company, PPL. In this system PPL pays all the direct medical and workmen's compensation claims. Rushton does not pay a premium to PPL, but instead reimburses PPL for all costs incurred. Our rule is to use cost under the current system (self-insured) as a way of determining the costs of accidents. The self-insured plan began approximately the same time as the experiment. Therefore, there were no premium payments in the costing of accidents nor could we estimate reduction in premium payments as a function of a decrease in accidents. A third potential fixed cost concerns the maintenance of roles or facilities for dealing with accidents. There is a safety director at Rushton, but he works across all parts of the mine. There are no real in-house medical facilities. In general, therefore, fixed costs are not included in costing accidents.

The variable costs are important in analyzing the effect of the experiment on accidents. There are categories of accident costs. First, if a person is injured he receives reimbursement for all accident costs. A second variable cost is the compensation expense. This reflects time lost because of an accident and any payment for permanent disability. If a permanent disability occurs (e.g., loss of eye), the individual receives a compensation payment based on a predetermined schedule

Table 12.2.   Accident Costs
*Average is calculated with a denominator equal to
the number of cost-incurring accidents. (Data are in
actual dollar costs.)*

	Period 1 1/73– 11/73	Period 2 12/73– 11/74	Period 3 12/74– 8/75	Period 4 9/75– 12/76
South				
Total	$ 1,716	$ 2,350	$50	$ 309
Medical	516	805	50	309
Compensation	1,200	1,545	0	0
Range of accident costs	16–17,000	17–2,332	50–50	100–108
Average	858	1,175	50	103
East				
Total	$43,793	$13,801	$3,458	$14,721
Medical	2,850	885	2,565	5,386
Compensation	40,943	12,916	893	9,335
Range of accident costs	11–41,500	24–13,409	9–3,386	25–14,277
Average	6,256	2,760	1,152	1,338
North				
Total	$47,772	$ 2,996	$52	$24,148
Medical	12,512	619	52	10,808
Compensation	35,260	2,377	0	13,340
Range of accident costs	5–47,369	7–2,931	52–52	40–20,000
Average	15,804	749	52	3,450

set up by the state. A third variable concerns costs related to being absent from work. These costs can arise from the effect of absenteeism on production or on the need to have a labor pool to replace absentee workers. In our analysis of economic data there is no significant relationship between absenteeism and lost production. In terms of a labor pool, Rushton never had a policy of hiring additional workers to offset absenteeism. Also, the number of lost-time accidents is quite low. Therefore, we have not included in accident costs any costs relating to lost production or absenteeism. For similar reasons we have excluded costs related to terminations due to accidents. There is no policy at Rushton to replace accident-related terminations. Replacements came generally from the existing work force. Eventually new people were hired, but not solely because of the accident.

Results. Table 12.2 presents the direct costs (medical and compensation) associated with the accidents at Rushton during the four periods. A word of caution is necessary before one interprets this table. The number of accidents from which the cost figures are derived is very small. Given what we know about the high variability of days lost, we expect that one accident can substantially change the picture of the comparisons across sections. Given these limitations, it is probably better to look at the general trends rather than at any detailed analysis. The most observable general trends are that the first experimental section has lower accident costs for all the time periods and that there is a slight tendency for these costs to decline over time.

Accident Data Summary

The accident data provide no conclusive evidence on whether the experimental section had an effect. This observation appears to be true whether we compare the first experimental section with the other sections in time periods 1 to 3, or whether we examine the effect of the mine-wide program. Fortunately (but unfortunately for assessing experimental changes) across the whole mine the accident record was good; the first experimental section in particular exhibited very low accident rates. Therefore, there was little room to move the experimental section to a better record. We do find an increase in accident rate over time from the control sections, but a rate increase also appears in the first experimental section. At time period 4 the accident rate is lower in South, but not appreciably.

Other factors might contribute to the character of the accident data. For example, changes in work force composition, especially between the baseline and period 2, may confound the analyses of accident data since accidents to some extent are explained by individual differences. However, we conducted an analysis of changes in section composition (Goodman, 1976) and found no difference from the trends reported above. Another possible problem was that foremen might report accidents to make the experimental section look good or bad. We found no evidence for this.

Perceptions of QOW Program Effects

Method. Another indicator of safety comes from the attitude questionnaire. One set of items in that survey included an assessment of the effects of the program. The basic question was, "What effect, if any, has the autonomous work-group program had on a variety of outcomes (e.g., safety production)?" The interviewer used a number of substitute terms (e.g., the "program," "the project going on in 2 South") as a way to clarify the AW concept. The respondent, using a five-point scale, rated: no effect, slight effect, some effect, great effect, or very great

Table 12.3.   Perceptions of AW Effects on Safety

	T_2 (6/74)		T_3 (10/74)	
	Union ($N = 39$)	Management ($N = 18$)	Union ($N = 55$)	Management ($N = 19$)
Effect				
None	10%	6%	11%	16%
Some	15	33	42	42
Great	75	61	47	42
Direction				
Negative	0	0	0	0
Negative-positive	0	0	0	0
Positive	100	100	100	100

	T_4 (4/75)		T_5 (8/76)	
	Union ($N = 64$)	Management ($N = 18$)	Union ($N = 84$)	Management ($N = 28$)
Effect				
None	2%	0%	19%	4%
Some	37	28	32	35
Great	61	72	49	61
Direction				
Negative	0	0	0	11
Negative-positive	0	0	0	0
Positive	100	100	100	89

effect. A follow-up question was used to determine if the effect was positive (i.e., better safety), negative, or some combination.

The question was asked four times: survey 2 (June 1974), survey 3 (October 1974), survey 4 (April 1975), and survey 5 (August 1976). The respondents' knowledge of the project and hence ability to respond varied over these time periods. Only 35% of the union respondents answered this question in time period 2. This is not surprising since the experiment was new and the results were not well-known. Management on the other hand had greater access to information on outcomes, such as safety, and over 85% responded. In period 5, when the program was minewide, more of the miners had knowledge of the project's impact.

Results. The data in Table 12.3 clearly indicate that people responding to the question feel the program had a positive effect on safety. (The "some effect" category is derived from responses of "slight" and "some effect"; the "great effect" category includes responses of "great" and "very great effect.") In general the perceptions of the union and management respondents are similar over the different time periods.

Summary. Most respondents viewed the program as positively affecting safety. If we divide union respondents into experimental and control, both groups endorse the positive effects of safety over time. Members of management, many of whom were not strongly committed to the program, also reported that safety practices had improved.

Violations and the Inspection Process

Method. Another measure of safety is the number of violations of both federal and state inspection laws. The general objectives of both governmment groups are the same—to improve the level of safety in the mines. Jurisdiction varies between the federal and state agencies, and the enforcement powers also differ. The federal inspector has a broader range of control, including maintenance of the equipment, dust levels, electrical systems, and so on. The state inspector focuses more on roof control issues. In terms of enforcement both can close down the mine and order changes to be made in compliance with the law. Only the federal inspector can initiate a fine for a violation.

Inspections are made on a quarterly basis. The inspector arrives at the mine unannounced. He goes in with the man trip to a particular section and checks a variety of dimensions, such as the level or amount of air, the condition of the machinery, the operation of machinery and fire-protection equipment. Then he inspects the larger environment around the immediate work area, such as escapeways, the belt, and so on.

During the course of his inspection the inspector might point out both minor violations that are easily corrected and serious violations that need immediate attention. When the inspector returns outside, he formally presents his notices of violations. A federal inspector writes dated notices for each violation, including information such as the section of the law violated, a brief description of the violation, the person served, and so on.

The state inspector fills out one form that includes his observations (e.g., is hoist machinery in good condition?) and a write-up on the ventilation, timbering, clearance, electrical wiring, and so on.

Since the federal inspector's violations carry a fine, which is a cost to the company, it is useful to follow the options that occur as a notice is presented to someone in management. At Rushton, management usually challenges the validity of the notice. Whether the company challenges the notice or not, it is forwarded to a district office and then

220 SAFETY

Table 12.4. Number of Federal Violations and Violations Rate

	Period 1 1/73–11/73	Period 2 12/73–11/74	Period 3 12/74–8/75	Period 4 9/75–12/76
Number				
South	14	13 (−7%)	13 (−7%)	10 (−28%)
East	19	42 (+121%)	18 (−5%)	15 (−21%)
North	8	28 (+250%)	8 (0%)	10 (+25%)
Rate				
South	0.06	0.06	0.08	0.03
East	0.09	0.18	0.11	0.04
North	0.04	0.12	0.05	0.03
No. of days	214	227	164	330

an assessment is determined by a formula that reflects the nature and severity of the violation, past company behavior in complying with violations, and the company's current attitudes toward compliance. The assessment is then returned to the company, which, in the case of Rushton, responds always by contesting the assessment in court. Eventually a judgment is made by the court. However, this judgment generally takes place several years after the notice is written.

There are a number of potential problems with the violation data that need to be mentioned. In terms of the quality of the data, different inspectors (either state or federal) with different decision rules may identify violations differently. This would lead to a bias; however, since the same inspector does all the sections in one time period, the bias would be the same across sections. If the 1973 inspector was a high notice writer, while the 1974 inspector was a low notice writer, the problem would be significant. The absolute difference would show "improvements" in the experimental period. Since we are examining relative improvement across sections, however, this problem can be managed. A related problem concerns obtaining information on the fines associated with particular violations. There is a long time period (in excess of a year) between the assessment of a violation and the court determination of the actual violation costs. Therefore, a considerable amount of data is missing on settlement costs per violation.

Results. Table 12.4 presents the federal violations recorded for the three mining sections for the four time periods used in the accident analysis. Data on actual violations, percent increase or decrease in violations from the baseline (in parentheses), and the rate of violations (per number of days) are presented.

Table 12.5.   Lost Production Time Due to Inspectors Closing
Down Sections (in shifts and rate)

	Period 1 1/73–11/73	Period 2 12/73–11/74	Period 3 12/74–8/75	Period 4 9/75–12/76
South	5 (0.007)[a]	6 (0.008)	0	0
North	5 (0.007)	7 (0.010)	2 (0.004)	0
East	5 (0.007)	13 (0.019)	0	0

[a] The number in parentheses is the number of shifts lost over potential shifts.

From these data we can draw several conclusions. In the first
experimental period (December 1973 through November 1974), when
the effects of the intervention were the strongest, there was a slight
drop in violations in the South section and a significant increase in the
other two sections. In the third period the two control sections reverted
back to their baseline level of violations. One of the sections has more
violations than South, the other less, and the range is in the order of
five violations. In the last period, we find a similar picture: the number
of violations in the experimental section matches one of the control
groups, the other section is slightly higher. Comparing the fourth
period against the baseline we find a reduction in the number of
violations in South (28%), a drop in the East section (21%), and an
increase in the North section (25%).

There is no evidence in the data that the changes are a function of
some constant bias, that is, inspectors in one period write more
violations than in another period.

We also examined settlement costs for federal violations. These
costs reflect the actual fine determined by the court, the cost for
management's time in court, and the lawyer's fees. Given the data that
were available on this question, we were not able to identify any
differences among the sections.

Another way the inspectors can exercise control is by closing down a
section: they have the right to close down a section and require the
violation to be resolved prior to starting up production again. This is a
serious action because of the production time lost. Table 12.5 shows the
number of shifts lost by each section for the four measurement periods.
The number in parentheses is the number of shifts lost over potential
shifts, which varies during the four periods. At the baseline the
sections are the same. In the first experimental period all sections
show an increase; the experimental section shows the smallest in-

Table 12.6. Number of State Violations and Violations Rate

	Period 1 1/73–11/73	Period 2 12/73–11/74	Period 3 12/74–8/75	Period 4 9/75–12/76
Number				
South	18	8 (−55%)	11 (−38%)	5 (−73%)
East	15	14 (− 7%)	10 (−33%)	5 (−67%)
North	12	15 (+25%)	11 (− 8%)	6 (−50%)
Rate				
South	0.08	0.03	0.07	0.015
East	0.07	0.06	0.06	0.015
North	0.06	0.07	0.07	0.018
No. of days	214	227	164	330

crease. In the third and fourth period, the number of shifts lost decreases virtually to zero.

Table 12.6 presents the data on state inspections. In the first experimental period the number of state violations in the South section is less than in the other sections and its own baseline. In the second and third periods there are no differences among the sections with respect to state violations.

Summary. The data on federal violations indicate that the sections were relatively similar during the baseline. During the first experimental period, when the intervention should have had its strongest effect, the experimental section remained essentially the same (there was a slight decrease). Violations in the other sections increased. In the last two periods there is no clear trend in violation data that can be attributed to the intervention.

The analysis of shifts lost due to the inspector closing down the section does not indicate any substantial advantage to the experimental section.

In the state violations, the South section performed better in the first experimental period. There are no differences among the sections in the remaining periods. It is difficult to attribute the general decline in state violations in these last two periods to the experiment. Since the mine-wide program was initiated in the fourth period, we might expect a change in that period, but not in period 3.

Overall there is a slight improvement in the experimental section (relative to the others) with respect to violations in the first 11 months of operation.

Table 12.7.   Global Rating of Section Safety by Federal and State
Inspectors (on a scale of 100)

Quarter	Experimental	Control E	Control N
	1974		
1	—	—	—
2	88	73	70
3	88	82	50
4	88	82	77
	1975		
1	88	82	77
2	—	—	—
3	90	85	76
4	—	—	—
	1976		
1	93	88	75
2	95	88	60
3	93	93	85
4	85	84	80

Outside Observers

Method. To gather more information on safety we interviewed
Rushton personnel who were responsible for safety across the mine and
the federal and state inspectors who regularly examined all parts of
the mine. The purpose of the interview was to get their global
judgment on the level of safety in the different sections. While ratings
from the mine inspectors reflected their activity of looking for violations and accordingly were related to the violation data found in Tables
12.4 to 12.6, this was offset by the global nature of the ratings which
reflected the overall quality of safety. Also, the other expert raters
from Rushton did not focus exclusively on violations.

The specific rating task was to evaluate the experimental and
control sections in terms of a 100-point scale. Excellent safety was 90 to
100, 80 to 89 was above average, 70 to 79 was average, and below 70
was poor. The interviews were conducted quarterly. Since the evaluation team was not at the site for most of 1973, no data were collected for
that period. Collection began in the second quarter in 1974. We were
unable to collect ratings in two quarters of 1975.

Results. Table 12.7 contains the average ratings for several raters
for each of the quarters. The raters agreed on approximately 75% of the

ratings. These men knew that an experiment was underway in 1974, and they knew which section was designated as the experimental section. According to the data in Table 12.7, the experimental section consistently received a higher rating than the other two sections. The qualitative interview comments confirmed that the inspectors and mine personnel saw the experimental section as operating at a higher safety level. The North section seemed to be consistently the poorest in terms of overall safety. The section was also operating in the poorest physical conditions, which tended to work against the high safety ratings. The East section by the end of 1976 was virtually the same as the South.

Summary. The data derived from the ratings indicate that the experimental section's overall safety record was better than the other two sections, although the East section was virtually identical to the South section in the last half of 1976.

It might be that the raters were reporting information in a way to make the experiment appear successful, either as a favor to management or to the union. My own observation is that relationships among the inspectors, the company, and the union were quite independent. In addition, the inspectors were not well acquainted with the program; the possibility that they would present selective information to highlight the experiment's features is most unlikely. The raters from the mine were knowledgeable about the experiment and had some interest in seeing it succeed, so their ratings could be biased. The only evidence for the validity of the ratings is that the raters exhibited a good deal of variability in their ratings across sections over time and that there was good convergence across the raters.

On-Site Observation

Method. On-site observations conducted during the course of this study were another source of information on safety. The goal of the on-site observations was to collect data on work behavior related to safety practices in the experimental and nonexperimental sections. Topics in the semistructured observation form included intershift communication, mantrip time, boss-worker interactions, as well as safety issues. Since the observers were not trained miners, the safety issues dealt with easily observable practices regulated by law. For example, the use of a torque wrench during the bolting cycle, whether the car operators changed their seats as they changed directions, the accumulation of coal dust along the ribs, whether the posts were in place, air level, and so on, represent the types of dimensions that observers recorded. Although these behaviors were a small set of possible safety practices regulated by law, they were visible to the inspectors and subject to fines. They represent a minimal set of practices that should be followed.

The observations began in the experimental year and continued through 1976. At first they were conducted several times a month, then on a six-week basis. In 1976 they were collected bimonthly. Each observation was recorded by the observer after he left the work section. More observation was done in the experimental section than in the control sections.

The on-site information was collected because it represents an independent data source on what was going on during the experiment. Its distinguishing feature is that is concentrates on behavior—what people do versus the attitude measures, which record people's beliefs or feelings about what they do. Although there are obvious advantages to this data source, it also has limitations. First, although we attempted to observe different crews at different times, we did not draw a statistical sample for observation times; therefore, the times we collected data might not have been representative. There is no easy solution to this problem. A large number of observations would have been too expensive. Our only recourse is to examine these data in the light of other indicators. Second, our presence as observers might have had a reactive quality. The only counter to this problem was that we were well-known (and I believe accepted) prior to the beginning of the observations and there was no formal recording of information during the observation.

Results. The summary of the on-site observation follows:

1. There were no significant improvements in safety practices in the South section during the first quarter of the experiment. During the observations there was evidence of timbering problems (e.g., props down), ventilation problems (e.g., curtains down), and improper practices (e.g., car operators not switching seats, and clean-up problems, such as excessive coal along ribs). Discussions with members of management who were visiting the section indicated that they viewed safety as not substantially improving. During on-site observations, informal discussions with some of the men also indicated safety levels had not substantially improved.

2. Relative to the other sections the experimental section probably had a slightly better safety record during the first quarter. If both experimental and control sections had a clean-up problem (e.g., coal on the runways), it was likely to be more significant in the control

sections. Housekeeping (e.g., cleaning up after dinner breaks) was likely to be better in the experimental section.

3. By the middle of the second quarter (1974) the safety levels seemed to have improved in the South section as compared with East and North. The observer of the experimental section reported:

> Ventilation seems to be OK. The car operators are switching seats . . . bolters are using the torque wrench . . . timbers seem to be in place . . . when they were knocked down the men reset them. . . . Housekeeping around the section seems pretty well cleaned up. . . . The only machinery-related problem I can see concerns the miner. . . . The water vents aren't working well, and therefore, there is a lot of dust.

4. Although there was some improvement in the experimental section, the observer did note differences among the crews, that is, some crews were more tolerant of safety violations than others.

5. The third and fourth quarters seemed relatively similar to the second quarter. The last observations in the experimental section were conducted in October (the national strike occurred in November 1974). Both observations reported favorable safety conditions. Cleanup, ventilation, safety practices, and housekeeping all seemed in compliance with the law.

6. On-site observations were initiated in the second experimental section in the first quarter of 1975. The on-site observer reported on January 22:

> There are a lot of potential violations: . . . tremendous amounts of coal dust have not been picked up . . . some of the curtains (for controlling the air) are down . . . also the boss in that crew reports that the miner operator in the previous crew probably had driven the miner past the last roof bolt.

Because this was a new section with a relatively large number of inexperienced miners, its operation along program lines was to take more time.

7. Other observations through the first half of 1975 indicated that South was the best section in terms of overall safety.

8. Through June 1976 the on-site observers reported that South was still the best section. There were, however, some signs in South of changes in minor safety practices. Posts were not always in position, more loose coal was visible, torque wrenches were not always used in the bolting operation. These changes were congruent with declines in other AW behaviors (e.g., intershift communications).

9. Of the other sections East was most comparable to South in positive safety practices.

10. At the end of 1976, South and East appeared to have the best safety practices; North showed some improvement, but did not perform at the level of South and East. The second experimental section was comparable to the North section in safety practices.

Summary. The on-site observations indicate that safety conditions were better in the experimental section. However, considered by itself, this data source must be cautiously used. The observation times were not drawn from a sampling plan, and results can be highly biased by problems of sampling error. At best we can say only that there was an advantage to the experimental section in the observed adherence to proper safety practices which were visible to the on-site observer.

DISCUSSION

There were six indicators of the level of safety. The first, the analysis of accident data, is fairly inconclusive. Although the South section had lower accident rates and costs, it started out with better performance in the baseline period, and the differences among sections were not appreciable. The second indicator, workers' perceptions of the QOW project's effects on safety, are clear. Both miners and management saw a strong positive effect. These data, however, are possibly affected by socially desirable response sets. Nevertheless, since both experimental and nonexperimental respondents as well as managers who were in favor, neutral, or opposed to the program all see it as improving safety, this problem is partially discounted.

The data on violations provide some information on the impact of the program on safety. In the first experimental period when the effect of the intervention should have been strongest, the number of violations substantially increased in the control sections, while slightly dropping in the experimental section. Given this relationship, it is difficult to assert with confidence that the experiment caused this difference between experimental and control. It would have been more conclusive if the experimental section's violations had dropped substantially, while the control sections had remained the same. Nevertheless, the high number of violations in the control sections indicate that the inspector was writing violations; the fact that no many were found in South suggests that miners were attempting to keep the section up to standard. This, of course, corresponds to other data we have on the South section.

The global ratings of overall safety by inspectors and mine personnel indicate that the South section was consistently better than the other sections. Although these ratings are not independent of the violations, they do provide a picture of overall safety practices. The mine inspectors' global ratings are particularly important since the inspectors were not likely to overstate safety performance. Their selection of South as the best safety section should be given some weight since their orientation was more to find problems than to praise. The last indicator, the on-site observer's report, also indicated improved safety practices as a result of the experimental intervention in the South section.

It is interesting to note that the subjective accounts of safety (e.g., attitude question, global ratings, on-site observer) view the impact of the experiment as greater than is found in the record data (e.g., accidents, costs, violations). This difference may be accounted for by these factors: (1) the record data pick up specific events at a specific time, while the subjective reports concern evaluations of safety over a period of time (e.g., several weeks); (2) inherent in the subjective scales is the possibility of distinguishing good and bad safety practices. The record data start with a situation of good safety practices (e.g., only two accidents in the experimental section in the baseline) and do not have far to move (i.e., to indicate better safety practices). Remember that the record data do not contradict the subjective data, they simply do not highlight differences.

Our general conclusion is that the experiment did affect safety behaviors, that is, the men in the South section put into effect safety practices that would prevent accidents. They were more pro-active toward safety than they had been prior to the experiment. The main evidence for this judgment comes from subjective measures, which focus on safety practices, rather than safety events (e.g., an accident). This conclusion is congruent with the structure of the program, which focused on safety practices. A training program provided knowledge about safety practices that previously was not available. Making the foreman's role safety, rather than production, minimized the negative reinforcement workers usually received from their bosses when they wanted to do safety work. The meetings provided formal feedback on how safety behavior matched safety goals;

they were a problem-solving arena where new safety practices were developed and offered a direct opportunity to reinforce good safety behavior. This is absent in most traditional safety programs. Lastly, the autonomous work-group concept increased workers' feelings of responsibility for achieving high safety levels.

There is no clear evidence that when the program went mine-wide (period 4) there were consistent improvements in safety. This conclusion is congruent with the fact that the intervention structures (e.g., training, modification of foreman's role) were not as powerful as they were in the initial intervention.

While safety practices did improve, the results should be viewed in their proper perspective. The main changes we observed were in safety practices relevant to minimizing accidents, but accident rates at Rushton were already low and the company as a whole was interested in improving safety independent of the experiment. Basically we acknowledge an improvement in safety as a function of the experiment. At the same time we feel some of the public claims (Trist et al., 1977) about safety improvements at Rushton have been overstated.

Job Skills

One of the major goals of top management in this QOW project was to develop the professional miner, a person with extended knowledge and job skills. The role of the professional miner would help to attract and retain the younger, better educated worker in Rushton's labor market. The general finding in this chapter is that the experiment increased the level of miners' job skills.

BASIC HYPOTHESIS

The basic hypothesis is that the experimental intervention will increase job skills. The introduction of formal training programs, modification of the foreman's role to include more teaching, and participation by the crews in section conferences were all designed to increase the miner's knowledge of his work. All these new institutions provided not only new knowledge over a long time period, but also opportunities to reinforce the newly acquired behavior.

The problem of determining whether the experimental induction increased job skills is the same we have faced in all the analyses where econometric models are inapplicable. Assessment in this context is further aggravated because we do not have any clear outcome measures, that is, we do not have a direct measure of job skills. Given these limitations, our strategy has been to examine multiple measures that are approximations of the job-skill variable and to compare the data from these measures between experimental and nonexperimental groups.

230

Formal Training

One way to assess the effect of the intervention on job skills is to catalogue the training opportunities given to the experimental group, but not to the control groups. Our analysis will focus on the South section since many observers felt its program was the best that was developed during the project.

The experimental group initially received a six-day training program spread over two months. The training took place in the classrooms at the mine on company time and covered both mining and safety practices. The teachers were members of the research team, mine management, and outside experts. A program such as this had never before been offered at Rushton; it was not offered to the control groups.

Section Conferences

Section conferences were another training medium created as part of the experiment. Day-long conferences (on company time) provided the opportunity to review past performance and to learn new ways to carry out future performance. In this sense these meetings were more dynamic learning opportunities than the classroom format used in the formal training. Another unique characteristic of the section conference was that while it facilitated development in mining and safety skills, it also served as an arena for testing communications skills, problem-solving skills, and conflict-management skills. During the first experimental period (December 1973 to November 1974) there were five section conferences. In the remaining periods (through December 1976) there were six. We observed all these meetings, and our transcripts indicated that they provided the men in the experimental section a variety of learning opportunities.

Job Switching

Job switching was another integral part of the intervention at Rushton. The basic idea was that during the shift the men would exchange jobs. This would provide opportunities for acquiring multiple skills and for moving toward the goal of becoming a professional miner. A crew with multiple skills also would be more flexible and responsive to changes in the mining environment.

Method. Two general procedures were used to measure job switching activities. First, we asked in the fourth (April 1975) and fifth

232   JOB SKILLS

(August 1976) attitude survey: "How many times have you exchanged jobs in the last __ months?" Since the question was asked in an interview setting we tried to be sure that the respondent was distinguishing between exchanging jobs to learn a new skill versus being assigned to some job because a crew member was absent (in all sections a foreman may assign someone temporarily to a job if a crew member is absent). Job switching in the experiment was a voluntary exchange between two crew members in order to learn new job skills. By asking this question we could determine whether switching occurred, on how many different jobs, and how often over a given time period. In the fifth interview we also asked a global question about how frequently job switching occurred in the crew.

The second procedure to measure job switching was the on-site observation. One item on the observer's form was to determine whether job switching was occurring.

Results. The fourth interview occurred during the second experimental period (December 1974 to August 1975). We asked the respondents how many times they had exchanged jobs (and on what jobs) since the experiment was initiated. All the members of the first experimental section had exchanged at least one job; 50% had exchanged on all possible jobs on the crew. Each crew member was averaging 3.6 exchanges per month. At the fifth measurement which occurred during the last experimental period (September 1975 to December 1976) all respondents had switched on at least one job. However, this time only 15% (as contrasted with 50% in the prior measure) had exchanged on all jobs. Also, the average number of exchanges per month per crew member had dropped to 2. The decline in job switching behavior does not mean that there was a decline in job skills. Quite the contrary, we would expect job switching to occur early and new skills acquired; then, less job switching occurred as a means of learning. The men still preferred their original jobs. Once knowledge about other jobs was acquired, we would expect them to spend most of their time in their original jobs. Job switching has other functions, such as breaking the monotony of performing one job. For this reason we would expect it to continue, but at a lower rate.

In response to the question of how often switching occurred in the crew (interview 5), the mean response was "sometimes" (3 on a 5-point scale) for miners in the experimental section.

Our on-site observations provide another picture of the job switching behavior. The following summaries are drawn from these observations:

1. When the experiment began in South there was no job switching. The men were to work in their own jobs, to implement some of the ideas in the training classes, and to practice some of the autonomous concepts before beginning any job switching. Most of the new learning opportunities during the early months in the experiment were found in the support job. This newly created position provided the job holder with opportunities to do things, such as laying track and switches, that he had not done before.

2. By the time the South section was considered fully autonomous (March 1, 1974), some job switching had begun.

3. On-site observations in the other sections (controls) during this first experimental period (December 1973 through November 1974) indicated that no job switching, in the experimental sense, was undertaken. If someone was absent in these sections, another miner would perform that job, but there was no mutual exchange to learn new skills.

4. Six months into the project we observed problems with job switching in the experimental section. Some men, particularly older miners, did not want to switch. Others told us they would switch only to certain machines. For example, one of the miners did not want to work on the bolter because it was too dangerous. The unwillingness to switch obviously placed constraints on the ability of others to exchange jobs.

5. These problems came to a head at a meeting in the first quarter of 1975 when a crew in South asked for the removal of their miner operator because he would not switch. The meeting was significant because it indicated that job switching was an important activity for this crew. We conducted an observation in that crew directly after a joint committee meeting on this issue and found the crew members relieved that they had brought this issue to the surface and optimistic that job switching would occur in the future.

6. At the end of the second experimental period (August 1975) observations in the control sections (East and North) indicated that no switching in the experimental sense was occurring. Observations in the South section indicate switching was occurring very infrequently.

7. In the last experimental period (September 1975 through December 1976) we did not observe any job switches when the on-site observations were conducted. This finding is not inconsistent with the survey data we reported earlier. In those data we found job switching had declined to around two switches a month per person.

We conducted only four on-site observations during this last experimental period, so it is not surprising that our observations did not map on to the job switching events.

Foreman's Training Role

Another experimental innovation was to separate production responsibilities from the foreman's job. His new role was to focus primarily on safety and to spend more time on planning and training activities. We conducted a series of on-site observations during the course of this study to determine among other things how the supervisor modified his role. A careful examination of the on-site observer's notes provides no evidence that the foreman engaged in any more training activities than he had done prior to the experiment. More of his time was spent on safety activities and observing the mining operation; the foreman had more slack time.

Summary. We have reviewed four training inputs that should have increased job skills. The formal training and section conferences provided the miners in the experimental section a unique opportunity for learning which was not available in other sections, and from our best information, in other mines in the industry. Although it was impossible to observe each crew each day, or even on some consistent sampling basis, to determine accurately how much job switching occurred, we do know from the survey items and on-site observations that it did occur through the end of the second experimental period, and then dropped off during the third period. It provided one way to acquire multiple skills. Lastly, we did not find any evidence that the change in the foreman's role substantially increased his training activities with the miners.

Perceptions about Job Skills

Method. Another way to determine the impact of the program on job skills was to gather opinions and beliefs on this subject. A number of different measures were introduced into the attitude survey. Three different questions were asked: (1) "What effect, if any, has the AW program had on job skills?" A response category from 1 to 5 was used to determine the level of effect (4–5 = great; 2–3 = some; 1 = none). The direction of the effect was also ascertained; (2) This question used a similar format, but asked about the effect of the training program on program results (e.g., productivity, safety, etc.); (3) This question was

Table 13.1. Perceived Effect of AW Program on Job Skills

	T_2 (6/74)		T_3 (10/74)	
	Union (N = 39)	Management (N = 19)	Union (N = 54)	Management (N = 19)
Effect				
None	10%	11%	17%	10%
Some	41	21	31	37
Great	49	68	52	53
Direction				
Negative	6	—	0	0
Negative-positive	—	—	—	11
Positive	94	100	100	89

	T_4 (4/75)		T_5 (8/76)	
	Union (N = 63)	Management (N = 16)	Union (N = 83)	Management (N = 28)
Effect				
None	3%	0%	23%	4%
Some	36	19	41	61
Great	61	81	36	35
Direction				
Negative	—	—	—	11
Negative-positive	—	—	—	—
Positive	100	100	100	89

open-ended and asked the respondent to describe the Rushton program in his own words.

Results. Table 13.1 presents the results for the perceived effects of the program on job skills. In general, both union and managerial respondents see the program as having a positive effect on job skills, with the managers giving a somewhat more positive endorsement. Union respondents tend to see the program's effect increasing as one moves from measurement 2 to 4. The shift of the percentages to the "some" and "no effect" categories in time 5 probably reflects the respondents' general disillusionment with the program, rather than a deterioration of job skills.

Respondents were also asked at time 5 whether the initial training sessions had an effect on the program's outcomes (e.g., safety). Table 13.2 shows that both union and managerial respondents viewed the training sessions as having some positive effects. A similar question

Table 13.2. Perceived Effectiveness of Training

| | T_5 | |
For Miners	Union ($N = 28$)[a]	Management ($N = 28$)
Effect		
None	15	0
Some	40	57
Great	45	43

For Foremen	Management ($N = 24$)
Effect	
None	21
Some	42
Great	37

[a] Union figure is for South section only

was asked about the training program for foremen, which was introduced to help them with their new role. Of the managers, 37% felt that training for foreman had a great effect on program outcomes, while 42% said that it had some effect.

Another question aimed at the respondents' perceptions of what the program at Rushton was all about. The semistructured format permitted the respondents to describe the program in their own words which were then coded. Tables 10.15–10.17 indicate that learning opportunities were an important part of the respondents' conception of a QOW project.

Summary. The opinion data show fairly clearly that the participants in the Rushton program felt job skills had been increased to *some* extent by the experimental interventions.

DISCUSSION

The data suggest that the experiment increased the level of skills in the experimental section. Although we cannot make this evaluation with an experimental design or through some multivariate process, it seems clear that the intervention introduced new structures that lead to more knowledge about mining and safety practices. This finding comes through whether we ask the people in the experimental section, miners in the control sections, management, or even outsiders, such as safety inspectors.

The form of our data permits us to say only that there was an effect. We cannot assess the magnitude. If we use the survey measures as a guide, *some* effect seems to capture the degree of change.

Our analysis of job skills has been in terms of the first experimental section. We focused on that section because on all accounts it was considered the best example of the experimental intervention, that is, the impact of change was clearer in that section. Training for the second experimental section was spread over a longer period of time, which in our judgement reduced its impact. Also, this section had fewer section conferences, therefore, its opportunities for job skills acquisition were fewer. In addition, the fact that the second section never adopted autonomous work group practices (e.g., job switching) to the same degree as the first section mitigated against major changes in job skills. In extending the program minewide, training programs were again spread over long periods (October 1975 to March 1976) and section conferences were not held frequently. Also, few of the autonomous practices, such as job switching, were adopted. In our judgment the mine-wide extension of the program did not lead to the development of professional miners.

CHAPTER FOURTEEN

Labor-Management Relations

Although it was not one of the explicit goals of the Rushton project, the improvement of labor-management relations is clearly an important part of any QOW project. Overall the QOW program had a mixed effect on labor-management relations. The experimental intervention contributed to improved attitudes of labor and management toward each other and these attitudes probably facilitated the process of labor-management relations from the initiation of the experiment to the mine-wide vote. At the same time the new QOW agreement created a new set of grievances that needed to be resolved. After the mine-wide vote, labor-management relations reverted to their baseline form.

A quick review of Rushton's labor-management history will put this topic into perspective. Rushton was started in 1965 as a nonunion mine. The UMWA's attempt to organize the mine resulted in a bitter struggle with management. Even after the company was unionized (1967), strikes continued as management resisted the union's development and the union attempted to establish its power base. In 1969 a new superintendent took over at the mine, and the management-union relationship was gradually re-evaluated. After 1969, the relationship moved to a new equilibrium in which the two parties accepted each other as legitimate institutions. There was still conflict; both institutions had different goals and the results of bargaining were zero-sum (wins for one party represented losses for the other).

In comparing the periods before and after 1969, we can say that the level of conflict was lower after 1969, and the focus was more on issues within the collective-bargaining agreement than on the validity of collective bargaining itself. The labor-management relationship, however, was still primarily adversary. When the project was introduced at Rushton in August 1973, a strike occurred over whether management could determine who was a member of the union's safety committee.

BASIC HYPOTHESIS

The basic hypothesis was that the QOW project would improve the quality of labor-management relationships. The rationale for this was as follows: the QOW project provided new opportunities for labor and management to work together, principally through the labor-management committee meetings; often the issues discussed in these meetings were compatible to both parties (for example, how to improve safety). This greater opportunity for cooperation contrasts with traditional labor-management contact, for example, in grievance meetings, where bargaining represents the mode of behavior. Given this greater interaction over more compatible issues, it was hypothesized that stereotypes, which hinder effective communication, would be broken and that better understanding would occur. Similarly opportunities for decision making in the more cooperative QOW project environment were hypothesized to lead to a more cooperative environment in traditional labor-management settings. This cooperative environment, then, might lead to improving the processing of grievances, reducing the frequency of and duration of strikes, and so on.

The basic methodological problem is to evaluate the effects of the experimental intervention on labor-management relations. Unfortunately, given the nature of the data, we cannot use multivariate procedures employed in the attitude and economic chapters. Also, in some cases (e.g., strikes), the analysis is at the level of the mine and no control groups are available.

Instead, the analysis strategy is to examine several independent indicators of QOW project effects on labor-management relationships to see if there is some convergence. Data were gathered on five potential indicators of the quality of labor-management relations at Rushton: traditional grievances, AW (autonomous work group) grievances, strikes, perceptions of QOW project effects on labor-management relations, and labor-management interactions. Convergence among these indicators would constitute evidence that the QOW project did affect labor-management relations. A divergence in the measures would occasion less confidence in attributing any effects to the program.

TRADITIONAL GRIEVANCES

Grievances represent one traditional measure of the character of labor-management relations. The grievance procedure is governed by the contract between the United Mine Workers of American and the Bituminous Coal Operators Association. The 1971 contract covered the year 1973 and most of 1974. The next three-year contract was effective on December 6, 1974 and covered the remainder of the experimental period. Although the grievance procedure differs slightly in each contract, this difference does not bear on our analysis.

The contract's formal grievance procedure is rarely followed at Rushton. It is unlikely that a grievance would be brought up between the union member and foreman as the contract provides (step 1). A more typical practice would be for the union member to talk to the mine committee, which, in turn, would talk with the superintendent. Generally grievances are handled by discussions between the superintendent and the mine committee (step 2). Few grievances get pushed to step 3, that is, to the commissioners (a representative from top management and a representative from the district). That meant that grievances at Rushton either were resolved or remained unresolved at step 2.

Method

The analysis of the frequency and content of grievances is one of the most difficult tasks in this evaluation effort. The reason is that neither the union nor management keeps formal records of all grievances. The only way to examine grievances, therefore, is through the superintendent's and grievance committee members' estimates of frequency and content. These limitations preclude any analysis by section. Only comparisons at the mine level between the baseline and experimental periods are possible. Here we are considering only traditional grievances, those that concern the interpretation of the labor-management contract. The next section looks at grievances that arose out of interpreting and implementing the new QOW contract.

Results

There were no differences between the baseline and the three experimental periods in the number of grievances processed. One to three grievances were filed each month. Of these, all were initially resolved or left undecided at step 2 in the grievance procedure (mine committee and superintendent). The shortest time required to reach an agreement during the baseline or experimental periods was one day. Union officers estimated that during the first experimental period there was a reduction from 18 to 12 months in the longest time needed to resolve a grievance. No estimates were available for the other two experimental periods. The average processing time (3 to 4 months) was the same for all four periods.

The content of grievances was also similar in the baseline and experimental periods. The majority of grievances concerned pay and benefits or job bidding. For example, several grievances concerned whether payments should be made to an employee for lost time due to a death in the family. A change in technology in one of the sections involved switching men to new jobs, this led to grievances about appropriate job rates. A few grievances concerned the foremen's right to work on certain jobs and the foremen's treatment of their men. Absenteeism became more of a grievance issue in 1975 and in 1976. Job bidding continued to generate grievances.

Since formal records were not kept and grievances unresolved at step 2 were not immediately pushed to step 3, the most difficult figure to obtain concerned the percent of grievances resolved. The status of grievances that remained at step 2 was left ambiguous. Our best estimate obtained from interviews with union officers and management was that the ratio of unresolved to resolved grievances was much the same throughout the four periods.

Summary

The number and content of grievances did not appear to differ between the baseline year and the three experimental periods. Our interviews with and observations of the members of the mine committee (i.e., the grievance committee) indicate that they were not only willing to challenge management through a grievance, but also firmly committed to win. Even in cases where the mine committee was not supported by the UMWA district, it prided itself in "taking on management" and in winning. In retrospect, the fact that the experiment did not affect the frequency of grievances seems reasonable. Since union and management are different political constituencies with different goals, there is no reason to expect either group to give up their political role. The union's role, in part, is to protect the rights of the worker and to secure as many benefits as possible from the company. It plays out this adversary role by initiating and winning grievances.

AUTONOMOUS WORK GROUP GRIEVANCES

The experimental document was, in effect, a second contract, which, as with any traditional labor-management contract, needed to be clarified and elaborated. We introduced the concept of AW grievances because the new document generated a series of problems between labor and management. In the most general sense these grievances required resources (time, energy, etc.) that would not have been demanded without the experiment, and their frequency, type, and resolution are worthy of examination as indicators of labor-management relations.

Method

The source of data for this analysis came from the transcripts of the steering committee meetings and the section conferences. These were collected at each meeting by a member of the evaluation team and then coded by a formal hierarchial procedure—beginning with meeting type, and date, and ending with codes for each interaction (i.e., who said what to whom). An elaboration of this coding system is presented at the end of this chapter.

AW grievances were defined as problems generated in the QOW meetings. They have nothing to do with the formal grievance procedure. The coding system permitted the identification of problems and their disposition. For this analysis we further categorized these problems or grievances into "document problems," "policy problems," and "other problems." Document problems represent disagreements between labor and management about the existing QOW document. For example, the document stated that the boss would no longer direct the work force on production issues. Not all of the bosses accepted this principle, and the issue appeared in the steering committee. The document also called for job switching, but some men did not want to switch. While this problem represented a conflict among the miners, it was still defined as a problem for labor and management to solve. Policy problems concerned elaboration or extension of the document. Many issues that evolved in the course of the experiment were impossible to anticipate. Extending the project to the second experimental section, determining an overtime policy for experimental and nonexperimental sections, developing a gain-sharing program are all examples of policy problems. The third category, "other," contains problems generated in the meetings. These deal with technical or procedural aspects of mining, such as how to improve safety, how to eliminate delays, or new ways to improve ventilation. Three dimensions of each problem were coded:

1. **The solution presented.** Whenever a course of action (such as buying a new tool) or a procedure for solving a problem (such as the development of a gain-sharing plan) was presented in the transcripts, it was coded as a possible solution.

2. **The solution agreed on.** Here the coding rule was to code a proposed solution as agreed on, when none of the principal actors disagreed with it. The position of the major figures in the union and management (e.g., the president, superintendent) was fairly visible. Neither union leaders nor top management officials were reticent about expressing opinions.

3. **The solution implementation.** Data for this coding came from the transcripts, on-site observations, and unstructured interviews with labor and management. When a course of action was attempted, but was not necessarily carried out or successful, it was coded as implemented. For example, job switching was implemented and persisted early in the experiment, while planning before the section was tried but never fully institutionalized. Both cases were coded as solution implemented.

Where at all possible in our study we have collected traditional reliability measures. Information, particularly about problem resolutions, however, required not only an intimate knowledge of the meetings, but also knowledge from the on-site observations and unstructured interviews. We found it difficult to format this information to permit some traditional reliability checks. So the codes about problems and their disposition represent consensus judgments by the authors of this chapter.

Results

Data presented in Tables 14.1 to 14.4 are divided into three experimental time periods used in other analyses. Unfortunately no baseline data are available since the evaluation team did not enter Rushton until late in the fall of 1973. Two other qualifications are necessary to interpret the tables. First, during the December 1974 to August 1975 period, plans for a mine-wide program were set up. This required the steering committee members to make a major investment in time to draw up a new document. The meetings involved solely in drawing up a mine-wide document were not included in Tables 14.1 to 14.4 because

Table 14.1. AW Problems (Grievances)—Steering Committee

	Number of Meetings in Time Period	Average Number of Problems per Meeting	Document		Policy		Other	
			Average Number per Meeting	Total	Average Number per Meeting	Total	Average Number per Meeting	Total
Period 2 12/73–11/74	1	3	0	0	3	3	0	0
Period 3 12/74–8/75[a]	3	2	0.67	2	1	3	0	0
Period 4 9/75–12/76	14	2.78	0.28	4	1.71	24	0.5	7

[a]A sample of four meetings from period 3 was reviewed, and averages were extrapolated to obtain these data.

Table 14.2. AW Problem (Grievance) Resolutions—Steering
Committee

| | Problem Type | | | | | | | |
| | Document | | Policy | | Other | | Total | |
	Total Number	Rate[a]	Total Number	Rate[a]	Total Number	Rate[a]	Total Number	Rate[a]
Problems discussed	6	—	30	—	7	—	43	—
Problems for which solution presented	5	0.83	24	0.80	6	0.86	35	0.88
Problems for which solution agreed on	1	0.16	19	0.63	5	0.71	25	0.63
Problems for which solution implemented	1	0.16	19	0.70	4	0.57	24	0.60

[a]Rates for agreement and implementation utilize the number of
solutions presented as a denominator.

they represent a special case and are not representative of the other
experimental periods. During this period only 3 out of 13 committee
meetings were nondocument meetings.

The second qualification is that problem solving represents only one
of the activities in the labor-management meetings. Our coding system
classifies the content of the meetings into: (1) feedback, where the
content focuses on providing committee members information on past
performance; (2) planning about future activities; (3) reviewing past
problems that have been resolved; and (4) solving new problems. Given
that solving problems is only one of the four content categories, it is not
surprising that the number of problems per meeting is relatively low.

Table 14.1 presents the data for the steering committee meetings by
problem area and by the disposition of the problem. The number of
steering committee meetings in period 2 was low because the major
focus of the project was in setting up the South section, and the section
conferences were the principal form of labor-management meetings.
As stated above we have eliminated the 10 meetings used to develop
the mine-wide document that occurred in period 3. Given the low
frequency of problems initiated, it is difficult to discern any trends. The
relative absence of "other" problems is congruent with the idea that
the steering committee dealt with document and policy issues, while
the section meetings dealt more with technical issues.

Table 14.3. AW Problems (Grievances)—Section Conferences

	Average Number of Problems per Meeting	Document		Policy		Other	
Number of Meetings in Time Period		Average Number per Meeting	Total	Average Number per Meeting	Total	Average Number per Meeting	Total
Period 2 12/73–11/74							
5	10.2	0.8	4	2.6	13	4.8	24
Period 3 12/74–8/75							
4	7	0	0	1.5	6	5.5	22
Period 4 9/75–12/76							
2	2	0	0	1	2	2	4

Table 14.4.   AW Problem (Grievance) Resolutions—Section
Conferences

	Problem Type							
	Document		Policy		Other		Total	
	Total Number	Rate[a]	Total Number	Rate[a]	Total Number	Rate[a]	Total Number	Rate[a]
Problems discussed	4	—	21	—	50	—	75	—
Problems for which solution presented	2	0.50	11	0.52	31	0.62	44	0.59
Problems for which solution agreed on	1	0.25	8	0.38	26	0.52	35	0.46
Problems for which solution implemented	1	0.25	8	0.38	25	0.50	34	0.45

[a]Rates for agreement and implementation utilize the number of
solutions presented as a denominator.

Table 14.2 presents information on the resolution of problems for
the steering committee—the presentation of a solution, amount of
agreement on a solution, and whether the solution was implemented.
Basically the table tells us that solutions were generated for most of
the problems, but that courses of action were agreed on and implemented more frequently for policy and other types of problems than
for document problems.

Table 14.3 captures the distribution of problems for the section
conferences. These meetings were attended by the entire experimental
section, sometimes union officers participated. From Table 14.3 we can
see that there were a large number of problems (relative to the steering
committee) in period 2, which is appropriate since the South miners,
the majority members in the section conference, lived out the experiment, and problems would be the most salient to them. Most of the
problems were classifed as "other" in that they dealt primarily with
technical issues, rather than with the document. It is interesting that
in the post-vote period (period 4) no document problems were initiated.
This, of course, might be due to the fact that many of the South miners
felt they were no longer in an experiment. The decrease in the
frequency of problems per section conference in period 4 may indicate a
decreasing identification with the program.

Table 14.4 presents information on how the section conferences
resolved problems. In general in the section conferences the rate of

agreeing on solutions and implementing courses of action was less than the rate in the steering committee. This lower level of problem resolution may be attributed to the fact that the section committee was too large to serve as a problem-solving group. More than 35 people participated in section conferences versus 20 for the steering committee. Also, the section conferences occurred in a classroom, a physical setting less suitable for problem-solving sessions. The steering committee meetings occurred in a conference room at a local motel.

Summary

AW grievances represent a measure of the character of labor-management relations. These particular problems or grievances are unique to and caused by the experiment. To that extent the program, through the AW grievances, changed the character of labor-management relations. While the number of problems is not large for either committee, these problems would not have been generated without the QOW program. Although the word ".grievance" carries a negative connotation, it is important to point out that discussing these problems had benefits as well as costs; that is, the more problems were resolved, the better labor and management felt about their ability to solve problems and the more the experimental program became successfully institutionalized at Rushton. On the other hand, the 29 meetings required a significant investment in time and energy, and the problem discussions—even those on technical issues—generated new conflicts and tensions. While it is difficult to identify a ratio between costs and benefits, we do know that the "implemented solutions" category is overstated. It does not reflect whether the course of action was successful or maintained over time. This stemmed from the problem (discussed in Chapter 19) that the structure of neither the steering committee nor section meetings was well suited to monitor or follow up on selected courses of action. The basic point, however, is that the program created a new set of problems or grievances for labor and management. The process of resolving these problems had benefits and costs for labor and management relationships.

STRIKES

Method

Strikes and the lost production time they cause represent another way to characterize labor-management relationships. Strikes can be

Table 14.5. Shifts Lost Due to Strikes (Total Mine)

	Period 1 Baseline 1/73–11/73	Period 2 12/73–11/74	Period 3 12/74–8/75	Period 4 9/75–12/76
Number of strikes: internal	2	0	0	6
Number of shifts lost: internal	36	0	0	156
Shifts lost/potential shifts	.018	0	0	0.059
Number of strikes: external	2	3	0	0
Number of shifts lost: external	12	252	0	0
Shifts lost/potential shifts	0.006	0.12	0	0

internally or externally induced. The former refers to walkouts generated by some conflict between labor and management at Rushton. The
latter includes walkouts, initiated by conflict between other mine
operators and locals, that have spread through the district. Pickets are
set up by outsiders, and the Rushton local, although not immediately
engaged in the conflict, respects the pickets. A QOW intervention
might affect internally induced, but not externally induced, strikes.

Results

Table 14.5 presents the information on strikes. During the baseline
period four walkouts occurred at Rushton. Two of the strikes were internally caused. The first, a single-day's stoppage, concerned a worker
allegedly caught sleeping at work and considered for firing. The union
objected to any disciplinary action and walked out. Three production
shifts were lost (3 crews × 1 shift). The man was not fired. The second
concerned the management's opposition to a particular union man becoming a member of the safety committee—a union committee that
monitors the company's safety practices. This strike lasted for 33
shifts. The miner elected to the safety committee remained on that
committee. Altogether 36 work shifts were lost in the two internally
caused strikes.

The other two strikes were externally caused. Pickets were set up by
the miners from other mines; as a matter of tradition these pickets are
always respected. Twelve work shifts were lost during these two
strikes.

In the first experimental period there were three strikes, all externally caused. One lasted for 9 shifts; the next was a week strike in August, which preceded the national coal strike. The last was the four-week strike over national contract negotiations.

In the second experimental period (after the national coal strike until the mine-wide vote) there were no walkouts. The third experimental period, beginning in the fall of 1975, marked a change in the frequency of internal walkouts. Three walkouts occurred. The first two concerned canopies which federal safety officials ordered to be placed on the continuous miner and shuttle (or ram) cars in the sections. Two men from the East section refused at two different times to work on cars with canopies. They walked out and the rest of the miners followed, as is the custom. In this walkout the controversy was really between the men and federal regulations. While the company asked for a variance and offered the men other work, the company was really a third party to this walkout. The canopies remained on the equipment and the two initiators of the walkouts worked on the cars for a time and then moved on to other jobs. The next walkout, in November, grew out of the canopy controversy. One of the crews claimed it had not been paid properly. They argued that the company had not accurately calculated the time that they had worked during the shift in which the walkout occurred. This grievance was resolved in the favor of the crew during a QOW steering committee meeting. After reviewing the foreman's work report, it was determined that the company was in error in calculating the pay.

The first quarter of 1976 was plagued by a series of walkouts. The first two related to absenteeism. In one case a man who had been absent returned to work without a doctor's excuse and was sent home. This initiated the walkout. In all of these walkouts the company refused to meet with the workers to discuss a settlement until they returned to work, as is the custom. In this dispute the employee in question produced the doctor's letter and returned to work. The second walkout occurred when a union member received a letter from the superintendent stating that further absenteeism would lead to dismissal. Union members objected to this action since it resembled a formal absenteeism policy, which they oppose, and they walked out. The policy indicated by the letter was never put into operation.

The third walkout was one of the most critical for the QOW project at Rushton. A bulldozer operator job was open. The senior man who bid for the job was not selected. A formal grievance was filed, and after some discussion, the mine committee and superintendent tentatively agreed to send the grievance for arbitration. However, the men walked out and put up pickets the next morning at Rushton and other mines owned by the Rushton president. Letters of intent to discharge were sent by the company to the picketers. The dismissals were withdrawn, but management removed two of the picketers from the mine committee and QOW committees. This brought a bitter attack on the company from the international. The final resolution included reinstating the men to their committee assignments; the senior man who was the subject of the strike received another job and an opportunity to learn the job he had bid on. Now he is on the bulldozer.

We label this third walkout as critical not because of the walkout itself, but because of the series of unilateral acts that followed the walkout, such as the pickets and the removal of elected union officials from committees. The objective in QOW programs is for joint problem-solving between labor and management. The unilateral acts in this strike pushed labor and management further into an adversary relationship, further reduced the saliency of QOW principles, and increased the tension between the company and certain portions of the work force and the international. No other strike activity occurred in 1976.

In April 1977 another walkout took place. The union claimed a foreman assaulted one of its members. A joint labor-management committee was called, but the men walked out. Management claimed that the foreman did not hit the man, but placed a finger on his chest. The men voted to stay out, and following a recommendation by the district, brought a civil action against the foreman. The strike lasted 77 days, the longest walkout during the period of the program. As the walkout continued the union challenged the company's no-work/no-talk policy, that is, the company does not meet with the union when they are on strike. Although there were several attempts within the membership to return to work, a vocal minority was able to prevent it. Finally, the district president met with the miners at the union hall and they voted to return.

This was the second critical walkout during the course of the project. The men lost a considerable amount in wages, while the company retained its no-work/no-talk policy and did not reprimand the boss. Nothing came of the civil action. As one reaction to their unsuccessful strike, some of the union officers drew up a letter withdrawing the local from the QOW program. Other union officers opposed the letter, so it was not formally sent. The union officers did announce, however, that they would not participate in any more labor-management meetings until the issue of further participation in the QOW program was discussed at their next regular union meeting. After that meeting

(May, 1977) the union withdrew an earlier motion (from the December 1975 meeting) that authorized the union officers to participate with management in developing a new QOW document. This action by the union was the second formal withdrawal (the negative mine-wide vote was the first) during the program's history.

Summary

Strike behavior is clearly a complex phenomenon. Walkouts occur for many reasons and the explanations range from explicit, rational, conscious reasons to unconscious feelings. Our primary purpose is not to delve into these levels of explanation, but to ask whether the experiment affected strike behavior. For that reason we shall examine only internally induced strikes.

An examination of Table 14.5 indicates a difference in strike behavior in the four time periods. No internally caused strikes occurred during the first two experimental periods (periods 2 and 3). Internally caused strikes do occur, however, during the baseline and in the post-vote period. The question is, to what extent is the apparent absence of internally caused strikes related to the experiment?

Since we cannot analyze differences in strike behavior in the traditional experimental design format, it is difficult clearly to relate the intervention to any changes in strike behavior. The next best strategy is to relate the strike behavior to other labor-management indicators to see if any trends are indicated. That analysis will wait for the conclusion of this section.

Given the limitation on making causal inferences, another strategy for interpreting these data is to examine the changes in strike behavior in terms of the qualitative-historical events in the different time periods. The QOW project created a new set of labor-management relationships early in the experiment. The two parties met in a new physical location; the composition of the two groups was different. For example, the president of the mine attended most of the QOW meetings and could implement decisions on the spot. These frequent meetings in a new social setting increased levels of understanding and cooperation. Although the adversary relationship continued during periods 2 and 3 and the union officials were still motivated to obtain as much as possible for their members, less planned hostility (e.g., picketing) occurred than in period 4. In period 4 the union officers were no longer equal partners in the QOW program. Their role was advisory after the vote; the obligation for joint action was less apparent. Conflict within the union hierarchy at period 4 was more frequent than in periods 2 and 3, that is, the union leadership was divided over whether to fight or to cooperate with management. This increased the propensity for aggressive behavior. Also, the general attitudes of the work force changed during period 4. It is important to remember that many of the walkouts were initiated in the work force and not from the union leadership. After the vote, attitudes toward the program degenerated in the first experimental section. The unilateral institution of the program by management after the vote alienated some of the work force. Our argument therefore is that, while some antagonism toward the program existed over all three experimental periods, the decline in support in period 4 created a climate more prone to fighting than to cooperating with management.

Other explanations for the no-strike behavior in periods 2 and 3 have been offered. Some have argued that in period 2 the miners anticipated a long national strike and remained on the job to maintain income. However, this argument is not supported by the events in 1977 when both a long strike and a national strike took place. Another argument is that, since walkouts are initiated spontaneously by individuals and not by the union leadership implementing some explicit union strategy, the motivations for walkouts are related more to managing tensions from work than the substantive issue in any grievance. This is a compelling argument. Indeed, we would expect some walkouts simply as a reaction to frustrations from work, especially given the environment of mining. Actually, it is surprising that no walkouts occurred in periods 2 and 3. We *do not* expect QOW projects to preclude strikes. We do expect, however, the new social arrangements in QOW programs to reduce the frequency of strikes. In periods 2 and 3 those mechanisms were working; after the mine-wide vote they began to deteriorate.

PERCEPTIONS OF QOW PROJECT EFFECTS ON LABOR-MANAGEMENT RELATIONS

Method

Two methods were used to capture the Rushton employees' perceptions about whether the program changed the character of labor-management relations. First, in the structured attitude survey respondents were asked to rate the program's effect from no effect (1) to very great effect (5) and whether the effect was positive or negative. The second procedure was to collect data from a semistructured inter-

Table 14.6. Perceived Effect of the AW Program on Labor-Management Relations

	T_2(6/74)		T_3(10/74)	
	Union (N = 94)	Management (N = 21)	Union (N = 88)	Management (N = 13)
Effect				
None	60%	43%	45%	15%
Some	34	33	38	46
Great	6	24	17	39
Direction				
Negative	38	0	54	14
Negative-positive	0	0	0	14
Positive	62	100	46	72
	T_4(4/75)		T_5(8/76)	
	Union (N = 92)	Management (N = 17)	Union (N = 82)	Management (N = 26)
Effect				
None	22%	6%	28%	8%
Some	49	41	56	62
Great	29	53	16	30
Direction				
Negative	30	0	28	12
Negative-positive	5	8	5	8
Positive	65	92	67	80

view on how the union and management leaders perceived the character of labor-management relations. These data were qualitative in nature and were collected annually and after major labor-management crises.

Results

Table 14.6 presents the results from the structured attitude survey item: "What effect, if any, has the AW program had on labor-management relations?" At T_2 (June 1974) the union respondents did not see a great impact from the program on labor-management relations. This is not surprising since the program at that time was just starting up and operating in only one section. In T_3 (October 1974), when two experimental sections were underway, slightly more than half of the union respondents identified a negative effect. This shift is congruent with the major event occurring at this time period, the introduction of the second experimental section. This created another situation where some miners were paid one rate, while others received a lower rate for the same work. The perceived inequities were highlighted by the fact that the high-wage earners had relatively low-work experience. In T_4 (April 1975) and T_5 (August 1976) measurement periods, more of the union respondents saw the program as having at least some effect. The effect was more often seen as positive than negative. The managerial respondents also saw the program as having some (versus a great) effect, and they viewed the effect as more favorable than the union respondents.

The second procedure we used to measure attitudes was to draw on semistructured interviews that were conducted with members of labor and management. These measures were typically taken annually or at critical events in the Rushton story.

At the end of the first experimental period (October 1974), the frequent contacts during the QOW meetings seemed to have enhanced the understanding and respect each party had for the other. Reflecting on this first experimental period, a member of management said:

> Since we have the labor-management committee meetings, we are in more face-to-face discussion with the men on the mine committee. . . . I think we have agreed on many issues now. . . . I feel those discussions in the labor-management committee have helped in conducting discussions with those guys on the mine committee. . . . This is an outcome of the labor-management committee. Before, it was very emotional.

The view from the union side is captured in the following response:

> I think . . . it's getting better. More of the decisions are being made here now [at the mine] . . . before things would go back and forth. . . . They'd never give us an answer . . . it would just go round and round. Since this program things have changed. They [top management] realize we put our pants on the same way. I think they trust us more than they did. We used to see top management only once in a while, now we see them a lot.

Both of the above quotes are representative responses gathered from managers and union officials involved in the grievance procedure. We can detect a spillover effect from the QOW meetings to the grievance meetings.

During the second experimental period the labor-management steering committee held 10 meetings to develop a mine-wide plan.

Many of the issues were controversial, adversary positions were evident, but a joint final document was completed. As the date of the major vote approached, a final steering committee meeting was held to make any necessary adjustments prior to the vote. The meeting took an unexpected turn, however, which to some extent became a precursor of coming labor-management events. Prior to the meeting in July of that year one crew from the second experimental section had been reprimanded in the superintendent's office for poor mining practices. The men claimed they should be paid for the time spent in the office. The company refused, stating that it had the right to reprimand workers and that paying would establish an unacceptable precedent. The union brought this grievance into the steering committee meeting and made it clear that settlement of the grievance (i.e., paying) would facilitate the vote. After an acrimonious afternoon discussion, the president agreed to pay, stating that the pay was justified since the time in the office was learning time. The union was elated with the decision. The superintendent said his position with the union had been undercut and was quite disappointed. The research team felt that the union's behavior indicated that a new work atmosphere had not been successfully instituted. The president, on the other hand, said:

> It was hot and heavy. . . . I felt there was a good solution that we could agree on. . . . There will be no precedent. I wanted to preserve the best aspects of AW . . . *if [you] have a confrontation you solve it* . . . [even if it wasn't] the right time to fit into Eric's [Trist] agenda.

Our view is that the union selected a strategic moment to win a benefit from management. The president of the mine was not going to jeopardize the program for a few dollars. This was one of a series of confrontations where the union was able to extract benefits in exchange for their support of the program.

In the third experimental period, management initiated a mine-wide program with the union officers as advisors. The scene began to mirror a more adversary than problem-solving behavior. Both forms of conflict resolution had been used in the past; the issue was one of emphasis. A member of the research team characterized relationships during the fall of 1975 in the following way:

> The union is now in a fight-flight syndrome . . . sometimes they fight sometimes they withdraw . . . fighting is a way to reassert the position of the union officers.

Another observer of the steering committee meetings, who was a member neither of labor nor management, said:

I can see _____ 's (a union official) strategy all over the wall. It's jab, jab, jab . . . look for more all the time. Let Hinks get angry, blow off some steam, and then Hinks will give in.

At the end of 1975 we asked the president his view of the current labor-management situation. He said:

The strikes brought to everyone's attention that communication was not too good. . . . It showed us that the adversary relationship was not under control.

We hadn't had strikes in the past couple of years. We had a spirit of cooperation when this program started. But the spirit has deteriorated after the vote. Now it was [them] against us. . . . It came up in the first meeting after the vote.

I tried to encourage a more consultative relationship, but Eric [Trist] said it would not work under the new situation.

The major strike over job bidding in April 1976 contributed to further deterioration in labor-management relations:

I think it's the program versus Blair [superintendent]. There's a lot of hatred by the men against Blair. Over the years Blair made an ass out of the men . . . they don't like it. [Union, April 1976]

We feel that some of the union officers are saying one thing in the QOW meetings and doing another thing with the men. Some of the feedback we get . . . tells us these guys were the perpetrators of the strike, of maintaining it. We told them we thought they were double dealing. [Management, April 1976]

We weren't getting anywhere . . . it was going to arbitration. That's baloney . . . I don't want the district to represent us. We've had enough of these short strikes . . . they're unnecessary. We'd give them one strike to end them all . . . can't just say we'll put it through arbitration. [Union, April 1975]

Senior man deserves training . . . he should get the job. The company just proved there is a nigger in the woodpile . . . can't fill jobs with young guys. [Union, April 1975]

Well, it tells me the atmosphere [of cooperation] we expected to create is not here. I know we've slid back . . . the whole atmosphere is not there. The program has not created loyalty between labor and management. The guys don't have confidence in the institutions we have defined. [Management, December 1975]

The second major strike took place early in 1977; at issue was whether a foreman struck one of the miners. It brought labor-management relations to their lowest point since the experiment was launched in 1973.

> The company wouldn't budge [in reprimanding foreman]; they just said [the incident] wouldn't happen again. They just don't bargain in good faith. We're going to withdraw from the program. It's the company's might versus us. The program is a mockery . . . they hold the hammer . . . it's the old way . . . it always goes back to might. [Union, May 1977]

Summary

The two attitude measures, at least on the surface, provide different pictures of the effect of the Rushton program on labor-management relations. The structured attitude measure indicates the program had some effect on labor-management relations. With the exception of the period when the second autonomous section was started, the effect was regarded as positive. The semistructured measure indicated an initial positive effect on labor-management relations, but after the vote the attitudes of labor and management toward each other seemed to deteriorate. By the first quarter of 1977 it was clear that relationships were at an all-time low.

The differences in the results can be attributed to the respondents, the formats of the instruments, and the timing of the measures. The semistructured form was used only with labor-management leaders who participated in the grievance and QOW meetings. Their responses were based on specific experiences in labor-management negotiation. The structured item was asked of all respondents. Our experience in the interviews was that the work force had little knowledge of the character of labor-management activities. Their referent in answering the questions was how the program affected union affairs, such as creating pay inequities, rather than the character of the negotiating relationships between labor and management. Another factor that creates differences between the results from the two measures is the timing of the surveys. There was more flexibility in using the semistructured instrument, particularly in tying it into major labor-management events, such as the strikes. In this sense the data from that measure are both more responsive and to some extent more contaminated by these events. The structured item was part of a larger survey. The formats of the two instruments also elicit different responses. The survey item generates a global evaluation response, while the semistructured item elicits more feelings and beliefs about specific events.

Our basic judgment is that the results, though different, are not contradictory. The picture we get from these measures is that the mechanisms of the program provided a new social arena for labor and management that contributed to better understanding and more problem-solving behavior. The introduction of the second autonomous section created feelings of inequity which became defined, at least by the union respondent, as a negative effect of the program on labor-management relationships. The deterioration of labor-management relationships reported after the vote comes from the viewpoint of the participants in the labor-management committees. The work force in general had little opportunity to learn about the character of these relationships, and their judgments were global in nature.

LABOR-MANAGEMENT INTERACTIONS

Thus far we have examined the quality of labor-management relationships through institutional indicators of conflict (i.e., grievances and strikes) and through individual perceptions. Another means for examining such relationships is through various analyses of the interactions that occurred between labor and management over the course of the experiment. As stated earlier, the QOW project provided new arrangements for labor and management to work together, principally through labor-management committees. The interactions that occurred (between labor and management) in these forums, and their patterns over time, provide important indicators of labor-management relationships.

A unique feature of our assessment work was that transcripts were developed from the major meetings. These were then coded and the data computerized, so that we could examine interactions between labor and management. We developed a record of who said what to whom. These data are invaluable in that they provide a record of what went on during the meetings, rather than someone's notes of the meetings. They are also important in that they provide an opportunity to measure what labor and management did, that is, how they behaved. In other words, the transcripts permit us to look at behavior, not just at reports of behavior or opinions about labor-management relations.

Our focus is on the interactions that occurred between the major constituencies attending the South section conferences during the four years of the study. We limited our examination to South section conferences because the experiences in South were the best prototype of a QOW project at Rushton. Also, the costs of coding all the meetings (steering committee and other section conferences) would have been too great, given other demands on our funds.

There are two labor constituencies, the autonomous work group (AW) and the union representatives (U). There is one management constituency (M) and the research team (RT). The major hypothesis, that labor-management relationships improved over the course of the study, will be examined through tabulations of the interactions that occurred between these constituencies. These tabulations can be used to examine both the quantity (i.e., amount) and content of interactions between constituencies over time. The major emphasis will be placed on interactions occurring between the autonomous work group-management and the union-management constituencies.

Method

The sample of meetings consists of all 11 meetings of the South section held between January 1974 and December 1976. Participants at these meetings included all 30 members of South's experimental crews and representatives of the 3 other constituencies. The management constituency consisted of 5 or 6 members of management, including the company president, mine superintendent, mine general foreman, safety director (or his assistant), training director, and sometimes the chief mechanic. The research team consisted of from 3 to 5 members. Finally, the union constituency included 5 to 7 elected local union officers. The total number of participants at any one meeting ranged from 40 to 55.

Data were collected by one of the two trained observers who were familiar to the meeting participants. The typical procedure was for the observer to sit at the rear of the meeting room (i.e., a classroom at the mine site) and take verbatim notes by hand of the proceedings, including the name of the speaker and what he said. These transcripts account for an estimated 75% of all interactions at the meetings. In addition to recording the meetings, the observer made a "map" of the general seating arrangement in the room and a roster of the participants. The completed transcripts were then coded for analysis.

The Coding and Analysis Scheme. Data were presented through the use of an "interaction process" called the group analysis package (GAP) coding scheme developed expressly for the QOW project evaluation. The coding system orders the data into four parts. First, the data were classified by meeting, then meetings were broken into quarters. Quarters were then coded for discussion content or episodes. The smallest unit in the coding system is an interaction—the content of what person A says to person B. A detailed coding system is available on request (cf. Bales, 1950).

The present analysis investigates patterns of interactions across meetings and does not include episodes or quarters (see pp. 242-248 for an analysis of problems in the meetings). A coded interaction or "act" consists of: (1) the initiator; (2) the intended receiver, and (3) any of three types of content codes—task, process, or special. See Table 14.7 for specific definitions and examples of the content codes.

Transcripts were coded independently by two trained coders. Coding differences were resolved by a discussion among the coders and the senior investigator. An example of a coded manuscript is presented in Table 14.8. Data were then keypunched, verified, and cleaned by a computer program called a "cleaner," which is designed to search for incorrect data specifications.

Analyses of these data required the tabulation of interactions according to a variety of specifications. A series of programs called GROUPLIB were written to generate such tabulations. The programs allowed the user to specify up to five-way tables of interactions. Using GROUPLIB, for example, it would be possible to tabulate all interactions between members of the union and members of management according to type and by meeting. These programs made it possible to examine the exact nature of interactions within each of the 11 meetings and hence explore hypotheses about changes in the quantity and quality of such interactions.

We shall use the data gathered and coded with the GAP to examine the quality of labor-management interactions over the course of the experiment. Our general strategy is to aggregate the interactions by the time periods utilized throughout this report. There were no meetings during the first time period, or baseline (January 1973 to November 1973), hence it is excluded from the remainder of this particular analysis. There were five meetings in period 2 (December 1973 to November 1974), 4 meetings in period 3 (December 1974 to August 1975), and 2 meetings in period 4 (September 1975 to December 1976). For each time period, interactions from all meetings were aggregated, so that the sum of all interactions in a time period is the sum of the interactions for all meetings in a time period. Hence, the periods provide the time parameter in the analysis. In addition, the actors have been grouped by constituency, even though it is possible to use the GAP to perform analyses on specific individuals (i.e., initiators).

The union officers were absent from two meetings in period 3. Their absence may be attributed to two factors. First, there were a large

Table 14.7. A Description of Interaction Codes

Task Codes

Problem identification (PI). These are statements that identify, clarify, focus on, or refocus on problems that concern the group. Example: "We have been having too many miner delays because of routine maintenance lately."

Asks orientations or gives orientations (AO and GO). These are statements that give or seek information about the problem. Example: "We have been short on timber supplies lately."

Asks opinions or gives opinions (AOP and GOP). These are statements that evaluate the task or characteristics of the task. Example: "I don't think taking pillars requires special learning."

Asks suggestions or gives suggestions (AS and GS). A suggestion is a statement that promotes an idea or course of action. Example: "I think we should begin maintenance at dinner time."

Asks procedural suggestions or gives procedural suggestions (APS and GPS). A procedural suggestion proposes a means of going about solving a problem. Example: "Let's vote on the idea."

Gives positive evaluation or gives negative evaluation (GPE and GNE). Expression of agreement or disagreement with the statements of another. Example: "Your idea is a good one."

Process Codes

Task performance strategies (TPS). These are statements about how the group does or should operate. Example: "We ought to have more inputs from the union at those meetings."

Positive and negative process statements (PPS and NPS). Process statements tend to raise or lower the esteem of another group member. They are generally statements of affect. Example: "Your union leaders do a good job for you."

Special Codes

Interruption (INT). Behavior that attempts or succeeds in stopping or changing the course of a discussion.

Positive and negative autonomous work group statements (AWP and AWN).

Positive and negative management statements (CP and CN).

Positive and negative union statements (UP and UN). Positive statements indicate support for or commitment to a subgroup. Negative statements express dislike for or alienation from the subgroup. Example: "How come the union is never wrong?"

Integrating role (IR). Brings information or problems that occurred in another solution to the attention of participants at the meeting. Example: "The union officers were not present at the last foremen meeting."

Summarizing role (SR). Summarizes and clarifies what has been said in the meeting. Example: "Thus far, we have decided to expand the program, the question is how?"

Table 14.8.   A Sample Meeting

Burton:	*We should deal with the roof problem first. That is more critical than the miner. It is important to get some good ideas about how to deal with the roof.*	Task performance strategy
King:	*Easy for you to say . . . you don't run the thing* [miner].	Gives negative evaluation
Floyd:	*Burton is right. The miner won't do us any good with rock on it.*	Gives positive evaluation Gives opinion
	[Pause]	
Burton:	*OK. Any other ideas?*	Asks orientation
Cox:	*Dangerous for bolter . . .* [tells of rock coming down]	Gives opinions
Prescott:	*Remember the last time we had roof problems, used more timber . . . water was the big problem then . . . slate roof . . . we also used different style bolts.*	Integrating role
Cox:	*More timber . . . good idea.*	Gives positive evaluation
Fisher:	*Agree.*	Gives positive evaluation
Floyd:	*Might make smaller cross cuts.*	Gives suggestion
Burton:	*Violates the mining plan . . . means would have to change cycle . . . inspectors would balk.*	Gives negative evaluation
Adams:	*OK. So the problem is that we are in slate . . . bad roof . . . in some places water is causing a slick bottom. Can either stay or move . . . depends on what we expect to gain by staying . . . will conditions improve?*	Gives opinion
Floyd:	*Up to the section to make decision, that's part of AW idea.*	AW positive Gives opinion

number of steering committee meetings during this period and concern was expressed by management about the number of hours being allocated to nonmining work; the second and most important reason was that by period 3 the South section had a clear identity and had developed its own leaders who represented their interests. In period 4, the union officers did not participate in any section conferences. This

Table 14.9. General Interactions by Each Constituency over Time

	Constituency			
	Autonomous Work Group	Union	Management	Research Team
Period 2 (5 meetings)				
Raw count	596	305	471	898
Number per meeting	119.2	61	94.2	179.6
Percent of interactions	26%	13%	21%	40%
Period 3 (4 meetings)				
Raw count	812	31	243	646
Number per meeting	203	15.5	60.75	161.5
Percent of interactions	48%	—[a]	14%	38%
Period 4 (2 meetings)				
Raw count	537	—[b]	357	203
Number per meeting	268.5	—	187.5	101.5
Percent of interactions	48%	—	34%	18%

[a] The union constituency was absent from two meetings in period 3.
[b] The union constituency was absent from all meetings in period 4.

was the post-vote period and their QOW activities were limited to the Mine Training and Development Committee (MTDC).

Results

Analysis of General Initiations. Table 14.9 was developed in order to examine the general pattern of initiations generated by the constituencies over time. The raw initiation is provided to give an indication of the absolute level of interactions on which the other entries are based. The second entry (interactions per meeting) is useful as an indicator of the relative contribution of a constituency to the meetings occurring in a time period. Finally, the percent of initiations indicates the relative contribution of a constituency to all interactions in a time period; this measure is an indicator of the propensity for a constituency to contribute to the meetings.

Table 14.9 reveals several relevant characteristics of the initiation patterns. An examination of differences across constituencies indicates that the research team, in period 2, was the dominant initiator in terms of both number of initiations per meeting and proportion of initiations generated in the period. This pattern changed over time. The average number of initiations per meeting decreased over time from 179.6 in period 2 to 101.5 in period 4. Similarly, the relative proportion of initiations attributable to the research team decreased from 40 to 18%. In contrast, the contribution of the autonomous work group increased from 119.2 to 268.5 interactions per meeting or from 26 to 48% of the interactions occurring in periods 2 and 4. There is no uniform trend for the management constituency as the amount of initiations decreases from period 2 to period 3 (i.e., from 21 to 14% of the initiations) and then increases sharply in period 4 (from 14 to 34%). The union constituency was absent from four of the last six meetings, hence trends cannot be identified for that constituency.

Although a variety of interpretations are possible, the above trends suggest that the relative contribution of the experimental group increased over time, which may indicate the learning of a new problem-solving role. In contrast, the amount of intervention of the research team decreased in period 4, which is congruent with their strategy of slowly withdrawing from the project. The decreasing-increasing trend of the management team is difficult to explain; we shall discuss this trend below with reference to the union's absence.

The data presented in Table 14.9 are misleading when one does not take into account the differences in the sizes of the constituencies. The number of initiations per person for each constituency in period 2 would be approximately 20 for the autonomous work group, 51 for the union, 94 for management, and 225 for the research team. From this perspective—the propensity of individual members to initiate—the contribution of the autonomous work group is clearly the least, followed in order by the union, management, and research team for all time periods but 4. In period 4, the individual contributions of members of management are greater than those of the research team.

The large size of the autonomous work group raises the issue of how the group's initiations are distributed across individuals. An analysis of the distribution of initiations for the autonomous group indicates that approximately 7 individuals, or 25% of the group, account for over 75% of the initiations in any given meeting. For example, in the first meeting only 11 of 30 members of the autonomous group were above the group average of 4 interactions per person per meeting. In addition, more than half of the members of the group did not have an initiation in the first meeting. This trend is evident across all 11 meetings. The distributions for the union, management, and research team, although somewhat skewed, are much more uniform. In these constituencies, a single member typically dominates, with the distribution across the remainder of the members being roughly uniform. In no case was there a meeting where a member of the union, management, or research team failed to contribute at least 1 initiation.

The skewed characteristic of the autonomous work group's distribution of initiations is important since it suggests that the position of the entire group can be represented by a subset. The failure of individuals outside the subgroup to participate indicates that the representation provided by the subgroup might have been adequate; that is, the subgroup's political position might have been shared by members of the constituency. If one considers only the actively participating subgroup in calculating the average initiations per person, the degree of participation of the autonomous group becomes similar to the per person participation of the other constituencies.

A third issue regarding the general pattern of initiations is the effect of the union's nonparticipation in periods 3 and 4 on the initiation propensities of other constituencies. In particular, it is reasonable to expect the absence of the union to affect the initiations of the other labor constituency, the autonomous work group. If both groups espouse the labor position, then the removal of the union group should result in a relative increase in autonomous work group initiations. Indeed, the absence of the union in part of period 3 and for all of period 4 may account for the comparatively large amount of initiations generated by the autonomous work group in periods 3 and 4. It is unlikely that the absence of the union is the only factor contributing to the increase, however. Comparing the percentage of initiations generated by the union in period 2 (13%) with the net increase in the autonomous work group's contribution from period 2 to period 4 (22%) leaves a difference of 9%, which cannot be attributed to the union's absence.

In summary, our examination of the general context of the meetings indicates a trend for the autonomous work group to contribute more to the meetings and for the research team to contribute less. Although the decreased participation of the union is a cause for the autonomous work group increase, it is probably not the only cause. The research team's decrease reflects a conscious decision in the post-vote time period to have management personnel, rather than themselves, conduct these meetings. We now turn to an examination of dyadic interactions and the quantity and quality of relationships between constituencies.

Analysis of Dyadic Interaction. The quantity and content of dyadic interaction between the labor and management constituencies may be used as another indicator of labor-management relationships. Dyadic interactions refer to direct interactions from union (or management) to management (or union). Quantity serves as an index of the amount of communication and joint problem solving that occurred between these

Table 14.10.   Content Category

Positive Evaluation Category	Gives positive evaluation Positive process statement Autonomous work group positive Management positive Union positive
Negative Evaluation Category	Gives negative evaluation Negative process statement Autonomous work group negative Management negative Union negative
Informational Category	Asks and gives orientation Asks and gives opinion Asks suggestions Summarizing role Integrating role Asks evaluation
Productive Category	Gives suggestion Gives procedural suggestion Task performance strategy

groups. In general, an increase in the amount of interaction within the labor-management dyads in a QOW context is a sign of greater communication and problem solving and hence improved labor-management relationships.

The content of dyadic interaction is another indicator of the nature of the joint relationship. The interactions, using the GAP, were classified into the four categories shown in Table 14.10. The *positive evaluation* category includes interactions that express approval of another's ideas or suggestions or that compliment and raise the esteem of others or their group affiliation. In contrast, the *negative evaluation* category contains both comments of disapproval about ideas or suggestions and derogatory criticism that lowers another's esteem or the esteem of their group. The *informational* category contains interactions that ask for or provide information for the function of orienting others about the specifics of an issue. The *opinion* category contains beliefs or opinions that an individual has with regard to the problem under discussion. Opinions differ from evaluations, in that the former represent evaluative statements directed to the group as a whole (e.g., "I do not think paying workers weekly will lower absenteeism."), while the latter are directed to specific others (e.g., "I agree with you that

Table 14.11. Dyadic Interactions by Constituencies over Time

	Labor-Management Dyads			Comparison Dyads	
	AW ↔ M	U ↔ M	AW ↔ RT	U ↔ RT	M ↔ RT
Period 2					
Raw count	121	271	200	164	781
Number per meeting	24.2	54.2	40	32.8	156.2
Percent of total interactions	5%	12%	9%	7%	34%
Period 3					
Raw count	281	19	824	31	71
Number per meeting	70.25	27.1ᵃ	206	15.5ᵃ	17.75
Percent of total interactions	16%	2%	48%	3%	4%
Period 4					
Raw count	672	—ᵇ	284	—ᵇ	10
Number per meeting	336	—	142	—	5
Percent of total interactions	60%	—	25%	—	1%

ᵃ The union constituency was not present at two meetings during period 3.
ᵇ The union constituency was absent from all meetings in period 4.
See p. 269 for discussions of symbols used in column heads.

weekly payment will not reduce absenteeism."). The *productive* category contains interactions that constitute specific suggestions or solutions to problems, suggestions about procedures for generating solutions, or ideas about how the group should operate as a problem-solving mechanism.

The two evaluative categories, positive and negative, are of particular importance for assessing the quality of labor-management relationships. Large amounts of positive or negative behaviors provide an indicator of the feelings that the constituencies in the dyad have for one another. Indeed, a general hypothesis is that the sentiments between labor and management should become more positive as a result of the program. Another useful indicator of labor-management relations is the productive category. One of the behaviors or activities sought in the project was joint problem solving among labor and management groups. An increase or decrease in the productive category over time would indicate progress, or lack of progress, in developing joint problem-solving behavior. The informational category is somewhat less important as an indicator in the present context of labor-management relationships. Although in a broader analysis of the problem-solving capability of the group, the informational category would be very important.

Table 14.11 provides data on the quantity of dyadic interactions over time. The first two columns—the labor-management dyads (AW-M, U-M)—are the primary focus. The remaining three dyads are for comparison purposes and show the amount of interaction between the labor-management constituencies and the research team. As before, the data on the union constituency are limited by their nonparticipation in the later meetings. There are three indicators in each cell of the table: (1) the number of interactions; (2) the number of interactions per meeting, and (3) the percent of total interactions in the time period that is accounted for by the dyadic interactions.

The raw counts are provided as an indicator of absolute amounts. The number per meeting entry indicates the average amount of interaction that occurred in a dyad for a specific time period. Finally, the percentage entry is particularly useful for examining the relative contribution of the dyadic interactions to all initiations and comparing across dyads for relative contribution to the meetings.

Prior to examining trends, it is useful to make several general observations about the data. First, the relative contribution of dyadic interactions to the total amount of initiations is quite small for most of the dyads (less than 20%). That means that more of the interactions are to the group as a whole than to any specific individual. Second, dyads containing the research team dominate the interaction patterns for periods 2 and 3. In period 2, the highest level of dyadic interaction occurs between the research team and management. In the next period, it is between the research team and the experimental group. This change may represent the growing identity and ability of the experimental group to play a major role in the section conference, and a lower need to rely on management. In period 3, the AW-management dyad exhibited the greatest interaction pattern.

Looking further at the trends within the labor-management dyads, it is evident that the amount of interaction between the autonomous work group and management increased sharply over time (from 5 to 60% of total initiations). Unfortunately, this trend cannot be examined fully for the union constituency. Comparing now across dyads in period 2, the amount of interaction between the autonomous work group and management is somewhat smaller than between the autonomous work group and the research team (5 versus 9%) or between management and the research team (5 versus 34%).

In period 3 the interaction between the autonomous work group and the research team still dominates that between the autonomous work

Table 14.12.   Profiles of Interaction Content within Dyads over
Time

	Labor-Management Dyads			Comparison Dyads		
	AW ↔ M	U ↔ M	AW ↔ RT	U ↔ RT	M ↔ RT
Period 2						
+ Evaluation	3	5	8	4	9
− Evaluation	16	12	6	10	7
Productive	11	15	16	21	11
Informational	47	51	51	38	54
Opinion	23	17	19	27	19
Period 3						
+ Evaluation	2	12	7	0	8
− Evaluation	6	0	3	0	1
Productive	9	0	15	6	7
Informational	68	69	64	81	73
Opinion	15	19	11	13	11
Period 4						
+ Evaluation	6	—[a]	14	—[a]	1
− Evaluation	6	—	4	—	0
Productive	5	—	13	—	2
Informational	61	—	50	—	97
Opinion	22	—	19	—	0

[a] Union constituency not present at meetings.

group and management (48 versus 16%). In period 4 the amount of interaction between the autonomous work group and management clearly dominates the amount of interaction between either the autonomous work group and the research team or management and the research team. Hence, relative to the comparison dyads, it is reasonably clear that the amount of dyadic communication between labor and management has increased. Again, some of the increase may be accounted for by the absence of the union (about 21%), but not all of it. These data suggest that the QOW program may have increased the amount of communication between labor and management, at least in the section conference context.

Table 14.12 presents data on the content of interactions within the labor-management dyads and the comparison dyads. The five rows of each time period correspond to the five content codes described above. The cell entries correspond to percentages of interaction in the dyad falling into the particular content category, so that if 10 out of the 100 interactions between the autonomous work group and management in period 2 were productive, the productive entry in the AW-M column for period 2 would be 10%.

Examining the trend in the autonomous work group-management dyads over time, it is apparent that content patterns changed relatively little. There are, however, several small trends. The amount of positive evaluation changed from 3% in period 2, to 2% in period 3, to 6% in period 4. In contrast, the amount of negative evaluation decreased from 16% in period 2 to 6% in periods 3 and 4. Similarly, the amount of productive interaction decreased from 11 to 9 to 5%. Concurrently, the amount of informational content increased from 47% in period 2 to 68 and 61% respectively in periods 3 and 4. The opinion category remains relatively the same. A comparison across columns of Table 14.12 suggests that the content profiles for all dyads are similar, with relatively large informational components and small productive and evaluative components.

Summary

These data on labor-management interactions provide a new way to look at labor-management relationships. We have learned the following from the analysis of this measure:

1. The experimental group (AW) increased its participation in the meetings over time. This increase is due to the absence of the union leaders in periods 3 and 4 as well as to an increased propensity for AW members to participate.

2. The distribution of participation within the AW group is skewed—only a small percent of the members account for the majority of the interactions.

3. The analysis of interactions between labor and management indicated an increasing level of interactions or communication. Again, the increase in interactions between the AW and management represents to some extent a compensation for the absence of union leaders in periods 2 and 3.

4. The content of the interactions are characterized by a high degree of information giving and receiving. There is a surprisingly low level of negative evaluations between labor and management. Also, if there is any trend in Table 14.12, it is a decline in the use of negative evaluations between periods 2 and 3.

We can further clarify this data by comparing it with our analysis of AW problems presented in the section conferences (see Table 14.3). Over time we find fewer problems initiated in the section conferences, yet the amount of AW-management (i.e., union-management) interactions was increasing. Is this a contradiction? Probably not, because the interactions recorded communication attempts and are primarily of the information, rather than the productive, category. Higher levels of productive interactions would be associated more with problem generation and resolution. This indicates, therefore, an increase over time in communication between labor and management and not necessarily an increase in problem-solving.

Another issue concerns relating the general decline of interest in the experiment in the post-vote period to the interaction pattern, that is, if the AW miners were less interested in the project, why do we see an increase in interactions? Are not these two reported findings contradictory? The apparent contradiction can be resolved as follows: Fairly consistent evidence across a variety of indicators measured a decline in commitment to AW practices in the post-vote period. The section conferences occurred in a special context that had been legitimated for three years. Since these conferences released the men from the regular mining activity for a day of discussion, the two conferences of the post-vote period were probably viewed as a welcome break from the daily routine. Given that participation was a legitimate activity, it is not surprising that the AW miners chose to participate.

The distinct trend from this analysis is that the AW miners increased their participation in section conferences over time. This increased participation is reflected in the communication exhibited between the miners and management over the three periods. The nature of the communication is informative rather than evaluative; evaluative interactions decline between periods 2 and 3.

DISCUSSION

The QOW program had a mixed effect on labor-management relations at Rushton, and the effects varied over the course of the project. From the company and union's points of view the project led to improved attitudes of labor and management toward each other and these attitudes probably facilitated the process of labor-management relationships during periods 2 and 3. The project also contributed to the absence of strikes during these two periods, but had no effect on the frequency, processing, or content of regular grievances. Members of the mine committee and management, however, felt that the process of resolving these grievances was easier during periods 2 and 3.

The program also changed the character of communication and problem-solving activity. We have reported an increased rate of interaction between labor and management, which is due to the committee structure created by the project. The communications, however, were more informational than evaluative in nature. The level of negative evaluative interactions declined from period 2 to 3.

On the negative side, the program led to a new set of grievances, which we have labeled "AW grievances." While some of these were resolved and provided a training ground for problem-solving, they also represented a cost in terms of time and energy that would not have occurred without the QOW program.

Another issue concerns whether the program changed the balance of power between labor and management. This is hard to determine since we do not have any good baseline data that would indicate a shift. Given these limitations, data from interviews with local labor leaders and management officials suggest that the company lost leverage against the union. The program and its success was important to the company president who was also the final decision-maker from the company's position in labor-management issues. It was clear, given his strong commitment, that he did not want to jeopardize the program. The union officials knew this and used this knowledge to gain concessions. Besides the grievance brought to the steering committee just before the mine-wide vote (see p. 256), after the vote in other crucial decisions concerning pay rates and qualification procedures the union was able to extract concessions on the basis that only a favorable decision would permit their cooperation in QOW program. Other evidence in the meetings documents that union officials knew they could use their participation in the program to extract concessions. We are not arguing that these decisions were good or bad, only that they are evidence of some shift in power.

Finally, it is important to view the costs and benefits of the program in light of the different experimental periods. The benefits were pronounced during periods 2 and 3 when the program was at its peak. As behaviors related to the program began to decline so did the quality of labor-management relations.

CHAPTER FIFTEEN

Implicit Goals and Unintended Consequences

In our discussion on effectiveness, we proposed two types of goals to be used in assessing the effectiveness of a QOW program—explicit and implicit. Explicit goals are those publicly agreed on by labor and management. We have examined these in the previous chapters. In this chapter we shall review some of the implicit goals and unintended consequences of the program, first from the point of view of the company and then from the view of the union. Implicit goals are those that have not been publicly agreed on, but they would be considered important by the major participants. These implicit goals are derived from our theoretical framework of an effective organization as one that must maintain itself both internally and externally (see Chapter 9). Our basic thesis is that any program will have both intended and unintended consequences. These unintended consequences will represent benefits or costs to the major participants. These unintended consequences may facilitate or hinder the internal or external adaptability of the organization.

THE COMPANY MANAGEMENT

Internal Consequences

The QOW program brought certain positive unintended consequences to the internal operation at Rushton:

274

1. The project's focus on training for the miners also benefited members of management and maintenance personnel who participated in the program. As observers and participants in the formal training program, section conferences, joint labor-management meetings, and so on, members of management had the opportunity to practice presentation and problem-solving skills. Although the miners were the object of the training, management reaped indirect benefits by participating in the program.

On a more formal basis, supervisory training was initiated in 1976 by the research team, and a subsequent supervisory-skills program was offered by an outside trainer. The focus on supervisory training arose after QOW discussions indicated potential problems in the supervisory area. The openness toward bringing in outside trainers was congruent with the values put on training during the project.

An elaborate training program for preventive maintenance was initiated during the QOW project. This program did not grow directly from any QOW discussions. Rather, it was a decision by the president to improve the operations of the mine. An interview with the mine president after the decision indicated that the values of the QOW project on training and on finding new ways to improve work influenced his decision to initiate the preventive maintenance program.

Our basic thesis is that the program had indirect effects on increasing the job skills held by management and maintenance workers. These changes were not initially planned in the design of the program. We consider them benefits in the sense that they probably contributed to the internal adaptability of Rushton.

2. Another benefit of the program was that it facilitated the movement of miners to managerial positions. In a sense the various meetings served as an identification and selection mechanism for new managerial personnel. Participation in any of these meetings provided some indication of presentation, problem solving, and other related leadership skills. Two of the members of the first experimental section moved into foremen's positions and another moved into a quasisupervisory role. Our argument is not that these individuals would not have moved without the program, but that the program probably increased their self-confidence about performing in supervisory jobs.

3. The program changed the character of the communication system at Rushton. Prior to the experiment, the vertical communication at Rushton was primarily one-way. The superintendent was the primary initiator for both his staff and the first-line supervisors. The staff, in turn, was the primary initiator of communication to first-line supervisors. During periods 2 and 3, from December 1973 to August 1975, the institutions of the experiment substantially changed the communication pattern. The various meetings provided communication contacts that generally had not occurred (e.g., between a miner and the president). The ratio of interactions also changed with a more reciprocal ratio between lower and higher status jobs. Instead of the superintendent being the sole initiator to the foreman, the pattern of initiation was more balanced. Also, the meetings increased the frequency of communication. We consider the change in the communication structure a benefit, in that it elicited more information about how to operate the mine effectively. It tapped information from people who, prior to the experiment, had no easy way to express their ideas. It was also a benefit to the extent that more reciprocal communication may have increased worker satisfaction and commitment to the firm. As opportunities to participate increase, the chances of increasing commitment to the firm are also enhanced. These benefits derived from the changes in the communication system were apparent prior to the vote. They gradually diminished during the post-vote period and are inconsequential now.

4. Prior to the experiment there was virtually no planning at Rushton. The mine was operated on a day-to-day basis. A major thrust of the change effort was to increase planning horizons at the crew, section, and mine-wide level. During the peak effectiveness of the program (prior to the vote) section conferences, foreman meetings, and meetings of the managerial staff served as planning mechanisms. We are not arguing that planning per se is good. But up until the time of the experiment there had been no planning at Rushton. Given the interdependent nature of the work, some increment of planning was probably beneficial. We doubt that the increases in planning activity had a direct traceable effect to any of the short-term economic indicators. Planning can, however, increase the internal adaptability of an organization and thus contribute to its long-run effectiveness.

The program also introduced certain costs within the firm.

1. The foreman's role was substantially changed. He was to be primarily responsible for safety. This change required dropping traditional activities (e.g., production) and learning new skills (e.g., planning and coordination). The change in role behaviors was ambiguous and

stressful for the foreman. Ambiguities—about how much he could direct the work force, whether he could make suggestions about work, when he should obtain opinions from the crew—characterized the foreman's role during the introduction of the QOW program. While it is difficult to determine whether this tension decreased the foreman's performance, the role ambiguity introduced by the change created psychological costs for the first-line managers that were directly attributable to the project.

2. Changes at the section and first-line supervisor level reverberated throughout the organization. Middle and upper middle management roles also had to change. People in these positions experienced even greater ambiguity and stress than that identified for the first-line supervisors. The ambiguity and stress were in part due to the changes in authority and decision making that gave more control to the miners. The stress was augmented by the lack of support given to these positions during the introduction of the QOW experiment. Another factor contributing to the stress was that many occupants of these positions were opposed to the QOW principles. Since they were constrained to adopt behaviors counter to their beliefs, tension increased. As with the foreman, this tension represented a psychological cost to management.

External Consequences

To be an effective organization Rushton had to deal successfully with a set of outside actors. There were some unintended consequences for Rushton's external relationships.

1. PPL owns Rushton through its subsidiary, Pennsylvania Mines Corporation (PMC). Although the major decisions about the QOW program were made at Rushton, the program could have affected the relationship with the parent corporation. We interviewed people at PPL and PMC and found that the program had virtually no effect on these organizations or on their relationship with Rushton. What is interesting is that PMC operates a number of mines for the utility company, and none of these had adopted any of the practices introduced at Rushton. Also, the president of Rushton owns several mines. There was no transfer of Rushton practices to these mines during the 1974 to 1977 period.

2. The federal and state inspectors are major actors in the Rushton scene. They visit Rushton frequently and have power to signifi-

cantly affect the mining operation. In general the program had little effect on the relationship between the inspectors and the company. Some inspectors seemed to be always in conflict with management; others were not. There was one exception: one state inspector viewed aspects of the program as contradictory to the law. He interpreted the program as not requiring the foreman to be responsible for activities at the face. This belief, which does not accurately characterize the program, continued to persist despite a series of clarification meetings with the inspector. In this case we know the program created more tension between the inspector and management. We cannot claim, however, that it led to more violations.

Job Attachment

Another outcome of the project for Rushton concerns job attachment behavior—absenteeism and turnover. Job attachment is considered here because it was never explicitly stated as a goal of the QOW project. It is clear, however, that job attachment is an outcome considered important by the company. If the QOW project reduced absenteeism, this would be considered a benefit. Improvements in job attachment represented an implicit goal for the company; changes in job attachment behaviors represented unintended consequences.

We are treating job attachment as a separate section in this chapter because quantitative data were available. Our attention will focus primarily on absenteeism. If a worker was late and missed the man trip (transportation to the coal face), he was considered absent. Data on turnover will be mentioned briefly since it occurs very rarely at Rushton.

Basic Hypothesis

The basic hypothesis is that absenteeism should have decreased as a function of the QOW program. The program provided the men greater responsibility in controlling their work, congruent with this was the responsibility to come to work. Also, the experiment provided feedback and potential reinforcement for good attendance records. A related factor is that most of the intervention focused on developing the work sections into an autonomous, cohesive group. One function of the group was to monitor and control group behavior (such as absenteeism). Therefore, absenteeism in the experimental section should have been reduced.

Methodology

Information on absenteeism came from the payroll and monthly bonus sheets. From these sources, which are quite reliable, absenteeism could be further classified into accident or nonaccident related absenteeism. Accident related absenteeism is discussed in Chapter 12. Nonaccident related absenteeism was further broken down into excused and unexcused. A person was excused if his absence was caused by illness or injury at work, a death or illness in his family, a doctor's appointment, jury duty, military reserve service, company business, and approved union business. In all of the above cases of excused absenteeism, the burden of proof remained on the worker. He had to supply written evidence of a sickness (from a doctor) or death in the family (from a funeral home) to have his absence excused. The distinction between excused and unexcused absences seemed to be strictly enforced. Another form of absentee behavior examined was single-day absenteeism. Here we wanted to see if there was a propensity to take single days off versus longer periods of time. We examined other ways to characterize distributions of absenteeism behavior (e.g., single day excused) and found no differences from the four indices presented in the tables. Other reasons for lost time (such as strikes) affected the whole work force and were excluded from this analysis since they were not related to the miner's individual decision to come to work.

The indices of absenteeism used in this analysis included: nonaccident absences, unexcused absences, excused absences, and single-day absences. These indices were calculated on a weekly basis in the form of a rate:

$$\text{The absenteeism rate} = \frac{\text{number of absences}}{\begin{matrix} 5 - \text{strikes} \\ \text{and holidays} \end{matrix} \times \begin{matrix} \text{number of} \\ \text{men in the} \\ \text{section} \end{matrix}}$$

The number of men in the section represents the potential maximum crew size. For example, the size of the experimental crew during the baseline period was six, during the experimental periods it was eight. For both control sections the size was six across the first 3 time periods and eight after the experiment went minewide. All 4 time periods—baseline plus 3 experimental periods—were used in this analysis.

The analysis of absenteeism followed three stages. First, we developed a model of absenteeism for each of the sections following the same procedure as discussed in the economic section. The purpose was to separate out the effect of the intervention from other variables that affected absenteeism. Our model included some of the variables in the production function, such as roof and runway conditions and type of mining, as possible predictors of absenteeism. We also introduced other uncontrollable variables to represent the start of hunting and fishing season, since Rushton is in a rural area where these activities are important. Our analysis of this model (absenteeism = coal and boney, roof condition, runway condition, type of mining, hunting season, fishing season) indicated very few significant predictors of absenteeism. The f statistics for the total model for each of the six predictors over several different absenteeism indicators (nonaccident absences, single-day absences, unexcused absences, excused absences) were insignificant.

Our second strategy was to test a more comprehensive model that included the uncontrollable factors (e.g., roof conditions) as well as individual differences (e.g., age, education). The individual difference variables were considered because they have been shown to bear on absenteeism. Since our analysis is on a section basis, rather than on an individual basis, we had to put variables, such as average age, education, and so on, in our model. That is, the individual level data had to be aggregated to the section level. Results from this analysis show few, if any, significant results. For example, out of 30 different models (6 sections; 5 indicators) the f statistic for only one model was significant. The general findings suggest that we are not able to specify a model that predicts absenteeism and that could have been (as in the economic analysis) used to control nonexperimental factors. The failure to develop an adequate model is partially explained by skewed distribution of the absenteeism variable. Also, our data files were set up by section on a weekly basis (i.e., all the uncontrollable variables were measured weekly), thus we lost information on our individual level variables (e.g., age), which were aggregated for the whole section. We had to use average age per section, rather than relate differences in age to individual differences in absenteeism.

Given these limitations we adopted a third analysis strategy: to examine rates of absenteeism across sections. The statistical test was an analysis-of-variance design using regression analysis.

Table 15.1.   Mean Absenteeism Rate by Section (Unadjusted)

	1/73–11/73	12/73–11/74	12/74–8/75	9/75–12/76
Experimental				
Nonaccident	0.030	0.032	0.047	0.056
Unexcused	0.010	0.012	0.014	0.025
Excused	0.012	0.013	0.027	0.031
Single day	0.026	0.023	0.024	0.049
Control N				
Nonaccident	0.020	0.033	0.027	0.069
Unexcused	0.006	0.013	0.009	0.023
Excused	0.009	0.011	0.015	0.045
Single day	0.021	0.027	0.018	0.046
Control E				
Nonaccident	0.043	0.052	0.068	0.088
Unexcused	0.016	0.024	0.026	0.028
Excused	0.015	0.008	0.028	0.058
Single day	0.036	0.043	0.040	0.054

Results

Table 15.1 presents mean absenteeism rate by section for the four different time periods. Again the focus is on the sections since they were the major object of the experimental intervention and were comparable work areas.

Table 15.2 presents an analysis using each section as its own control, that is: Was the rate of absenteeism during the experimental periods similar to or different from the baseline (i.e., the control period)? This question was asked for each section. In Table 15.2 t values are presented where there are significant differences, $p < .05$; a positive value indicates the absenteeism rate was greater than the baseline. The data indicate that there was: (1) no decrease (or

Table 15.2.   Comparison of Absenteeism Rate to Baseline Period
(January 1973 to November 1973) within Section

	12/73–11/74	12/74–8/75	9/75–12/76
		Experimental	
Nonaccident	—	—	$t = 3.08$
Unexcused	—	—	$t = 3.54$
Excused	—	$t = 2.041$	$t = 2.70$
Single day	—	—	$t = 2.77$
		Control N	
Nonaccident	—	—	$t = 6.28$
Unexcused	—	—	$t = 4.12$
Excused	—	—	$t = 6.05$
Single day	—	—	$t = 2.89$
		Control E	
Nonaccident	—	$t = 2.188$	$t = 4.28$
Unexcused	—	—	$t = 2.35$
Excused	—	—	$t = 5.80$
Single day	—	—	$t = 2.09$

increase) in absenteeism in the experimental section, (2) no increase
(or decrease) in the control sections, and (3) an increase for all sections
across all four indicators during the last experimental period.

Table 15.3 presents an analysis of absenteeism among the South
section, using the East and North sections as controls for each of the
time periods. The t values identify whether East and North were
significantly different from South. The basic trends in these data show
that East had consistently higher absenteeism than South over all four
time periods for most of the indices, and the absenteeism rates for
South and North were similar.

One problem in this analysis is that the work force composition of
the sections may have differed between the baseline and experimental
periods. Since individual differences can affect absenteeism rates, we

Table 15.3.   Comparisons of Other Sections to Experimental
Section

	1/73–11/73		12/73–11/74		12/74–8/75		9/75–12/76	
	Control E	Control N	Control E	Control N	Control E	Control N	Control E	Control N
Nonaccident	$t = 1.98$	—	$t = 2.43$	—	$t = 2.64$	$t = 2.50$	$t = 2.45$	—
Unexcused	$t = 2.03$	—	$t = 2.76$	—	$t = 2.97$	—	—	—
Excused	—	—	—	—	—	—	$t = 2.61$	—
Single day	—	—	$t = 2.97$	—	$t = 3.79$	—	—	—

Note: $t = 1.98$ means that the absentee rate in Control E is significantly greater than in South for that time period, $p < .05$. No entry means there are no significant differences between South and the control section.

developed an adjusted baseline work force composition by the work location of people at the beginning of the first experimental period. That is, if a person was in South in the first experimental period, we created a data set that put that person in South during the baseline. Analysis of the adjusted data set did not change the results reported for absenteeism.

Summary

The data show that absenteeism rates for the experimental section did not decrease and in the third experimental period (September 1975 to December 1976) increased, following the pattern of the other sections. Compared to the other sections, East had higher rates across all time periods. South rates were similar to the North rates across all periods. These results hold consistently across all four indicators.

The basic question is whether the experimental intervention had an effect on absenteeism. No evidence supports the hypothesis that the experiment, at least during the first two experimental periods, lowered absenteeism.

There are a number of possible reasons why the absenteeism rates did not change in the experimental section. First, it could be said that since the rates were relatively low, there was no room to reduce them in some significant way; that is, zero absenteeism was unlikely, given the nature of the working conditions and the individualistic nature of the miners. Perhaps the absenteeism rates in the South section were close to their lowest potential level. This explanation might have some validity for the first two experimental periods but not for the fourth period (September 1975 to December 1976) where the rates increased.

A second explanation is that although the men in the first experimental section accepted greater responsibility, the focus of this responsibility was more on decisions about mining or safety conditions than on coming to work. A review of the section meetings shows that data on absenteeism were presented by the research team. Yet there is no evidence that the miners defined absenteeism as a problem nor did they propose some course of action. This is the critical issue. Reduction in absenteeism comes about not simply because the men like the QOW program or assume new responsibilities, but only when the group defines absenteeism as a problem and identifies paths to solve that problem.

Absenteeism was discussed, primarily in the third experimental period, when the climate was in an adversary, rather than a problem-solving mode. Some solutions were proposed (union officials talked to chronic absentee individuals and a research team member interviewed these individuals), but there was little follow-through. Our point is that absenteeism had not been identified as a joint problem for labor and management, and there was no systematic program developed to deal with absenteeism.

The third explanation concerns why absenteeism increased in period 4, rather than why it did not decrease. In period 4 (the third experimental period) we found deterioration in the miners' identification with the QOW project and an increasing level of tension between labor and management. Both these conditions worked against job attachment and for increased absenteeism. Some of the increases might be attributed to the 1974 contract, which permitted more legitimate days off (i.e., excused absences). If the new contract had an effect, there would be an increase only in the excused category. But this is not the case. Also, if the contract explained changes in absenteeism, the effects should appear in period 3 (December 1974 to August 1975) as well as in period 4 (September 1975 to December 1976).

Turnover

As previously mentioned, there is very little turnover at Rushton. In the first experimental section, there was one voluntary quit in the baseline and no quits in the next three periods. In East there was only one quit and none in North. For the six other people who left the experimental section from January 1973 to December 1976, one retired, two left because of health problems, and three moved to better jobs (e.g., foreman). In East four people left due to sickness, accidents (i.e., one fatality), or retirement. In the North section only one person left due to an accident. In conclusion, there was very little turnover, voluntary or involuntary, before the experiment, and little room, if any, for the experimental intervention to change turnover rates. The most basic conclusion is that the experiment did not affect job turnover.

THE UNION

The explicit goal of the union in participating in the Rushton project was to improve safety at the mine. Our analysis shows that the project had a positive impact on safety practices. Outcomes, such as improvement in earnings, greater job satisfaction, and greater job skills were explicit goals in the original Rushton document that were also supported by the union.

The following analysis of the union's implicit goals uses the same pattern as the discussion of implicit goals for management. Like the company, the union is an organization that must maintain itself internally and externally if it is to survive.

Internal Consequences

1. The training aspect of the QOW project at Rushton placed the union officers in an environment for learning presentation and problem-solving skills. The steering committees and section conferences were important training grounds for the union leaders. Another aspect of the project was participation in regional QOW conferences. This activity required union officers to make presentations and answer questions in large public gatherings. These were unique experiences for practical leadership training that occurred only because of the project.

2. The project also provided opportunities for upward movement. One of the union officers who played a major role in the QOW project ran for a district office. Knowing this individual, I would guess that he would have tried to move up in the union hierarchy whether there was a program or not. But the program provided him special training opportunities. It also made this individual visible at the international

and district level. For example, he was selected by the international to work on one of the UMWA convention committees. This recognition would not have occurred without the QOW program. The basic point is that the QOW project facilitated the movement of miners to higher positions within the union hierarchy.

1. The program also exacted certain costs within the union. The introduction of a QOW labor-management committee substantially increased the frequency of interaction between labor leaders and management. Typically the meetings were held at a local motel where steaks were the usual luncheon fare. These activities fostered conflict between the union leadership and their constituency. The frequent association between management and union officers outside the traditional bargaining arrangement raised feelings of distrust in the union membership toward their leaders. One of the union officers claimed he lost a subsequent election because of his association with the program. We have found no evidence to substantiate that claim, but the conflict or tension between leaders and members was real.

2. The program also created conflict within the union membership by placing union members against their brothers. The program introduced change in one pilot section. This led to differences in pay and resources among the sections. Men were receiving different pay for doing the same work. These differences were further aggravated when the second experimental section was put on line. The inequities created by the experiment within the work force were visible and caused tension within the union.

3. Another unanticipated consequence was that the program created challenges to the influence-power structure of the union by increasing the level of cohesiveness within the experimental section. When votes relevant to QOW issues occurred at the local union hall, this group appeared en masse; in the past most of these men had not attended meetings. (The rate of participation in regular union affairs was not affected by the experiment.) The point is not that this emerging power structure was good or bad, but that it represented a challenge to the existing power structure, and thus, a potential source of conflict.

External Consequences

1. The project also had unexpected consequences on the union's relations with outside groups, such as the international. Most of the activity at Rushton occurred at the local union level, while the final legitimation came from the international. This poses an interesting dilemma. At the local level, union and management have a mandate to innovate. Yet the international may view the local QOW project as only experimental and temporary (quite independent of the success of the project), especially if the new labor-management innovations are considered beyond the boundaries of future collective-bargaining agreements. Another dilemma is that the local union officers need expertise to play out their role in QOW meetings. Gain sharing is an example of a topic that requires outside expertise. A project such as Rushton, however, was only one of many issues facing the international. Often the international did not provide expert services when they were needed. Both dilemmas, especially the second, were a source of conflict between the local and international. The local union officers continually complained about the lack of international support. Their complaints seem justified since the international rarely contributed to the project. This conflict or tension is directly attributable to the program. A similar situation characterized the district-local relationship, but the source of tension was modest compared to the international-local relationship.

2. In Chapter 14 we reviewed the data on union-company relations, primarily from the company point of view. In this section we shall interpret the results from the union perspective. The program did not affect the frequency, duration, or content of grievances, but union leaders felt that the process of working through grievances was easier during the periods of the experiment prior to the vote. The number of AW grievances, of course, substantially increased because of the program. This represented both a benefit and a cost. The benefit was that resolving the grievances provided an opportunity to test out new problem-solving skills, since the steering committee's orientation was more problem-solving than bargaining. The cost was that the AW grievances were sources of conflict, so the level of tension between labor and management increased. We have argued that the absence of strikes was partly attributable to the QOW arrangements. In general, we also feel that the absence of strikes (given that the right to strike was available) was beneficial to the union in terms of minimizing income loss. Some might argue that strikes can be functional in enhancing the union's status or bargaining position relative to management. But the situation at Rushton from December 1973 to August 1975 did not seem to call for that kind of behavior. The union during that period had been reasonably successful in gaining benefits for its members within the scope of the QOW project. Specifically, the key benefit to the union was that the program increased the union's leverage or power over management. This occurred because the union officers realized the president wanted the program to go, and they traded on this point to extract concessions. Also, the program permitted them to deal directly with the president, rather than with the superintendent who was more experienced in bargaining with the union and more willing to take a hard line.

CONCLUSION

I have enumerated some of the major and unintended consequences that accrued to Rushton and to the union. Some of these consequences were beneficial in terms of enhancing internal and external adaptability; some of the consequences were costs to these two organizations. In this chapter the best we can do is to identify these costs and benefits. We cannot objectively say that increased conflict between union leaders and their constituencies cost less than the benefit of getting more control over management, or that the increased level of training experienced by upper level managers counterbalanced the strains brought about by the change. It is up to the reader to introduce his or her weighting scheme. In Chapter 16 we shall look at the tangible costs and benefits of the program. A procedure for estimating some of the intangible benefits will also be discussed.

CHAPTER SIXTEEN

Cost-Benefit Analysis

This chapter presents a cost-benefit analysis of the Rushton QOW project. Cost-benefit analysis techniques have not generally been used by people involved in organizational intervention and change. This chapter, therefore, is a significant innovation in the evaluation of organizational interventions. A principal value of cost-benefit analysis is that it forces one to think through the costs and benefits of a program, that is, this type of analysis focuses on the incremental flow of costs and benefits caused by the experimental intervention. Much of our analysis thus far has concerned single dimensions, such as productivity or safety. An advantage of cost-benefit analysis is that it forces us to consider multiple dimensions. Too often behavioral scientists consider a program's relative benefits without considering carefully the relation of those benefits to the program's costs. In this chapter we shall examine the costs of setting up the Rushton QOW project, as well as the costs of operating the project.

Our perspective in this analysis is to identify the flow of the principal benefits and costs in order to understand the impact of the project. The final relationship between net present value of benefits and costs is, therefore, *not* the critical issue. Throughout this book we have stressed that the Rushton project was truly an experiment into uncharted areas. The results of the cost-benefit analysis for Rushton should not (although I fear it will) be used to judge whether a project like Rushton should be undertaken. Rushton is one of the first in a series of experiments. We need to review the costs and benefits of the entire series before we can make any judgments about the continuation of QOW projects.

CONCEPTUAL ISSUES

Here we shall review decisions that were made in the process of the cost-benefit analysis and that determine the final figures.

1. Level of analysis. In this cost-benefit analysis the company is the unit of analysis; that is, we shall determine the costs and benefits from the point of view of the owners of Rushton. This level of analysis is used for these reasons: (1) The focus of the project was on changing outcomes at the firm level. The company, therefore, was the relevant unit of analysis; (2) A cost-benefit analysis at the firm level provides information to critical decision makers in other firms. At the present time the decision to undertake a QOW experiment is made at the company, rather than government level; company decision makers need to know the potential benefits and costs of a QOW project to their organization. A societal level of analysis, for example, would not be relevant to that decision-making perspective. If we were analyzing a national program of QOW projects, the societal level might be the appropriate unit of analysis.

While the firm is the appropriate level of analysis, the nature of the experimental intervention creates some problems in assessing costs and benefits. At Rushton there was no single mine-wide intervention. All the changes were introduced at the section level and at different times in different forms. This presented the problem of using either the first experimental section for the cost-benefit analysis or aggregating the costs and benefits of each section to arrive at some mine-wide figure. The former was inappropriate since the plan called for a mine-wide project, but the latter approach combines different time periods and interventions.

We resolved the problem of determining the costs and benefits mine-wide, although the interventions were conducted at the section level, by using the first experimental section as the prototype of the intervention. All the other sections were treated as if they had the same costs and benefits as the first experimental section. This permitted the most optimistic statement of the relevant benefits and the most realistic statement of the costs necessary to achieve those benefits. Following this rule, if a specific set of costs were necessary to maintain or operate the first experimental section, then four times that number was the operating cost for the whole mine, using the four sections as our definition of a mine-wide program. Clearly, the multiple of four was not always the appropriate way to identify costs and benefits minewide. In some cases economies of scale appear, for example, in the area of investment costs (those costs incurred when setting up the project). Here we estimated the investment costs from the actual costs incurred in setting up the QOW program minewide.

2. Determination of Costs. The principle of opportunity costs was used to determine the costs of activities generated by the experiment. The opportunity costs for a particular activity refer to the highest foregone costs of performing that activity. To illustrate the principle, let us examine the costs of participation in QOW meetings, a major cost item in the Rushton project. One participant in the meetings was the outside research team which received a daily consulting fee. Should this fee be charged to the project? Applying the opportunity-cost idea, if the firm did not hold the meeting (i.e., there was no experiment), the fee paid to the consultant could have been used for other purposes. The opportunity cost is then the amount of the fee and should be considered a cost of the experiment.

Another example, also using the opportunity-cost principle, leads us to a different decision. The superintendent of the mine also attended the QOW meetings. The superintendent is paid an annual salary from which we could derive a daily rate. It is clear, however, that his daily wage is not tied to any specific activities. The superintendent performs a variety of tasks of varying importance in assuring effective operation of the mine. One would expect that an effective superintendent would allocate his time across tasks according to their relative importance. While his absence for a year might well result in losses far in excess of his salary, his absence for brief periods of time need have no noticeable effect on productivity because relatively inconsequential tasks go undone. It is our judgment that this is an accurate characterization of the supervisor's job at Rushton. Thus, the opportunity cost of his time (that is, the loss in production due to his attendance at QOW meetings) is quite small, and we accordingly find the daily wage an inappropriate measure of the value of the supervisor's time. Given the evidence of a high degree of slack within the job and within the jobs necessary to manage the mine, we are arguing that the foregone activity (that which he would do if he were not at the meeting) is *not* equivalent to his wage for that day. More specifically we are arguing that the opportunity cost is zero and we therefore do not cost the experiment for the superintendent's participation in the meeting.

The opportunity-cost rule requires: (1) identifying an activity that is directly related to the experimental induction and (2) determining the economic value of the foregone activity. The source of funds is not critical in using this rule: whether the government or the company pays for an experimental activity is not important. What is critical is the opportunity cost of the experimental activity.

3. Types of Costs. There are two general types of costs included in this analysis—investment costs and operating costs. Investment costs represent the initial outlay required to set up an experimental section. At Rushton most of these costs were derived from the many meetings used to set up the project. The six-day training meetings for the miners generated a cost for all four sections, as did the foremen's meetings, which were set up to help the foreman learn his new role.

Operating costs represent the routine expenses necessary to maintain the potential benefits from the experiment. This would also include the costs of certain meetings. For example, the Rushton experiment was structured on labor-management problem-solving meetings; therefore, these meetings were necessary to maintain the project over time. Steering committees, joint labor-management committees, section conferences, and management meetings continued over the life of the project, but at a rate considerably less than occurred in setting up the project. Because of this factor, we considered the first year's meetings as investment costs and subsequent meetings as operating costs. The major portion of operating costs, however, did not come from meetings. The program changed the wage structure and the size of the crews.

4. Valuation of Foregone Production. Thus far we have reviewed the principle for costing and the types of costs. Another important issue in the determination of costs was how to deal with foregone production. The design of the Rushton experiment included training meetings and section conferences which met for the entire work day and precluded any production. The question was how to value this lost production.

The opportunity-cost principle provides a solution to this problem, namely, that the foregone benefit of production is equal to the revenue from production less the royalty to the landowner. This result is based on the following rationale: If coal is not produced one day, it is there the next to be recovered. Thus, the royalty to the landowner is not lost and will be paid when the coal is produced. However, the costs of overhead are paid whether the coal is mined or not. Similarly, wages are being paid for meeting attendance, but no production is occurring. To recover the lost coal in the future, someone will have to be "hired" and overhead costs will have to be paid. Therefore, in any meeting directly related to the experiment in which the section was completely closed for production, we used revenue per unit less royalty to the company as the value of the foregone production.

Other meetings related to the experiment that required participation from a few individuals in each work area (e.g., steering committee) lasted for a whole day, others lasted only a few hours (joint labor-management meetings). Applying the preceding argument, we determined the loss in production incurred due to the absence of these individuals (see Chapter 11) and considered it a cost of the meetings. These meetings did not close down a section, but production can be affected when the crew size is reduced. Thus, the cost of individuals attending meetings was the value of the additional production that would have been achieved if they had remained at work in the section.

5. Determination and Type of Benefits. The primary rule in the determination of benefits was to ascertain whether the experimental intervention led to improvements in the principal goals of the Rushton QOW project. Benefits in this analysis are either tangible or intangible. The most obvious tangible benefit is productivity. An increase in productivity would be classified as a tangible benefit. A corollary variable would be a reduction in downtime. For example, if the men planned their work better and this, in turn, increased the absolute amount of time in production, then the increased coal produced would be valued as a benefit. The valuation of increases in production proceeds in the same way as the valuation of lost production discussed above, that is, we use the increase in revenue less the royalty to the landowner as the value of added production.

Improvements in safety also can be treated as benefits. The hard safety indicators, such as accidents, had very low frequencies, and there was, therefore, little variation among sections. At the same time there was evidence that safety practices did improve. Since no direct dollar value was assigned to these practices, we classified safety as an intangible benefit and developed a special procedure to evaluate its worth (see pp. 297-300).

Another goal of the project was to increase job skills; the data suggest that this did occur. For evaluation, however, this benefit could be treated either as a tangible or an intangible benefit. If it led to changes in productivity, it would be an indirect benefit with increased skill leading to increased productivity. Such an increase in productivity would be counted as a tangible benefit of the increased skill level. But if it were seen as something valuable in itself, it could be classified as an intangible benefit, that is, holding its effect on productivity constant—a better educated work force would be more flexible and adaptable and perhaps viewed as more valuable by a mine manager. Since we found no evidence in any of our data supporting the impact of increased job skills on short-run productivity and since the increased job skills may enhance organizational adaptability, we classified it as an intangible benefit. Whether managers would actually place a value on job skills as an intangible benefit was to be subjected to empirical verification.

In our discussion of effectiveness we noted the implicit goals in the

Rushton project. Better communication within the firm and better relationships with outside organizations (e.g., regulatory agencies) could be classified as intangible benefits. Although these outcomes are important, we have not included them in our analysis for two reasons: (1) the method we developed to measure intangible benefits can only deal with a small number of intangible factors and (2) we think safety, job skills, and attitudes are the most important factors and should be valued.

6. Other Issues. A cost-benefit analysis needs to specify the time stream for the flow of benefits and costs. Although the determination of this period is somewhat arbitrary, we have chosen the remaining life of this mine, which is 15 years. We expect the costs and benefits to flow for that period once the intervention is intact, assuming continuing effort to maintain the effectiveness of the intervention. We discuss below the procedure for projecting the costs of this continuing effort.

Another issue is the discount rate to be used to determine the present value of the costs and benefits. Since Rushton has a special financial relationship with its owner, the utility company, it is hard to get a traditional return-on-investment indicator. We have initially selected the mine's borrowing rate as one discount rate. However, sensitivity analysis will be conducted with other rates to determine the character of the net present value of costs and benefits.

METHODOLOGY

As we have indicated, four sets of variables must be measured in conducting the benefit-cost analysis. They are the costs of introducing the experiment (investment costs), the costs of continuing the experiment once the intervention was completed (operating costs), and the benefits (both tangible and intangible) from the intervention. These variables must be measured for each year from the start up of the experiment to the termination of all benefits and costs of the experiment. We used the remaining 15-year life of the Rushton mine as the period over which the benefits and costs would accrue. After obtaining the costs and benefits for each year, we expressed them in present value terms, using our chosen interest rate. The present value is simply the sum of money which (if received now) would, with accrued interest, be sufficient to pay all costs over the duration of the project and pay exactly the stream of benefits estimated for the project.

Investment Costs

The costs of introducing the experiment include all nonrecurring costs of introducing the mine-wide intervention. Included in this category are steering committee meetings, foremen meetings, joint labor-management committee meetings, section conferences, training meetings, costs of the research team, and so on. For this category we used the actual costs of setting up the mine-wide program from the four sections at Rushton. Meetings such as section conferences or steering committee meetings were considered part of investment costs for the first year.

Operating Costs

The costs of continuing the experiment included the costs of increased crew size and increased wages and other expenses needed to maintain the effectiveness of the intervention.

In measuring the costs of increased crew size, it was necessary to correct for any reduction of inside general workers or mechanics that occurred because of the larger crew size. Our procedure for determining the amount of this reduction was as follows: We determined from past records the average number of inside general workers or mechanics assigned per section prior to the experiment. This figure was subtracted from the six additional men (two for each crew) permanently added to the section because of the experiment. Since additional specialists (i.e., skilled inside general workers) were assigned to the sections over and above the six workers after the experiment was underway, these individuals were included as additional inside general costs.

It was difficult to make a precise estimate of the number of additional crew members because there was no information in the baseline. It was also difficult to get mine personnel continually to report the assignment of extra men during the experiment. To deal with this issue we analyzed the costs generated by the additional men in terms of the best (lowest cost) and worst estimates. We also had the superintendent independently estimate the number of additional inside general workers hired because of the experiment. His estimate is within the range of our other estimates.

To cost out this category we reflected the absolute increased wage costs of the additional men. Since miners in the experimental sections received top wages, however, it was also necessary to add on the differential wage cost (i.e., crew costs at top wage minus crew costs without the experiment).

Other major operating costs included the research team (fees and travel) and meeting costs (section conferences, steering committee). The costs attributed to lost production were determined by examining the effect of AW downtime in the production function. That is, the estimated production with and without the downtime indicates the "cost" of the program due to the value of lost production.

In computing the expense required to maintain the effectiveness of the experiment, we took the South section as representative. We used the costs in South to generate the costs in the other work areas. Also in developing these operating costs it was clear that they might change over time. Therefore, we adopted the following rule: The actual costs for South from 1974 through 1977 were considered as representative of the results for the first three years. Costs in 1977, which were lower than in the preceding experimental years, were used to represent the costs over the remaining life of the experiment. These results were multiplied by four to obtain mine-wide costs. We used the sections as the focus of the cost-benefit analysis since they were the primary object of the experiment, and it was possible to trace both costs and benefits to these work units.

Benefits

The experiment had two types of benefits: (1) the value of increased production resulting from the experiment and (2) the value of intangible benefits.

Production Benefits. Chapter 11 contains a presentation of the procedures we used in determining whether an increase in productivity occurred. To do this, we used the estimated production function for the control section to predict how much output would have been achieved without the experiment with the resources and physical conditions encountered in the experimental section. This amount is deducted from the actual production in the experimental section to determine the change in productivity.

A difference in production arising from the experiment can be the consequence of an increase either in productivity or in the use of resources. An increase in productivity simply means that more output is achieved with a given level of resources. With an increase in resources, such as the permanent addition of two men to the section, production would be expected to increase even if no increase in productivity occurred. Such an increase in the use of resources might be warranted, even in the absence of a change in productivity, since the added production might generate sufficient revenue to more than pay the costs of expanding the use of resources. It is important, then, to examine the effect of increasing resources in the form of additional crew members. At the same time it is important to remember that the change in crew size was only one part of a total intervention. The effect of crew size must be interpreted within the context of the total change effort.

To estimate the effect of changing crew size, we used the production function for the control section and predicted output both with the standard-size crew and the experimental-size crew. The difference in these two amounts was an estimate of the effect of expanding crew size. This analysis also permits identifying the effect of the experiment on productivity independent of crew size. The sum of the two gives the total effect of the experiment on production.

We used South from 1974 through 1977 as representative of the production results that the experiment would yield during the first three years of a section. We used South 1977 as representative of the steady state of production changes achievable over the remaining life of the experiment. These results were then multiplied by four to get the mine-wide equivalent benefits of the experiment. South was selected as the prototype section because the most comprehensive form of the intervention was introduced in that section and we believe future QOW experiments in mining would adopt those experimental practices.

The valuation of the increased output was obtained by deducting the landowner's royalty from revenue per ton produced. In principle, revenue per ton should equal the price of unprocessed coal at the mouth of the mine. However, the Rushton mine is owned by an electrical utility, and revenue per ton is set equal to average cost per ton produced. We have taken this average cost per ton as representative of the market price that the utility would pay for coal.

Intangible Benefits. A problem in any cost-benefit analysis is dealing with costs and benefits that are not easily reducible to some monetary form. In the preceding discussion we concentrated on those consequences of the QOW program that were easily translatable into dollars and cents. This approach has obvious limitations since it leaves out a set of outcomes that are an important part of the evaluation of the benefits and costs of a QOW project. To deal with these problems we have developed a technique that permits assigning monetary values to outcomes that are not easily reducible to a dollar form.

The objectives of the Rushton project included greater productivity, earnings, job satisfaction, job flexibility, and safety. The first two objectives can be analyzed in dollar terms, but the other three cannot. Some aspects of safety behavior, such as accidents, can be costed; the major safety changes at Rushton, however, were in greater adherence to safety practices and standards—behavior important for the firm, but not easily translated into a monetary form. In order to expand the scope of our cost-benefit analysis, a decision-making technique was developed to generate monetary values for the objectives of job flexibility-training, job attitudes, and job safety. This technique was composed of a series of descriptions of underground coal mines. Each description included different combinations of the intangible dimensions we wanted to value. The problem for the decision maker was to determine how much he would pay for each mine. By looking at how different combinations of intangible benefits were valued, it would be possible to reduce these intangible dimensions to some monetary value. The respondents were mine managers who had some experience in the purchase of coal mines.

The decision-making task required the respondent to behave as if he were a manager in the coal mining industry faced with the problem of buying a coal mine. Much of the valuation of the mine, such as the value of equipment, buildings, and recoverable tons, had already been estimated by a mining engineer. The respondent's job was to estimate how much he would pay for three intangible factors—job flexibility-training, job attitudes, and safety practices. The specific question was how much more money, if any, would a respondent pay for these intangibles over and above the engineer's estimate? It was made clear that these intangibles were in the class of good will. *They did not have any direct effect on productivity.* Any direct effect of the three intangibles had been factored into the engineer's estimates.

The respondent was given booklets that described a series of mines that were for sale. The descriptions were identical except for variations in job flexibility-training, job attitudes, and safety. The following describes three levels of job attitudes:

1. **High:** The results from a recent attitude survey at this mine showed that the men liked their jobs, work groups, and supervisor. This mine ranks in the top 10% of all similar mines in the country in terms of positive attitudes toward the job and the company. Jobs were seen as less repetitive, the work groups more innovative, and supervisors less directive. There is a high degree of cooperation within the crew and among crews in a section. In general, the men had a good deal of enthusiasm at work. If machines were down, they would assume the responsibility themselves to find other work that had to be done.

2. Medium: The results from a recent attitude survey showed that the men were neutral (neither liking nor disliking) in their attitudes toward their job, work group, and supervisor. In comparison with other mines their attitudes toward their company, job, and supervisor seemed about in the middle (fiftieth percentile). There was about average cooperation within the crew and some attempt to coordinate activities among crews in a section. The men were neither very enthusiastic nor negative about their work.

3. Low: The results from a recent attitude survey showed that the men at this mine were negative in their attitudes toward their job, work group, and supervisor. In comparison with other mines, this mine ranks below average (thirtieth percentile) in positive attitudes toward their supervisor, job, and company. Their jobs were seen as repetitive, the work groups were not particularly innovative, and their supervisor was fairly directive. There was minimum cooperation within a crew and little attempt to coordinate activities among crews in a section. There was little enthusiasm about work. If a machine was down, the men waited for their supervisor to direct them.

Similar descriptions were generated for job flexibility-training and job safety. In developing descriptions for each level we used the state of affairs in the South section (prior to the vote) to anchor the high level. For example, if the South section had one lost time accident for a given year, the high safety-level description would state that there were only four lost-time accidents (one accident times four sections). From these three intangible dimensions, which were described in three levels, 12 descriptions of mines were generated. The descriptions included a mine high on all three dimensions; one low on all three; one high on job flexibility, but low on attitudes and safety; as well as other combinations. We decided not to generate all combinations because it would have been difficult to obtain and motivate our respondents for a period sufficient to rate them.

The respondents were high-level managers in the mining industry who were involved in decisions pertaining to the acquisition of mines. Four respondents participated in the rating task, which required 30 to 40 minutes. One of these individuals was familiar with the Rushton project.

There was a surprising convergence among the raters who agreed on about 75% of the judgments. In general, they would not pay anything over and above the mine engineer's estimate (fixed at $7 million) unless job attitudes in the mine were high. Given high positive attitudes, it was different combinations of low, medium, and high levels of job flexibility-training plus job safety that then affected the additional amount the "buyer" would pay for the mine.

The managers were willing to pay 5 to 10% over the estimated value of $7 million for the mine with high job flexibility-training, high job safety practices, and high positive work attitudes. The next combination—low job flexibility, high safety, and high positive attitudes—received 5% over the mine engineer's estimate. The only other viable combination was high flexibility and high attitudes, which received 2 to 5% over the engineer's estimate.

Since the "high-high-high" condition represented the conditions at Rushton during the peak of the experiment (prior to the vote), it was used to represent the intangible benefits of the project. The range of values attached to this condition was $350,000 to $700,000.

RESULTS

We shall now explain how the figures for the estimated annual investment costs, operating costs, and gross benefits were obtained and then discuss the estimated net benefits of the experiment.

The total investment costs for the mine-wide program were $189,100 (in 1976 dollars). As explained earlier, these costs were generated from steering committee meetings, section conferences, foremen's meetings, joint labor-management committee meetings, and training sessions; they included salaries for the consultants as well as transportation, food, and lodging expenses. The time wages of production workers were viewed as an inappropriate measure of the opportunity cost of their time. Instead, the appropriate measure was the loss in production that occurred due to their attendance at training meetings. The amount of lost production was estimated from the production function, and the simplest computational procedure was to deduct these losses from increased production when calculating benefits of the experiment. Therefore, we have incorporated these losses in calculating benefits, rather than incorporating them in investment costs. This is merely an accounting convenience and does not affect the net valuation of benefits presented later in this chapter.

Operating costs included increased wages to production workers, the wages to the extra workers permanently assigned to the experimental section, the salary of supervisory personnel hired due to the experiment, and the costs of meetings required to maintain the effectiveness of the intervention. In determining the cost of the two additional workers permanently assigned to the experimental section,

Table 16.1.   Costs of Additional Miners (1976 Dollars)

Major Category of Costs	1974	1975	1976	1977	1978–1988
Extra inside general (East as control)	249,000	251,000	251,000	251,000	251,000
Extra inside general (North as control)	130,000	131,000	131,000	131,000	131,000
Extra inside general (hired)	297,000	300,000	300,000	300,000	300,000

it was necessary to account for the reduction, if any, in the use of inside general workers and mechanics in the experimental section.

Two procedures were used to estimate the difference in the number of inside general workers before and after the experiment. The first was to determine the difference between the six additional men assigned to the section because of the experiment and the number of inside general workers who would have been assigned anyway. The latter figure was developed from the number of additional men assigned to the two control sections (East and North) in 1974 and 1975 before the vote. These were the only data available on the assignment of inside general workers; it came from a data system that we introduced, and therefore, was unavailable in the baseline. Since the control sections differed in terms of the number of men that would have been assigned regardless of the experiment, Table 16.1 presents a high and low estimate for the cost of additional workers. The costs in Table 16.1 also include extra inside general men who would have been assigned to the experimental section in addition to the six permanent crew men. The second procedure was to determine the difference in the total number of inside general workers employed by the mine before and after the change and to attribute this difference to the experiment. The results of using this procedure are reported in Table 16.1.

There was no change in the number of mechanics employed by the mine when the experiment was introduced. Since the extra workers in South would not be expected to substitute for mechanics, this result is consistent with our expectations. Therefore, no adjustment was made in the cost of mechanics to the South section.

During the course of the experiment there were additions to management in the safety and training areas. From our discussion with top management, the hiring of these individuals was in part attributed to increased work loads generated by the experiment.

Table 16.2.   Other Operating Costs[a] (1976 Dollars)

Major Category of Costs	1974	1975	1976	1977	1978–1988
Additional managerial time	1,000	5,000	6,000	6,000	6,000
Wage rate differences	40,000	16,000	16,000	16,000	16,000
External consulting	—	4,000	4,000	4,000	2,500

[a]Lost production is treated in Table 16.3.

Therefore, a portion of a man year was allocated to operating costs.

Since the experiment provided that everyone get top wage rates, the costs of the additional wages were calculated. Similarly the costs for the external consultants were included in other operating costs (see Table 16.2). Those costs related to lost production were deducted from the benefit side, as previously explained. Operating costs for 1978–1988 were estimated on the basis of what it would be required to maintain the experiment at the 1977 level, since the level of meetings and their associated costs in 1977 were expected to continue. Some level of external consulting was also considered necessary to maintain the project.

It was anticipated that benefits of the experiment might accrue in three areas. The major effect was expected to be an increase in production arising not only from increased output per unit of time that production was occurring, but also from a reduction in delays, so that production would be underway during a larger portion of the shift. It was also thought that the experiment might potentially decrease absenteeism and the use of production supplies.

When we modeled delays using regression analysis, we found that delays were related to working conditions, but that the amount of delays, after controlling for conditions, did not change with the introduction of the experiment. We concluded that the experiment did not affect delays, so that there were no benefits from this source. Likewise, when we modeled absenteeism using regression analysis, we found no significant relationship between absences and mine conditions and no significant difference in the absentee rate between the experimental and control sections. We concluded that absences were not attributable to mine conditions and that the experiment had no effect on th rate of absence, so no benefits derive from this source.

To determine whether supply costs were affected by the experiment,

Table 16.3.   Gross Benefits
   (in $000)

	Productivity Benefit	Crew-Size Benefit	Total Benefit
Control South 73			
Model 3	557[a]	1025	1582
	409[b]	787	1196
Model 4	913	2150	3063
	629	1642	2271
Control ENSENEN			
Model 3	307.6	3419	3786.6
	182	2619	2801
Model 4	(219)	3915	3696
	(269)	2290	2721

[a]The top number is discounted at 5%.
[b]The second number is discounted at 10%, using $11.568/ton.

regression analyses were conducted using data before and after the introduction of the experiment in East and North. Unfortunately data were not available on usage of supplies in South prior to the introduction of the experiment. When we tested for supply usage before and after the introduction of the experiment, no consistent differences were found. Therefore, we concluded that the experiment had no effect on supply costs.

Tangible benefits to the company of the experiment, if any, derive from changes in the quantity of coal produced. To predict coal production in the absence of the experiment two different models are used with two different control groups giving four sets of predictions. Production function models 3 and 4 were used. These models differ in the treatment of the extra men in the crew as explained in Chapter 11. The control sections used were South 73 and ENSENEN. The advantage of using South 73 as the control is that any persistent, but unmeasured, differences across sections will not affect comparisons in a given section before and after the introduction of the experiment. If such unmeasured differences are not present, then the ENSENEN predictions will be more accurate because the ENSENEN estimates are based on a larger number of observations. Since the possible importance of unmeasured differences is unknown, we present both sets of estimates. We are inclined to place greater reliance on the estimates based on South 73 since our tests in Chapter 11 for

Table 16.4.   Net Present Value
(in $000)

	Tangible Benefits			Intangible Benefits	
	High	Medium	Low	High	Low
Control South 73					
Model 3	(332)	(1378)	(2167)	700	350
Model 4	1149	102	(686)	700	350
Control ENSENEN					
Model 3	1873	826	38	700	350
Model 4	1782	735	(53)	700	350

homogeneity of the production functions across sections indicated that the function differed across sections.

The estimated gross benefits, presented in Table 16.3, are subdivided into a productivity effect and a crew-size effect using the procedure explained previously. The benefits are calculated by multiplying tons times the price (cost per ton) and then determining the present value using a 5 or 10% discount rate.

The difference in crew size for this calculation is taken to be one man per shift. While two extra men per shift were permanently assigned to the experimental section, this resulted in a reduction in the number of inside general people assigned to the section. The experimental section used an average of two less inside general men per day than East and four less than North. Therefore, we have taken an average of three men per day or one man per shift as the reduction in inside general men used in South.

It is clear from Table 16.3 that the crew-size effect is a major source of benefits from the experimental change regardless of which model or control group is used. It should be emphasized however that the change in crew size is an integral part of the experiment and both effects need to be jointly examined.

Finally, in Table 16.4, we present the estimates of net tangible benefits of the experiment. These are broken down by model and control group with high, medium, and low estimates for each. The discount rate used in the calculations is 5%. Since the mine can borrow at the prime rate plus 2%, this figure approximates the borrowing rate of the mine after removing the effects of inflation from the prime rate. The estimated intangible benefits are also included.

The divergence among the benefit estimates in Table 16.4 reflects several factors. First, it is difficult to obtain precise estimates of the effects of the experiment on production. The production function does not fit the data perfectly because of both the effects of unmeasured variables and the errors of measurement in observed variables. These factors are present in any statistical analysis. The second reason for divergence among the benefit estimates is that relatively small changes in output generate large changes in revenue. For example, a 5% increase in output across four sections is roughly 800 tons per week. A change of this magnitude results in an increase in revenues over the life of the mine that amounts to a present value at a 5% interest rate of approximately $4 million. An error as small as 5% reflects a very accurate prediction. In fact, our standard error estimates (reported in Chapter 11) with South 73 as a control indicate that a prediction error as large as 5% would occur an average of two-thirds of the time. Therefore, none of the estimated differences reported in Table 16.4 can be considered statistically significant because they are due primarily to predicted gains in output that are not statistically significant.

Third, in Table 16.1 it was demonstrated that the costs of the additional inside general laborers was substantial and also subject to variation. The variation was caused by the difficulty in making a precise estimate of the additional number of men added to the experimental section. Therefore, this variation must be reflected in net present value estimates. Under tangible benefits, the high, medium, and low categories in Table 16.4 represent, respectively, the low, average, and highest estimate of the additional labor costs presented in Table 16.1. That is, low additional labor costs yielded high tangible benefits, and so on.

The intangible benefits are estimated from our decision-making instrument discussed earlier in this chapter. The range of intangible benefits estimated for a mine that exhibited the characteristics of the South section prior to the vote was $350,000 to $700,000. These figures are presented in Table 16.4 separately from the tangible benefits.

We have argued previously that South 73 was the most reliable comparison group. Model 4 is preferable to model 3, in that it more accurately reflects the contribution of extra men to the experimental section. Model 3 says average productivity per man does not change as additional crew members are added. Model 4 permits the productivity of the additional crew members to vary. If we use South 73 as a control, we find positive net present values for the high and medium conditions in Model 4. The low condition has a negative net present value. Looking across all models and all conditions, the trend is positive. If we added in the intangible benefits (using the high estimate), the results would be more positive.

DISCUSSION

The purpose of this chapter is to assess the costs and benefits of the Rushton QOW project. Table 16.4 indicates a positive net effect, but with a good deal of variability. Slight changes in predicted output from the control models could eliminate all the benefits. Still, over all, our best estimate is that the effects are positive.

The real purpose of this analysis is not to draw out the bottom-line assessment. Rather it is to understand the effect of the experiment on the flow of costs and benefits it generated. For example, in the productivity analysis we demonstrated that changing crew size—an important part of the experimental intervention—had an effect on production levels. In examining operating costs, it also appears that the additional inside general workers were a large item. Our view is that the 1973 decision concerning adding two crew members should have paid more attention to the relationships among crew size, costs, and productivity.

Much has been made of the decision to pay top wage rates to the miners. Although that decision was congruent with asking the men to learn multiple jobs and to assume more responsibilities, some observers of the Rushton project perceived the decision to be quite expensive. However, the value of this type of analysis is that it puts that decision in perspective. Relative to other expenses, the additional wage costs were not substantial.

Another issue generated by this analysis concerns estimates of intangible benefits. In many cost-benefit analyses, the researchers focus on the measurable outcomes and briefly comment on the intangibles. In this analysis we propose that the intangible benefits are important and that they can be translated into dollar estimates. Our experience is that the judges were reasonably consistent in what combinations of benefits were valuable and what combinations were not.

We have argued that the value of the cost-benefit analysis is that it identifies the different flows of benefits and costs that relate to the design of the Rushton project. The validity of this analysis, however, rests on the several assumptions that have guided it. First, one important assumption is that our estimated production functions are valid. We have spent a tremendous amount of time on these estimates and feel that they are good statements about the production process at Rushton, with Model 4 being a reasonable theoretical model. Second, the use of control groups is critical to cost-benefit analysis. Our best judgment, through extensive analyses, is to use South 73 and ENSE-NEN. A review across all the models and controls in Table 16.4 indicates a trend toward positive benefits. Third, the estimate of extra men is an important part of the cost-benefit analysis. This estimate eludes precise estimation because the necessary information was not collected in the baseline. We have treated the issue by identifying a range of acceptable estimates.

Instead of using estimates of the costs and benefits of each section, we assumed that South could function as a prototype of the other sections. It could be argued that we should not have used the best section. Our belief, however, is that if another QOW experiment were conducted in a coal mine, it would introduce a design parallel to that of the South section versus that of any other section at Rushton. Also, we wanted to identify a flow of costs and benefits that might be representative for other QOW projects in mining.

Other assumptions underlying our analysis could be challenged, but it is unclear that this would affect our conclusion. For example, we might have used a shorter project life time. However, if we had used 10 instead of 15 years, the net effect would have been similar. It is also possible that the consultants' fees should not have been carried through the fifteenth year. We felt that for the program to survive, however, some external help was necessary. Also, the amount we included for this operating cost was small and would not substantially affect the figures in Table 16.4. Another issue concerns whether we should have used cost per ton (as a measure of price), rather than actual market price. Again this decision represented our best judgment of what a benefit flow meant at Rushton (since this company did not sell its coal on the market and used cost per ton as its price).

We can conclude with the following observation: This analysis is the first, or one of the first, cost-benefit examinations of a quality of work experiment. It is valuable in that it provides additional information on evaluating the Rushton project. It is *not* meant to represent the final answer. We never expected that there would be some precise estimate that would convince managers to initiate (or not to initiate) other QOW experiments. In retrospect, if we had doubled our investment in the evaluation by building new data systems or doing more analyses, our estimates would probably not be very different from what we have reported. It is important to remember that companies are not generating data systems for QOW evaluations. With certain modifications we take the data that is available. Then we develop theoretical models and use statistical techniques, where appropriate, to formulate reasonable estimates. We did this in the Rushton case, and our best judgment is that the experiment probably had a small positive effect.

PART FOUR

ANALYSIS OF ORGANIZATIONAL CHANGE

IN THIS CONCLUDING SECTION IT IS IMPORTANT to step back and take a broader view of the Rushton experiment. Basically we want to move from what happened to why it happened. This was dealt with briefly in the results chapters. Here we want to elaborate on the question of why certain changes occurred, while others did not, and identify some lessons learned from the Rushton experience. First, we shall review why changes did or did not occur, present an analysis of the diffusion of the experiment to the whole mine, and then highlight those aspects of the Rushton experience that might be applicable to other organizational settings.

Clearly there were changes at Rushton that were traceable to the experimental intervention. These changes occurred in the first experimental section during the period from December 1973 to August 1975. Why did these changes occur? What factors contributed to these changes? Can any principles be generalized to other settings?

CHAPTER SEVENTEEN

Institutionalizing and Sustaining Change

To understand why change occurred at Rushton and what factors contributed to that change we need an analytic framework to guide our analysis.

KEY VARIABLES

Three classes of variables are important to understanding the Rushton experience:

1. The changes in work behavior or "new forms of work behavior" themselves.

2. The psychological processes that determine whether the new behaviors will be adopted.

3. The antecedent conditions that change the nature of the psychological processes.

I shall examine each of these concepts and then move toward describing their interrelationship. Our objective is to develop a framework that will assist in explaining why change occurs in experimental interventions such as QOW projects.

New Forms of Work Behavior

The term "new forms of work behavior" refers to a behavior that became institutionalized after the experimental intervention and whose origin can be traced directly to the intervention. An institutionalized behavior is one that persists over time without some form of direct and/or immediate external control. Let us assume we wanted to institutionalize intershift communication behavior: we wanted the miners between shifts to exchange information that would enhance the technical coordination of the work flow. If a miner talked with his counterpart between shifts because he was under surveillance from his boss (direct control) or because he was getting paid each time he talked (immediate control), his behavior might persist over time, but we would not consider it institutionalized because it occurred solely through a direct and immediate external control. New forms of behavior, following our definition of institutionalization, occur when the behavior is rewarding in its own right and/or is normally sanctioned by some relevant group. If intershift behavior persisted because the miners felt communication between shifts helped them in their jobs or because their work group expected that behavior to be performed, we would label that behavior as institutionalized or as a new form of work behavior.

Psychological Processes

Psychological processes refer to those psychological factors that influence whether a worker decided to adopt a new behavior and to continue that behavior. Basic to any experimental intervention is whether the subject of the change will adopt and experiment with the proposed behavior. Once the adoption decision occurs, the individual, through various forms of feedback and learning, decides to continue or to reject the new work behavior. The miner then is treated here as a decision-maker who can choose, for example, to work in ways that are safer than others or to communicate with his counterparts during shift interchange. Why does he make this choice? What factors affect this decision?

One factor that bears on his choice is his perception of his own ability to perform a new behavior. This requires matching his own estimate of his capabilities with the demands of the task. The subjective judgment that he is capable of performing the new behavior seems to be a necessary condition for engaging in that behavior. It is unlikely that a miner will adopt a new mining practice if he does not understand how to do the new behavior or if he does not feel able to perform that behavior. Another factor is the miner's perception of whether adopting the new behavior (e.g., communicating between crews) will lead to desirable outcomes (e.g., recognition from peers). A related factor is the relationship between the new behavior and undesirable outcomes, for example, adopting a new mining practice might lead to more difficult work, which would be labeled as undesirable. Our assumption is that for the new behavior to occur its net benefits must be seen as more attractive than the net benefits from the current behavior. We also acknowledge that attractiveness or undesirability of these benefits and costs varies across individuals.

This picture of the miner as a decision maker is consistent with a variety of current theories of work behavior (Mitchell, 1974). We are proposing these factors only as a way of thinking about how the change process occurs. Our picture is not one of the rational decision maker cranking out rational choices from perfect information and a known preference function. Rather we see the decision-making processes occuring in the context of limited rationality. The decision to communicate between shifts or to wear safety glasses occurs in the context of limited information, limited preferences, and a decision role using a satisfying, rather than an optimizing, strategy.

Antecedent Conditions

Understanding how individuals make choices is not sufficient to understanding why change occurs. In the context of an organizational experiment there are antecedent conditions that may significantly affect the psychological processes. Two particular dimensions are important. First, the intervention at Rushton was made up of a series of new structures. The training program, modification of the foreman's role, the new pay system are all examples of new structures. To understand the change process at Rushton we need to link the effects of the new structures to the factors identified as part of the individual's decision-making process. For example, to what extent do changes in the pay system or in committee structure affect such factors as perceived capability of performing a new behavior, the perception that the new behavior will lead to rewards, the perception that the new behavior will lead to costs, or the perceived net benefits of the new behavior compared to an alternative behavior? It is by tying the specific structural changes to the decision-making process that we can understand why change occurs.

The second dimension that bears on the understanding of change in the Rushton study consists of changes instituted on the work group or section level and the effects of these changes on the individual decision processes. Our thesis is that the structures (e.g., pay system, training, section conferences) and the process by which they were introduced

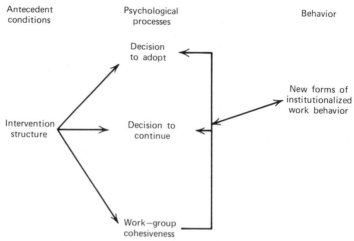

Figure 17.1 Framework for institutionalization.

have a direct effect on the nature of the work group. Changes in the work group, particularly in terms of levels of cohesiveness, in turn affect the individual decision processes. If the norms of the work group sanction job switching and the group is cohesive, the individuals will be under strong pressure to adopt job-switching behavior. In this case the behavior may be adopted quite independent of the rewards intrinsic to that behavior.

Figure 17.1 summarizes the major variables in our framework to explain change processes. The basic paradigm is that the intervention introduces new structures that directly affect the choice processes (i.e., the decision to adopt and to continue) and the nature of the work group. Changes in the work group, in turn, can modify the choice processes. Changes in the choice process lead to adopting new forms of work behavior. (See Goodman, Conlon, and Bazerman, forthcoming, for a more elaborate discussion of institutionalization.)

EXPLANATIONS

In this section we shall apply the framework to understanding why changes did occur in the Rushton experiment. The following eight points relate the intervention structure to changes in the group structure and to changes in the choice processes.

1. The formal training program, the section conferences, and the foremen's meetings substantially increased the miner's knowledge of new mining practices and safety procedures. Knowledge about safety laws is a precondition for improving safety behavior. This information also increased the miner's understanding of the work behaviors required under the autonomous work group program and thus enhanced his perceived ability to perform the behaviors.

2. Opportunities for feedback were increased. New social arrangements in the form of section conferences and mini-labor-management meetings provided constant feedback to the workers about their performance (accidents, violations, production, costs, etc.). Now the miners knew how they were doing. Previously this type of information was infrequently given to foremen. Without feedback it is difficult to change one's behavior.

3. The QOW program brought a new set of rewards to the workers. The men were given greater levels of responsibility and assumed these new levels. Greater pay was tied to taking this greater responsibility. The section conferences and other meetings provided a direct opportunity for management, union officers, and the research team to recognize and reinforce changes in the workers' behavior on such items as safety or intercrew coordination. Through job switching the men had the opportunity to develop new skills. As one miner said:

> I don't have to just run the car all the time . . . yesterday I did brattices [ventilation work]. . . . I've learned how to lay track.

Through the committeeman role in each crew, some of the men were able to test their leadership skills. Two committeemen from the experimental section eventually became foremen. The point is that the structure of the program created a new set of rewards—some related to membership in the experimental group, others to the worker's performance—that reinforced change. These rewards were built into the context of work, rather than solely mediated by some external agent. Reinforcement of a new form of work behavior moves the behavior from a trial adoption stage to an institutionalized behavior.

4. The experiment removed many of the negative incentives attached to work behavior. A major problem in mining is close supervision and constant pressure for production from the bosses. The work of a miner is relatively autonomous, even without an experimental program. These supervisory practices increased tension at work. By changing the foreman's role to concentrate on safety and buffering the foreman from production pressures from his boss, the source of tension between supervisor and worker was removed. As one miner said:

There's no one breathing down your back any more—you make your own decisions.

The above points indicate the program's effects on individual miner's decision-making processes. However, changes were going on simultaneously to make the section in which the individual miner worked more cohesive. The more cohesive the group, the more it could affect the worker's behavior.

5. The program reduced conflict among the crews by providing greater opportunity to communicate (and thus coordinate) as shifts were changing. Section conferences and mini-labor-management committee meetings were used to resolve problems between crews (e.g., who should do clean-up).

6. There was an attempt to change the basis of performance evaluation from the crew to the section. The rationale was that section-wide evaluation should minimize within-crew competition. All these program changes created an opportunity for cohesiveness to develop.

7. The autonomous work group concept led to greater interaction among the men, greater opportunities to make joint decisions, and greater control over their environment. This, in turn, led to more positive feelings about work and stronger identification with the experimental program. Again this is another necessary condition for the development of a cohesive group.

8. The first experimental section was launched with an intensive set of meetings. This helped create a strong section identity and also increased the feelings of cohesiveness.

Points 5 to 8 explain changes in the crew and section which, in turn, affected individual performance in the first experimental period in the South section. The stronger feelings of group cohesiveness developed because of experimental changes that placed new forces on the men to adhere to the concepts of the program (e.g., autonomy—one crew asked that its boss be removed because he was being too authoritarian) and to work toward the program objectives (e.g., safety).

We can summarize our explanation of why the experimental program caused changes at Rushton by looking at intershift communication (an immediate behavior) and safety practices (a final behavior). Intershift communication was clearly a new form of work behavior, since it did not occur prior to the intervention. It was an explicit aspect of the intervention structure, and it has persisted over time in the absence of any direct surveillance device. Why did this behavior become institutionalized? First, the miners received information in the section conferences of what was expected in intershift communication. Since the nature of the behavior is simple, all the miners would probably understand the communication about it and feel capable of performing it (one critical factor in the choice process). Second, the new activity cost little to perform; it simply required saying, "The continuous miner is in X room," "The hose is broken off the car," or "Rock dusting needs to be done on the fourth belt." Therefore, strong opposition to it was unlikely. A possible reward for the new behavior was that the miner's job would be easier. Knowing the jobs to be done or the equipment's location beforehand would make his job smoother. Given this choice, with potential rewards and virtually no costs, it is not surprising that the miner would adopt intershift communication. We must now trace the change process from the adoption decision to institutionalization. When intershift communication was adopted, did it set up a stream of reinforcements that would facilitate institutionalization? Our view is that only insignificant rewards were attached to intershift communication. We concluded this after three years of observing how miners start work. In the nonexperimental sections, where no intershift communication occurred, the men knew where to find their equipment; they knew the general mining plan from the day before and simply followed the cable to the machine. Even a novice miner could tell if the belt was not dusted. For these regular activities intershift communication did not, therefore, provide a great advantage. Intershift communication was an advantage only in exceptional cases, such as when a piece of machinery broke down as the shift ended and a part was needed. Overall, however, no stream of reinforcements followed the communication activity itself. Why then did it persist? As Figure 17.1 indicates, changes in group structure can affect choice behavior. In the case of intershift communications we think this was the major predictor. When the program started, intershift communication was defined as part of autonomous work groups. As the number of autonomous work group activities (especially meetings) increased so did the miners' identification with their section as an autonomous work group. We feel that this identification with the section and with its norms facilitated the institutionalization of intershift communication.

Our analysis of safety-practice behavior follows the same pattern. What caused this change in safety practices? Although the training program provided knowledge about safety, this was a common feature of all safety programs. What distinguished the Rushton program was that the motivational state of the workers also was changed. This happened in several ways: (1) Making the foreman's role safety, rather than a production-oriented role, minimized the negative reinforcement workers usually received from their bosses when they wanted to do safety work; (2) The meetings provided formal feedback on how safety behavior matched safety goals; (3) The section meetings provided a problem-solving arena where new safety practices were developed; (4) The meetings also provided a direct opportunity to reinforce positively good safety behavior. This is absent in most traditional safety programs; and (5) The autonomous work group concept increased the worker's feelings of responsibility for achieving high safety levels.

Two Other Explanations

While the framework we have presented can account for the change to new forms of work behavior, we should review two other explanations.

First, members of the South section volunteered to participate and this led to some level of selection bias. We were aware of this problem and questioned these people about their decision to volunteer. Most of the men volunteered to get more money, to learn new skills, or to stay in their current section. Their motivation to participate in the experiment was not based on their interest in its ideological aspects (e.g., greater autonomy). Indeed most knew little about the new program. Since practical (e.g., more money), rather than ideological considerations, affected participation, the volunteer section bias cannot be the principal predictor. Also, it is unlikely that selection bias would be a major explanatory variable several years into the project. It is clear some level of selection bias did exist since volunteering, of itself, indicated a level of receptivity to new forms of work organization. We feel, however, that selection bias was not strong, that the program did not select out those high in need for autonomy, and that the structures in the experiment and the identification with the experimental group were the major predictors of the new forms of work exhibited during the first 20 months.

A second explanation for the change to new forms of work behavior is that subjects in an experiment react because they are in an experiment, rather than because of any features of the experiment (this is often labeled the "Hawthorne Effect"). In the Rushton situation both within the firm and in the external media, the experimental group was subject to a great deal of attention which could stimulate a Hawthorne type of reaction. However, the experiment at Rushton prior to the vote covered a 20-month period. It is unlikely that the reactive features of an experiment (in this case a Hawthorne effect) could account for the results we have reported after this length of time.

WHY WAS THE CHANGE IN THE FIRST EXPERIMENTAL SECTION NOT SUSTAINED?

Although the QOW project at Rushton was initially successful, it was not sustained over time. Program changes and policies can be expected to evolve over time, but the argument here is that Rushton's program changes and policies did not remain viable institutions.

To analyze the reasons for this, we shall separate our question into two parts: (1) Why was the change that had successful consequences in the first experimental section not sustained over time? (2) Why was the project not successfully extended to the rest of the mine? (This question will be discussed in Chapter 18.)

In the chapters depicting the historical development of the Rushton project and in the results chapters we documented a gradual decline in the new forms of work behavior, especially during 1976 and 1977 in the South section. During those years, most of the men discussed the program in the past rather than present tense. Our on-site observations indicated declines in previously institutionalized behaviors, such as intershift communication and safety practices. Comparing the transcripts of the section conferences in 1974 with those in 1976 reveals a substantial change in interest in the QOW program. Here we want to explore this decline, again using the framework developed for explaining the persistence of new forms of work behavior. The basic premise is that declines in new forms of work behavior represent a choice by the miner. These choices, in turn, are affected by the characteristics of the intervention structure and the structure of the work group section.

The following factors contributed to the decline of the autonomous work group institutions in the South section:

1. The meetings, particularly the section conferences, were curtailed in 1975 and 1976. These meetings were a critical part of the intervention structure and an important source for feedback about past performance. Information on safety, production, costs, and other AW outcomes were reviewed. Without this feedback it was impossible to identify deviations from AW practices and to generate corrective actions. The meetings also had increased the men's identification with the section and with the program by enhancing intercrew cooperation,

reducing conflict, and providing opportunities for interaction. Fewer meetings tended to decrease section and program identification, which had been a powerful mechanism for affecting choice processes. Lastly, the meetings provided reinforcements, often in the form of recognition, for following AW practices. A decline in reinforcements withdrew an important source of motivation from the South section and preceded the decline in AW behaviors. Following the framework (Figure 17.1), the basic argument is that changes in the intervention structure directly reduced the level of reinforcements for new forms of work behavior and changed the level of group-section identification, which further reduced the incentive to perform the new behaviors.

The meetings were curtailed partly because new events were capturing the time of the research team. The unexpected opening of a new section (1974) as an experimental section represented a major time commitment. Planning for and extending the project minewide required another major commitment. Given a limited set of resources, the research team could not deal with both the new demands and the South section. Another reason for curtailing the South section meetings was management's objections to the proliferation of meetings that had affected production in 1974 and 1975. Why there was no concerted effort to provide attention and reinforcement to the South section, especially after the vote, is not clear. For example, short meetings led by at least one member of the research team on a crew-by-crew basis would have provided the necessary contact and not substantially affected production. We feel that this reduction in the number of South section meetings changed the motivators available to men in that section and subsequently their behavior. Other mechanisms to sustain the South section's identity with the program were available within the constraints provided by the management.

2. An analysis of the South experimental section conferences held in 1975 and 1976 indicates that many of the miners perceived these meetings as ineffectual. The basic complaint was that a lot of talking occurred, but few decisions were actually implemented. This reaction could simply have been a symptom of the men's growing discontent with the program. On the other hand, one of the basic themes of the meetings during these two years had been the problem of following through on decisions made in the meetings; decisions reached in one section meeting would still not be implemented by the following meeting. There were no mechanisms built into the structure for change to test for initial consensus, to implement the proposed change, to feed back on its progress, or to take some corrective action. The more the miners perceived the meetings as ineffectual, the less the meetings

served as reinforcers of the choice of maintaining the new form of work behavior and of identification with the section and program characteristics.

3. The character of the success in the South section indirectly contributed to its decline. Basic changes occurred in the areas of safety, job skills, and work attitudes. These changes, however, were in less quantifiable dimensions, such as better safety practices and a cleaner section. Since accident rates were already low, there was not room to demonstrate improvement by a change in accident rate. Job skills and job attitudes are important organizational variables, but saying that job attitudes increased significantly at the $p < .05$ level is not the same as saying that production went up by 15%. The latter change, and its economic implications, is clearly understood. Although changes in attitudes are important, our point is that the South section did not produce any dramatic changes in those areas valued by outsiders. Our assumption was that an increase in production (e.g., 15%) would have attracted the attention of PPL and other mines and resulted in more attention for the experimental group. This, in turn, would have heightened feelings of group identification, thus reinforcing some of the new forms of work behavior. The character of the success can generate new forces in the organization's environment to maintain the newly adopted behavior. Although there were clear and important changes in the South section, they did not attract the active interest of outside constituencies (e.g., PPL, the international union, etc.).

4. The vote rejecting a mine-wide autonomous work group program clearly reduced the viability of the program in the South section. From its inception in December 1973, the South section had been the object of criticism from the other miners who claimed that pay rates and other privileges enjoyed by the experimental section were inequitable. Initially, this hostile environment probably contributed to the solidarity of the South section. However, the vote was a statement by the union membership to stop the program. While the management attempted to extend the program to other areas of the mine, a good deal of ambiguity existed for the members of the South section as to whether they were an autonomous group or not. In the first formal announcement after the vote, management retained the right to direct the work force and wages were to be paid according to the contract. At the same time statements in the Mine Training and Development Committee meeting indicated that the original experimental sections were to continue operating in an autonomous mode. Signals to revert back to the old way of mining conflicted with signals that the program was still going on (e.g., training for the other sections, reinstating the

INSTITUTIONALIZING AND SUSTAINING CHANGE

high pay rate, etc.). These changes in the intervention structures created ambiguities that worked against maintaining the new forms of work behavior. A related point is that the outcome of the vote raised questions about the legitimacy of the experimental program. Up to the time of the vote, the Rushton project was a joint labor-management endeavor; the vote signaled its end. The issue then for the men was whether it was legitimate to behave autonomously when the union did not support the program.

5. While there was a surprising amount of stability (i.e., low turnover) in the first experimental section, there were changes in personnel. Two of the foremen left for other jobs at the mine during the period after the vote. (They were replaced through promotion by men in the experimental section.) Other men also moved to more responsible jobs (e.g., belt examiner). These job movements and the subsequent replacements were natural occurrences, but created a problem since the replacements received no special training and did not have the same training as the original experimental members. Consequently the new workers tended to dilute further the original impact of the QOW program. As the framework suggested, to adopt a new form of work behavior a miner must: (1) understand and feel capable of performing that behavior, (2) identify the rewards and costs associated with that behavior, (3) perceive a net gain for performing the new behavior over the old one. The failure to develop a mechanism to orient the new miners in the program's behaviors and norms or to encourage adoption of AW behaviors contributed to the decline of AW behaviors. As a result original members, who because of fewer meetings, the vote, and so on, were less committed to the program now interacted with new members, men who had never engaged in program behavior.

6. There were few, if any, new experimental structures successfully introduced in 1975 and 1976 to sustain the new forms of work behavior over time. The project at Rushton went through many phases, including the initial introduction of the experiment into a pilot section, an adoption phase in which the new behaviors were tried. As the first year progressed, there was the institutionalization of many of the new behaviors. It was likely that some backsliding (i.e., a tendency to revert to behavior resembling the original set of work behaviors) would occur at this point, partly because the novelty and value of the rewards had decreased as well as because the research team was less involved. (Backsliding would probably have occurred even if the vote had been positive.) In order to counterbalance this regression, it was important to introduce new structures.

Why was there a decrease in the successful introduction of the new structures? By 1976 the effective size of the research team was reduced to two individuals, and they were spending less time at the mine. These lower time commitments and the broader set of problems inherent in a mine-wide program left little time to introduce new structures. Second, as we have previously said, the climate at the mine after the vote was not conducive to trying new forms of work organization. Third, the attempts to introduce new structures were superficial. For example, in 1976 a goal-setting program for foremen was introduced; they were to estimate monthly production and use this as a guide and motivational device for getting production out. By the end of 1976 monthly estimates were not being generated, and we found no evidence in selected interviews with foremen and managers that any estimates were being used. Why did this happen?

The research team saw goal setting as an important new structure, yet it was never accepted as valuable by the foremen. The estimates were difficult to make because they required forecasting physical conditions (roof conditions) and other variables that affect production. Often the superintendent would adjust estimates that he felt were wrong. Most important, the setting of production goals by the foremen did not include their crew members' commitment. From the goal-setting literature it is clear that the relevant individuals (in this case the crew or section) must be identified, they must understand the goal and the paths to goal, accept the goal as obtainable, see some valued outcomes for reaching the goal, and make some commitment, preferably public in nature, to reach these goals. Few of these conditions were met in the Rushton case. There are other examples where the research team introduced new structures (e.g., a deployment model and a planning model) that never became institutionalized.

7. The failure of the project to diffuse successfully throughout the whole mine contributed to the decline of the new forms of work behavior that had been institutionalized in the South section. There is an interesting relationship between diffusion and institutionalization. Diffusion refers to the spread (adoption) of innovations (new forms of work) in new social settings (other parts of the mine). As diffusion occurs and the new behaviors are institutionalized there is a tendency for these behaviors to reinforce those in the area from which diffusion originated. The South section did not operate in a vacuum. It was influenced by the activities of the other sections. If the QOW program had been successfully extended to other sections, even after the vote, many of the work practices and values developed in the South section might have been sustained.

8. The failure to introduce a gain-sharing plan significantly contributed to the decline of new forms of work behavior in the experimental section. A plan was introduced in October 1977, but this was well

after the union withdrew from participation in the program. Of all the issues of the program during 1975, 1976, and early 1977, the gain-sharing program—particularly the failure to introduce this program—was one of the most salient. It was a rare event for me to visit the mine without having many of the miners in the South section ask me for their bonus check. It was an important symbol. Why? In the first place it was a visible reward. Increasing autonomy, decision-making skills, and so on, are abstract ideas. Getting more money is a well understood and desirable outcome for the miners. Secondly, the interest in gain-sharing began to grow in the second and third year of the project. Our guess is that the novelty of the project as well as the marginal value of some of the rewards from the project were decreasing. For example, the attractiveness of job switching may decrease over time as the novelty of learning a new job decreases. We expect that as these rewards decrease in value that the search for new outcomes, such as a bonus, increases. Third, the initial program was based on a mutual reciprocity between labor and management with gain sharing as a clear measure of this reciprocity. Members of the experimental section believed their production had improved and some bonus was expected. Since a gain-sharing program could not be devised and allocated in three years, it was not surprising that the miners did not feel committed to meet their AW obligations. The failure to deliver an operative bonus plan reduced the need for the men to reciprocate—this was particularly true after the vote when the program was labeled management's program.

Since the gain-sharing plan is a critical issue, it might be useful to explore why it was not instituted. The first reason is that setting up a gain-sharing plan in a mine is inherently a complicated problem. In the economic section we pointed out that many exogenous factors (e.g., roof and runway conditions) affect production. If a particular baseline level of production is set, but the following year brings substantially different physical conditions, then the baseline is not a good mark to estimate productivity gains. A mine poses a much different problem than a manufacturing plant which has a stable technology and environment. Setting up a mine-wide bonus system is a complicated task.

The second factor is that none of the members of the research team had any substantial experience in setting up gain-sharing plans. Given the complicated nature of the problem, this was a severe drawback. Also, because they felt they had sufficient knowledge, they did not consult any pay-system experts. The result was a series of proposals from the research team that were either sent back for revision or never really understood by the mine's president. The idea of giving a bonus was not at issue; from all our information, the president was willing to pay. The real problem was in developing an understandable and technically feasible plan, presenting it to all the parties, and getting it approved. Responsibility for this rested with the research team because: (1) the local union felt unable to contribute to the design and had publicly assigned its role to the research team and (2) management, lacking expertise in the area, had also employed the research team.

The gain-sharing program was also delayed because our evaluation team was late in providing the appropriate data. It is true that we were responsible for processing the economic data. It is also true that, because of the complicated process of setting up this information system, we always lagged a year behind, that is, 1974 data were available in 1975. While there was a delay in generating data, the statement, "We have to wait for Goodman's data before setting up a gain-sharing plan," was more a rationalization than a reality. The real problem in setting up a gain-sharing plan was to develop a model of what that plan would be like. How was the baseline to be determined? How were exogenous variables to be dealt with? How were savings from purchasing to be dealt with? How were savings from purchasing to be handled that really were outside of the program? These were the tough questions that were not and still have not been answered. So while "Goodman's data" were necessary, it was not the crux of setting up a gain-sharing plan.

A fourth reason concerns Rushton's owner, PPL. Since the bonus decision would establish a precedent for other PPL operations, the plan had to be approved by them. Getting a commitment from PPL represented a potential delay. However, I attended meetings at that company where the bonus was discussed and my view is that the idea of paying a bonus had been approved by PPL.

To conclude this discussion on the failure of the program to be sustained over time we can make the following observations: The paradigm to explain why new forms of work organization become institutionalized also explains why proposed structures do not last over time. Factors 1-8 indicate that some intervention structures (e.g., section meetings) lost power over time to influence the workers' choice processes to continue QOW behaviors. The failure to successfully introduce new structures (e.g., gain sharing) to revive interest worked against the institutionalization of the program. The failure to successfully maintain the original experimental structures or to introduce new structures reduced the frequency of feedback, quality of feedback, and the level of reinforcements. The decline of the section meetings, the vote, and the failure to socialize new members reduced work group section identification and cohesiveness, which had been an important source for sustaining the program. This reduction in feedback, reinforcement, and work-group cohesion contributed to the workers' decision not to continue the QOW program behaviors.

CHAPTER EIGHTEEN

Diffusion of the Experiment within Rushton

By the first quarter of 1976 the quality of work program at Rushton had been extended minewide. As we have noted in the results section, the new intervention initially had some effect on attitudes and behavior, but the effect was not as pronounced as it had been in the first experimental section. At the end of 1976, however, the data from our periodic interviews, on-site observations, and the labor-management committee meetings indicate that the program was not a viable institution. If the president of Rushton had withdrawn from active involvement at that time, the program would not have continued. Program structures, such as the labor-management commit-tees, did not have a life of their own that would enable them to continue as integral parts of Rushton's operations without their initiator and chief supporter (that is, the president). There was no person at the mine, respected by both management and labor, who could have administered the program after the external research team had gone. Most important, our interviews with management and union leaders as well as with the men in the first experimental sections indicate that they did not see a program going on at Rushton at the end of 1976.

In the first quarter of 1977 the results of a major strike confirmed our original belief that the program was no longer viable. After the strike the union formally withdrew from participation in the Mine Training and Development Committee, which was the major struc-ture where both labor and management could forward the program's objectives.

Understanding the decline of the program is as important as understanding its success—perhaps even more important. As a point of review let us return to March 1975 when there was a discussion and a perceived motion either to extend the experiment to the whole mine or to drop it. This challenge from the union was presented to management at a section conference shortly after the union meeting. Management rejected the all-or-nothing proposal, but was willing to consider extending the project. At the next union meeting it was discovered that a formal motion had not been made. After discussions among union members, the steering committee, management, and the research team, it was agreed that a new document specifying the operation of the QOW program in the whole mine would be drawn up by the steering committee and voted on by the union. From April to August the committee worked to develop the mine-wide program; this culminated in the August 1975 vote.

The "no" vote was the key factor in preventing the successful diffusion of the QOW project at Rushton. The 79 to 75 vote was not close in the following sense: all the members of the first experimental section, most of those in the second section, and some of the other members associated with the labor-management committee probably voted yes. That number would account for most of the "yes" votes. Almost all the voters who rejected the program, then, were not directly involved with it. That is, the majority of those not in the program and to whom the program was to be extended voted against it. The vote can then be characterized in three ways: (1) This was the first vote that really reflected mine-wide sentiment since it was the first time the "whole" membership voted. All other votes included only about 20 to 25% of the union membership; (2) Those people who had experienced and received the benefits of the QOW program were positively disposed toward it; and (3) A majority of those people outside the experimental sections rejected the program as a mine-wide plan. Why did the vote come out the way it did?

ANALYSIS OF THE "NO" VOTE

Before we analyze the vote it will be useful to revise the framework presented in the previous chapter. That model of how change occurs states that intervention structures affect individual choice processes that lead first to the adoption and then institutionalization of new forms of work behavior. Extending the project to the whole mine is an exercise in diffusion. Diffusion is the process of extending an innovation to members of a new social system—in the Rushton case this refers to the rest of the mine.

The Diffusion Process

Introducing the concept of diffusion in our framework only requires a slight adjustment. Basically, there are a set of diffusion processes that moderate the effect of the intervention structures on the psychological processes related to the adoption decision. Once the adoption decision is made, the inherent characteristics of the intervention structure are the major factors affecting the decision to continue the new form of work behavior that eventually may become institutionalized. The first question in diffusion then is whether members in a new social system will adopt the innovation? Once they have adopted the new behavior, the inherent characteristics of the behavior (e.g., intershift communication) and the environment primarily determine (through reinforcements) whether the behavior will be continued. Figure 18.1 diagrams that relationship. As the reader will note we believe that the diffusion process can also affect the decision to continue. Changes in the diffusion communicator, message, and so on, could enhance or inhibit continuing the new form of work organization. However, the critical factors in the decision to continue are the reinforcements built into the intervention structure.

Before we begin applying this framework, it is useful to delineate the elements in the diffusion process. The first is the *communicator*. Prior research (Oskamp, 1977) has shown that the credibility and attractiveness of the communicator may affect attitudes toward and

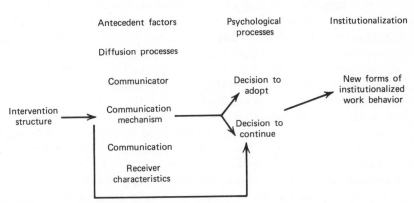

Figure 18.1 Diffusion framework.

the propensity to adopt the new form of work behavior. The second is the *mechanism* by which information about the innovation is transferred to the potential clients. Third is the inherent character of the *communication*. This, as with all the diffusion elements, is affected by the structure of the intervention. For example, if the experimental structure is a new piece of technology, then the substance of the communication would be concrete in nature. If the structure is a set of ideas, then the communication would be more abstract. The fourth element is the characteristics of the *receiver*. If the innovation is in conflict with basic attitudes and beliefs held by the receiver, the diffusion process will be limited. The following is an analysis of how these elements in the diffusion process contributed to the "no" vote.

The Communicator. The formal communicators in the attempt to extend the program minewide were the members of the research team. These individuals were not well known by the miners in the nonautonomous sections. They were perceived as the "professors from Penn State," and it is fair to say that they were not seen as highly credible communicators. The local union officers also served as communicators. However, none of the union officers at Rushton were able to influence substantially the opinions of a majority of the union members. Since we have been at Rushton, we have never observed any union leader who could shape a majority opinion. Moreover, none of the powerful union officers had fully embraced the QOW concepts. On management's side, the president was actively involved in the diffusion process and his opinions seemed to be listened to by most of the union members. None of the other managers did, or perhaps could, play a major role as a pro communicator. Some of the managers in the foreman ranks took a negative stance toward the program. Since most foreman at Rushton are respected by their crews, their position was influential. Our observation is that, with the exception of the president, there was no effective advocate of the program. Indeed some effective communicators argued against the program.

Mechanisms. After the decision to extend the program to the whole mine was made, several mechanisms were initiated to accomplish that purpose: (1) The steering committee met to draw up a new document; (2) A series of communication meetings were held with members in the nonautonomous work areas; (3) A limited foreman exchange program was initiated; and (4) The union meeting prior to the vote was to be used to explain the new document.

These four mechanisms will now be discussed in detail.

The steering committee met approximately twice a month from April through July 1975. Members of this committee worked to design a new document reflecting the operation of the whole mine. The steering committee was clearly the appropriate body to initiate the new document since its role had always been to initiate new policy for the project. Nevertheless, a discussion of some aspects of the committee structure and the substantive issues it discussed will give some insights into the "no" vote.

The membership of the steering committee had remained largely unchanged since the initiation of the project. Even after the union election, some of the defeated officers remained on the committee; this drew some negative criticism from men in the mine. The issue of composition became important as the focus turned to a mine-wide plan. At this time the steering committee was not really representative of the whole mine: there was a disproportionate representation from the mechanics section and no representation from the cleaning plant. Since the focus was now on the whole mine, representation from the whole mine would probably have been useful. A related point concerns the rotation of miners on the steering committee. We observed that once people had attended steering committee meetings they seemed to understand the program better and be more favorably disposed toward it. The relative lack of circulation of steering committee members prevented exposing more people to the operation of the program. Thus the diffusion process was limited.

Another steering committee issue concerned the focus of its activities in drawing up the document. The inside mining sections, their pay rates, and the paths to qualify for those rates received much attention from the committee. Surprisingly little time was given to work areas (e.g., the cleaning plant) that did not fit neatly into the autonomous scheme. The fact that less time was spent on these areas probably contributed to some extent to the negative vote. Workers in such areas did not see the plan as fitting their needs.

Another substantive issue concerns a grievance introduced in the last steering committee meeting before the vote. The grievance concerned whether a crew would receive payment for time spent in the superintendent's office after their shift was completed. Our interest is not in the grievance itself, but rather in its introduction at this time into the steering committee. From the union's point of view the introduction of the grievance prior to the vote gave the union leverage for a favorable resolution—"Support our position or the men will not vote for the program." From another point of view the grievance focused attention away from the implementation of the program. While we cannot say definitively that the introduction of the grievance significantly affected the vote, it did represent a major turnaround in the work the steering committee had done. It highlighted the ever present conflict between QOW values and traditional labor-management values. Symbolically it raised questions about the real commitment of the parties to the program.

We can conclude this discussion of the steering committee with the following observations: the steering committee was the appropriate mechanism to develop the new document for a plant-wide program. During the four months of drawing up the document the members worked hard and were able to resolve some difficult issues. Our analysis then is not to demean in any way the operation of this group. In many ways it was a model labor-management committee. Rather, we want to highlight some issues of the committee's operation: First, we feel that the composition of the committee detracted from its effectiveness as a diffusion mechanism. Our analysis pointed to its static and nonrepresentative character. Second, the committee tended to neglect work areas that did not fit neatly into the autonomous program. Third, a continual dilemma existed about including traditional union issues (e.g., grievances) in groups primarily organized to deal with QOW problems. The traditional issues took focus away from the QOW issues, and the effectiveness of the QOW groups was lessened.

The second major mechanism for introducing the program was a series of communication meetings with men who were not part of the AW sections. The purpose of the meetings was to present segments of the document and to obtain feedback from the men for subsequent modifications. The initial meetings were run by the research team and organized by shifts. Therefore, more than one section was represented at each meeting. The second series of communication meetings was run by selected union officials; the participants were usually from only one rather than several sections. The meetings were conducted primarily in June and July.

Our evaluation of both series of meetings is that they were not very effective. During the first series the men were primarily talked to; there was little systematic feedback from the men to the research team. Also, the research team used no systematic mechanism to evaluate the effectiveness of the meetings. The second series of meetings was designed to put the union officials and men together without any outsiders (e.g., management, research team). We attended one of these meetings with a member of the research team, and our observations confirmed the general estimate that the meetings were not significantly changing beliefs about the program. This was partly due to the lack of a dominant opinion leader among the union officers or one who thoroughly embraced QOW concepts.

Another factor contributing to the ineffectiveness was the lecture versus group-discussion format used in most of the meetings. In general, the literature suggests that the former approach is less effective than the latter in generating commitment.

Another strategy used in diffusing the project was to have foremen from the nonautonomous sections observe the workings of an autonomous section. This procedure was based on the idea of modeling, that is, by observing others' work behaviors and the potential benefits from them, the observer is more prone to experiment with the new work methods. Unfortunately, only a few foremen participated, and these were only single observations. The strategy could have been a viable one, but its limited application at Rushton reduced its effectiveness. Our interviews with foremen who had visited the South section indicated that the exchange was ineffective. They felt that their way of mining was better and that South's only distinctive quality was its two extra men.

The union hall during the regular monthly meeting represented another arena to discuss the new document and influence acceptance of the program. In the August meeting prior to the vote, the document was to be reviewed and a representative from the international was to present the international's endorsement of the program. Instead, attacks from some members of the local against the program prevented any systematic review of the document. It seems unlikely that the events at the union hall changed any attitudes toward the program.

We conclude our analysis of the diffusion mechanisms with the following observation: there was too much reliance on one mechanism—communication and persuasion. The exchange program (using a modeling mechanism) might have worked if it was started earlier and if it could have occurred when clear differences between autonomous and nonautonomous crews could be demonstrated. An alternative to a communication-persuasion approach would have been to let the men adopt some of the AW practices prior to the vote—experiencing the benefits of an AW section (experiential mechanism) might have influenced voting behavior more than discussing its advantages. In any case, the use of multiple mechanisms, rather than reliance on one, is most important.

Communications. The character of the communications used to diffuse the program in some ways detracted from the effectiveness of the diffusion. First, the major document describing the program was long and complex. It was very unlikely that any miners would sit down and read it. Second, the substance of the communications was abstract, rather than concrete. It is inherently more difficult to diffuse an innovation that rests on abstractions, instead of on concrete objects or tasks. Communicating about the structure of an autonomous work group is a difficult task especially because mining is fairly autonomous to begin with. Describing greater skills, autonomy, and responsibility as benefits is also not easy to do with an audience that prefers concrete objects. The structure of the program, therefore, led to an abstract set of communications that made it difficult to identify the net benefits of the new program over the old.

A third factor was that most of the communications were onesided; the virtues of the program were proclaimed, but rarely were the disadvantages discussed. This heightened feelings of suspicion that nullified the impact of the communication. A frequent reaction to all the one-sided communication was that something must be wrong—that there must be "a nigger in the woodpile," as several of the men said. This type of reaction makes sense when we remember that labor-management relationships in the past were frought with conflict and suspicion. Why should management offer all these advantages without getting something for itself?

Receiver. Some union members expressed low levels of trust toward management because of previous labor-management conflicts. Rushton is a relatively young mine, and the bitterness generated by organizing the mine is still salient. These feelings made it difficult for management to initiate any new proposals, not just the QOW proposal.

Also, some miners were alienated by the original project. Walton (1975) has pointed out that a star envy phenomenon occurs when a pilot experimental section is subject to a great deal of attention. There were numerous accounts of the Rushton project in national newspapers and magazines. The quality of work conferences gave members of the experimental section the opportunity to travel around the country to talk about the Rushton experience. Jealousy toward an experimental group inhibits diffusion of an experiment. At Rushton negative attitudes toward the program were not solely due to the attention received by the South section. We have already documented the strong feelings of inequity generated by the pay rates in the first two experimental sections. These feelings also acted to inhibit the diffusion of the program. In addition, the men not in the first two experimental groups had not volunteered to participate in the program. This was another indicator that few people were positively disposed toward QOW concepts—the majority were either neutral or negatively disposed—therefore, the task of changing attitudes was a difficult one. It is clearly easier to move beliefs and behavior in a congruent rather than incongruent direction. Also, those not volunteering might have felt the need to justify their original decision and thus were less susceptible to change.

Another important factor is that our discussion of receivers includes members of both the union *and* management. The Rushton project was pioneered by one man, the company president. Most of the managers were not committed to the program; their beliefs and behavior were not modified by the diffusion process. That some bosses did not push their members for a "yes" vote also has to be included in the discussion of the vote.

Structure of the Intervention

A number of provisions in the proposed structure also affected the vote. First, there was a qualification clause. It stated that miners would get the top rate for 90 days and then be judged by a qualification committee as to whether they could perform the jobs specified in the document for that top rate. This was a new twist. The prior experimental groups received top rate without any qualification "test." This provision provided a stumbling block. It aroused feelings of inequity and some feelings about being able to pass the "test." Although it was demonstrated and communicated that almost all workers would qualify, the perception of having to take a qualifications test hurt the chances for a favorable vote.

The wage provision called for a top rate; during the 1974 labor negotiation, however, more jobs in the section qualified for the high rate as a contractual right. Now the bolters, miner operator and helper, and mechanic received top rate in the nonexperimental sections with only the car and support men at a lower rate. The inducement of more money now affected fewer people than when the first experimental section was launched. Although an argument was offered by the research team that a vote for the project would help one's brothers receive more pay, it had a hollow ring. We found few miners motivated by the idea of supporting the program to help others. Actually those at the top rate saw little to gain and, more importantly, something to lose as new responsibilities were added.

Another provision concerned the rate structure for those outside the sections. Some of the surface workers perceived the document as limiting their opportunities for higher rates because they could only exchange among certain sets of jobs. Other groups, such as the pumpers, were dissatisfied with their rates. The document also did not build any incentive for the mechanics. As a result, specific provisions of the document raised feelings of inequity and thus prevented some workers from supporting the whole document.

In summary, prior to the vote no strongholds of support for the program existed among Rushton's major groups: management, foremen, local union officials, and membership. In fact, some groups held negative attitudes due to earlier labor-management conflicts and perceived inequities in the initial experimental program. Certain provisions of the document were highlighted and became a source of conflicts. Finally, the method of diffusion relied on a communications model that was unlikely to bring about major changes in beliefs or values. The characteristics of the communicators, the mechanisms for transferring information, and the characteristics of the information detracted from a successful diffusion.

ANALYSIS OF THE POST-VOTE DIFFUSION

A number of factors contributed to the unsuccessful extension of the QOW program after the vote:

1. The decision by management to extend the AW concept throughout the mine reduced the effectiveness of a mine-wide program. The president of the mine (Warren Hinks) firmly believed in the advantages of giving greater autonomy and responsibility to the work force and viewed the August 20 vote as close, with "almost one-half" of the members supporting the program concepts. He felt, therefore, that if he operated within the context of the contract, he could and should extend the QOW concepts into the rest of the mine. He also stated that he did not want to deprive those who wanted the program. Those who voted against the program he felt lacked an understanding of what is "good for the working man" and once they experienced the program they would recognize its merits.

The major issues raised by this decision concerned the president's right to make it and its potential consequences. The president clearly had the legal right within the context of both his office in the corporation and the labor-management agreement. Company presidents can decide who should be trained and when. Also, the UMWA contract permits training, a labor-management advisory committee, and a wage rate structure not less than in the contract. Although the president clearly had the legal right to extend the project, he did not necessarily have the social or psychological right. At the outset of the program an agreement was signed by the company and union presidents that described the QOW project as a joint effort; each party had the right to withdraw and thus to terminate the agreement. In addition, the concept of joint ownership was stressed throughout the operation of the program. If the idea of joint ownership had been taken in its literal and/or symbolic sense, the August 20 vote would have indicated the union's decision not to continue and the end of the program.

It could also be argued that the vote cancelled out the labor-management program and that the new program instituted by management was different. This position, however, seems to stretch the point, since the actors and institutions were relatively the same before and after the vote.

It is not easy to rationalize away the fact that a social or psychological contract existed between labor and management about the joint aspects of this project, both in terms of initiation and termination. Management's unilateral decision to continue the program after the vote alienated some members of the nonautonomous section despite the fact that the union officers were willing to cooperate with management. The degree of alienation is difficult to assess since it was not possible to reinterview the miners after the vote, and since the company's offer of top wages plus two extra support people per crew probably minimized any immediate negative reactions. From the data we were able to gather later, those originally opposed to the program held their views more strongly after management's unilateral action.

With the decision to diffuse the program by authority as a background, the question then became: Will the intervention structures be able to cause the institutionalization of new forms of work behavior?

2. Extending the program mine-wide, rather than work area by work area, reduced its effectiveness. Interestingly, one of management's objections to the mine-wide program proposed by the union (in March 1975) was that it takes a lot of intensive work to get a section or work area up to program standards. Yet after the vote the program was introduced minewide.

Since a lot of effort was needed to train an autonomous section, introducing the experiment to the whole mine drew heavily on resources. The mine-wide plan required autonomous training for at least six work areas. One consequence of this was that training for the sections was spread over a long period of time. As mentioned earlier, the more the meetings were spread out, the less effective the training was. Spreading the training out also worked against developing a group or section identity with the program. This group identification and cohesiveness was important in institutionalizing the new forms of work behavior. Intensive training and section meetings had helped to develop this identification in the South section; it was never developed in the other areas.

To summarize: The choice of a mine-wide program, rather than sequential introduction of the program, taxed already limited resources and spread the training over a long time period. A sequential program would have provided greater attention to each area and thus might have facilitated learning, identification with the program, and change. Since the sequential plan might have required paying all the miners top rates, even though some were not in training, the costs of both programs would have been similar, but the impact on institutionalization would probably have been greater with a sequential plan.

3. The number of section conferences held for each of the work areas was considerably less than those held for the South section at the experiment's beginning. As we have argued, the initial success of the South section was built on the men's close identification with their work area and the program. The decline of QOW institutions in the South section and the lack of them in the other sections after the vote was partly attributable to the decline in the number of section meetings. A related point concerns the perceived value of the section meetings. In late 1976 and early 1977 some men refused to go to section meetings. This was partly attributed to the fact that they saw little value in them.

4. The inducements for the workers to participate in the program were less than when the experiment began in 1973. Because of a change in the national coal contract (1974) more members of a crew received the top rate, so fewer crew members benefitted from the top-rate provision in the mine-wide program. Also, the expansion of the program to a mine-wide basis required hiring additional miners, most of whom were relatively inexperienced. These miners, often referred to as "yellow hats," filled the extra support positions in the (formerly) nonautonomous sections. Their lack of experience complicated the process of setting up the new program. In the original experimental section, the additional support people were experienced miners.

5. There was considerable ambiguity over the meaning of autonomy in the post-vote period. Some signals from management indicated that the mining sections should adopt the autonomous work practices exhibited by the first experimental section. Other signals from management and the research team indicated that the mining sections should determine their own level of autonomy. In either case it was difficult to know what was the expected behavior.

6. The program model did not fit all the mine's work areas, including such dissimilar work areas as the cleaning plant, the pumpers, the mechanics, and so on. Since the original program was designed to fit the unique technological configurations of the mining sections, there was a need to individualize the program to fit the different areas. The autonomous work group concept is not necessarily generalizable to fit all work areas. Although the research team analyzed some technological features of different areas, we saw no evidence of new program structures to fit these different areas. The focus from the beginning of this project was on the mining sections, and it has remained there. The failure to tailor the program to the different work areas probably reduced the possibility of introducing work changes in these areas.

7. A mine-wide program required the cooperation of all levels of management. Interviews collected in the last quarter of 1975 and throughout 1976 indicated that certain members of the mine management, critical to the installation of the program, were uncooperative. Although these individuals did not support the program from the beginning, the effect of their lack of support was not critical until the program was extended to the entire mine. A mine-wide program requires coordination of multiple work areas and follow through. These individuals were in important decision positions that influenced the operation of the mine-wide program.

The research team tried unsuccessfully to "bring these individuals around" through individual and group counseling sessions. Some of these men held value positions quite opposed to the quality of work concepts. It was unlikely that their values could have been changed. Also, the meetings were held sporadically and thus were not terribly effective.

8. An operative gain-sharing plan might have encouraged the adoption of new forms of work behavior. The failure to institute a gain-sharing plan hurt the extension of the program at Rushton. This was true for the original autonomous sections as well as for those involved in the post-vote program. Lack of a gain-sharing plan was taken as a negative symbol of management's role in the program. While paying a bonus itself would not have sustained the program, it would have been an important stimulus to extending it.

9. The role of the union had changed in the post-vote period. The union was no longer a coowner of the project. Adversary behavior, rather than problem-solving behavior, grew more frequent in the labor-management meetings. A rash of strikes occurred in late 1975, early 1976, and early 1977. These strikes created tensions that further separated labor and management. This situation of growing tension between labor and management and little identification with the QOW program did not foster the extension of new forms of work behavior. Also, the international no longer provided any support for the project. This occurred for a variety of reasons: the project was no longer jointly run by the union and management; there was a tremendous amount of political turmoil within the international; and by the end of 1976 several of the project's contacts within the international had left for other jobs.

In summary, we argued earlier that a new form of work behavior becomes institutionalized after a miner has adopted the new behavior and decided to continue it over time. These decisions require some net benefit inherent in the new behavior, that is, the intervention structure has to create a situation where there is a net advantage in performing the new behavior. We have also argued that the intervention structure can modify work group structure, providing a cohesiveness which, in turn, can cause the adoption of new forms of work organization. In the post-vote intervention, none of these conditions were present. Group and program identification did not develop. The nature of the intervention structure was sometimes ambiguous and at other times not suited to special work areas. After the men voted against the program, but management persisted in setting it up, the environment for change was no longer benign. Some of the miners were antagonized by management's unilateral action. Growing labor-management strife and the lack of management commitment stifled the research team's ability to institute changes. The results of the post-vote activities were not surprising.

CHAPTER NINETEEN

Critical Issues in Designing QOW Experiments

This chapter explores some of the critical issues in designing QOW experiments, building from analyses already presented as well as from aspects of the Rushton case that have not yet been discussed. The basic strategy is to evaluate the features of the Rushton design and then to generalize, wherever possible, on how variations of these design issues may be incorporated into other QOW projects. Chapter 20 will examine implementation issues.

The Rushton experiment was an example of a major system intervention. Multiple aspects of that organization were changed. Modifications in the goals, pay system, authority, decision-making, communication, and so on, were part of the experimental design. Although the following analysis is based on the Rushton experience, some of these design issues will appear in most QOW experiments.

Goals

The Rushton design incorporated an explicit statement of goals. This seems to be a desirable strategy for two reasons: (1) it tests the intentions of the participants by creating a certain level of commitment for them and (2) it provides one basis for evaluation. We organized our analysis of Rushton around the stated goals of safety, productivity, earnings, job skills, and job satisfaction. If these were the desired goals, then the success of the project could be judged on the extent to which these goals were realized. It is important to note, however, that a QOW project will have consequences in areas other than those encompassed by the explicit goals. For that reason we introduced the concept of implicit goals in our evaluation.

Another important issue is the type of goals included in the QOW contract between labor and management. Common goals are those that are equally accepted by labor and management. Safety is an example of a common goal at Rushton. This type of goal should evoke cooperative behavior. Complementary goals are tradeoff goals, such as productivity or wages. Each of these goals represents the interest of one party; by achieving one goal the other goal can be satisfied. Complementary goals often evoke bargaining or adversary behavior, while common goals are more congruent with joint problem-solving behavior, which is a necessary ingredient in all QOW experiments. Since adversary behaviors are incongruent with QOW projects, projects built solely on complementary goals will probably be less successful than those that include some common goals. The safety goal at Rushton provided a unifying focus for labor and management.

Pay System

The autonomous work group concept required that the union miners assume greater responsibility in directing the work and that they perform multiple jobs. Because of these increased inputs, it was deemed appropriate to change their pay. Each member of the experimental section received the top rate. This decision was a major source of conflict throughout the experiment.

There are a number of issues raised by this payment scheme. First, pay was not related directly to services rendered. The top rate was paid at the outset, before the men had assumed more responsibility or had learned multiple jobs. There was, then, no incentive goal for the workers to aim toward. In other autonomous work group experiments (Walton, 1975) payment was tied to the number of jobs an individual could perform. That is, contributions and rewards were related and provided more incentive for the worker to switch and exchange jobs in order to receive a higher rate. One of the reasons that job switching in the Rushton project never became fully institutionalized may be attributed to the payment scheme.

Second, the pay system was clearly the source of feelings of inequity across the sections. Pay was a valued reward; the pay differences between the experimental and nonexperimental section were quite visible. Relating the pay system more closely to the jobs that were performed might have modified feelings of inequity between sections.

For example, the design of the second AW mining section generated strong feelings of inequity because inexperienced miners were receiving top wages. If a pay-related-to-skills system had been instituted, the "green" miners would not have received top wages for some time.

A third issue concerns the precedent established by the pay system and its impact on diffusing the experiment to other sections in the mine. The original document, which included provisions for the new pay system, was defined initially as an experiment. The word experiment implies something temporary and open to change. Indeed one of the major sources of conflict during the negotiations for a mine-wide document concerned whether the pay system for the first experimental section would apply if the program were extended to the whole mine. The president contended that decisions made for the first experimental section were not binding. The union, on the other hand, advocated that the whole mine get top rates. A compromise was included in the document for a mine-wide program. However, controversies continued about the pay rates and the paths to get these rates. This source of disagreement contributed in part to votes against the program in August 1975. The point is that the experiment created a precedent that was not easily forgotten by the union. Therefore, the design of a pay system for a pilot experiment must not reflect solely the demands of that setting. The pay system must be designed so that it will facilitate the diffusion of the QOW program within the total organization, and so that it will be congruent with the jobs throughout the organization.

Gain sharing is another feature of the payment system. We have already indicated that the failure to generate a gain-sharing plan between 1974 and the fall of 1977 contributed to the decline of QOW institutions in the first experimental section and to the difficulties in extending the project throughout the mine.

The first issue is whether gain-sharing plans are necessary in QOW projects: Is some form of monetary reward needed to sustain a QOW program over and above the immediate rewards attached to the program? Some researchers argue that gain-sharing plans are not necessary. The opportunities in the program for greater responsibility, autonomy, and job skills are sufficient to maintain worker participation in the project. In the Rushton case the individual workers received many nonmonetary benefits (e.g., training). Others argue that some monetary rewards are necessary and that the value of intrinsic rewards, such as greater opportunity for decision-making for the worker, is sometimes overstated.

Our position is that any major new form of work organization project will require some gain-sharing program. Since the scope of such a program would affect the total operations of the firm, not exchanging any resulting productivity gains or cost savings would lead to feelings of inequity, and the viability of the program would be attacked. Also, despite all the arguments for the value of greater participation, workers, such as the men at Rushton, are attracted by dollars and cents. Some gain-sharing distribution over time, then, would help maintain the project. A third reason for instituting some plant or company-wide program is that it focuses attention on the total operations of the firm. In order for a company-wide bonus to occur, all the different work areas must cooperate. One advantage of a company-wide program, such as the Scanlon Plan, is that it elicits more intrafirm cooperation and provides the workers with more knowledge about the firm. This, in turn, improves their capabilities as decision makers.

The development of gain-sharing plans is another issue. Using either monetary or nonmonetary payments, most plans are complicated and require some level of expertise. The goal is to set up an equitable plan that will be responsive to worker inputs and that will last over time. This is not a trivial task. We believe that specialists need to be brought in to develop this plan. Most specialists in organizational change are not specialists in gain-sharing plans. A plan at Rushton might have been set up with outside help.

Another issue concerns the form of the gain-sharing plan. There are a variety of different forms of monetary plans at the plant or company-wide level (see Lawler, 1971). Another option would be to develop a plan based on allocating nonmonetary benefits. Additional training on company time, extended benefits (e.g., health), time off with pay, could be some of the benefits exchanged. The Bolivar QOW project has used such a scheme (Maccoby, 1978).

Job Switching

One of the structural changes at Rushton was job switching; it also appears in other work restructuring projects. The purpose of job switching was to build job skills and thus create more work group flexibility and greater variety at work. At Rushton some job switching did occur as the project took hold, but it began to decrease in the post-vote period (see Chapter 13). As an institution, it was never diffused to the other areas because of several factors. In most unionized work places, seniority determines access to the most desirable jobs. Job switching replaces seniority and usually requires that the person with the best (highest status) job work on a lower status job at times. Thus, a major reward from work is withdrawn. Switching in an interdependent group, such as a mine, requires that everyone switch. Yet there were individuals (e.g., older workers) who did not feel capable of performing certain jobs. Resistance of some of the less able work group members confounded the job-switching process.

Another factor inhibiting job switching was in its implementation. Job switching was outlined in the section conferences, but little was done in the mine to facilitate it. Also, no information system existed to identify how often switching occurred.

Since job switching is likely to be incorporated in other work restructuring projects, it is important to review factors that would facilitate it: Some incentive for the unskilled worker to shift is necessary. This might mean simply providing a new learning opportunity or tying pay into skills. Some incentive is also needed for the multiskilled worker. This high-status worker needs some rewards for switching to low-status jobs. A special high rate for knowledge of all job skills, plus opportunities to learn new skills (such as training skills) might motivate this worker to participate in switching. It is also necessary to remove negative incentives surrounding the switching process. At Rushton production demands dominated opportunities to exchange. If production was poor on a given shift, switching was less likely to occur. When switching is seen as a desirable behavior, production demands must be buffered on a regular basis. Individual preferences for switching also must be managed. At Rushton some crew members could not, or did not, want to switch. In the cases where older workers do not want to switch or where switching might increase accidents, special procedures are necessary. This puts constraints on switching in an interdependent work group, which switching across groups or across sections might resolve. Given all these complications, it is unlikely that introducing job switching will be a smooth operation. Therefore, at least two implementations are important: (1) you need data about how often switching occurs (a good feedback system) and (2) facilitators need to be on the scene to make the process work, that is, to manage switching opportunities within and between groups.

Training

A major part of the change at Rushton was to move men toward being professional miners through training. Since active training efforts are important to most QOW projects, it is useful to highlight some of the issues generated by the Rushton training program.

There were several training formats. A major effort was the six-session formal training given to the sections to initiate the experimental program. In addition, section conferences and other labor-management meetings served as training sessions. The research team made some effort to train the trainers (management personnel within the firm responsible for training). Lastly, there was some training in the sections.

Formal Training. The design of a training program represents a series of decisions. The most basic concerns: What do we want to change? The formal program at Rushton focused primarily on changing information about safety laws and about mining practices. An alternative approach might have been to focus on changing attitudes toward safety and work practices. However, many more powerful learning mechanisms built into the overall change program dealt with attitudes; therefore focusing on information-giving was reasonable.

A second issue in training design concerns timing. Should the training be concentrated over a relatively short period of time or spread out? Training for the South section was concentrated into two months. Subsequent training for other sections was spread over a longer time. It is our observation that more concentrated training facilitates: (1) the development of the autonomous concept and (2) the workers' identity with an experimental section. As members conceived motivational forces was an important part of the program, there into this program became more powerful. Given that increasing these motivational forces was an important part of the program, there probably were certain advantages to a concentrated training.

At a more microlevel we could have asked "How much time during a given day should be allocated to training?" This dilemma was not easily resolved. The miners were not used to sitting in a classroom. Therefore, a full-day session was probably too long. On the other hand, because of the 24-hour crew schedule and the transportation time to and from the coal face, it was not efficient or practical to bring three different shifts together for a half day. A full-day session seemed to be the practical alternative. In other QOW projects, this question must be asked in the light of the workers' span of attention for training and the economics of training large groups of workers.

Another training issue concerns the method of instruction. The lecture was the primary method used with some small group problem-solving sessions. Given that the major objectives were to impart knowledge about safety laws and regulations, this format seems appropriate. Other methods, such as developing special written material tailored to the men's reading level, were probably not appropriate, given the small size of the program. While the lecture method fit the expressed objectives of the training and the cost considerations, it limited the possibility of feedback from the students (the workers) about what they were learning and of providing reinforcement. Although the training probably helped to improve safety levels, at the same time we observed no consistent efforts to facilitate learning through other processes, such as obtaining feedback and providing reinforcement.

Section Conferences. Section conferences were a logical continuation of the formal training sessions. In them past behavior was reviewed, current problems were identified and solved, and future behavior was planned. As compared with the training sessions, these conferences put more emphasis on problem solving as a form of learning. However, since more than 30 people attended each meeting, problem solving as a group was difficult. Bringing the section together fostered section identity, yet the group was too big for effective problem solving. Attempts in most meetings to work in smaller groups were not terribly effective because no group decision-making skills had been developed. If groups are to engage in problem-solving activities, some training in these skills, including observation and feedback to the group about behaviors that facilitate problem solving, seems appropriate. Some QOW projects have used specialists to help in this area. Perhaps if the research team had focused more attention on developing problem-solving skills among the men and less time in facilitating problem-solving through their leadership behavior, more learning might have occurred in these conferences. I am not arguing that the section conferences were ineffective. They were *very* important mechanisms for developing section identity, which was a powerful motivation force in this project. The critical issue concerns developing problem-solving skills for the workers. This cannot be done easily in large groups. A possible strategy would have been to select (or elect) three to five potential problem-solving leaders from a section. These individuals would receive special problem-solving, discussion-skill training. (It is not appropriate to detail that training here—for more detailed information see Maier, 1963.) The important feature would be to tie that training knowledge into the specific day-to-day problems that confront the workers.

Role of Evaluation. Another issue relevant to training concerns the role of evaluation. Most texts on training advocate stating in behavioral terms what the students are expected to learn, developing measures to assess whether this behavior was learned, and actually doing the assessment. Since the training was to be ongoing, systematic information such as this gathered at the first session would have been helpful in designing subsequent training sessions and section conferences. Instead, there was no systematic analysis of the first training program or of the effectiveness of the section conferences in the Rushton project. Failure to collect this information formally reduced the opportunities to redesign the formal training sessions or section conference.

Training the Trainers. A basic problem in a change effort initiated externally is to train internal personnel to sustain the program. At Rushton the training director, his assistant, and the safety director were the objects of this training. In both our judgment and that of the trainees, the training did not enable them to take over the internal operation of the program. This occurred for two reasons: First, the research team initiated most phases of the project and ran many South section meetings. There was little opportunity for the "insiders" to practice new skills. Their (research team) role began to decrease only after the August 1975 vote. And second, the training that did occur focused more on drawing up a meeting agenda than on the problem-solving skills needed to run a meeting. These kinds of skills require on-the-job coaching. The need to train the trainers has to be one of the keys to maintaining a program over time. Dependencies on the external consultant must be reduced early in a QOW project. The external consultant will still be needed over the long course of the experiment, but it is open to question whether that external role should play as dominant a part as it did in the Rushton experience.

Training in the Section. Another aspect of training concerns on-the-job training in the mining section. Most of the program changes in mining, safety, and organizational practices were explained in the classroom or in the section conferences. However, to achieve these changes in behavior in the work place, training must also occur at the coal face. For example, planning practices were new behaviors initiated by the research team at Rushton. Some learning relevant to these behaviors can occur in the classroom setting. However, acquiring planning behaviors can only occur through systematic instruction at the coal face. There was little, if any systematic training at the section level. The following prescription is suggested: verbal commands are not enough to bring about behavior change, especially if the new behavior is novel. Some "hands on" training is necessary. This means that a new behavior is acquired through modeling or through some direct behavior modification. The error is to remain in the classroom too long.

DESIGN OF LABOR-MANAGEMENT COMMITTEES

While labor-management committees are an integral part of many QOW projects and are often the key to a project's success, their design has received little attention. The steering committee at Rushton, composed of members from labor and management, was the major mechanism for designing and extending the QOW project. It served as the policy-making, decision-making, and coordinating body. Although other joint labor-management committees focused on the day-to-day technical and coordination problems in a particular work area, our analysis will focus on the steering committee. In general the comments also apply to the smaller joint committees.

Membership

What should be the composition of the labor-management committee? At Rushton the membership included an equal representation from labor and management. Labor members are drawn from the elected union officers and the elected grievance and safety committees. Management was represented by the major line and staff positions (e.g., president, superintendent, safety director). One consequence of this method of generating members was that, except for natural job movement and some changes in union officers by way of election, the membership remained relatively the same from the beginning of the experiment. Since the union officers in this mine were more often found in outside jobs (e.g., maintenance), the union members of the committee were not representative of the mine. Most members from management were also from outside jobs. Only one foreman participated in the committee, and he was from the experimental section. As a result, the work force was not well represented on either side. This probably limited the diffusion of the project. If members of the nonautonomous inside sections had participated in the design and monitoring of the project, there might have been greater understanding of the experimental concepts at the time of the vote.

Should the members be appointed or elected? At Rushton members were appointed; in other projects they have been elected. It is difficult to answer the appointment versus election question in isolation from other factors. First, we have argued above that *representativeness* is important in QOW committees. This could be achieved by either an appointment or elective procedure. Second, some continuity is necessary in a QOW labor-management committee. At Rushton virtually the same people remained on the committee. At Rushton virtually the same people remained on the committee. Circulating new people into the committee would have provided new perspectives and socialized the new entrant in QOW concepts. Annual elections to replace the total membership would probably have been undesirable because of the break in continuity. Representativeness with some circulation of membership are the two critical factors in composition; they could be achieved through appointment or election.

The principal advantage of an election is that it involves the whole work force. Focusing attention on a project in its early stages should facilitate its diffusion. An election could also be used as a way to explain QOW concepts and to test how other areas of the organization feel toward the project. In the long run elections provide a way for the whole work force to participate in the project. This should facilitate some level of commitment. An election is also a legitimate mechanism for changing membership; in the Rushton system there was no agreed upon method to change members.

What is an optimal size? There is probably no simple answer to this question. At Rushton approximately 20 people were on the committee. Conflicting goals make the size of the committee a complicated question. From a political point of view the union, and perhaps management, would probably want broad representation as a means of keeping its members informed and maintaining control of the project. From the point of view of effective decision-making, large groups are not desirable. To resolve these conflicting goals we propose that in the initial stages of a project the policy labor-management group be a broad representative body of different labor and management constituencies. The major function of this group would be to establish overall policies. The specific studies or development of these policies would be delegated to smaller task forces drawn from the larger group. In this way the political and decision-making goals could be accomplished with integrated groups of different sizes.

Mechanisms

Who should lead the labor-management group? At Rushton the research team members were the principal leaders throughout the course of this experiment. We think that this is an undesirable practice. The external consultants should play a major role only in the initial few months of a project and not over such a long time period. The committee leader should be drawn by way of rotation from labor and management. This gives both parties another investment in the project. It also provides training for the committee leaders, a critical factor in sustaining the program over time. In addition, this arrangement would leave the external consultant free to observe and improve the functioning of the group.

What kinds of leadership roles should be performed? Research about small groups stresses two functions: a task and a process function. The task function concerns those activities needed to reach the group's goal. In the Rushton project this could have meant labor and management developing a new document for a mine-wide QOW program, or solving a technical problem, such as reducing the number of flat tires on shuttle cars. As the group moved toward its goals the resulting strain and tension among its members would be minimized through the process function.

A basic question is to what extent these roles or functions should be played out in labor-management committees. One position, which characterizes the meeting interactions at Rushton, emphasizes the task function (see Chapter 14). Given the basic institutional differences between labor and management, process interventions, in this political environment, are considered inappropriate. Another position emphasizes the process role where a trained observer of group dynamics continually feeds back information to the group on how it is progressing, whether people are listening, and how it is dealing with conflict. The process consultant might, for example, expose value differences as a way of facilitating group problem solving.

There is a dilemma in selecting between the task and process roles. While the QOW program labor and management committees represent problem-solving arenas rather than places for traditional bargaining, labor and management still represent different constituencies. They have different values and goals. The political aspect of their relationship is a reality. Therefore, it is likely that a number of different agenda will be operative during a labor-management meeting. We believe that the institutional nature of the labor-management role places some constraints on how far the process role can be introduced in these committees. For example, the union representative's behavior in a meeting is affected by local membership pressures. His behavior might be dysfunctional for the labor-management committee but not for his relationship with the membership. In this case, where political constraints affect behavior, we would argue that some forms of process intervention are not really beneficial. On the other hand, there are behaviors not tied to political constraints which do affect how well the group solves problems.

The process functions we visualize would insure that everyone has an opportunity to speak, that minority opinions are aired, and that the group make explicit the problem it wants to solve before thinking of other choices. One graduate student on the research team, Mel Blumberg, did play out this type of process role. In the labor-management committee meetings he would encourage individuals to talk who had not been recognized or encourage those who were discouraged with a course of events to express their point of view. The president of Rushton played out a principal process role in translating some of the research team's ideas to the miners. These types of intervention, however, were at a minimum at Rushton.

To summarize this argument, we think that the mix between task and process roles needs to be considered in designing a QOW project. Although it will be limited by political constraints, some level of process intervention can facilitate group problem solving.

What structures facilitate problem solving? A dominant activity of these labor-management committees was to resolve problems ranging from very technical subjects to the structure of the program itself. In any problem-solving process there is a natural cycle to be followed. The problem is identified, some search for information occurs, choices are generated, and a solution is selected. After the solution is implemented, results occur, a feedback mechanism is implemented, and the problem is either resolved or reconsidered. The structure of the meetings at Rushton was well suited up to the phase in the cycle where a solution is reached, but did not lend itself to implementing or monitoring the results of the decision. Therefore, some other mechanism was needed for feedback and corrective action. In our observation such a secondary structure was not devised at Rushton. One persistent problem with the committees was the lack of follow-up on decisions. Decisions made at one meeting often were not fully implemented when the next meeting occurred. The point of raising this issue is not to criticize the committee's structure, but to suggest that a secondary structure would have completed the problem-solving cycle.

The secondary structure could have been in the form of a problem expeditor or of a subgroup from the major committee which examines the implementation of a decision and then provides corrective feedback.

How should decisions be resolved? At Rushton decisions were worked out through discussion and compromise. The membership at any meeting was fluid and rarely was concerned that management and labor be in equal numbers. Voting was never used as a method to resolve decisions. Although we do not have any empirical evidence, the consensus mode of operation seemed to be a preferable strategy. Formal voting would have reinforced institutional affiliations (union membership), and there would have been very strong pressures to vote along party lines. Once this had happened the labor-management groups might have reverted to the more traditional collective bargaining mode.

Content

What is the role of traditional labor relations in QOW committees? Labor-management committees are created to design, implement, and monitor QOW activities in a cooperative relationship, with mutual problem solving representing the mode of operation. Traditional collective-bargaining issues, such as grievances, are handled through procedures set up in the national collective-bargaining agreement. Processing a grievance involves an adversary relationship with bargaining representing the mode of operation. Excluding traditional collective-bargaining issues from QOW relationships is bound to create a spillover effect. A bitter battle over a grievance, for example, probably will reduce the effectiveness of problem solving in a QOW meeting since some representatives of labor and management generally appear in both settings. On the other hand, if grievances are included in QOW sessions they might drive out discussions of QOW problems. This occurred at Rushton. Also, grievances might be introduced into QOW discussions as a way to get special settlements that were not attainable under the traditional grievance procedure. In a number of instances at Rushton the union brought up a grievance in a QOW meeting at a strategic time. The bargain was—resolve the grievance in the union's favor and the union will support management's position in a QOW problem. Although this was a reasonable bargaining position from the union's point of view, it was not an optimal way to develop problem-solving capabilities between labor and management.

The problem then is to design a labor-management QOW committee that deals with this dilemma. It is most important to note that the inherent conflict between the cooperative mode of QOW committees and the adversary relationship in the traditional collective bargaining set up cannot be eliminated. The adversary relationship derives from institutional structure, and it will not go away. Although it has been argued that QOW projects will eventually push labor-management relationships to a new level of cooperation, the conflict between a cooperative mode and the adversary mode will continue. We must conclude, therefore, that the dilemma will persist and cannot be designed away.

There are, however, some ways to reduce the magnitude of the dilemma. The first and most obvious is to keep the two institutions as separate as possible. At Rushton it was a mistake, I think, to allow grievances into the steering committees. Since the probabilities of a favorable judgment were higher because of the QOW concept and the different management personnel in attendance, it was to the union's advantage to bring significant grievances in front of this committee. Consider the case just before the major vote in August 1975 when the union brought a grievance to the steering committee with the indication that a favorable judgment would facilitate the vote. This behavior benefited the union, but detracted from working on QOW problems. Along with separating the issues discussed, it would also be useful both to hold grievance or negotiating committee meetings and the QOW committee meetings in different locations and to minimize the overlap in memberships. A related strategy would be to develop norms within both groups (e.g., grievance committee, steering committee) to keep the issues separate. Recognizing that there will be a spill-over effect and dealing with it explicitly in the QOW group will help to minimize it. This will force the QOW committee, in particular, to take a hard line on what it will or will not discuss.

Another approach is to improve existing labor-management relations, procedures, and practices. The most common direction of spill-over will be for issues not resolved in the traditional collective-bargaining arena to get pushed over to the QOW committee. At Rushton one of the dominant spill-over problems concerned the job-bidding and job-selection procedure. The more an operative procedure can be worked out for bidding and selection through collective bargaining, the less spillover will occur. It is not possible to develop procedures that will eliminate conflict, but improving existing labor-management operations improves the chances that a QOW program will survive.

SOCIO-TECHNICAL-ECONOMIC SYSTEMS

To close this section on design issues, we shall review the intellectual premises guiding this project. The research team is a major exponent of the socio-technical orientation. Basically this holds that an organization is an integrated complex of systems and that intervention into only one system (e.g., the social system) will in the end be ineffective. The argument is that joint optimization of both the social and technical systems is a way to increase organizational effectiveness. Reviewing the Rushton experience, however, reveals much more emphasis on social-organizational interventions than on the technical system. Although the attempts at Rushton to improve planning and the communications system within the mine should have had some bearing on the effectiveness of the technical system, there was little focus on specific mining practices, such as the mining cycle and mining equipment; consequently, no major changes in productivity occurred. The failure to innovate in the technical system is not surprising. Most social scientists are not sufficiently acquainted with the technology of a particular site to enable them to make major technical breakthroughs. This would necessitate having a technological expert as part of the intervention team. There was one mining engineer in the research team, but because of other commitments he was not able to spend significant portions of time at the mine.

Hiring a technical expert is not the only way to make technological innovations. Various employees can also serve as resource persons on small task forces assigned to specific technological problems. The section conferences at Rushton were too large to be effective problem-solving devices and met outside, versus inside the mine, where the technological problems exist. Task forces which spend considerable time in the mining sections experimenting with new technological choices represent a more viable alternative.

Another idea is that the socio-technical framework should be extended to be a socio-technical-economic framework. Besides looking for the optimum fit between the technological and social systems of a firm, organizational designers need to consider how that fit bears on the firm's economic system, since all three systems are interdependent. In other words, it is conceivable that an intervention structure would complement a firm's social and technical system, but be detrimental to its economic system.

At Rushton, little attention was given to the economic feasibility of the proposed organizational innovations. In some cases the effect was trivial, but in others it was substantial. Adding two extra supply men to each section was a major recurring cost. It was not clear that each shift needed two extra men or whether one extra man, or some other combination, would have been just as effective. Clearly, organizational innovations need to complement the organization's economic system, or, at least, their impact on the economic system needs to be assessed. We are *not* arguing for a cost-benefit analysis of each proposed structure, since we do not believe that economic feasibility determines the acceptability of a new structure. We do believe, however, that a new structure affects the economic viability of the organization, and, therefore, some approach toward optimization of the social, technical, and economic systems seems appropriate.

CHAPTER TWENTY

Critical Issues in Implementing QOW Experiments

Introducing a quality of work experiment in an organization is a complex task with many unanticipated consequences. In this chapter we shall identify some of those problem areas. These are derived from the Rushton experience, but have appeared in other QOW experiments (Goodman and Lawler, 1977). Resolving these implementation issues is critical to the success of any QOW experiment.

PROBLEM AREAS

First-Line Supervisors

A basic theme in most QOW projects is giving workers more control over their environment, usually in the form of more responsibility. It has been argued that changes in control do not really redistribute responsibilities from one segment of the organization to another, but instead expand the total influence structure for all jobs. However, many jobs *are* changed, and stress on the job is increased for certain positions. This is a fairly general occurrence across most QOW sites. The first-line supervisor in particular is initially affected the most. At Rushton his traditional activity of supervising production was withdrawn, and responsibility for new and unfamiliar activities was introduced (e.g., planning). As a consequence, job stress increased. This, in turn, may have affected the

359

supervisor's performance and acceptance of the work restructuring effort.

Foremen's meetings were introduced at Rushton to help the boss make the transition to his new role. These meetings were designed to alleviate stress by allowing the foremen to share their feelings and to support them in their new roles. While the meetings provided a useful format for alleviating tension, they did not clearly help the foreman learn a new set of role behaviors. Consider the task of planning which is both complex and abstract. How do you teach a foreman to plan? Verbally imploring him to change or providing a supportive atmosphere is clearly not enough.

When new behaviors were required, we would suggest more emphasis on a behavioristic and/or modeling system to induce change. After the program had been introduced, a trainer would be with each foreman during work. The trainer first would model the new forms of work behavior, and then the foreman would engage in the behavior. Reinforcements would be provided to support the new behavior. A reinforcement schedule needs to be planned over a sufficient time period to insure some level of institutionalization. Meanwhile other activities were used to extinguish old behaviors. This "hands on"—on the job training—approach is necessary if new behaviors were to be adopted.

At Rushton the training director and his assistant did work with the foremen. But the program for this was not systematic. There was no analysis of which behaviors were to be performed and which were to be extinguished and no systematic modeling to illustrate the new behaviors. Most importantly, there was no reinforcement schedule to bring the new behaviors in place. The basic theme running through all our analyses is that changing behavior is very complex. Reliance on some form of verbal communication is not enough. It is necessary to: (1) illustrate the desired behavior, (2) identify paths to performing that behavior, and (3) reinforce its performance.

Middle Management

Changes at the first-line supervisor level reverberated throughout the organization. Not only did the foremen's jobs change, so did the jobs of middle and upper level managers. Unfortunately, at Rushton, as well as at other sites, the project is initiated from top management and is implemented at the lower levels of the organization. Middle and upper level positions are sometimes ignored.

Nevertheless, these jobs are changing and require that certain activities be given up and new skills be acquired. People in these positions experience ambiguity and stress similar to that identified for the first-line supervisor. This, in turn, can affect performance and the acceptance of the program.

This implementation problem occurred at Rushton. It was further compounded by the fact that some individuals in these positions were against the work restructuring program prior to its installation. The stress for these individuals was even higher since they had to adopt behaviors that they opposed. As a consequence, these individuals were never integrated into the program, and there is some evidence that they worked against it.

The approach at Rushton to resolve this issue was to hold some management and counseling meetings. These, however, were run sporadically and had the same thrust as the foremen's meetings we discussed. They were probably more effective in alleviating stress than in introducing new forms of work behavior. Although alleviating stress was necessary to facilitate learning, attention needed to be focused on the new behaviors. These required careful analysis to help the trainer describe or model them. As noted, a systematic plan is needed for all this; occasional meetings between middle management and the research team are not enough. A carefully planned training program with opportunities for feedback and follow up is necessary to deal with the conflict that the middle and upper level management positions are likely to experience.

Personnel

A QOW experiment may also create stress in staff functions, such as personnel. Many of the experiments require special forms of expertise not found in most personnel departments. Often, therefore, the strategy has been to use external consultants. This calls into question the effectiveness of the personnel area and leads to resistance from these individuals. Although at Rushton this did not occur because the personnel division was understaffed and undertrained and because the staff saw the project as a way to learn, in other sites (see Goodman and Lawler, 1977) stress and conflict was created in personnel as a function of the intervention.

This problem suggests the need for developing a resource person—an in-house expert—who will have skills to sustain the project over time. This individual may or may not come from personnel and would require some degree of classroom training as well as on-the-job training with the external consultant. The major task for this individual would be maintaining and initiating QOW projects for the organization. Again this would be a complicated new role that could not be learned by hearing about it. The inside consultant would have to be systematically trained by the outside consultant through on-the-job experiences.

Total System Commitment

It is an old adage that "commitment from the top" is needed to launch any major organizational project. Some minimal level of commitment to QOW goals, however, is necessary throughout the total organization in implementing any experiment. Rushton— where there was strong commitment from the president, but not throughout management or union leader ranks—is a good case in point. The president's strong commitment precluded any explicit disagreement over participation or in implementation from the managers. We expect that QOW projects started because of the values of a single decision-maker are likely to experience difficulties in persisting over time.

Some type of diagnosis of the congruence between QOW goals and employee values is necessary prior to launching any experiment. This is a critical step because most projects require changing some basic values. At Rushton the changes toward greater responsibility and autonomy were contrary to the values held by some members of management. Since these individuals could greatly affect the outcome of the project, a realistic question is whether the project should have been undertaken. The dilemma is interesting: On the one hand, there was strong commitment from the top, on the other hand there was no commitment among those individuals who affected the project's day-to-day operation. Creating commitment from these individuals is not a trivial task. At issue is changing some important values that are exceedingly difficult to change.

There is no easy resolution to this problem. One option is to begin a QOW project only if there is a reasonable probability of getting commitment at all relevant levels. This requires a good understanding of the organization and its personnel. However, given the drive to do QOW projects and the difficulty of finding sites, it is hard to reject an organization because of its lack of commitment. Some social scientists advocate insuring commitment prior to beginning a major intervention. Generally this would mean starting at the top and developing a set of goals and philosophies about

QOW projects. These principles would then be moved down through the organization as part of a ratification process. Understanding, acceptance, and commitment would be required before the principles would be presented at a new level. Such a top-down procedure has been introduced in some organizations (Hill, 1971). It is time consuming, costly, and, if it is to be effective, it requires a fair amount of expertise and resources.

In the Rushton case it was not until a year into the experiment before an effort was planned to bring the beliefs and interpersonal relationships among top management of the mine in line with the objectives of the QOW project. While no one knows what the optimal time is for insuring continued commitment to a QOW project, it is relatively clear that commitment must be demonstrated by the central and peripheral actors, and it should occur relatively early in a project.

The second question concerns the methods for obtaining commitment from individuals who might be neutral or negative toward a QOW project. At Rushton one member of the research team worked with individuals or with small groups attempting to improve understanding of their relationships with each other, especially as they bore on the operation of the QOW program. This type of process intervention represents one strategy; clearly others are available. There is no good evidence to suggest that one method is better than another. Rather, two factors should be considered when reviewing methods for obtaining commitment. One concerns the skills and experience of the intervener. The level of skills and experience in changing individual beliefs and attitudes should determine whether change can be undertaken and what methods should be used. At Rushton the research team member had not had a lot of experience in this type of change work. The other factor concerns the reinforcement schedule attached to the learning sessions. The learning sessions focused on the modification of some basic beliefs and values. This type of change is quite demanding and generally requires a systematic reinforcement schedule over time. At Rushton there was no regular program to modify the beliefs of top managers. Consequently, the managers holding neutral or negative beliefs changed little.

Another strategy is to acknowledge in the beginning that commitment will not be possible and then to develop explicit organizational mechanisms (in the form of new communications and decision-making channels) around the uncommitted individuals. This strategy is possible when the uncommitted individual does not have a direct relationship to the experiment. At Rushton, if the purchasing agent opposed the program, the consequences for its long-run operation would not be significant. If the general foreman (above the foremen) were opposed, it would have negative consequences for the long-term operation of the program.

Union Relationships

In our analysis of implementation problems the focus has primarily been on management. Introducing a QOW project, however, has consequences for the union.

Union Leader-Member Relationships. The labor-management committee is the principal mechanism for integrating union and management efforts in most QOW projects. Through frequent meetings participants have reported developing a better understanding of each other, a consequence that should facilitate traditional labor-management negotiations. On the other hand, the frequent association between management and union officers outside the traditional collective-bargaining arrangements did raise feelings of distrust in the union membership toward their leaders at Rushton. This, in turn, encouraged the leaders to behave in any way that was dysfunctional to the program, but that enhanced their position with their men. We see this as an inherent conflict built into the operation of the QOW committee. Understanding and recognition that the problem will occur is probably the only way it can be confronted.

Member Relations. At Rushton the change was introduced in a particular section. The pilot project strategy was used and will be used in other QOW projects. This strategy had two implications for the internal function of the local union. First, the experimental section was different from the other sections in terms of pay for the same work and other resources. These differences generated feelings of inequity and led to conflict among the union members. Given the need for solidarity, tension among union members has a dysfunctional consequence for the union. Different approaches to the pilot project strategy are discussed later in this chapter.

A second unanticipated consequence was that the experiment created a new potential power structure within the local union. In the Rushton project some of the experimental groups voted en masse at union meetings; in the past most of these men had not attended meetings. The point is not that this emerging power structure was good or bad, but that it represented a possible challenge to the existing power structure, and thus, was a potential source of conflict, insecurity, and resistance.

Local-International Relations. Most activity in quality of work experiments such as Rushton occurs at the local level, while the final legitimation comes from the international level. This poses an interesting dilemma. On one hand, at the local level union and management have a mandate to innovate. On the other hand, especially if the new labor-management arrangements are considered far beyond the boundaries that could be incorporated in a future collective-bargaining agreement, the international may view the local QOW project as only experimental and temporary, quite independently of the success of the project. Without long-run legitimation, the local project is unlikely to survive. This can result in conflict between the local and international if the local wants the project to continue.

Another dilemma is that QOW projects such as Rushton require resources and support from the international. The international is concerned with all the mines within its jurisdiction as well as organizing new mines. Rushton is only one mine competing against many other larger mines for the international's resources. Again this seems to be an inherent conflict between the local and international. It was a major source of tension between these two groups at Rushton.

Another unanticipated consequence is that political activities within the international can affect the viability of the local project, again quite independently of the success of the project. The political battles in the UMWA headquarters affected the degree of support the international provided to the Rushton project. This, in turn, probably affected the successful expansion of the program. When the international staff contributed to the Rushton project (e.g., in drawing up the mine-wide document), the contributions were viewed as positive by all parties. However, the total amount of support was quite low.

There are no simple solutions to resolve the tensions between the local and international brought about by the QOW project. I believe the tensions are inherent in structural arrangement between the local and international. However, a strong commitment by the international leaders to a QOW project and an accessible sponsor in the international who can coordinate local and international activities with respect to a QOW project seem to be necessary conditions for the project's long-run viability.

It should be noted that relations between corporate headquarters and local plants can parallel international-local union relations. This was not true at Rushton, where although the mine is part of a larger corporation, most of the decisions were made by the mine president. In other organizational arrangements with more centralized decision-making, conflict may occur between the local plant QOW activities and corporate policy.

Individual Differences. A problem at Rushton and in all QOW projects is how to introduce organizational change and at the same time be responsive to individual differences. The change program at Rushton called for greater levels of responsibility and autonomy; this did affect worker behavior. These changes, however, were not equally valued by all workers. Some individuals might perceive opportunities for greater responsibility and control to be threatening, rather than beneficial.

We consider this an implementation issue since it is unlikely that one can design *a priori* a program that will reflect individual differences. As the program evolves some mechanism is necessary to permit people to choose. At Rushton the mine-wide document acknowledged the worker's right not to participate in an autonomous work group framework. However, this did not really provide the worker a choice. If his work group chose to go autonomous did he have any choice other than to leave the group? Group pressures in a relatively autonomous group would be too great to let any individual operate nonautonomously. Also, at Rushton there was neither a specific mechanism nor a specific time for the individual to make this choice.

Dealing with individual differences requires two mechanisms: one for making a choice and one to determine how often the choice should be expressed. The mechanism would probably take different forms in different places. At a minimum it should provide each work group member a "secret ballot" (known only to external consultant) to express his or her preferences for participating in some QOW arrangement. From this information the consultant would have to decide whether an individual should move or the structure be modified. My own observations are that a strong experimental group will not tolerate deviants. The timing of individual difference expressions would have to be arbitrary; once a year is probably a reasonable period. Programs, such as Scanlon Plans, usually call for an annual expression of preferences to continue.

CRITICAL PROCESSES

In concluding this chapter two processes, institutionalization and diffusion, are reviewed. These are selected because they are the two critical processes in any QOW intervention. The effectiveness of any project will depend on the degree of institutionalization and the degree of diffusion within the organization.

Institutionalization refers to the process by which new structures persist over time without some form of external surveillance. The idea is that a worker would first decide whether to adopt a new form of work behavior. The next step is whether to continue that behavior. Over time, if the new behavior is internalized (i.e., becomes a value in its own right) or the reinforcement schedule continues, then the new form of work behavior will tend to persist and become institutionalized. Diffusion refers to the process by which a new form of work behavior is spread to other areas of the social system. At Rushton it refers to the spread of the intervention throughout the mine or to other mines.

These two processes are conceptually highly interrelated. For diffusion to occur the new structure needs to be spread *and* institutionalized. At Rushton this would have meant that the new forms of work behavior had become institutionalized in the nonexperimental sections. Therefore, institutionalization is included in the definition of diffusion. Also, once diffusion occurs, institutionalized behavior is likely to be reinforced. For example, the nonexperimental sections' acceptance of the QOW program would have exerted forces on the original section to maintain the program. Similarly, other mines adopting the Rushton program would have created forces on Rushton to continue in the program.

Institutionalization

For institutionalization to occur the individual must first decide to adopt the new behavior. This decision will be affected by the net gain of performing the new behavior instead of some alternative behavior. The individual will then choose whether to continue in that behavior. This choice will be a function of the positive or negative consequences of adopting the behavior, the strength of the expectation that there will be a net gain in performing the behavior (an expectation which might persist despite negative consequences), and other forces (e.g., work group pressures). Over time if the behavior becomes internalized and/or the reinforcements derived from the behavior or work group continue, the behavior will become institutionalized. Antecedents to the adoption, continuation, and institutionalization of the behavior are the character of the intervention structure and of the work group.

A number of factors will facilitate the institutionalization process:

1. The nature of the new behavior, in terms of what it is and how to do it, should be visible to the employees. At Rushton the act of communicating about work between shifts was a visible and understandable behavior. This new form of work behavior became one of the most persistent structures at Rushton. Planning before the shift was not an understandable behavior for the work force at Rushton and never became institutionalized. When dealing with a less visible or more abstract behavior the intervener must do more than tell the employee that the behavior should be performed. We have argued that detailed analysis and on-the-job modeling of the new behavior is necessary if it is to become institutionalized. Section conferences are not enough.

2. The proposed behavior must be perceived as connected to some valued reward. Although this point seems obvious, we saw many instances at Rushton where the connection was not made. This was due to discrepancies in understanding between the research team and employees as to whether the proposed new structures held positive benefits. These discrepancies originated from two sources: First, the research team sometimes did not distinguish between company benefits and personal benefits. Company benefits are advantages that accrue to the firm, while personal benefits flow to the individual. Greater coordination, work group flexibility, and so on, are really company benefits. Greater pay or security is an advantage to the work force. We would argue that one reason planning before the shift, for instance, had never taken is that it offered no immediate personal benefits. Second, discrepancies also originated in the way the research team and workers valued certain rewards. Autonomy and responsibility were major values for the research team. However, not all workers subscribed to these values.

3. The worker must receive some feedback about how congruent their new behaviors are with the expected behaviors. That is, some feedback mechanism is necessary to bring the actual and intended behaviors together. It is unlikely that the foreman's first try at planning behavior would correspond to the expected behavior.

4. The workers must receive reinforcements on some periodic basis after the adoption decision. If a worker engages in job switching, some reinforcement must follow. In designing a job-switching program, therefore, one must not only specify how to do the behavior, but also build in a reinforcement schedule. The reinforcements may flow from the intrinsic characteristics of the behavior or from the periodic extrinsic reinforcements.

5. Negative incentives attached to the new behavior must be minimized. These were a major problem in implementing the job-switching procedures. For example, job switching required men in high status jobs to relinquish their standing; some workers simply did not want to switch for this reason.

6. Development of work group norms for the new behavior is essential in the institutionalization process. If the work group supports the new behavior and is cohesive, a powerful force can be brought to bear on the institutionalization of the new behavior.

7. The research or consulting team must receive feedback about whether the new behaviors are being adopted. Introducing change is not a one-shot endeavor. Once a new practice is introduced, it needs to be continually modified. Without feedback this modification process cannot be undertaken. At Rushton feedback systems did not provide effective monitoring of the changes introduced. Throughout this project there were discrepancies between expected and actual behaviors. (See Goodman, Conlon, and Bazerman, forthcoming, for a more detailed discussion.)

Diffusion

Diffusion is one of the most critical dimensions of any QOW project. While each project is interesting in its own right, whether it can stimulate other organizations to participate is an important question. In the Rushton case, no other mines have agreed to adopt a related program. Yet one purpose of the Rushton project was to motivate other mines to adopt QOW projects.

Diffusion can occur at four levels: within a plant or site, within sites in the same firm, within the industry, or within the country. We shall explore each of these, but with more emphasis on within-plant diffusion.

The models of diffusion and institutionalization are highly related. Diffusion requires institutionalization of structures in new locations. The major difference is in the "front end," where diffusion focuses more on whether a new structure will be adopted, while institutionalization refers to whether the new structure will continue or persist over time. Our basic strategy has been to examine how the intervention structure affects whether the individual adopts a new innovation. The process works in the following way: the intervention structure determines the diffusion processes. These refer to the nature of the communicator, the mechanisms for diffusion, the nature of the communication, and the receiver. The interaction between these factors determines whether the adoption decision will occur. Once the individual tries the new behavior, the rewards inherent in that new behavior (e.g., intershift communications or forces from the work group) will become over time more powerful than the diffusion mechanisms in influencing the decision to continue that behavior.

At Rushton we saw the problems of within-plant diffusion. The vote and the difficulties with the post-vote diffusion point up the need of a strategy for diffusion. The following factors may be generalized to other settings:

1. The characteristics of the intervention structure are a major determinant of the diffusion process. A major problem in most QOW projects is the failure to deal with the process of diffusion in the initial design of the project. Since these intervention structures have been discussed in Chapters 17 and 18, in this chapter only a few illustrations will be presented:

(a) The use of the pilot project strategy can inhibit diffusion. Given the problems of gaining acceptance, the risks in a new experiment, and the need for learning, the initial use of a pilot strategy makes sense. Over time, however, differences between the pilot and other work areas cause tension either because of jealousy or real inequities. In either case the tension inhibits the diffusion process. An obvious solution to this dilemma is to move the QOW project quickly from the pilot to the other work areas. Another strategy is to begin with at least two pilot projects. The two projects would support each other and appear less deviant (i.e., more workers involved would signal more acceptance).

(b) The design of reward systems can also facilitate diffusion. The decision to adopt or participate in a QOW project depends on the decision-maker's belief about the net gain of such a choice. At the time of the Rushton vote, there were no significant concrete benefits (e.g., major pay differentials) for participating. The existence of an operational QOW gain-sharing plan might have influenced the diffusion process at Rushton. It is my judgment that the long-term viability of QOW projects will depend on the viability of a gain-sharing plan.

(c) The design of the QOW labor-management committee systems isolated the experimental and nonexperimental sections at Rushton. Greater opportunities for the nonexperimental miners to learn about the experiment through participation in its design and implementation might have influenced diffusion.

2. The character of the diffusion processes can also affect diffusion:

(a) The communicators for the diffusion should be highly attractive and/or credible to the work force. This seems to be a necessary condition for diffusion. The enlistment of opinion leaders in the process should facilitate diffusion. These conditions were relatively absent at Rushton.

(b) The communication meetings were the primary mechanism of diffusion. In our analysis of these meetings we pointed out that reliance on a single mechanism and one built on the communication-persuasion model limited the diffusion at Rushton. The use of multiple mechanisms based on different models (e.g., modeling, operant) should facilitate the process.

(c) The content of what is to be diffused cannot be too abstract. The concept of "autonomous work groups" is quite abstract and difficult to diffuse, particularly for the population under study. Essentially, the content must be understandable and be perceived as different from the existing state of affairs; that is, the nonexperimental subjects must perceive the practices in the experimental section as different from their own practices, beneficial, and also as achievable.

3. The attitudes of the receiver obviously filter the information and thus affect the decision to adopt the behavior. There were factors prior to (anti-management feelings held by union organizers) and after the intervention (arbitrary implementation of the program after the "no" vote) that affected the receiver's attitudes and beliefs. In general there were strong negative attitudes toward the diffusion process that inhibited diffusion. Unless these attitudes changed, diffusion throughout the mine was unlikely. The basic point is that strategies must be undertaken to modify the receiver's attitudes prior to any diffusion strategy.

Within-company diffusion has been most thoroughly analyzed by Walton (1975), and his analysis makes a useful parallel to our discussion of within-plant diffusion.

He mentions that lack of compatibility between the organization that adopted the QOW experiment and the prospective organization can inhibit diffusion. In our framework this would mean that the nature of the communication about the intervention structure would be incongruent with the beliefs held by the receiver about his own organization. Walton also suggests that confusion over what is to be diffused inhibits diffusion. By this he means that the communicator selects the wrong message (one that is either too abstract or too

CRITICAL ISSUES IN IMPLEMENTING QOW EXPERIMENTS

operational) and diffusion is inhibited. This parallels our analysis of how communication content can affect diffusion processes. Union opposition, another within-company restriction on diffusion, has a similar effect on within-plant diffusion. The framework and strategies for within-company diffusion then are similar to those for within-plant diffusion. The underlying issue of whether the new behaviors will be viewed as a net gain and adopted is the same. The need to define the similarities and differences (in attitudes, beliefs, work, etc.) between the old system and the system being diffused is still a necessary activity.

Diffusion within an industry, although based on the same processes discussed, is clearly different. It involves organizations that are physically and organizationally separate. In many cases the organizations are competitors.

The most typical within-industry diffusion mechanism is the demonstration project model. Here a firm in a particular industry participates in a QOW program as a demonstration project for that industry; hopefully other firms will copy the practices of that demonstration site. At best, this mechanism generates some awareness, but little commitment to adopt the experiment, primarily because the demonstration site is atypical. Rushton is not a typical mine; it is small, not encumbered by a large bureaucratic structure, and led by a man willing to experiment. It is not representative of the industry, but then no single site is likely to be representative. It is not surprising that the Rushton project did not have a major diffusion impact on the coal mining industry.

Another mechanism—one adopted at first by the Rushton research team—was to have two demonstration sites: Rushton and a second mine with dissimilar characteristics (e.g., different size and technology). The idea was to make the demonstration projects more representative. If both projects were successful, there would be more compatiblility (in terms of organizational characteristics) between the communication about the new intervention and any proposed receivers. While the two-mine study is a preferable mechanism (unfortunately, the second mine declined to participate because of internal problems with the local union), it really deals with the awareness of an innovation, not the commitment to adopt it.

Another strategy is to design a mechanism that insures awareness and commitment to adopt. To achieve the latter some opinion leaders from other firms must be involved in the design, monitoring, or evaluation of the new project. This could occur under the auspices of a trade association. The critical issue is that direct involvement in the demonstration projects by nonparticipants should facilitate the commitment to participate.

A diverse set of centers at the national level are trying to diffuse ideas relevant to QOW experiments. Each center uses different strategies for diffusion. Some rely primarily on conferences, others provide newsletters, still others are activists trying to get labor and management together. The latter centers now provide consultation in the design, training for, and the implementation of these projects. Since our experience has been primarily at the organizational level and since the QOW projects are relatively new, it is difficult to evaluate diffusion attempts at the national level. Our assumption is that the basic processes identified in the discussion of diffusion are applicable at the national level.

CONCLUSION

The purpose of Chapters 19 and 20 has been to identify the critical issues that make a difference in success of any QOW project. Issues in the design, implementation, and processes of change have been identified. Anyone, whether they be union, management, or organizational-change specialists must deal with these issues and questions: How does one design a labor-management committee? How do variations in these designs fit into different types of union-management structures and/or QOW experiments? How do rewards systems need to be restructured to be congruent with the QOW design features? How are new behaviors to be adopted? What is the appropriate model? How does one design projects where institutionalization and diffusion occur?

It is clear that the answers to these issues and questions are not easily obtained. I have taken one step by trying to delineate the major issues or questions. The next step, whether one is practioner or theorist, is to develop some type of framework for understanding the critical processes in organizational change. Some preliminary frameworks have been identified in the last section of this book. Next some alternative design configurations have been identified; no single design will be the most effective. The next step must be taken by you—to experiment with some of the new proposals, to identify new issues, and to elaborate on the theoretical processes.

Epilogue

I am writing this short concluding section in the first week of January 1979 to give the reader the most current picture of the state of affairs at Rushton and to indicate new developments for 1979. There is also a brief identification of the major events that occurred between the end of our historical account in December 1976 (Chapter Eight) and the beginning of 1979.

There is now *no* functioning quality of work program at Rushton. The major institutions have disappeared; training and development committee meetings (which generated the overall policy for the program) are not called; and the joint committees that coordinated inter-crew activities are no longer used. Intershift communication, foreman planning and goal-setting activities, job switching, intramanagement coordination meetings, and other parts of the Rushton program are not operational. The research team has left the mine.

The following observations were drawn from a set of interviews and observations conducted at the mine near the end of 1978.

One miner said: "There is no program now. We have a boss. He tells us what to do. Before, when the mine was down, we would service it and roof dust . . . we did things before the boss said anything . . . now we wait for him."

The picture, then, is that the major institutions and roles that had been created by the experimental intervention and had existed for more than 3 years were not in existence in December 1978. This does not mean, however, that the mine remains as it was in 1973 when this experimental project was initiated. Once major interventions are introduced into an organization, it must move to a new equilibrium. Such is the case at Rushton. The miners at Rushton were extensively trained through the QOW program. Almost all the men have learned to do the other jobs in the crew. As one miner said: "I learned a lot. . . . We still put on the belt together and do it without any outside

374

help. . . . I can run most of the other pieces of equipment . . . look around, the other guys can do it too."

This training and additional knowledge has led to a more flexible work force. The men still know and use the technical aspects of good mining and safety practices. Also, the men who were part of the experiment had a unique set of experiences with the benefits and costs of new forms of work organization. Organizations are not static entities. We expect that modification in the Rushton organization will evolve over time. Our interviews indicate that the miners are reasonably sophisticated about the advantages and disadvantages of the Rushton QOW program as well as the factors that detracted from its long-run viability. This knowledge should be invaluable in shaping new organizational forms in the future.

The purpose of these few paragraphs is to give the reader a quick status report of what Rushton looks like today. Simply stated, the basic institutions are gone, but the effect of these institutions on some of the mining (e.g., moving a belt) and safety practices still persists. The new organizational arrangements are gone; the new technical knowledge of mining and safety practices remains.

Before we turn to the future, I will provide a brief summary of the major events between January 1977 and January 1979. Nineteen seventy-seven started the same way that 1976 ended (Chapter Eight). The major institutions continued to slowly erode. The Mine Training and Development Committee meetings were the major sign that the program was still in operation.

A 10-day strike in March 1977 dealt a major blow to the program. The union alleged that a foreman hit one of its UMW members, and the miners walked out. As the strike continued, tensions between union and management grew. There were many issues underlying the strike. The foreman in question had been the subject of numerous complaints (e.g., he performed work prohibited by the contract) by the union over the course of the experiment. Others felt that it was unfair that a foreman could hit a man and not be fired when firing was company policy if a union member were to hit a foreman. Still others wanted to attack the company's "no work, no talk" policy during walkouts. They felt that a prolonged strike might force management to talk to them.

Eventual pressures from the district, loss of income, and individuals wanting to return to work led to a resumption of work. However, after this strike, nothing was resolved in favor of the union. The foreman remained on the job. He apologized to the worker but was not disciplined.

This infuriated some of the union members. As one member said, "The men feel the company did not bargain in good faith—they wouldn't budge. They called us liars . . . it's their might versus us. . . . The AW program is a mockery."

The union membership shortly after the strike rescinded a motion, made in December 1975, that permitted their officers to work with management in designing a QOW program. This action represented the union's formal withdrawal from the program.

The research team and management tried to continue the program by forming a Mine Communication Committee. The contract created this Committee to deal with training and safety matters. At Rushton the committee focused on the company's current training for UMW members and on the gain-sharing program. Developing a gain-sharing program to pay out some of the gains achieved by the experiment became a major activity of the research team. In 1977, a one-shot bonus was paid to all employees (labor and management).

The national coal strike began in December 1977 and continued until March 1978. By the time work began again, there was no significant attempt to revitalize the program; most of the original research team had departed from Rushton.

There are some potential organizational innovations currently being planned at Rushton that might influence the future structure and activities at the mine. The new national contract permits incentive plans in underground mines. Pennsylvania Mines Corporation (which owns Rushton) recently asked me to help them design a wage incentive system that might be used in their mines.

Rushton has been selected as the first mine to implement the system. After interviewing a random sample of the Rushton work force about their opinions on incentive plans and extensive discussions with management, a plan has been designed. The wage plan now will be presented to the Mine Communication Committee and then to the work force prior to a union vote on the plan.

Hopefully, we have learned from the problems encountered in diffusing the QOW program minewide. Although the core of the plan is a straight productivity-wage plan, some organizational modifications are introduced *to complement the plan.* These modifications, which include mechanisms to increase or improve intercrew cooperation, productivity suggestions, safety practices, etc., are built on some of the innovations proposed during the original experiment, a sign that the mine is still being affected by the quality of work program.

APPENDIXES

Description of Some Major Instruments

1. Organizational Description Interview

This is a structured interview that includes questions on: organizational demographics, organizational structure, specialization of functions, authority structure, documents, products, technology, control systems, communication systems, decision structure, personnel policies, environment, and so on. (59 pages)

2. On-the-Job Observation Booklet

This is an observational instrument of job activities and job environment developed at the Institute for Social Research at the University of Michigan (ISR). It includes measures of safety hazards; environmental conditions, such as noise, temperature, cleanliness, and so on; job characteristics, such as autonomy, variety, feedback opportunities, control, and so on. Ratings are done on 5 to 7 point scales; some scales are in the semantic differential format. (21 pages)

3. Union Description Interview

This is a structured interview that includes questions on: union demographics, organization of the union, history of labor-management relations, grievance procedure, bargaining process and proposals, launching the agreement, character of labor-management relations, performance of local, and so on. (25 pages)

APPENDIX TWO

Derivation of the Means Test

The test developed here compares mean output per period between the experimental and control units, while controlling for differences in the values of all independent variables. The test is designed to place as few restrictions as possible on the form and properties of the production function in the experimental unit. Operationally, the test involves substituting observed values of the independent variables from the experimental unit for the estimated production function of the control group. The test then compares mean production per period predicted from the function for the control group with the mean actual production from the experimental unit. It is assumed that observations are available for N periods for the control group and T periods for the experimental unit.

We observe the values of the dependent variable generated in the experimental unit. Call these y_e and let the mean of these be:

$$(1) \qquad \bar{y}_e = \sum_{t=1}^{T} \frac{y_{et}}{T}$$

We assume that y_{et} is normally distributed with mean $\mu_{e,t}$ and variance σ_e^2. In general $\mu_{e,t}$ will be functionally dependent on values assumed by the vector of exogenous variables $(\underset{\sim}{x}_t)$ in the experimental section at time t, but it is not necessary to specify the form of that function for the test described below. Mean output in the experimental section is then normally distributed:

$$(2) \qquad \bar{y}_e \sim N\left(\mu_e, \frac{\sigma_e^2}{T}\right)$$

$$\text{where } \mu_e = \sum_{t=1}^{T} \frac{\mu_{e,t}}{T}$$

380

The vector of values (y_c) of the dependent variable in the control group is observed with a different matrix of exogenous variables $\underset{\sim}{Z}$. Let $\underset{\sim}{Z}$ have dimension $N \times P$; there are N observations on P variables in the control group. Let $\underset{\sim}{X}$ have dimension $T \times P$ where there are T observations on the vector of P independent variables, and the ordering of variables is the same as in $\underset{\sim}{Z}$. The assumed model for the control group is linear in $\underset{\sim}{Z}$; the residual is assumed to exhibit first order serial correlation:

(3) $$y_{et} = \underset{\sim}{Z}_t \underset{\sim}{\beta} + e_t$$

where

$e_t = \rho e_{t-1} + u_t$

$u_t \sim N(O, \sigma^2_c)$

If the matrix $\underset{\sim}{X}$ were to occur in the control group, the model in Equation 3 implies:

(4) $$y_{pt} = \underset{\sim}{X}_t \underset{\sim}{\beta} + v_t$$

where $v_t = \rho v_{t-1} + w_t$

$w_t \sim N(O, \sigma^2_c)$

That is, y_{pt} are the observations on the dependent variable that would have occurred if the set of independent variables observed in the experimental unit had also occurred in the control group. The test procedure will be to predict the y_{pt} and to compare the mean of the prediction to $\bar{y}_e$, the mean of the observed values in the experimental unit.

Since β and ρ are unobservable, maximum likelihood estimators are obtained from Equation 3. These will be denoted $\hat{\underset{\sim}{\beta}}$ and $\hat{\rho}$. The mean of the predicted values is:

(5) $$\hat{\bar{y}} p = \bar{\underset{\sim}{x}}' \underset{\sim}{\beta}$$

where $\bar{x}$ is the vector of sample means of the variable in $\underset{\sim}{X}$ (i.e.,

$$\bar{x}_i = \frac{\sum_{t=1}^{T} x_{it}}{T}$$ Since the $\hat{\underset{\sim}{\beta}}$ are consistent estimators of the β, the

asymptotic expectation of $\hat{\bar{y}}$ is:

(6) $$\mathscr{E}(\hat{\bar{y}}_p) = \bar{\underset{\sim}{x}}' \mathscr{E}(\hat{\underset{\sim}{\beta}}) = \bar{\underset{\sim}{x}}' \underset{\sim}{\beta} = \mu_p$$

In taking the above expectation, it is assumed that the prediction period T is finite and that the mean of the exogenous variables in $\bar{\underset{\sim}{x}}$ are nonstochistic. The sample, n, from which β is estimated, is permitted to go to infinity for a fixed T. The asymptotic variance of $\hat{\bar{y}}_p$ is:[1]

$$(7) \quad \text{Asy Var} (\hat{\bar{y}}_p) = \frac{1}{n} \text{plim} \, [\sqrt{n} \, (\hat{\bar{y}}_p - \mu_p) \, \sqrt{n} \, (\bar{y}_p - \mu_p)]$$

$$= \frac{1}{n} \text{plim} \, [\sqrt{n} \, (\underset{\sim}{\bar{x}}' \, \hat{\beta} - \underset{\sim}{\bar{x}}'\beta) \, (\underset{\sim}{\bar{x}}'\beta - \underset{\sim}{\bar{x}}' \, \beta)']$$

$$= \frac{1}{n} \underset{\sim}{\bar{x}}' \, \text{plim} \, [n \, (\hat{\beta} - \beta) \, (\hat{\beta} - \beta)'] \underset{\sim}{\bar{x}}$$

$$= \frac{\sigma_c^2}{n} \underset{\sim}{\bar{x}}' \, \text{plim} \, \left(\frac{Z^{*\prime} \, Z^*}{n} \right)^{-1} \underset{\sim}{\bar{x}} = \frac{\sigma_c^2}{n} \underset{\sim}{\bar{x}}' \, \overset{-1}{\underset{\sim}{\Sigma}}{}_z^* {}_z^* \underset{\sim}{\bar{x}}$$

$$= \frac{\sigma_c^2}{n} K^*$$

where $Z^*_t = Z_t - \rho Z_{t-1}$.

Thus, asymptotically:

$$(8) \qquad \qquad \hat{\bar{y}}_p \sim N(\mu_p, \frac{\sigma_c^2}{n} K^*)$$

The asymptotic variance can be consistently estimated by $\frac{\sigma_c^2}{n} \hat{K}^*$ where

$$K^* = -x' \, (Z^{*\prime} \, Z^*)^{-1} x' \text{ and } Z^* = Z_t - pZ_{t-1}$$

The goal is to test whether the difference in means, d, is significant.

$$(9) \qquad \qquad d = \mu_p - \mu_e$$

and the proposed test statistic is:

$$(10) \qquad \qquad \hat{d} = \hat{\bar{y}}_p - \bar{y}_e.$$

Obviously the limiting expectation of $\hat{d}$ is d and the asymptotic variance of $\hat{d}$ is $K^* \frac{\sigma_c^2}{n} + \frac{\sigma_e^2}{T}$.

Thus, asymptotically:

$$(11) \qquad \qquad \hat{d} \sim N \left(\mu_p - \mu_e, \ K^* \frac{\sigma_c^2}{n} + \frac{\sigma_e^2}{T} \right)$$

[1]See Cooper, J. Phillip, "Asymptotic covariance matrix of procedures for linear regression in the presence of first order autoregressive disturbances," *Econometrica, 40*, 2, 305–310, March, 1972.

The goal is to make a minimal set of assumptions about the experimental unit. To avoid estimating the $\mu_{e,t}$ which are functions of $\underline{x}_t$, we will assume $\sigma^2 = \sigma^2_e = \sigma^2_c$. Then the variance can be estimated using the data from the control group. The appropriate test statistic is then:

(12)
$$\frac{\hat{d} - d}{\sigma^2_c \left(\hat{K}^* + \frac{1}{T} \right)}$$

This statistic is distributed asymptotically as the unit normal. This is the test statistic used in the text of Chapter 11 for the means test.

References

Campbell, D., and J. Stanley. *Experimental and quasi-experimental design for research*. Chicago: Rand-McNally, 1966.

Dunlop, J. "Policy decisions and research in economics and industrial relations." *Industrial and Labor Relations Review, 30*(3), 275–282, 1977.

Epple, D., E. Fidler, and P. S. Goodman. *"Estimating economic consequences in organizational effectiveness experiments."* (Working paper.) Pittsburgh: Carnegie-Mellon University, 1977. (Unpublished manuscript.)

Goodman, P.S. *Rushton quality of work project*. (Baseline Report.) Pittsburgh: Graduate School of Industrial Administration, Carnegie-Mellon University, 1975.

Goodman, P. S. *Rushton quality of work project*. (Interim report.) Pittsburgh: Graduate School of Industrial Administration, Carnegie-Mellon University, 1976.

Goodman, P. S., E. Conlon, and M. Bazerman. "Institutionalization of planned organizational change," in B. M. Staw and L. L. Cummings (Eds.). *Research in organizational behavior*, Vol. II. Greenwich, Conn.: JAI Press, forthcoming.

Goodman, P. S., and E. E. Lawler. *New forms of work organization in the United States*. (Monograph for the International Labor Organization.) Geneva, Switzerland: 1977.

Goodman, P. S., and J. M. Pennings (Eds.). *New perspectives on organizational effectiveness*. San Francisco: Jossey-Bass, 1977.

Goodman, P. S., and J. M. Pennings. "Critical issues in assessing organizational effectiveness," in E. Lawler, D. A. Nadler, and C. Cammann (Eds.). *Organizational assessment: Perspectives on the measurement of organizational behavior and the quality of working life*. New York: Wiley–Interscience, 1979.

Hill, P. *Towards a new philosophy of management*. New York: Barnes & Noble Books, 1971.

Jenkins, G., D. Nadler, E. E. Lawler, and C. Cammann. "Standardized observations: An approach to measuring the nature of jobs." *Journal of Applied Psychology, 60,* 171–181, 1975.

Johnston, J. *Econometric Methods, 2nd Ed.* New York: McGraw-Hill, 1972.

Lawler, E. E. *Pay and organizational effectiveness: A psychological view.* New York: McGraw-Hill, 1971.

Maccoby, M. "The Bolivar project—productivity and human development." Washington, D.C.: Harvard Technology Project, 1978. (Unpublished manuscript.)

Maier, N. *Problem-solving discussions and conferences.* New York: McGraw-Hill, 1963.

March, J. and H. Simon. *Organizations.* New York: Wiley, 1958.

Mitchell, T. "Expectancy models of job satisfaction, occupational preference, and effort." *Psychological Bulletin, 81,* 1053–1070, 1974.

Oskamp, S. *Attitudes and opinions.* Englewood Cliffs, N.J.: Prentice-Hall, 1977.

Tannenbaum, A. S. *Control in organizations.* New York: McGraw-Hill, 1968.

Trist, E., G. Higgins, H. Murray, and A. Pollock. *Organizational choice.* London: Tavistock, 1963.

Trist, E., G. Susman, and G. Brown. "An experiment in autonomous working in an American underground coal mine." *Human Relations, 30,* 201–236, 1977.

U.S. Department of Labor. *Productivity Indexes for Selected Industries, 1976 Edition.* Bureau of Labor Statistics Bulletin 1938, 25.

Walton, R. "Explaining why success didn't take." *Organizational Dynamics, 3,* 2–22, 1975.

Index

387

Soc
HD
8039
M62
LL6258

DATE DUE

OCT~~1980~~	~~APR 16 1985~~
~~NOV 10 1980~~	~~DEC 13 1997~~
~~NOV 01 1985~~	
~~DEC 01 1988~~	
~~1995~~	
~~JUN 16 1995~~	

MP 728